VALUES OF HAPPINESS

www.haubooks.com

VALUES OF HAPPINESS

TOWARD AN ANTHROPOLOGY OF PURPOSE IN LIFE

Special Issues in Ethnographic Theory Series

Edited by

Iza Kavedžija and Harry Walker

Hau Books
Chicago

© 2016 Hau Books

Hau Books Special Issues in Ethnographic Theory Series (Volume 2)

The Hau Books Special Issues in Ethnographic Theory Series prints paperback versions of pathbreaking collections, previously published in Hau: Journal of Ethnographic Theory.

Cover and layout design: Sheehan Moore

Cover Photo © Skye Hohmann

Typesetting: Prepress Plus (www.prepressplus.in)

ISBN: 978-0-9861325-7-5
LCCN: 2016959208

Hau Books
Chicago Distribution Center
11030 S. Langley
Chicago, IL 60628
www.haubooks.com

Hau Books is marketed and distributed by The University of Chicago Press.
www.press.uchicago.edu

Printed in the United States of America on acid-free paper.

Table of Contents

List of Contributors

Joanna Cook is an anthropologist at University College London. She is the author of *Meditation in modern Buddhism: Renunciation and change in Thai monastic life* (Cambridge University Press, 2010) and the coeditor of *The state we're in: Reflecting on democracy's troubles* (Berghahn Books, 2016), *Detachment: Essays on the limits of relational thinking* (Manchester University Press, 2015) and *Southeast Asian perspectives on power* (Routledge, 2012).

Matthew Engelke is Professor of Anthropology at the London School of Economics and Political Science. He is the author of *A problem of presence: Beyond scripture in an African church* (University of California Press, 2007), which won the 2008 Geertz Prize for Anthropology of Religion and the 2009 Turner Prize for Ethnographic Writing, and *God's agents: Biblical publicity in contemporary England* (University of California Press, 2013). He is coeditor, most recently, of *Global Christianity, global critique* (with Joel Robbins), a special issue of *South Atlantic Quarterly* (2010). He has run Prickly Paradigm Press with Marshall Sahlins since 2002, and was editor of the *Journal of the Royal Anthropological Institute* from 2010 to 2013.

Dena Freeman is a Senior Visiting Fellow in the Department of Anthropology at the London School of Economics. She has carried out research in Ethiopia for over twenty years and has written about cultural change, inequality, marginalization, happiness, religion, and development. Her most recent book is *Pentecostalism and development: Churches, NGOs and social change in Africa* (Palgrave 2012).

Katy Gardner is a Professor of Anthropology at the London School of Economics where she is currently Head of Department. Her published works include *Global migrants, local lives: Travel and transformation in rural Bangladesh* (Oxford University Press, 1995); *Age, narrative and migration: The life histories and the life course amongst British Bengali elders in London* (Berg, 2002); and *Discordant developments: Global capitalism and the struggle for survival in Bangladesh* (Pluto Press, 2012). She has also written a book on Anthropology and Development (*Anthropology and development: Challenges for the twenty first century*, with David Lewis, Pluto Press, 2015) and is the author of several novels and a collection of short stories.

Iza Kavedžija has worked in Japan on meaning in life, motivation, life choices, aging, and the life-course. She is currently a Lecturer in Anthropology at the University of Exeter. Her monograph *Meaning in life: Tales from aging Japan*, based on her work with older Japanese, exploring their experiences of aging, narrativity, and wellbeing, is forthcoming with University of Pennsylvania Press. She is currently carrying out research examining practices of contemporary art production among a community of young avant-garde artists in the Japanese city of Osaka.

Michael Lambek holds a Canada Research Chair and is Professor of Anthropology at the University of Toronto. He carries out the majority of his fieldwork in the Western Indian Ocean and is the author or editor of a dozen books, most recently *The ethical condition* (University of Chicago Press, 2015), *A companion to the anthropology of religion* (edited with Janice Boddy; Wiley-Blackwell, paper edition 2015), and *Four lectures on ethics: Anthropological perspectives* (with Veena Das, Didier Fassin, and Webb Keane; Hau Books, 2015).

Joel Robbins is Sigrid Rausing Professor of Social Anthropology at the University of Cambridge. Much of his recent work has focused on the anthropological study of values.

Charles Stafford teaches anthropology at the London School of Economics and is also the publisher and editor of *Anthropology of this Century*. He is a specialist in cognitive anthropology and the author of *The roads of Chinese childhood* (Cambridge University Press, 1995) and *Separation and reunion in modern China* (Cambridge University Press, 2000), and the editor of *Ordinary ethics in China* (Bloomsbury, 2013).

C. Jason Throop is Professor of Anthropology at University of California, Los Angeles. He has conducted ethnographic fieldwork on pain, suffering, empathy, and morality on the island of Yap in the Western Caroline Islands of Micronesia. He is the author of *Suffering and sentiment: Exploring the vicissitudes of experience and pain in Yap* (University of California Press, 2010) and the coeditor of the volumes *Toward an anthropology of the will* (Stanford University Press, 2010) and *The anthropology of empathy: Experiencing the lives of others in Pacific societies* (Berghahn Books, 2011).

Henrik Vigh is Professor of Anthropology at the University of Copenhagen. He has researched issues of youth and conflict in both Europe and Africa and has written extensively on issues of social crisis, conflict, and mobilization. He is the author of *Navigating terrains of war: Youth and soldiering in Guinea-Bissau*. His current research investigates the intersection between war and crime focusing on the transnational movement of cocaine through militant networks in West Africa.

Harry Walker has worked in the Peruvian Amazon on a range of topics including personhood, materiality, exchange, shamanism, law, sport, and social change. He is an Associate Professor in the Department of Anthropology at the London School of Economics and Political Science. His monograph on the Amazonian Urarina, *Under a watchful eye: Self, power and intimacy in Amazonia* (University of California Press, 2013), explores the emergence of personal autonomy through intimate but asymmetrical relations of nurturance and dependency. He has recently published on the apprehension of formal law and its relationship to ritual practice, and coedited a recent special issue on Amazonian appropriations of documents and bureaucracy. He is currently carrying out research on conceptions of justice and injustice.

Values of happiness

HARRY WALKER and IZA KAVEDŽIJA

"Tell me how you define happiness, and I'll tell you who you are!" So concludes one survey of the concept's treatment by Western philosophy over the past two millennia (S. Bok 2010: 54), testifying not only to the diversity of ways in which happiness has been understood—even just within our own intellectual heritage—but also, and more importantly, to its role as what we might term a diagnostic of forms of life. How people conceive of, evaluate, and pursue (or not) happiness can reveal much about how they live and the values they hold dear. An ethnographic inquiry into happiness, we argue, offers a unique window onto the ways in which people diversely situated in time and space grapple with fundamental questions about how to live, the ends of life, and what it means to be human.

The idea of happiness—however defined in its specifics—makes a claim about what is most desirable and worthwhile in a person's life. It purports to be an all-inclusive assessment of a person's condition, either at a specific moment in time or in relation to a life in its entirety; it expresses a hope that the various aims, enjoyments, and desires that characterize a life—though they may often conflict with each other—may ultimately be harmonized, or somehow rendered coherent (White 2006). For most people in the West today, happiness is about feeling good; it denotes a preponderance of positive over negative affect, and a general sense of contentment or satisfaction with life. It is inherently subjective, consisting of people's evaluations of their own life, both affective and cognitive (Diener 1984; Argyle, Martin, and Crossland 1989). This is, of course, but one of many ways in which the term has been understood—and, like all others, says much about the social, economic, and political conditions in which it emerged.

Insofar as the study of happiness necessarily draws together considerations of meaning, values, and affect, it could be seen to lie at the very heart of the anthropological endeavor. Indeed, while the term itself has only very recently returned to fashion in academic circles, there is a real sense in which the underlying questions in which it deals have long been subjected to the ethnographic gaze: about the diverse ends that people pursue and how they seek fulfillment; about the structure of motivation and action; about the relationship between the sensuous and the moral. Since Durkheim, anthropologists have recognized that people are generally happiest in those moments when they feel most connected to others—hence, perhaps, the overwhelming interest in the ebb and flow of kinship, not to mention the power of those liminal moments in which social barriers melt away to produce an integrated, often joyful sense of *communitas* (see also Freeman, Walker, Robbins, this collection). Anthropologists have also long been acutely aware of the diversity of ends for which people strive, many of which may stand in a complex relationship to happiness (reproducing the lineage, say, or attaining the status of ancestorhood); not to mention their passion for engaging in a bewildering variety of projects and practices, from the Nuer's enthusiasm for oxen to the fervor of the kula ring (cf. Lambek 2008: 143). As Marshall Sahlins (2006) pointed out, moreover, there is more than one possible "road to affluence," because there exists more than one way of narrowing the gap between human wants and the means to satisfy them. And on the whole, desiring little would seem more conducive to living well than producing much in order to meet escalating material desires.

Given its unique ability to unravel what matters most to people and why, the relative silence of anthropology in the face of the recent "happiness turn" (Ahmed 2010) in the social sciences is all the more striking. As the most cursory glance reveals, the topic of happiness has achieved an extraordinary prominence over the course of the past decade, not only in academic research, but also in popular and public discourse. Bhutan's now-famous "Gross National Happiness" index has been widely heralded as an alternative to gross national product and other conventional measures of prosperity and growth for arriving at policy decisions and measuring progress; the idea has captured the attention of governments around the world,[1] and indeed the United Nations General Assembly has now passed a resolution that happiness should have a greater role in development policy, encouraging member states "to pursue the elaboration of additional measures that better capture the importance of the pursuit of happiness and well-being" (United Nations News Service 2011).

Placing happiness at the center of public policy is not, of course, a new idea; after all, the pursuit of happiness is famously enshrined in the French Constitution and the US Declaration of Independence. Bentham's utilitarian "science of happiness" was intended to be a means by which governments could measure the expected pleasures and pains resulting from policy proposals and select those that would produce the greatest net happiness. His ideas, though influential, were not adopted at the time in part because of the obvious difficulties of directly measuring something as intangible as happiness. In recent decades, however, psychologists and economists have made increasingly sophisticated attempts to overcome this problem, producing ever more refined sets of instruments and techniques, with ever more influence on governmental policy.

At the very heart of their methodology lies the deceptively simple procedure of asking people more or less directly, in the context of a survey or questionnaire, how happy they are; or how satisfied they feel overall with the lives they lead.[2] Such a procedure is useful because it produces results that are easily quantifiable, and which lend themselves to systematic comparison. Nevertheless, the

---

1. In Britain, for example, Prime Minister David Cameron has identified happiness as a "key challenge" for politicians everywhere, and he announced in November 2010 that it would be a major governmental objective to be regularly measured in the national statistics (BBC 2006).

2. The "happiness turn" has probably made the greatest impact in the fields of economics and psychology, with increasing numbers of economists proposing happiness indices and self-reported wellbeing as alternatives to measurements such as income or gross national product; and with growing interest among psychologists in "mental health" rather than illness, including the development of positive psychology. Both groups tend to measure "subjective wellbeing," which is often used synonymously with happiness or as a broader measure which encompasses it. Involving both cognitive judgments and affective reactions, measurements of subjective wellbeing typically try to capture both the momentary pleasurable sensation and an evaluation of one's life as a whole (for an overview of measures see S. Bok 2010: 33–34). Typical survey questions might include the following: "Overall, how happy did you feel yesterday?" "How much purpose does your life have?" "How satisfied with are you with your life these days, on a scale of 0 to 10 where 0 is 'not at all' and 10 is 'completely satisfied'?"

potential limitations of such a method should immediately also be apparent, perhaps especially to an anthropologist. We may well ask: Just how reliable are such responses, and what exactly do they reveal? As Sara Ahmed has pointed out, the model of subjectivity on which this research relies is a quite specific and somewhat peculiar one, "where one knows how one feels, and where the distinction between good and bad feeling is secure, forming the basis of subjective as well as social well-being" (2010: 6). What do people really understand by happiness anyway? Why should we assume respondents are all talking about the same thing? What if happiness means vastly different things from one place to the next, perhaps to the extent that the meanings contradict one other?

There are still broader concerns: Even if we could identify precisely what is meant by the term, is happiness really the best or most desirable goal? It has been suggested by some that happiness as such is illusory, or at best a side-effect; indeed, that pursuing happiness directly can only lead to further unhappiness, especially when it becomes a kind of duty (e.g., Bruckner 2011). In any case, what about other desirable goals for policy—or grassroots struggles for that matter—such as freedom, equality, or social justice? Why is maximizing happiness a better aim than, say, alleviating poverty or enhancing "capabilities" (e.g., Sen 2008)?[3] In a trenchant critique of the "happiness industry," William Davies (2015) decries the fact that a particular concept of happiness as something objective, measurable, and capable of being administered is rapidly gaining currency among the global elite, as well as increasing numbers of policy makers and managers, and mobilized in ways that potentially expand forms of surveillance and social control. He suggests that the current concern with happiness grows out of a particular scientific utopia originating in the Enlightenment, but gaining real traction in the late nineteenth century, in which "core questions of morality and politics will be solvable with an adequate science of human feelings" (ibid.: Loc114). A promise, that is, that a science of subjective feeling will prove the ultimate tool for working out how to act, both morally and politically. It must be emphasized, though, that the aim of making public policy "scientific"—and thus divorced from any specific moral or ideological foundation—is

---

3.   Robert Nozick (1990: 117) writes: "We want experiences, fitting ones, of profound connection with others, of deep understanding of natural phenomena, of love, of being profoundly moved by music or tragedy, or doing something new and innovative, experiences very different from the bounce and rosiness of the happy moments".

not without practical consequences, and—as we argue below—is certainly not apolitical.

The rapid spike of interest in happiness over the past decade or so would also seem to have much to do with the nature of twenty-first-century capitalism. Western economies increasingly depend on psychological and emotional engagement with work and commerce, but find this ever more difficult to sustain in a context of rising inequality and alienation. At the same time, increasingly sophisticated consumer technologies for monitoring and quantifying people's moods and feelings are enlarging the opportunities for surveillance and "expert administration" of their lives, and beginning to generate the promise of a new, "post-neoliberal era," in which the market is no longer the primary tool for this capture of mass sentiment (Davies 2015: Loc172). The techniques of positive psychology are thus mobilized in order to bring emotions and wellbeing within broader calculations of economic efficiency.

Whether for these or other concerns, anthropologists have had little to contribute to these prominent debates. There is a certain suspicion of happiness as an essentially bourgeois preoccupation, increasingly associated with a neoliberal agenda, and potentially at odds with emancipatory politics. To this we might also add that the discipline has often gravitated toward more "negative" forms of human experience, such as suffering, pain, or poverty (Thin 2008; Robbins 2013a). As a result, to the extent that "cultural" factors, including issues of translation and comparison, are taken seriously in the wider cross-disciplinary literature, discussions tend to be dominated by cultural psychologists and economists, who often have a more quantitative orientation, and may prefer to direct efforts toward refining the questionnaires used to gauge levels of happiness in a population.[4] We firmly believe that disengagement from one of the most important and high-profile recent developments in cross-disciplinary research and public debate would be a grave error. While beyond the scope of this introduction, many of the findings of happiness studies—from both cultural psychology and economics—are of significant interest and relevance for anthropology, as Neil Thin (2012) has shown at length in his excellent overview. It is important to note that the methods and techniques of happiness research have already been

---

4.   For discussions of intercultural differences in the constitutive elements of happiness, beyond the apparently differing "levels" of happiness reported, see, for example, Mishra (1994); Camfield et al. (2009); Kan, Karasawa, and Kitayama (2009); Bull et al. (2010); Lu (2010); Oishi et al. (2013).

subjected to extensive critical scrutiny, with many of the most thoroughgoing and elaborate criticisms coming from within the field itself.[5] Moreover, some practitioners have explicitly tried to encourage more input from anthropologists, acknowledging the need for—and possible advantages of—more nuanced ethnographic approaches (e.g., Diener and Suh 2000; Suh and Oishi 2004: 221). While our approach does not preclude critique, nor does it take critique to be the paramount goal; our intention is to open up rather than foreclose debate with happiness studies, engaging the field on our terms, but in a constructive and inclusive manner.

The approach we pursue in this collection is thus ethnographic, first and foremost. Owing to the sheer volume of work on the topic, we felt it especially important to develop an approach from the ground up, as it were, led by ethnography rather than the findings and assumptions of other disciplines, for it is precisely in this way that anthropology might have something genuinely original and interesting to contribute to cross-disciplinary discussions and debates. It is significant that none of the contributors to this volume employed the strategy of asking people directly about happiness as a central part of their research. This may be, in the end, what most distinguishes our approach from that adopted by the happiness studies community. Needless to say, while this avoids some of the problems faced by studies reliant on self-reporting, it raises other problems of its own. One is that we are simply unable to contribute to the vast enterprise of gauging comparative levels of happiness around the world, or indeed quantifying in any way "how happy" people are. The problem of how we can know or infer (let alone describe) the internal psychological states of others has gained renewed attention in recent years, especially in light of recognition that in some cultural contexts, the concealment of one's "true" thoughts or emotions may be deemed desirable or inevitable (see, e.g., Robbins and Rumsey 2008; Keane 2015: 125). Our focus here, then, is not on gauging or comparing levels of happiness, but on how happiness figures as an idea, mood, or motive in people's day-to-day lives: how they actually go about making their lives happier—or not—whether consciously or otherwise, in ways conditioned by dominant social values as well as an array of aims and aspirations that are potentially conflicting.

While happiness is not necessarily an easy topic for anthropology, given its notoriously elusive quality, we hope to show why it is nevertheless an important

5.   For an overview of some of these problems, see D. Bok (2010: 30–37). The validity of measures is discussed at some length by Dolan and Peasgood (2010).

and promising one. In what follows, we direct attention to a number of themes we consider particularly relevant to an ethnographic approach, including considerations of scope, virtue, and responsibility in gauging how happiness is conceptualized and how it comes to figure in people's actions and judgments; the link between happiness and values; the nature of happiness as a moral mood; and, finally, issues of temporal orientation, including senses of happiness as a receding horizon, a pursuit or promise more virtual than actual, ever so slightly out of one's grasp.

QUESTIONS OF HAPPINESS

Despite the general dearth of dedicated ethnographic treatments, the past few years have witnessed the emergence of a handful of engagements with happiness and the related topic of wellbeing from an anthropological perspective (e.g., Corsín Jiménez 2008a; Berthon et al. 2009; Mathews and Izquierdo 2009a; Miles-Watson 2010; Jackson 2011, 2013; Johnston 2012; Thin 2012; Fischer 2015).[6] These works suggest—contrary to the assumptions of some social scientific researchers—that there is no single or unified "pursuit of happiness"; or as Gordon Mathews and Carolina Izquierdo put it, "Happiness is not one thing; it means different things in different places, different societies, and different cultural contexts" (2009b: 1). This conclusion finds increasing support from the work of cultural psychologists, although systematic cross-cultural comparison to date has been overwhelmingly structured around the contrast between so-called "individualistic" and "collectivistic" cultures, with one of the more oft-repeated findings being that happiness in the latter context (paradigmatically East Asia) is more a matter of collective welfare, social harmony, or fulfilling one's duties than it is of individual achievement, sensory pleasures, or positive evaluations of the self (see, e.g., Lu 2010; Selin and Davey 2012). The emerging anthropological literature also draws attention to three important observations that resonate strongly with the present collection: that happiness in general is best understood as intersubjective and relational (Thin 2012); that even pleasure, as

---

6. Several of these authors explicitly prefer the term "wellbeing" to "happiness," largely on the grounds that the former includes objective elements or measurements such as quality of life, and as such lends itself more easily to cross-cultural comparison. Happiness is more "experience-near," being intrinsically linked to a person's own evaluation of his or her life.

a universal human experience, is informed by cultural expectations (Clark 2009: 207); and that wellbeing throws into relief the difficulty of considering both social realities and human virtues simultaneously (Corsín Jiménez 2008b: 180). In other words, studying happiness requires attention to the social and cultural as well as moral and political dimensions of human experience.

To this end, we find it especially useful to consider happiness in relation to values, or what *matters* to people, in three interrelated senses. Firstly, happiness is not only imagined very differently across cultural contexts—and indeed within specific contexts by differently situated actors—but is also itself quite differently valued, that is, evaluated as more or less important according to circumstances.[7] In other words, happiness may not be an unquestionable good in every social context, let alone the ultimate good. Secondly, happiness is itself intrinsically evaluative. To say that one is happy is to make a positive evaluation or overall assessment of one's condition; typically in a way that purports to take into consideration the whole multiplicity of aims a person may have. Thirdly, happiness cannot therefore be separated from the spectrum of cultural values in relation to which it becomes meaningful, and which necessarily inform the process of evaluation. As the contributions to this collection show, a range of values may be seen to promote happiness, in the conventional sense of good feeling: from peaceable sociality and the absence of worry to financial success or the security of one's family. Whether these values actually do promote happiness is another question; and such values can also be potentially contradictory, as we discuss further below.

While it can be useful and important to consider what happiness "is," including how it is imagined or (in some cases, perhaps) achieved, we are equally concerned in this collection with how happiness "works," or what it "does": how it enters into people's lives, leading them to choose one path over another—and what it reveals about those people in the process. We draw on the strengths

---

7. Thus Catherine Lutz (1988: 167) observes that on the Micronesian island of Ifaluk, in stark contrast to those American approaches to child rearing and emotion which elevate happiness to an important position, the Ifaluk view happiness/excitement as something that must be carefully monitored and sometimes halted in children. In other, more extreme cases, individual happiness can be envisaged in direct opposition to broader ideals of the good life, as in the case of the Jain renouncers described by James Laidlaw (2005). Jainism, he argues, "devalues worldly well-being to the extent of institutionalising, and recommending for the spiritually advanced as a telos of religious life, the practice of fasting to death" (ibid.:158).

of ethnography to explore how notions of happiness may give rise to or de-limit possibilities for action, entering as motives into personal projects, along-side the range of other goals, aspirations, or values that may together comprise specific conceptions of a life well lived, or worth pursuing. As such, we hope to reveal something of people's attempts to create good in their lives (Robbins 2013a: 457): how people strive to make not only their own life happier, but also the lives of those around them, often within challenging or even downright hostile circumstances.

HAPPINESS IN TRANSIT: SCOPE, VIRTUE, RESPONSIBILITY

The currently dominant conception in the West considers both happiness and its pursuit to be largely private matters. That is, happiness is best understood as an interior state of an individual actor, or what one prominent spokesperson of the "new science of happiness" suggests can be glossed as "feeling good—enjoy-ing life and wanting the feeling to be maintained" (Layard 2005: 12). This state might best be achieved by those same individuals, acting in their best interests, cultivating relationships with others, and so on. Yet this has not always been the dominant understanding, and may in fact be a relatively recent development. In the ancient world, happiness was understood with reference to a far broader conception of human flourishing, or *eudaimonia*, implying a relatively objective evaluation of a whole life, with particular reference to the practice of virtue: a happy life, simply put, was a life of virtue. Those who promote the modern conception point out that the two contrastive definitions are not necessarily in conflict; after all, as Richard Layard (ibid.) reminds us, doing good makes you feel good. Nevertheless, the relationship between *eudaimonia* and *hedonia* con-tinues to structure many recent debates in the field (see also Engelke, Walker, this collection).

The transition from the ancient conception of human flourishing to the modern understanding of happiness as an inner psychological state, a feeling or mood, might in some ways be understood as a gradual process of interioriza-tion that recalls venerated anthropological discussions of concepts of personhood (e.g., Mauss [1938] 1985). There seems to be an analogy of sorts to the kinds of transformations often thought to have taken place whereby some idea of a dis-tributed, relational, or "dividual" person, construed as constituted by her relations with others (e.g., Bird-David 1999), is progressively replaced by a more "modern" conception of an autonomous, self-contained "individual," who is now seen to exist prior to relations rather than constituted by them. As Charles Taylor (1989) has made clear, insofar as the self is constituted in and through the taking of moral stances, such notions of personhood are intimately connected to ideas of the good.

Looking back more broadly at how happiness has figured through the history of Western civilization, it is evident that a succession of monumental changes have taken place. As Darrin McMahon (2006) demonstrates in a magisterial study, the idea of happiness as an aim suitable for (and potentially available to) everyone—that is, something potentially within the grasp of each individual and attainable largely through his or her own actions—is indeed a highly culturally specific idea that only came into being as late as the eighteenth-century Enlightenment. In the tragedies of the ancient Greeks, happiness could only be achieved through some miraculous, divine intervention or blessing; it was deemed to be beyond human agency, a matter of luck or fortune, fragile and highly contingent upon external conditions (Nussbaum 2001). After Socrates, Plato, and Aristotle, happiness came to be seen as a final end (Annas 1993: 12, 39); and with the latter two thinkers in particular, the responsibility for happiness began to shift to human beings themselves—in this case, as something to be attained through virtuous behavior, and thus partially within one's control. It was thus only under the stable conditions of small, democratic city-states, during the "Golden Age" of Periclean Athens, that happiness came to be envisaged as a realizable human goal. During the precarious conditions following the demise of the city-state, a widespread sense of insecurity coincided with the popularity of the ideas of Zeno and Epicurus (S. Bok 2010: 48). Despite their differences, both these schools emphasized personal control and agency, and envisaged happiness as independent of external goods: whether through virtuous living aligned with the natural order of the world, in the case of Zeno's stoicism; or through reaching a state of tranquility, recognizing that many of our desires are idle or misplaced while taking pleasure in life's simple enjoyments (McMahon 2006: 47–64). For the ancients since Socrates, in other words, happiness was not in conflict with virtue (Annas 1993: 449) and could be expected as a reward for virtuous living: a possibility, even if a rare or exclusive one.

For Christian thinkers such as Augustine and Thomas Aquinas, true happiness was not possible in life but only in heaven (S. Bok 2010: 71), even though virtue remained central: "Happiness remained a telos, an end, and virtue the principal means to guide the way. But whereas the ancients had conceived of virtue as almost entirely of human striving, won only by the efforts of a happy few, Christians understood virtue as a divine gift, obtainable, in theory, by all" (McMahon 2006: 137). A much later formulation, a modern one, drew from these ideas the promise of universal deliverance attainable for all, as well as the notion of human responsibility for one's own happiness. In the eighteenth century, these ideas came together to form a particular vision of happiness as something all people deserved (ibid.: 230). At the same time, its connection to virtue weakened. This gave rise to a more receptive attitude toward good feeling and pleasure, with significant long-term consequences. Some thinkers of the time, including those utilitarians interested in "the greatest happiness of the greatest number," attempted to resist the dissociation of happiness and virtue. John Stuart Mill, for example, whose work is often considered to be more subtle than Bentham's calculus, includes virtue among the pleasures, along with music and health (Nussbaum 2010: 85). Nevertheless, the connection between the two did not arise naturally from their system of thought, but rested instead on "the moral capital of the past" (McMahon 2006:230). The incongruity to which this gave rise was addressed explicitly by Kant, who saw happiness—already understood by that time as pleasure or good feeling—as opposed to both reason and morality (Annas 1993: 449). In Kant's words, "Making someone happy is quite different from making him good" (1996: 90).

Once the ties of happiness to virtue were no longer seen as binding, many thinkers (Tocqueville, for instance) considered the pursuit of individual happiness—through focusing on private pleasure and wealth, for example—as being in tension with the wider social good, and perhaps ultimately damaging for the actual realization of happiness (McMahon 2006: 341). We thus arrive at the modern conception of happiness, and with it the particular range of concerns most debated by happiness scholars today, particularly those with an interest in applying happiness research to public policy.

If we now consider this (necessarily schematic) historical overview in light of the existing comparative literature on happiness across cultures, as well as the contributions to this collection, some key themes emerge which are of particular interest in formulating an anthropological approach to happiness. In particular, we suggest that happiness can be considered as a triangulation of scope, virtue, and responsibility: three axes, as it were, along which the concept varies in significant ways, and in relation to which it may be apprehended and interrogated.

Firstly, then, the *scope* of happiness is always constrained or delimited in some way, such that we may usefully ask *who* can hope or even expect to be happy, and to what extent, and why. It is noteworthy that the ancient Greek conception of happiness as dependent on good luck and fortune, or favorable external circumstances, is also found in many other parts of the world (see, e.g., Lu 2001; da Col and Humphreys 2010); and that the English term "happy" is apparently used far more loosely—and is thus potentially more accessible as a condition—than its equivalents in other languages, including Polish, Russian, German, and French (Wierzbicka 2004; see also Oishi et al. 2013). Among the Amazonian Urarina, anyone can achieve the ideal state of tranquility, though it is rarely lasting (Walker, this collection). Most migrants from Sylhet in Bangladesh consider happiness attainable, even if their expectations are not fulfilled all that often (see Gardner, this collection); though happiness seems destined always to elude the young militiamen from Guinea-Bisseau (Vigh, this collection). What is more, the scope of happiness can also vary in terms of pertaining primarily to an individual or a group. It is clearly the former on Yap—hence its ambivalence (Throop, this collection)—while among people of the Gamo Highlands in Ethiopia, happiness is inconceivable in isolation and arguably pertains to the group as a whole (Freeman, this collection).

Secondly, happiness always stands in a particular relationship to *virtue*: for instance, as the goal of virtuous action, or as its precondition; or as severed from virtue altogether. This relationship lies at the heart of at least two crucial questions: What kind of life will bring happiness? And, how is happiness morally evaluated? One has the impression that the life of the retired Swiss farmer Willi discussed by Lambek (this collection) was a happy one largely because it was characterized by virtuous activity. Similarly, for British humanists, virtue—or being "good without God"—is central to how they understand the promise of (secular) happiness (Engelke, this collection). On the other hand, virtue scarcely enters into the calculations of the young Guinea-Bissau militiamen in pursuit of hedonic pleasure (Vigh, this collection); while happiness is in tension with virtue on the island of Yap insofar as it impedes attunement to the suffering of others (Throop, this collection).

Thirdly, happiness implicates specific forms of *responsibility*. It raises the question of who is responsible for the happiness of whom, and in what ways they may be held accountable. The notion that individuals are responsible for their own happiness is without doubt one of the most politically significant features of the modern conception, and goes some way toward accounting for its embrace by the purveyors of neoliberalism—even if this is only part of the story, as Cook shows here in her analysis of increasing political interest in mindfulness in Britain. Similarly, for the British humanists described by Engelke, assuming full responsibility for one's own happiness in the here and now is crucial for living well, and for creating purpose in life. In other contexts, emphasis may be placed on the duty to care for the happiness of others. It is widely maintained that East Asian conceptions of happiness in particular are deeply social and relational and may have little to do with individual achievement (Kitayama and Markus 2000; Kan, Karasawa and Kitayama 2009). Like the collectivism/individualism dichotomy itself, this may be an oversimplification, especially in a contemporary context of rapid individualization and changing social values. As Stafford shows (this collection), some Chinese today are struggling with the issue of whose happiness they should strive for: whether their own, that of their aging parents, or their children. Moreover, they must deal with the fact that while Chinese parents are still expected to take some responsibility for the marriage choices of their children, they may be no less successful at forecasting the future happiness of their children than they are at forecasting their own.

The issue of responsibility is also in many ways at the core of Hannah Arendt's analysis of that crucial moment of transition in which the right to the pursuit of happiness was inscribed in the framing of the American Constitution. Arendt ([1963] 1999) argues that the original concern of the founders was squarely with "public happiness," an eminently political conception associated above all with participation in public affairs, or an individual's laying claim to public power—in recognition of the fact that people could not be altogether "happy" if their happiness was located and enjoyed only in private life. This soon gave way, however, to the later concern with "private happiness," associated with the rights of subjects to be protected by the government. Arendt laments what she describes as "the conversion of the citizen of the revolutions into the private individual of nineteenth-century society . . . this disappearance of the 'taste for political freedom' as the withdrawal of the individual into an 'inward domain of consciousness' where it finds the only appropriate region of human liberty" (ibid.: 140). Yet whereas Arendt saw the currently dominant "private" conception of happiness as depoliticized, we would argue that it is in fact eminently political, albeit indicative of a different kind of politics.

THE COMMENSURABILITY OF VALUES

Happiness researchers working in or influenced by the utilitarian tradition take happiness to be the greatest good and ultimate end of life. From the perspective of the utilitarian ideal of greatest happiness for the greatest number, the concept itself is relatively unproblematic, being closely associated with pleasurable feeling, and constituting the one "ultimate goal that enables us to judge other goals by how they contribute to it" (Layard 2005: 113). In other words, happiness offers a single, ultimate good that can be measured and under which all other goods may effectively be subsumed. Yet as we have just seen in considering the history of the idea of happiness in Western civilization alone—and as the articles in this collection show in a comparative, contemporary context—the notion of happiness as the ultimate end or highest value has hardly been undisputed.[8] Indeed, some scholars—Amartya Sen among them—have raised important questions about how we should judge the goodness of human lives, and in particular whether other key concerns, such as freedom, can really be seen as subsidiary to utility (or happiness), as relevant only insofar as they determine or enhance it.[9]

The argument for value pluralism—that there may be many different values held dear to people and that they are not necessarily commensurable, as they make different demands on us and thus cannot be reduced to a common medium of

---

8. Bentham identified happiness with pleasure, considered to be homogeneous and differing only in duration and quantity, whereas Mill (whose ideas are somewhat closer to those of Aristotle) considered pleasures as differing not only in quantity and duration, but also in kind or quality, thus distinguishing between "higher" and "lower" pleasures. According to Nussbaum (2010: 85), it is this latter approach that forms the basis of the most modern discussions of pleasure among philosophers. Layard (2005) rejects as faulty the distinction between qualitatively different pleasures, or what he refers to as the happiness of experiences, arguing that certain kinds of pleasures have a more long-term effect on our happiness, while others only increase our happiness short-term. He rejects as paternalistic any qualitative differentiation of pleasures that results in enumeration of goods: "We ought never to say: this is good for you, even though it will never make you or others feel better. On the contrary, if we want to measure the quality of life it must be based on how people feel" (ibid.: 113). This is a powerful and persuasive argument, and its apparent simplicity makes it an appealing tool for public policy.

9. Sen (2009) questions the claim that happiness is the supreme good and ultimate goal because it alone is self-evidently good, arguing that how people feel should not necessarily be the ultimate yardstick, given people's well-documented abilities to adapt to hardship, and that they may have good reason to subject their own positive feelings to critical scrutiny. He nevertheless acknowledges that the achievement of other things that people may value may influence their sense of happiness, because people take pleasure in success in achieving their objectives; and that happiness can thus have indicative merit insofar as it reveals whether people are succeeding or failing to get what they value and have reason to value.

pleasure or utility—has been made forcefully by Isaiah Berlin, among others. This critique can be situated within a broader philosophical debate around value, one that has recently begun to attract greater anthropological attention. A central question concerns the relationship between the multiple values held in high regard, whether across social groups or within them: whereas monists argue that values can be seen as working harmoniously together—either because they can be subsumed under a higher value or because the important values support each other—pluralists tend to see them as fundamentally at odds, as some values may preclude pursuing others seen as of equal worth (Robbins 2013b: 100). It should come as no surprise that many anthropologists, deeply concerned with cultural specificity, find their position to be closer to value pluralism, and may feel discomfort at suggestions of any one value being a universal metavalue or ultimate end. Nevertheless, as suggested by recent anthropological discussions around the topic (e.g., Graeber 2001, 2013; Lambek 2008; Otto and Willerslev 2013; Robbins 2013b), the debate itself remains unresolved, and neither side can easily be dismissed.[10]

Value pluralism rests on an assumption that certain values are simply irreconcilable. Berlin was concerned that if the highest values of different people are at odds, then conflict may be inevitable; his suggestion recalls a more general statement by Weber that "the various value spheres [or values] of the world stand in irreconcilable conflict with each other" (1946: 147, cited in Robbins 2013b: 100). The articles in this collection, however, point to a different conclusion: while it may be difficult to endorse the possibility of any universal metavalue that allows for reconciliation of all lower values, the position that irreconcilability implies conflict is an oversimplification. We propose that values may well be incommensurable, and yet not stand in any direct conflict. In the everyday world of practical ethics, people routinely make judgments involving incommensurable values in a straightforward, formal, or schematic manner.

Instructive here is Michael Lambek's (2008) work on virtue and value, which argues that while economic values rest on an assumption of commensurability, ethical values are incommensurable and subject to judgment rather than choice. Nevertheless, historically speaking,

it is the nature of society, culture, or mind to posit or require some absolute standard of value or a meta-value that could provide a sound and universal measure

---

10. For example, Ronald Dworkin (2011) has recently made a forceful case for the unity of value.

of things. . . . There is a dialectic in human history between establishing absolute
values against which everything else is relative and to be measured, hence rendered commensurable to one another, and discovering things that render those
absolutes relative in turn. (Lambek 2008: 147)

In most societies there is a pressure to establish some overarching value as the
ultimate one, even though, historically, these values do not remain uncontested.
Two important lessons can be drawn from these observations. Firstly, the in-
commensurability of values need not imply total conflict, or the impossibility
of communication or translation between them; it presents instead a "partial
barrier" that can be navigated daily through judgment. In bringing the focus
back to everyday moral practice and decision making, this point is echoed by
several contributions to this collection (Freeman, Stafford, Vigh, among others).
Secondly, economic values are by definition commensurable, and market logic
calls for commensurability across different spheres of social life. This insight
is important, because it goes to the very heart of the question of why happiness has received such extraordinary attention across the social sciences over
the past decade or so. We suggest that as monetary value became increasingly
problematic as the basis for this market commensurability, happiness has proved
appealing to many because it appears to offer, in the form of an ultimate end,
precisely such commensurability. In other words, it is because of its potential
for translating across apparently diverse ends that happiness as a metavalue has
proved so powerful and alluring, while at the same time remaining thoroughly
embedded in—even further entrenching—a market logic.

Opposing the utilitarian conception of happiness as the highest end, a forceful argument for the multiplicity of values has recently been made by Robert
and Edward Skidelsky (2012). These authors list seven basic goods (health, security, dignity, personality, friendship, harmony with nature, and leisure)—notably excluding happiness, at least in the modern sense of a pleasant state of
mind, which they argue is not a good in itself, as everything depends on what
one is happy about. In this way, they effectively seek to renew the link between
happiness and virtue. They emphatically defend their substantive account of the
good life against the charge that it is potentially paternalistic, or even dangerous, by directly challenging the liberal assumption of "neutrality": the assumption that policy makers should refrain from making positive statements about
the way people should live, or creating policies with positive content, on the
grounds that doing so leads to authoritarianism. It is the legacy of John Rawls,

in particular, that only those principles necessary for people of different tastes and ideals to live together harmoniously should be embodied and promoted by a liberal state. The Skidelskys argue that this neutrality is largely fictional: "A 'neutral' state simply hands power to the guardians of capital to manipulate public taste in their own interests" (ibid.: 12). The refusal to state values clearly, in other words, fosters policies that are far from neutral in consequence.

Rather than the value pluralism represented by the Skidelskys, it is value monism that has been most closely associated with the danger of slipping into authoritarianism (Robbins 2013b: 102). Outside this particular debate, happiness discourse in economics and policy making may have acquired such power and prominence precisely because of the way it manages to evade both of these issues. It promises a unified value—the translatability and uniformity so very useful for policy making and measurement—while avoiding substantive claims about the nature or content of happiness, which is often defined simply in subjective terms. Whereas it could well be argued that the major flaw of this discourse is its conceptual emptiness, it must be remembered that this is precisely what makes it so versatile, flexible, and, ultimately, more powerful. A similar point is made by Cook (in this collection) in her analysis of the multiple meanings of "mindfulness." Metavalues in general, as anthropology has taught us, are most effective when they are not clearly defined. As Lambek observes in relation to religious values: "Rappaport argued that . . . [they] do their work best when they are stripped of informational content and specificity. Ultimate sacred postulates like 'God is one' may be deeply meaningful to their adherents but they are effective and enduring because they are referentially empty and unfalsifiable" (Lambek 2008: 144). We propose that "happiness," as it currently figures in the rising discourse of happiness studies, acquires its power precisely from its elusive definition.

HAPPINESS AS A MORAL MOOD

Are moral considerations external to happiness? Is there a conflict, in other words, between what it is morally right to do, and what is conducive to one's happiness? Or does happiness necessarily include, even depend on, being virtuous or morally upright? Insofar as happiness is considered to be a mood, feeling, or emotion, it has been relatively isolated from considerations of morality in recent work. Some of the reasons for this were touched upon above: the decoupling of happiness and virtue led to a view of the former as standing in tension with the wider social good. For some thinkers—most notably Kant—there is necessarily a conflict, in deciding what to do, between one's own happiness and the demands of morality. Within psychology, while researchers have been eager to emphasize the importance for individual happiness of rich social relationships, happiness (unlike, say, gratitude) is not considered to be prosocial; instead it is thought to occur primarily when (good) things happen to the self.[11] It can also occur when good things happen to another, although such reactions seem to require a prior social relationship, as when one is happy for a friend's success.

Nevertheless, according to some philosophers at least (Max Scheler for instance), happiness can be an affective motive of moral action. Ethnographically, there seems to be a close relationship between happiness and the interests of others. Among the Pintupi of Australia, for example, to be happy is to be shown affection and concern, and to show it to others. Because people represent their happiness as deriving from relations with "relations," there is in fact a very close connection between what it means to be among "kin," to be related, and to be "happy" (Myers 1979). Several of the contributions to this collection would similarly suggest that people are indeed often happiest precisely when they are attuned to others (see also Thin 2012). Successfully managing one's moral obligations may in fact be crucial for happiness: as among the Kuranko of Sierra Leone, for whom wellbeing is described as "dependent on an adjustment or balance between our sense of what we owe others and what we owe ourselves" (Jackson 2011: 195). After all, as Jarrett Zigon and Jason Throop put it, "a good deal of moral experience is about the care of relations," or what they term "being-together-with" (2014: 9).

The extent to which pleasure and virtue conflict, or reinforce each other, is a largely empirical question—still unresolved—that anthropology is perhaps uniquely well situated to answer. In any case, the contributions to this collection converge in suggesting that "real" happiness is not only highly relational—subsisting in the affective dimension of social relationships—but *other-oriented*. The direct pursuit of one's own individual happiness very often fails (e.g., Vigh, Stafford, this collection); on the other hand, in those cases where some form of happiness is actually achieved, it is often a result of actions carried out either

---

11. Some studies focusing on the effects of happiness on decision making even indicate that positive moods correlate with less generous or empathetic behaviors, or a higher degree of selfishness (Tan and Forgas 2010).

for or *by others* (e.g., Engelke, Freeman, Walker, this collection). The pursuit of happiness, we might conclude, is best left in the hands of those who care for us.

TEMPORALITIES

A final, though no less important, dimension of happiness concerns its temporality, or orientation in relation to the perception and social organization of time. Happiness clearly allows for multiple temporal vantage points: someone's overall condition could be evaluated at a particular moment in time, over a stretch of his or her life, or over that life as a whole (the perspectives taken by, respectively, Kavedžija, Vigh, and Lambek in this collection, for example). Happiness can also contain within it both long-term and short-term components (Walker, Robbins, this collection)—while the sources of happiness may themselves change dramatically over time, even over the space of just a few years (Freeman, this collection). A further key issue may be, as Lambek (this collection) puts it, "the way the temporal and the ethical dimensions intertwine."

Happiness is sometimes seen as pertaining to the distant past, imbuing memories of past times or events; or as located in the future, something for which one hopes or strives. Alternatively, it may be construed as immanent and immediate: as the British humanists profess, "the time to be happy is now" (Engelke, this collection). Wherever it is temporally located, happiness seems closely linked to a sense of "right orientation," a feeling that one is headed in the right direction. Of course, this allows for the distinct possibility that when people get what they want, they may cease to be happy (Bruckner 2011). Happiness can function as a powerful source of motivation, one that shapes the way people's lives are oriented toward certain horizons and not others. This may be true even when the pursuit of happiness itself becomes a kind of moral duty, as it arguably has in the modern West (see also Cook, this volume). To the extent that happiness is future-oriented, and to the extent that people's actions may be seen as motivated by this goal of future happiness, it is particularly interesting to consider the emerging body of work by psychologists demonstrating that humans are exceedingly poor at predicting what will make them happy, or, more precisely, how happy some given event or thing will actually make them in the future (Gilbert 2007; see also Stafford, this collection). Moreover, according to a number of studies conducted across widely different social contexts, people are surprisingly resilient in the sense that their self-proclaimed happiness levels remain relatively stable throughout their lives (D. Bok 2010). Even life-changing events, both positive and negative, affect their subjective wellbeing only temporarily, and it soon restabilizes at its "default" level. How, then, should we account for the wide range of actions ostensibly motivated by the pursuit of happiness, but which rarely if ever result in its achievement? The rational choice theory favored by economists (not far removed from utilitarianism) can only discount these efforts as misguided, based on the faulty reasoning to which humans are regrettably prone (Kahneman and Thaler 2006: 221). Our position, by contrast, is that studying these motivations in a broader sense involves placing the values of happiness alongside other those values seen as comprising or leading to it, as well as those seen as equally if not more important. It is in this way that we can understand the risky, reckless, and often futile pursuits of happiness of the young militiamen described by Vigh (this collection), for example; or the migration stories of young people from Bangladesh, as described by Gardner (this collection), whose expectations are not infrequently frustrated in their pursuit of a better life.

One question that arises, both philosophically and practically, is whether there is anything "real" about happiness. If it always "illusive" (Vigh, this collection), or imagined, endlessly deferred, and elusive when pursued outright (Gardner, this collection), where is it located? Happiness, we might suggest, provides a sense of orientation; like a horizon it delimits a space of action and understanding, even as it recedes from view. Situational and contingent, it brings some things into focus while occluding others, and adds a sense of depth to the mundane and everyday. As Hans-Georg Gadamer observed, speaking of historical consciousness: "To acquire a horizon means that one learns to look beyond what is close at hand – not in order to look away from it but to see it better" ([1975] 2006: 304).

The elusive or virtual quality of happiness would not make it any less real in its consequences, or capacity to orient people's actions. In many contexts, happiness may be seen as a worthwhile aim; in others it may be seen as lowly, selfish, or in competition with other values. Some of these evaluations will inevitably affect the way people direct their actions and imagine their futures. In contexts where happiness is valued highly, as in the West, the objects and aims with which it is associated will themselves typically be evaluated highly. This is what Ahmed (2010) calls the "promise of happiness": if you do "this," happiness will ensue. Conversely, "this" must therefore be good; and "you," as the kind of being who is guided by it, must therefore be good too. We can thus read Ahmed's observation as suggesting a crucial link between the temporality (and futurity) of happiness and its valuation. Depending on the values of happiness, as they stand in relation to other values, the social world takes its form: people's actions, plans, and motivations are offered to them along with their moral consequences.

CONCLUSION

One of the central challenges of anthropology is to recognize the potential diversity of human ends and to understand and interpret how people strive collectively to reach a balance between the different ends they value. These need not be commensurable, and may require a continuous exercise of moral judgment (Kavedžija, this collection); they may not all point to happiness. And yet, happiness seems strikingly well suited as a starting point for inquiring into what gives lives a sense of purpose or direction, or how people search for the best way to live—even in dire and hostile circumstances. For happiness is often something to be achieved—or not—by living a life of one kind or another. In contemplating the diversity of images revealed through ethnographic inquiry, we have suggested that happiness might usefully be considered in terms of questions of scope, virtue, and responsibility. Happiness may not always be seen as available to everyone, nor need it even be considered the property of a single individual; on the contrary, it may be construed as part of the uninterrupted flow of social life, an inherently relational quality not reducible to an individual person. Moreover, happiness always stands in a particular relationship to ideas of virtue, and at a greater or lesser distance from it; just as it always implicates specific forms of responsibility: who, ultimately, is responsible for the happiness of whom, and in what ways they may be held accountable.

Happiness always involves an evaluation of sorts: of one's condition at a moment in time, or of a life as a whole, or of several interpenetrating lives. As such, it is intrinsically linked to questions of value, both in terms of the cultural values that inform and enable the process of arriving at a positive assessment; and in terms of how happiness is itself evaluated in relation to that multiplicity of aims, desires, or experiences that may comprise one's conception of a full, good, or meaningful life. On the island of Yap, for example, happiness is less socially valued than suffering, which elicits empathic concern (Throop, this collection), while in the Ethiopian Gamo Highlands, by contrast, suffering is seen as unnecessary misery, whereas happiness consists of smooth and peaceful social relations—formerly achieved through the constant joking and interaction which ensured "present moment consciousness" and discouraged isolation, though increasingly through Pentecostal religious gatherings (Freeman, this collection). A different sense of changing values in China, and competing visions of family life, call into question the relative importance of individual and family happiness, as well as different possible evaluations of progress and material prosperity (Stafford, this collection). Among Japanese elderly, happiness can only be understood in relation to values of sociality, self-development, and responsibility to others (Kavedžija, this collection), while for British humanists, happiness involves a shared commitment to the Enlightenment values of secular reason (Engelke, this collection). Recent political interest in mindfulness in Britain reveals an indisputable affinity between individual happiness and the self-governing values of neoliberalism, and yet the experiences of mindfulness practitioners themselves reveals a broader and more diverse set of motivations and experiences (Cook, this collection). Happiness is bound up in the values of connectivity for Bengali migrants (Gardner, this collection), and in flexible, self-directed work, freedom from trouble, and the cultivation of a "style of life" for the Peruvian Urarina (Walker, this collection). For the retired Swiss dairy farmer Willi, it is his adhesion to the values of hard work and political engagement that underpins his achievement of a happy life (Lambek, this collection). For young militiamen in Guinnea-Bissau, happiness is closely related to social worth and status, or "becoming somebody," along with the values of stability and solidarity (Vigh, this collection).

An ethnographically grounded inquiry into happiness directs attention to what actually matters to people, or what gives life a sense of meaning and purpose, and it does so in a number of useful ways. To be clear, the answer to such a question of what matters most need not always be happiness, at least not in the sense of a pursuit of sustained good feeling. Our suggestion is rather that asking after happiness and its valences can offer a powerful way of understanding how diversely situated people grapple with fundamental questions of how to live, questions of value, motivation, and purpose; how they negotiate and reconcile their obligations to others with their sense of duty to themselves; and how they imagine their future, including how it feeds into their present and becomes their past. If value brings universes into being (Graeber 2013), the values of happiness go some way toward constituting the worlds of lived moral, political, and emotional experience, and an examination of those values may reveal to us their outlines and contours. We hope readers will find in the essays that follow a sense of worlds both familiar and unfamiliar.

ACKNOWLEDGMENTS

The present collection emerged from a workshop held at the London School of Economics and Political Science in January 2013, entitled "Values of Happiness: Ethnographic Perspectives on Living Well." The workshop was supported by the LSE Annual Fund. We are grateful to all those who participated, and especially to Neil Thin for his contributions as discussant. We would also like to thank Charles Stafford, Giovanni da Col, and two anonymous reviewers for their insightful comments and suggestions on this introductory chapter.

REFERENCES

Ahmed, Sara. 2010. *The promise of happiness*. Durham, NC: Duke University Press.

Annas, Julia. 1993. *The morality of happiness*. New York: Oxford University Press.

Arendt, Hannah. (1963) 1999. *On revolution*. London: Penguin. .

Argyle, Michael, Maryanne Martin, and Jill Crosslandl. 1989. "Happiness as a function of personality and social encounters." In *Recent advances in social psychology: An international perspective*, edited by Joseph P. Forgas and J. Michael Innes, 189-203. Amsterdam: Elsevier Science Publishers.

BBC. 2006. "Make people happier, says Cameron." May 22, sec. Politics. http://news.bbc.co.uk/1/hi/uk_politics/5003314.stm.

Berlin, Isaiah. 1969. *Four essays on liberty*. Oxford: Oxford University Press.

Berthon, Salomé, Sabine Chatelain, Marie-Noëlle Ottavi, and Olivier Wathelet, eds. 2009. *Ethnologie des gens heureux*. Paris: Éditions de la Maison des Sciences de l'Homme.

Bird-David, Nurit. 1999. "'Animism' revisited: Personhood, environment, relational epistemology." *Current Anthropology* 40: 67–91.

Bok, Derek. 2010. *The politics of happiness: What government can learn from the new research on well-being*. Princeton, NJ: Princeton University Press.

Bok, Sissela. 2010. *Exploring happiness: From Aristotle to brain science*. New Haven, CT: Yale University Press.

Bruckner, Pascal. 2011. *Perpetual euphoria: On the duty to be happy.* Translated by Steven Rendall. Princeton, NJ: Princeton University Press.

Bull, Torill, Mary Duah-Owusu, and Crystal Autry Andvik. 2010. "'My happiest moment is when I have food in stock': Poor women in northern Ghana talking about their happiness." *International Journal of Mental Health Promotion* 12 (2): 24–31.

Camfield, Laura, Kaneta Choudhury, and Joe Devine. 2009. "Well-being, happiness and why relationships matter: Evidence from Bangladesh." *Journal of Happiness Studies* 10 (1): 71–91.

Clark, Scott. 2009. "Pleasure experienced: Well-Being in the Japanese bath." In *Pursuits of happiness: Well-being in anthropological perspective,* edited by Gordon Mathews and Carolina Izquierdo, 189–210. New York: Berghahn Books.

Corsín Jiménez, Alberto, ed. 2008. *Culture and well-being: Anthropological approaches to freedom and political ethics.* London: Pluto.

————. 2008. "Well-being in anthropological balance: Remarks on proportionality as political imagination." In *Culture and well-being: Anthropological approaches to freedom and political ethics,* edited by Alberto Corsín Jiménez, 180–98. London: Pluto.

da Col, Giovanni, and Caroline Humphreys. 2012. "Introduction: Subjects of luck—contingency, morality, and the anticipation of everyday life." *Social Analysis* 56 (2): 1–18.

Davies, William. 2015. *The happiness industry: How the government and big business sold us well-being.* Kindle edition. London: Verso.

Diener, Edward. 1984. "Subjective well-being." *Psychological Bulletin* 95 (3): 542–75.

Diener, Edward, and Eunkook M. Suh. 2000. *Culture and subjective well-being.* Cambridge, MA: MIT Press.

Dolan, Paul, and Tessa Peasgood. 2010. "Measuring well-being for public policy: Preferences or experiences?" In *Law and Happiness,* edited by Eric A. Posner and Cass Sunstein, 5–32. Chicago: University of Chicago Press.

Dworkin, Ronald. 2011. *Justice for hedgehogs.* Cambridge, MA: Harvard University Press.

Fischer, Edward F. 2015. *The Good Life: Aspiration, Dignity, and the Anthropology of Wellbeing.* Stanford: Stanford University Press.

Gadamer, Hans-Georg. (1975) 2006. *Truth and method.* Translated by Joel G. Weinsheimer and Donald G. Marshall. Second, revised edition. London: Continuum.

Gilbert, Daniel. 2007. *Stumbling on happiness.* London: Harper Perennial.

Graeber, David. 2001. *Toward an anthropological theory of value: The false coin of our own dreams.* New York: Palgrave.

———. 2013. "It is value that brings universes into being: Postscript." *HAU: Journal of Ethnographic Theory* 3 (2): 219–43

Jackson, Michael. 2011. *Life within limits: Well-being in a world of want.* Durham, NC: Duke University Press.

———. 2013. *The wherewithal of life: Ethics, migration, and the question of well-being.* Berkeley: University of California Press.

Johnston, Barbara R. 2012. "Vital topics forum: On happiness." *American Anthropologist* 114 (1): 6–18.

Kahneman, Daniel, and Richard H. Thaler. 2006. "Anomalies, utility maximization and experienced utility." *Journal of Economic Perspectives* 20 (1): 221–34.

Kan, Chiemi, Mayumi Karasawa, and Shinobu Kitayama. 2009. "Minimalist in style: Self, identity, and well-being in Japan." *Self and Identity* 8 (2–3): 300–17.

Keane, Webb. 2015. *Ethical life: Its natural and social histories.* Princeton, NJ: Princeton University Press.

Kitayama, Shinobu, and Hazel Rose Markus. 2000. "The pursuit of happiness and the realization of sympathy: Cultural patterns of self, social relations, and wellbeing." In *Subjective well-being across cultures,* edited by Edward Diener and Eunkook M. Suh, 113–61. Cambridge, MA: MIT Press.

Kant, Immanuel. 1996. *Practical Philosophy.* Edited and translated by Mary J. Gregor. Cambridge: Cambridge University Press.

Laidlaw, James. 2005. "A life worth leaving: Fasting to death as telos of a Jain religious life." *Economy and Society* 34 (2): 178–99.

Lambek, Michael. 2008. "Value and virtue." *Anthropological Theory* 8 (2): 133–57.

Layard, Richard. 2005. *Happiness: Lessons from a new science.* Second revised edition. London: Penguin.

Lu, Luo. 2001. "Understanding happiness: A look into the Chinese folk psychology." *Journal of Happiness Studies* 2 (4): 407–32.

———. 2010. "Chinese well-being." In *The Oxford handbook of Chinese psychology,* edited by Michael Bond, 327–42. Oxford: Oxford University Press.

Lu, Luo, Robin Gilmour, Shu-Fang Kao, et al. 2001. "Two ways to achieve happiness: When the East meets the West." *Personality and Individual Differences* 30 (7): 1161–74.

Lutz, Catherine. 1988. *Unnatural emotions: Everyday sentiments on a Micronesian atoll and their challenge to Western theory.* Chicago: University of Chicago Press.

Mathews, Gordon, and Carolina Izquierdo, eds. 2009a. *Pursuits of happiness: Well-being in anthropological perspective.* New York: Berghahn Books.

———. 2009b. "Introduction: Anthropology, happiness, and well-being." In *Pursuits of happiness: Well-being in anthropological perspective*, edited by Gordon Mathews and Carolina Izquierdo, 1–19. New York: Berghahn Books.

Mauss, Marcel. (1938) 1985. "A category of the human mind: The notion of person; the notion of self." Translated by W. D. Halls. In *The category of the person: Anthropology, philosophy, history*, edited by Michael Carrithers, Steven Collins, and Steven Lukes, 1–25. Cambridge: Cambridge University Press.

McMahon, Darrin, 2006. *The pursuit of happiness: A history from the Greeks to the present.* London: Allen Lane (Penguin Books).

Miles-Watson, Jonathan. 2010. "Ethnographic insights into happiness." In *The practices of happiness: Political economy, religion and wellbeing*, edited by John Atherton, Elaine Graham, and Ian Steedman, 125–33. Abingdon: Routledge.

Mishra, Ramesh C. 1994. "Individualist and collectivist orientations across generations." In *Individualism and collectivism: Theory, method and application*, edited by Uichol Kim, Harry C. Triandis, Çigdem Kagitçibaşi, Sang-Chin Choi, and Gene Yoon, 225–38. London: Sage.

Myers, Fred R. 1979. "Emotions and the self." *Ethos* 7 (4): 343–70.

Nozick, Robert. 1990. *Examined Life: Philosophical Meditations.* New York: Simon and Schuster.

Nussbaum, Martha. 2001. "The fragility of goodness: Luck and ethics in Greek tragedy and philosophy." Revised edition. Cambridge: Cambridge University Press.

———. 2010. "Who is the happy warrior? Philosophy poses questions to psychology." In *Law and happiness*, edited by Eric A. Posner and Cass Sunstein, 81–113. Chicago: University of Chicago Press.

Oishi, Shigehiro, Jesse Graham, Selin Kesebir, and Iolanda Costa Galinha. 2013. "Concepts of happiness across time and cultures." *Personality and Social Psychology Bulletin* 39 (5): 559–77.

Otto, Ton, and Rane Willerslev. 2013. "Introduction: 'Value as theory': Comparison, cultural critique, and guerrilla ethnographic theory." *Hau: Journal of Ethnographic Theory* 3 (1): 1–20.

Robbins, Joel.. 2013a. "Beyond the suffering subject: Toward an anthropology of the good." *Journal of the Royal Anthropological Institute* (N.S.) 19 (3): 447–62.

———. 2013b. "Monism, pluralism, and the structure of value relations: A Dumontian contribution to the contemporary study of value." *Hau: Journal of Ethnographic Theory* 3 (1): 99–115.

Robbins, Joel, and Alan Rumsey. 2008. "Introduction: Cultural and linguistic anthropology and the opacity of other minds." *Anthropological Quarterly* 81 (2): 407–20.

Sahlins, Marshall. 2006. "The original affluent society (abridged)." In *The politics of egalitarianism: Theory and practice*, edited by Jacqueline Solway, 79–98. New York: Berghahn Books.

Selin, Helaine, and Gareth Davey, eds. 2012. *Happiness across cultures: Views of happiness and quality of life in non-Western cultures*. Ebook edition. Dordrecht: Springer Netherlands.

Sen, Amartya. 2008. "The economics of happiness and capability." *Capabilities and happiness*, edited by Luigino Bruni, Flavio Comim, and Maurizio Pugno, 16–27. Oxford: Oxford University Press.

———. 2009. *The idea of justice*. Cambridge, MA: Harvard University Press.

Skidelsky, Robert, and Edward Skidelsky. 2012. *How much is enough? The love of money and the case for the good life*. London: Penguin.

Suh, Eunkook M., and Shigehiro Oishi. 2004. "Culture and subjective well-being: Introduction to the special issue." *Journal of Happiness Studies* 5 (3): 219–22.

Tan, Hui Bing, and Joseph Forgas. 2010. "When happiness makes us selfish, but sadness makes us fair: Affective influences on interpersonal strategies in the dictator game." *Journal of Experimental Social Psychology* 46 (3): 571–76.

Taylor, Charles. 1989. *Sources of the self: The making of the modern identity*. Cambridge, MA: Harvard University Press.

Thin, Neil. 2008. "Realizing the substance of their happiness: How anthropology forgot about *Homo Gauiusus*." In *Culture and well-being: Anthropological approaches to freedom and political ethics*, edited by Alberto Corsín Jiménez, 134–55. London: Pluto.

———. 2012. *Social happiness: Theory into policy and practice*. Bristol: Policy Press.

United Nations News Service. 2011. "UN News—Happiness should have greater role in development policy—UN member states." July 19. http://www.un.org/apps/news/story.asp?NewsID=39084.

Weber, Max. 1946. *From Max Weber: Essays in sociology.* Translated by Hans H. Heinrich, New York: Oxford University Press.

White, Nicholas. 2006. *A brief history of happiness.* Malden, MA: Blackwell.

Wierzbicka, Anna. 2004. "'Happiness' in cross-linguistic and cross-cultural perspective." *Daedalus* 133 (2): 34–43.

Zigon, Jarrett, and C. Jason Throop. 2014. "Moral experience: Introduction." *Ethos* 42 (1): 1–15.

CHAPTER ONE

Ambivalent happiness and virtuous suffering

C. JASON THROOP

> *One of the fundamental fantasies of anthropology*
> *is that somewhere there must be a life really worth*
> *living.*
>
> – David Schneider, 1967

This sardonic reflection on one of the core fantasies motivating anthropological fieldwork is found in a brief two-page foreword that David Schneider penned to introduce Roy Wagner's book *The curse of the Souw* (1967).[1] The statement, classically Schneiderian in terms of its deeply ironic tone and scope, could very well have served as a preface to Schneider's own ethnographic research on Yap, however. As a member of the Harvard Yap Expedition—one of twenty-one "expeditions" launched as part of the Coordinated Investigation of Micronesian Anthropology (CIMA)—Schneider was required to contribute ethnographic data that would help to better understand, and ideally "solve," the problem of "rapid depopulation" on the island. During the period of Japanese colonial rule, depopulation had accelerated to such an extent that in 1924 "the Japanese

---

1. Joel Robbins (2013) references this same quote as a means to illuminate critical differences between so-called "savage slot" and "suffering slot" ethnography.

delegation to the League of Nations Permanent Mandates Commission was criticized regarding the 'alarming' danger of 'extinction' of the Yapese native population" (Bashkow 1991: 195).[2] As Ira Bashkow notes, at this time perhaps the

> most famous anthropological statement on de-population in indigenous com-
> munities was that of W. H. R. Rivers, who had argued that "underlying" the
> "more obvious causes" of depopulation, such as "the new diseases and poisons,"
> was a "psychological factor": the "loss of interest in life" caused by colonial dis-
> ruptions in the religious and economic institutions that had previously motivated
> vigorous native pursuits. (Bashkow 1991: 187)

A strikingly similar perspective was voiced, Bashkow observes, by Japanese co-lonial administrators, who, in responding to the League of Nations commis-sion, had "apparently convinced themselves that 'psychologically, the natives were absolutely indifferent to . . . their extinction'" (ibid.: 195). That the Yapese themselves may have no longer been able to hold on to the belief that their own lives were "really worth living," and that there could be significant psychologi-cal "factors" at the root of such a radical form of world-collapse, established the backdrop against which Schneider's fieldwork on the island was cast.

While Schneider's research eventually led him to the conclusion that "the population had begun a 'slow but steady' increase" and that "the Yapese suf-fered no Riversian 'loss of the will to live'" (ibid.: 227), as his fieldnotes attest, he was deeply unsettled by his inability to attune to the affective expectations and responses of his Yapese "informants" as he tried to establish "rapport" with them. In contrast to the tonality of many of his own idealized romantic and hu-manistic impulses prior to entering the field, Schneider discovered quite quickly that the Yapese "were not blissfully sexual, nor loyally communal, nor politically easygoing, and not by a long stretch were they egalitarian" (ibid.: 226). Nor were they, in any straightforward sense of the term at least, "happy."

---

2.   Estimates of precolonial population on the island range anywhere from 28,000 to 50,000 inhabitants (Hunt, Kidder, and Schneider 1954; Schneider 1955; Labby 1976). By the time of the first census conducted by the Catholic mission in 1899, however, the population had shrunk to just under 8000. Yap's population reached an all-time low during the American Navy's first census in the wake of the Japanese occupation in 1946, with merely 2478 inhabitants (Hunt, Kidder, and Schneider 1954; Egan 1998).

A LIFE REALLY WORTH LIVING

What makes a life "really worth living," and what, if anything, does "happiness" have to do with it? As detailed in Walker and Kavedžija's introduction to this collection, the relationship between understandings of happiness as *eudaimonia* (a form of human flourishing) or *hedonia* (a specifiable emotional feeling) has structured many debates about happiness in contemporary social scientific and philosophical accounts. From a phenomenological perspective, however, "happiness" is taken to be an *intermediary phenomenon* (Throop 2009a; cf. Jackson 1998) that manifests neither strictly in terms of a generalized capacity for flourishing nor as an interiorized state. It is considered instead a modality of being, a felicitous form of attunement, attachment, and attention, which orients persons to themselves, others, events, situations, and the world in particular sorts of ways. To put it differently, happiness in such a view is understood as an existential orientation to self, other, and world, rather than as a particular mode of living well or feeling good.

As Michael Jackson (2011) argues when speaking of the related concept of "wellbeing," however, such felicitous attunements are never settled states of existence (see also Jackson 2013; cf. Corsín Jimenez 2008; Mathews and Izquierdo 2009; Thin 2012). They arise and dissipate, flow and ebb, constrict and expand in ways that are never simply coterminous with, nor necessarily predictable from, the dictates of culturally constituted expectations and desires that inform putatively shared understandings of what constitutes the parameters of a good life or the discernible qualities of hedonic feelings. Rather, such positive attunements are always haunted by "insufficiency and loss," as well as by a basic "condition of existential dissatisfaction" that marks the ever-present discontinuities "between who we are and what we might become" (Jackson 2011: ix).

That we could be happier, that things that should make us happy sometimes do not, that we are not happy in the right way, measure, or degree, that some forms of happiness may be incommensurate with other forms of joy we may yet equally desire, that our happiness is not shared by others, that our own happiness may actually diminish possibilities for happiness in others, or, even worse, that it may only be possible by means of others' unhappiness and suffering—all of these are existential possibilities that not only inhabit the background of any foregrounded experience of happiness (see also Vigh, this collection), they also at times break through to unsettle and transform it. Happiness in the context of those concrete specificities of situated encounters in which singular and complex beings engage with one another and their surrounding world is thus seldom experienced without some degree of ambivalence, ambiguity, and instability.

THE SPIRIT OF HAPPINESS

Having witnessed the effects of cultural dissolution at the hands of four differing colonial administrations (Spanish, German, Japanese, and American), Schneider's adopted Yapese "father" embodied in a particularly striking way the tonality of despairing "unhappiness" that seemed to permeate everyday life in the wake of the US Navy's "liberation" of the island. As Bashkow describes it,

> Annually performing ceremonies that no one else remembered, Tannengin regarded the forgetting of customs as an actual threat to Yapese survival, because words to be spoken to the spirits were "lost and cannot be recovered." Lamenting depopulation—the people had died around him—he wondered if the spirits of fertility had not already "all gone away from Yap." (1991: 211)

And indeed, as Schneider's "father" well knew, the "words to be spoken to the spirits" were of paramount concern given that they not only facilitated communication with them but also helped to ensure their "happiness." As Schneider later famously observed, when confronted with a significant problem, the "head of the lineage" must divine "to locate a happy ancestral spirit, and on finding one, . . . [beseech] that ancestral spirit to intercede on behalf of its living lineage with the generalized spirit who can effect the cure for the illness, improve the fishing, make the woman pregnant, and so on" (1984: 15–16). Such efforts to discern and maintain the relative "happiness" of spirits, Schneider argued, were considered crucial to ensuring the wellbeing of individuals, families, and communities alike.

Concern for the "happiness" of spirits was also echoed in the reflections of Liffer, one of two women on the island who was known to still be able to communicate with spirits at the time at which I conducted the bulk of my fieldwork in the early to mid-2000s. In her late eighties, thin with short well-cropped hair, sharp features, and penetrating dark eyes, Liffer spoke quietly, but with a confidence that reflected the fact that people had approached her cautiously for many years, with respect, knowing that she had the ability to communicate with spirits (*ngathaliy*). When recounting her life story to me, Liffer recalled that the spirits (*thagiith*) first came to her when she left her natal village to move in with her husband and her husband's family. Her own family had not blessed the marriage and had cut off all ties with her in the wake of her decision to marry a man they did not first approve of. Liffer was only nineteen when all of this happened (about a decade prior to Schneider's arrival on the island). Not long after her family abandoned her, Liffer became terribly sick and remained incapacitated for the better part of three months.

As her illness showed little sign of abating, her mother-in-law, who had kept a close eye on her throughout her affliction, decided that her sickness was a symptom of *ngathaliy*. Since her mother-in-law had some previous experience calling the spirits, she offered to help. Frightened but unsure what else to do (or in fact if she had any choice in the matter), Liffer accepted the offer. Sitting down facing her directly, her mother-in-law looked deep into her eyes and instructed her not to resist, before beginning to utter in a repetitive and rhythmic fashion the phrase *moey moey* ("come, come"). As the spirit entered her body, Liffer recalled yawning and feeling a cold sensation running down the length of her spine, and then apparently nothing more until the spirit left her.

When she regained consciousness, her mother-in-law explained that the spirit who possessed her was her deceased father, who said that he had come on account of the sickness from which his *kanaawoq* ("host"; literally "path") was suffering. The spirit then explained that the way to cure her sickness was for Liffer to return to her natal estate and to have her family make sweet-scented flower necklaces, as well as gather food and other valuables that could be then used to propitiate him. When her natal family eventually complied with the spirit's request, her father's spirit was *falfalaen'* ("happy"), she reported, because there were now "good feelings in the estate" (*feal' ea laen ii yaen' ko tabinaew*). Her father's spirit had been acting out of "compassion" (*runguy*) for her, she explained, and was not "angry" (*puwaen'*) at the other members of her family who had abandoned her. Other spirits may and do act quite differently, however. The happiness of spirits is, it seems, a precarious achievement.

PRECARIOUS HAPPINESS

As Sara Ahmed (2010) points out in her excellent book on the topic, the instability and contingency of the English term "happiness" is captured in its etymological roots. The lexeme is derived from the Middle English word "hap," a term that refers to chance. In its earliest derivations, the word "happy" originally referred to "having 'good 'hap' or fortune,' to be lucky or fortunate" (ibid.: 22). According to Ahmed, the term "happy" was first used to refer to chance and contingency, to the fact that something beyond our control has happened to us—in this particular case, something good. Ahmed suggests, however, that the inherent contingency once tied to the meaning of the term "happiness"—its precariousness—has been slowly lost over time. No longer thought to be exclusively connected to unpredictability and chance, happiness has become deemed an internalized condition or state of being that can be cultivated or produced through our actions, choices, efforts, and work. As such, happiness is now deemed a state of the self that is produced through the self's efforts. A failure in happiness can thus quite easily be read back as a failure of the self.[3]

A primary goal of Ahmed's theoretical interventions into contemporary understandings and uses of happiness is to reclaim the contingency entailed in its original formulations. In so doing, she hopes to expand its range of possibility. She also aims to show how "unhappiness" can significantly unsettle and reveal aspects of our taken-for-granted assumptions about the world that may in fact limit the range of possibilities for happiness in the context of our own and others' lives. In this respect, she argues, "we need to think about unhappiness *as more than a feeling that needs to be overcome*" (ibid.: 217). It is only when this happens, she suggests, that we can, "witness happiness as a possibility that acquires significance by being a possibility alongside others . . . [and accordingly] can value happiness for its precariousness, as something that comes and goes, as life does" (ibid.: 219). In Ahmed's estimation, such a view of happiness is only rendered properly visible, however, when the variable "'worldly' question of happenings" that define the limits, contingencies, and possibilities of happiness is given careful consideration.

---

3. With the global circulation of psychiatric mood disorders, and the psychopharmaceutical management and "enhancement" of moods to fit within a range of the "happy," an ongoing diagnostic accounting of such failures of the self (which we should also note all too easily takes attention away from other political, social, and economic failures) is quite arguably one of the defining marks of our contemporary situation. To preserve the integrity of the self's wellbeing, the locus of failure is increasingly construed as one of neurobiological deficiency or malfunction (see Rose 2006).

WORLDLY HAPPENINGS

Paer was a large woman with pure white hair in her late sixties living in a mid-caste village on the east coast of Yap. Married three times, with four children, and recently widowed, she walked with a visible limp that required her to use a cane to get around. On this particular day, Paer sat on the veranda of her house, avoiding my gaze, looking out over her garden. She had planted this garden close to the house, she explained, to reduce the distance she had to walk to get food when her grandson was visiting. Her leg was hurting a lot these days and it was just not possible for her to get to her favorite taro patches and gardens without some help.

Her present pain seemed to be evocative of the traces of past suffering, however; at that moment our conversation shifted rather abruptly, I thought, to her memories of gardening for the Japanese soldiers during the war. "During that war, there was great suffering that was put upon us," she exclaimed.

> Very great suffering that the Japanese gave to us. We all stayed and we all worked. And there was work and that is how it went. We went to work and we all, we all cooked for them . . ., so in the morning we ate [whatever we could] and then off to work . . . in the gardens [to get] food for the Japanese.

After a long pause, my field assistant Manna interjected, "Very hard work was put in." "Very hard," Paer continued.

> Those Japanese I tell you, very hard work there. You could not . . . because . . . you were working it didn't matter . . . you see, you would work and [even if] there is pain in your back and you cannot stand up, you are told to return to work because they are watching . . . and they will beat you.

While the suffering associated with Japanese forced labor camps was brutal, the end of the war did not, however, mark the end of Paer's pain. "Myself, my life, there has been very intense suffering in my life, from long ago [before the war] to present." Not only did she lose her first husband in a car accident, but her efforts to pursue renewed possibilities for living were shattered yet again when her second husband beat her so badly that she had to end the marriage and return to her parents' village. While unwilling to say much about those years, she explained that through it all she somehow managed to find the wherewithal to keep going for the sake of her children. After a few years of struggling to make do in her parents' village, she eventually met the man who would become her third husband. While they, too, often struggled, argued, and fought, his final succumbing to cancer was perhaps the most devastating experience of her life.

While Paer believed that she had done the best she could have given the circumstances that were thrown her way, she had reached the limit of what she could bear. As she confided,

> I got married and I became pregnant, myself and my children, we lived together, . . . [and] I helped my [family's] and my children's life [as best I could]. But [then] there was my [last] husband who died so right now there is nothing that I can do, I stay and I wait for the time that I will [die].

Reflecting upon her situation in the wake of her third husband's passing, she characterized herself as having lost the ability to "hope." "I usually try a bit you know," she explained,

> [but] now I have no more responsibilities [my husband is dead and my children have grown] . . . if there is something [to do], I make every effort to do it . . . [if] there is something [to do] I try my best to garden . . . [for instance] if there is someone [visiting] who is hungry I don't like that they will [go] hungry, but, at present I am [mostly] living idly, perhaps I have lost hope, or I don't know what.

The fact that she had worked, endured, and persevered in the face of suffering was for Paer, as it was for many of the people I spoke to in the context of my research, something of significant moral worth (see Throop 2010a). Regardless of its perceived moral value, however, such experiences did not in the end bring her "happiness." They only resulted in her experiencing on a daily basis, now that she was close to the end of her life, a painful loss of hope.

ATTUNEMENT, ATTACHMENT, AND ATTENTION

Key to phenomenological approaches to lived experience is the idea, first articulated by Edmund Husserl ([1913] 1962), that individuals are continually shifting between differing "attitudes"—or what Clifford Geertz (1973) termed "perspectives"—in the context of their engagements with their social and physical worlds. It is by means of what Husserl termed "acts of phenomenological modification" that individuals come to transform their orientations to experience: from despairing to hopeful perspectives on a given situation, for example (see Throop 2003, 2010a, 2010b, 2015; Duranti 2009a, 2009b, 2010).

Differing phenomenological modifications can, however, have greater or lesser transformational effects on the experience of particular objects, acts, events, and persons. Some modifications are radical enough to transform an experience of an object to such an extent that it is no longer experienced as the "same" object at all—shifting between the incommensurable images of the Rubin Face/Vase Illusion being one good example. Other modifications may be quite subtle, however. Such attenuated shifts in perspective include everyday and ongoing fluctuations in attention by means of which different properties of an object come into focus: noticing the smooth surface of an actual vase after appreciating its amber coloring, for instance. Subtler modifications are also entailed in those moments where an object is experienced as the "same" object existing under different conditions through time—such as when it becomes apparent that the same vase placed in different lighting is actually a hue of brownish-red (see Throop 2015).

Whether radical or subtle, such shifts in orientation to objects of experience necessarily involve what are often unnoticed alterations in forms of understanding, feeling, emotion, and mood that color the experience of a given object, action, event, situation, or person moment by moment. Such everyday acts of modification Husserl termed "intentional modifications" (see Husserl [1913] 1962; Duranti 2009a, 2009b). In Husserlian terms, "intentional modifications" refers to *the ways* in which consciousness is directed toward given objects of experience (e.g., intentionality).[4] "Intentional modifications" implies, in short, that consciousness constitutes objects of experience by means of particular, and shifting, acts of judgment, feeling, sensing, imagining, remembering, anticipating, or perceiving.

The surrounding world is never a neutral canvas upon which subjects freely paint their experiences, however. The world itself also draws us in, has a hold on us, and pulls our attention toward it. Attention, as Husserl argued, is "pulled" or "affected" by worldly happenings, events, situations, and relations (Husserl [1918–26] 2001; see Throop and Duranti 2014). Accordingly, depending on the context, at any given moment, we may be drawn to notice or engage with certain

---

4. The term "intentional" is used here in reference to the phenomenological concept of intentionality, which refers to the "aboutness" of consciousness as directed toward particular objects of experience.

aspects of a given situation and not others. We are thus, as Jarrett Zigon argues, attuned to the "diverse and particular relationships that make possible the vast diversity of ways of living we find in the social world" (2014: 22).[5]

Happiness, as a form of attunement and intentional modification that transforms perspectives on the world, thus organizes attention in particular sorts of ways. Happiness brings attention to certain aspects of the world that would not otherwise be noticed in other emotional or mood-inflected orientations. It also covers over aspects of the world that would be disclosed in other, non-happy modes of being. As such, happiness significantly shapes the contours of the world, as well as those possibilities for action, attachment, attention, and attunement that are encountered within it. According to Ahmed (2010), who also productively draws from Husserl in her approach to happiness, such modes of "affective interest" shape the horizons of an individual's embodied experience, cares, and concerns, and the range of practical actions enfolded within them.

To say that happiness is a form of attunement that organizes attention, redefining what is salient and desirable, in the process reconfiguring the experience of particular situations, interactions, persons, or objects, is another way of saying that happiness establishes horizons. The phenomenological notion of *horizon* highlights the existential fact that humans are necessarily embodied, finite, and positioned beings who are never able to exhaust their experience of the world in which they are emplaced, "as there is always something more yet to come, a side yet to see, an aspect, quality, action, or interaction yet to experience" (Desjarlais and Throop 2011: 90). Happiness, its pursuit or realization, thus significantly organizes what it is that individuals attend to, how they attend to it, as well as what they ignore. It is, of course, necessary in this regard to recall that particular

---

5. My use of "attunement" throughout this article resonates strongly with Zigon's articulation of the concept, which builds directly upon Heidegger's original formulation (ibid.). As Heidegger explains, "Attunements are the fundamental ways in which we *find* ourselves *disposed* in such and such a way. Attunements are the '*how*' [*Wie*] according to which one is in such and such a way. Certainly we often take this 'one is in such and such a way'. . . . as something indifferent, in contrast to *what* we intend to do, *what* we are occupied with, or *what* will happen to us. And yet this 'one is in such and such a way' is not—is never—simply a consequence or side-effect of our thinking, doing, and acting. . . . And precisely *those* attunements to which we pay no heed at all, the attunements we least observe, those attunements which attune us in such a way that we feel as though there is no attunement there at all, as though we were not attuned in any way at all—these attunements are the most powerful" ([1929/30] 1995: 67–68).

horizons are defined *for us*, as much as *by us*, and that social, cultural, political, economic, and historical processes are always significantly at work in partially shaping the sedimented, habituated parameters of particular lifeworlds. This includes affectively configured horizons as well.

HORIZONS OF HAPPINESS

Over the course of my fieldwork, Tamag, a short and athletic man in his late fifties, had become a close friend whom I often visited whenever I had the chance to make the thirty- to forty-minute drive up to the northern municipality of Maap. Known for his good-natured affability, Tamag was a thoughtful, socially astute observer, with much to say about the contemporary challenges Yapese communities are facing. During one such visit, sitting together in the comfortable shade of his newly built rest house (*koeyeeng*) overlooking the ocean, I listened intently as Tamag reflected on the difficulty he and others were having motivating the village youth to participate in community work projects, such as their village's current effort to replace the roof on the village men's house (*faeluw*). The problem, Tamag suggested, was one of *falfalaen'* ("happiness"). Rather confused by the statement, I asked him to elaborate. Whereas community work had traditionally been a nonnegotiable obligation that took priority over all other considerations, he explained, for the younger generations it seemed that the self-sacrifice implicated in such community-mandated forms of service was increasingly at odds with the youth's growing desire to feel only "happiness" (*falfalaen'*) in their lives. While it was certainly enjoyable to feel "happy" (*falfalaen'*), a major problem with aspiring to be happy at all times, Tamag lamented, was that individuals who are always happy will never directly embody suffering (*gaafgow u fithik ea dooway*). Without directly experiencing suffering, he reasoned, an individual will never be able to effectively cultivate feelings of *runguy* ("compassion") for others who may yet still be suffering.

All of this was not to say, Tamag reassured me, that there were not times in his own life when he felt *falfalaen'* or desired to be "happy." In fact, he fondly remembered moments of playing with friends and cousins during his childhood as times when he felt some of his greatest contentment. The fact remained, however, that such experiences of "happiness" were fleeting and contingent affairs that arose in the wake of an absence of responsibility to and for others. Experiences of *falfalaen'* did not, therefore, in his estimation, significantly impact his attachments and obligations to friends, family, and community. Such moral bonds were instead defined, he believed, by his experiences of *suffering-for* others in the context of effortful work in the village and for his family (see the discussion in Walker and Kavedžija's introduction to this collection on the axes of "virtue" in relation to "happiness").

Even though still at times sought after and valued modes of being, "contentment" and "happiness" (*falfalaen*) were in Tamag's case modes of attunement that limit horizons of compassionate responsivity to others in the community who may be suffering (*gaafgow*). One of the key logical assumptions undergirding his reflections was that if an individual is *falfalaen* ("happy"), he or she is not focused on the wellbeing of others. The attention of such "happy" individuals will not be drawn, as Ahmed might say, to others' "unhappiness." Individuals who are *falfalaen* are instead characterized as focusing their attention solely upon their own success, wellbeing, and comfort. Social attachments are thus neglected in the wake of happiness's horizon. In short, a key moral question arising in the face of such forms of self-focused happiness is: If others are still suffering, how can you claim to be happy?[6]

THE UNHAPPINESS OF HAPPINESS

According to Ahmed, conventionalized forms of happiness that give shape to particular "horizons of experience" are affective forms of orientation that often

---

6.   It is interesting to note in this regard that the Yapese term that can be most easily glossed as "selfishness" (*fal'ngaak*) can be literally translated as "his or her goodness-wellbeing." Why would goodness or wellbeing be directly associated with self-centeredness? There are a number of cognate Yapese morphemes that carry the connotation of "good" or "well" (*fal, feal', faal,* and *fael'*) that are also used to designate morally problematic states of being. These include *fal'ngaak* ("selfish"), *fal'fal'l'ugun* ("liar, falsehood"), and *fael'* ("to fool someone"). On the positive end of the spectrum are the terms *faalngin* ("propitious act, abstention, or sacrifice"), *fal'eag* ("to create, build, or repair"), *fal'egin* ("to fix or mend"), *falaaqaab* ("fortunate, lucky"), and *falfalaen* ("happiness, contentment"). Even in the case of these more positively valenced terms, however, there are notable connotations of lack, contingency, imperfection, and sacrifice implicated in them. Bridging between these polarities is the term *falaay,* which may refer to either "beneficial medicine" or "harmful magic" depending on the context. That the same morphemic root is used to designate terms for happiness, good fortune, beneficial medicine, harmful magic, falsehood, and selfishness is quite striking and not, I think, arbitrary.

result from an unquestioned inheritance. The normative standards, values, and assumptions embedded in such affective orientations narrow the horizon of what counts as happiness for any given individual or group (cf. Laidlaw 2008). Conventional forms of happiness recurrently focus our attention to particular objects, actions, and situations and not others, in the process bringing definition and prominence to particular possibilities and relations and not others. If particular horizons of experience are defined by such an affective narrowing of attention, then, Ahmed asks, "what kind of world takes shape when happiness provides the horizon?" (2010:14). And perhaps more pointedly, whose happiness counts in the shaping of such a horizon?

"The promise of happiness is what makes certain objects proximate, affecting how the world gathers around us," Ahmed suggests (ibid.). And yet, on the flip side, happiness also causes objects and others to recede from our view. Most significantly, this includes those objects, others, and situations that threaten to diminish our happiness. As Ahmed explains,

> Happiness might play a crucial role in shaping our near sphere, the world that takes shape around us, as a world of familiar things. Objects that give us pleasure take up residence within our bodily horizon. . . . To have "our likes" means certain things are gathered around us . . . [conversely] awayness might help establish the edges of our horizon; in rejecting the proximity of certain objects, we define the places that we know we do not wish to go, the things we do not wish to have, touch, taste, hear, feel, see, those things we do not want to keep within reach. (2010: 24)

Happiness augments attachments to felicitous objects as much as it diminishes attachments to infelicitous ones.

Facing toward some horizons and away from others, happiness is a form of attunement, attachment, and attention that foregrounds some events, relations, and objects, while necessarily backgrounding others. Walking quickly past a homeless man on the street while averting our eyes, turning the channel on the TV so as not to hear about the latest onslaught of tragic news, avoiding "touchy subjects" in conversations with family and friends, dwelling in the happiness of places or times now long past or in the future possibility of a happiness yet to come—all are routine ways that happiness is guarded and guards, thus limiting and defining our proximity to the suffering of others or to those unhappy situations or relations that might threaten happiness (even if such happiness is only ever an anticipated goal). Happiness may mask the roots of suffering as well. As Ahmed argues, "Happiness can work to cover over unhappiness, in part by covering over its causes, such that to refuse to take cover can allow unhappiness to emerge" (ibid.: 87).

Happiness can define and narrow worldly horizons, thus excluding others, objects, events, and acts from a person's purview. It can also cover over or mask unhappiness and its roots. As Lauren Berlant (2011) claims, the very pursuit of happiness as a means of attaining "the good life" may also be implicated in forms of "cruel optimism," wherein objects of desire become themselves the primary obstacles to present and future flourishing. Happiness is, however, only one of many possible experiences of "affect" that may be attached to the "structure of relationality" characterizing Berlant's view of optimism. As she explains,

> Whatever the *experience* of optimism is in particular, then, the *affective structure* of an optimistic attachment involves a sustaining inclination to return to the scene of fantasy that enables you to expect that *this* time, nearness to *this* thing will help you or a world to become different in just the right way. But again, optimism is cruel when the object/scene that ignites a sense of possibility actually makes it impossible to attain the expansive transformation for which a person or a people risks striving. (2011: 2)

Even though Berlant explicitly distances herself from Ahmed, whom she sees as dealing primarily with emotion and not "affect," that is, with "the feeling of optimism itself" rather than the diffuse and uneven atmospherics implicated in the "optimism of attachment" (ibid.: 12), she certainly seems to share her suspicion that happiness may be implicated in binding people to particular "modes of life that threaten their well-being" (ibid.: 16). Her analysis of the global obesity epidemic as a form of "slow death" is one powerful example.

A SLOW DEATH

> This disease is terrible . . . it is just a terrible disease . . . it doesn't . . . the one thing
> I don't like about it is that it doesn't just kill you right there. It slowly, you know,
> . . . kills you little by little. One body part goes, then this, this, this, this . . . same
> . . . same . . . and that is worse . . . that is the pain . . . painful part of it.

The once assertive, self-assured, and at times intimidating young man whom I often saw stumbling around town in a half-drunken stupor, always sporting his ubiquitous sunglasses and baseball cap, had been reduced at the time that he uttered these words to a skinny, glassy-eyed, feeble man now facing the very real possibility of his own death. As he spoke these words to me, lying there on his hospital bed the day before he was to leave for Guam for treatment for his failing kidneys (Yap State Memorial Hospital has no dialysis machines), all of Chep's previous bravado and intensity seemed to have been drained from his being. As he explained to me, his diabetes had progressed to the point where his right leg had been amputated above the knee, his eyesight was steadily deteriorating, and his kidneys were failing. He also had a "bad heart" and there were problems with his "veins," which were not, as he put it, "letting enough blood through." As a result, he was suffering from shortness of breath. He could barely sit up in bed without feeling dizzy and faint. Standing up was simply out of the question.

As we spoke together in the poorly lit space of his hospital room, Chep knew that he did not have long to live, and, tragically, he was right; he died a few months later in a much better lit hospital room in Guam. Largely immobile, weak, at times disoriented, in constant pain, and unsure of his future, Chep spent much of his last days contemplating the events and circumstances that led up to the onset of his illness. As he recalled,

> My diabetes I think it is definitely the . . . the lifestyle the way I used to have to uh . . . do things . . . I think . . . ah . . . alcohol is the one thing that is not good for that . . . and I had so much alcohol when I was growing up . . . and . . . like twenty years or the last twenty years when I started drinking before I stopped . . . it didn't bother me at the time. I didn't even feel anything. And I kept on doing it and people kept telling me, "Hey, you have to slow down, you're sick . . ." "Who said?" . . . um . . . I really, I really, I really don't know when . . . until I knew that I could not do it . . . I was so sick, I couldn't do it . . . so [it is only then that] I stopped.

The simple truth was that Chep enjoyed drinking. It did not matter to him if the doctor told him to stop because he was sick or if he happened to hurt or disappoint his family when he was drunk. (He would often abandon his wife and children, disappearing for days when off on a bender.) The bottom line was that drinking made him "happy." It made him feel like his life was really worth living. When he was drunk, he asserted, he was *falfalaen*'—all of his worries, anxieties, and concerns faded away. That is, until his diabetes progressed to the point where he was far too sick to even consider taking another sip. By that point, however, his possibility for second chances had run out.

The tragic results of Chep's abiding in the "happiness" that he experienced while drinking resonated with what many voiced to be the narrowly present-focused temporal horizon that experiences of *falfalaen*' are prone to engender. Indeed, when people spoke to me about "happiness," their own and others', they often characterized it as a fleeting state of being in which one is no longer adequately oriented to either past or future concerns. To be *falfalaen*' in *this moment* is thus to forget the suffering of the past, not only one's own suffering but also the suffering of others, one's family, one's community, and one's ancestors. It is to forget Schneider's "father's" concern for the happiness of spirits. The restricted temporal reach of experiences of *falfalaen*' also obscures its precariousness in the face of an always-unpredictable future. It thus also covers over the contingency of happiness, as Ahmed would put it.[7]

In contrast to the narrow temporal horizons that *falfalaen*' putatively foregrounds, experiences of suffering (*gaafgow*) are understood to offer an extended existential vista onto both past situations and future happenings. Suffering, its avoidance, and "suffering-for" the benefit of others were in fact explicitly held to give rise to possibilities for appropriately planning and thinking through what can be done in the present in the service of bettering one's family's and community's position in future generations. Suffering was also a way to tangibly connect one's present suffering with the suffering of others who have also worked to better those material and social conditions that define an individual's, family's,

---

7.   A similar such ambivalent characterization of the narrow temporal horizons of happiness is also detailed in Catherine Lutz's classic ethnographic work on emotions on the nearby Micronesian atoll of Ifaluk. As Lutz observes, in Ifaluk, "happiness/excitement" is often seen to be a "dangerous, socially disruptive" emotion (1988: 145). "In this regard, the concept of *ker* (happiness/excitement) plays what is, from an American perspective, a paradoxical role. Happiness/excitement is an emotion people see as pleasant but amoral. It is often, in fact, *im*moral because someone who is happy/excited is more likely to be unafraid of other people. While this lack of fear may lead them to laugh and talk with people, it may also make them misbehave or walk around showing off or 'acting like a big shot' (*gabos fetal*)" (ibid.: 167). Accordingly, whereas "American approaches to child rearing and emotion elevate happiness to an important position, setting it out as an absolute necessity for the good or health child (and adult), the Ifaluk view happiness/excitement as something that must be carefully monitored and sometimes halted in children" (ibid.).

or community's contemporary existence. This includes the day-to-day efforts of those who suffer alongside each other in the present, as much as it does those whose past suffering has paved the way for current possibilities for prosperity and wellbeing. Indeed, each "estate" or *tabinaew* within a given village in Yap, along with all the various house foundations, taro patches, and gardens associated with it, was traditionally understood to be invested with particularized histories and ranks that reflect the labor of differing successive clans upon the land (see Labby 1976; Schneider 1984; Throop 2010a). "The place established by estate ancestors within this order," Jim Egan observes, was directly "bound to the land upon which they lived, imbuing its soil with essences that were passed on to the very taro grown within it" (1998: 45).

Suffering was thus generally deemed virtuous by local standards to the extent that it helped to orient individuals, families, and communities to future horizons of possibility and past legacies of effortful sacrifice. In so doing, suffering defines extended horizons of experience, and accordingly gives rise to possibilities for "hope" (*athapaag*). This is not the hope that suffering will be transformed without remainder into future happiness. It is instead more akin to the hope that Jackson (2011) sees as rooted in an existential dissatisfaction that traverses the expanse of who we are, who we have been, and who we might yet still become.

Recognizing past suffering, acknowledging the ongoing suffering of others, as well as being attuned to the ever-present possibility of an arrival of unwanted future suffering, are each aspects of the moral worth of *gaafgow* ("suffering") that actively bring into relief the precariousness of "happiness," as well as its limited intersubjective and temporal scope. "Happiness" (*falfalaen'*), while still at times valued, falls short in its capacity to organize horizons of experience that enable those forms of belonging, caring, and striving that best define moral modes of being in Yapese communities. It is important to note here, however, that the sense of precariousness articulated in such ambivalent moral framings of *falfalaen'*, especially when understood against the background of virtuous suffering, is rather differently pitched than Ahmed's call to value the "hap" of happiness—that is, its fragility and instability. For Ahmed it is precisely the "hap" of happiness that illuminates its value in disclosing possibilities. From a Yapese perspective, such precariousness is instead understood to be a temporal attribute of happiness that problematically narrows possibilities for social connection, responsibility, and care—possibilities that extend well beyond the contingencies of present relations and situations to those of previous and forthcoming generations.

THE BEING OF HAPPINESS

The precariousness of happiness, whether it is considered a desired or problematic aspect of its phenomenological manifestation, evokes again questions about the relation between *feeling* and *being* happy. If feeling happiness can lead us astray, is it possible to live a good life without happiness? Are Areliving a good life and living a happy life commensurable as modes of being? As Ahmed points out, for Aristotle, who took happiness to be an ultimate good or virtue, happiness cannot be "reduced to good feeling" (2010: 36). Rather, "happiness or *eudaimonia* refers to 'the good life' or the virtuous life, which is a life-long project" (ibid.). To say that happiness is not reducible to a specifiable good feeling in Aristotle's view is not to say, however, that happiness does not involve feelings (see also Lambek, this collection). "The virtuous agent will not only feel pleasure and pain where appropriate, in relation to the right objects, but will also experience the right amount of such feeling, where the right amount is the 'mean', which means not too much or too little" (Ahmed 2010: 36). The relationship between feeling and being happy, that is, between *hedonic* and *eudaimonic* perspectives on happiness, is one that pivots not only on the relative degree to which happiness can be understood to saturate a given moment of existence, but also on the temporal expanse of happiness itself (what Walker and Kavedžija term in their introduction to this collection the "scope" of happiness). If the good life is a "life-long project" and happy feelings are precarious and fleeting, then clearly, while the experience of happiness may be considered by some to be a necessary condition of living well, it can never in itself be a sufficient one. In short, there must be more to life than happiness if life is to be lived "well." And yet, is it really accurate to say that the experience of happiness is always temporally and situationally bound to such an extent that it cannot be anything otherwise than fleeting and ephemeral? What of happiness that extends within, between, and beyond generations? What of the happiness of spirits?

If happiness is a felicitous modality of being, a form of attunement, attachment, and attention that orients us to others, events, situations, and the world in particular sorts of ways, how might the horizons of "happiness" variously expand or contract? In terms of its positively inflected affective tonalities, happiness as a hedonic experience certainly ranges in duration, focus, and intensity as it manifests in particularized emotional experiences and more diffuse moods. When it is experienced as an emotion, happiness is a narrowly temporally bounded and positively valenced embodied feeling that is registered at an intensity that is strong enough to both catch and direct our attention to specific and specifiable contexts, situations, occurrences, objects, actions, and people. As an emotion, happiness is often, though not always, also reflexively available to us. We not only feel happy; we may recognize that we are happy. We may also recognize what or who is causing us to feel that way.

Happiness is not always so clearly rendered nor closely tethered to the immediate contexts in which we find ourselves enmeshed, however. It may in fact be distinctly decoupled from them. We may find ourselves feeling happy for no good reason or encounter others who seem happy despite the horrible circumstances they are in. We may also remain only vaguely aware of our happily mooded state as we move through obstacles and challenges with an ease that is not normally possible for us. In these contexts, happiness arises in situations that should evoke unhappiness or perhaps other more neutral or negative feelings. This form of happiness, as Ahmed terms it, is "unattributed happiness" (2010: 25). In my terminology, this would be an instance of happiness expressing itself as a mood (Throop 2014).

Seldom the endpoint of our reflection, moods are instead the existential medium through which our reflections take shape (Throop 2012, 2014). As E. Valentine Daniel suggests, moods connote "a state of feeling—usually vague, diffuse, and enduring, a disposition toward the world at any particular time yet with a timeless quality to it" (2000: 333). As a vague, yet enduring, "disposition toward the world," a mood provides the existential expanse within which reflection is deployed. To be in a mood is thus to inhabit a vague and diffuse orientation toward the world that suffuses our every perception, action, and reaction to it. In short, mood is our being, being affected and attuned (see Throop 2009a, 2009b, 2012, 2014).

Accordingly, when we are "in" a mood, let's say a "happy mood," the line between our subjective experience and the intersubjective world that surrounds us is often significantly blurred. As Geertz famously observed,

> Moods vary only in intensity: they go nowhere. They spring from certain circumstances but they are responsive to no ends. Like fogs, they just settle and lift; like scents, suffuse and evaporate. When present moods are totalistic: if one is sad everything and everybody seems dreary; if one is gay everything and everybody seems splendid. (1973: 97)

In this sense, happy moods are atmospheric. According to Ahmed, an atmosphere is "a feeling of what is around, which might be affective in its murkiness or fuzziness, as a surrounding influence which does not quite generate its own form" (2010: 40). And yet, the atmospheric quality of a happy mood is only ever made tangible from a particular point of view. As Ahmed argues, "If we are always in some way or another moody, then what we will receive as an impression will depend on our affective situation" (ibid.). In this capacity, we can understand a happy mood to be a dispersive and ongoing mode of attuning our attention to salient aspects of our own and others' ways of being, as well as to the situations within which we find ourselves emplaced. This is true, however, as much for happy moods as it is for unhappy ones.

ATMOSPHERIC AMBIVALENCE

Even despite the moral problematization of the horizons of *falfalaen'* in Yapese communities, individuals' everyday dealings often disclosed what seemed to me to be traces of tangible moods of happiness that were legible in stories, jokes, and exchanges between family and friends. Simple forms of copresence also often bore the glimmers of subtler forms of happy attunement. Moments of sitting quietly together on the veranda with a family member, attending a celebration, barbecue, or traditional dance, or even enjoying the taste of a good betel nut with a friend were all situations that seemed to be palpably imbued with an atmospheric mood of happiness. The presence of infants and toddlers also seemed to soften and yet enliven the mood of those caring for them, again bringing into being possibilities for experiences that might fall into the range of the felicitous. Moments of satisfaction arising in wake of having participated in a particularly successful fishing trip or when having completing a given work project were also often intersubjectively discernible, even if subtly so. For the most part, however, such moods were seldom if ever explicitly remarked upon. Nor were they brought up as examples of *falfalaen'* ("happiness"). When people did explicitly comment upon such moods, they almost always did so indirectly through deploying an idiomatic metaphorical allusion to fair meteorological conditions: for example, *Ke manigiil yifung ea doba* ("There is excellent weather today").

While talk of experiences of suffering came with relative ease for the majority of people I knew, most individuals had difficulty talking openly about their experiences of *falfalaen'*. In fact, even when I asked people directly about it, by far the most typical response was for individuals to simply deny that they had experienced much, if any, "happiness" in their lives. In the words of Tina, a hard-working woman in her early sixties who was suffering with chronic pain in her back, hands, and knees,, "I don't think there is anything in my life that brought me much happiness. . . . There is a lot of sadness in my life, lots of sadness and suffering, perhaps I have forgotten about the happiness since there was so little of it."

Of those few individuals who did have something specific to say about happiness, many spoke of experiences they had during their childhood. Being carefree and unencumbered by the responsibilities, duties, and expectations of adulthood stood out for them as a time in their lives when they were *falfalaen'*. Having limited social obligations, having fun, and playing were often fore-grounded as being key to their experience of "happiness" at that particular time in their lives. As Buulyal, a single woman in her late thirties, phrased it,

> In my life, the only time I remember feeling *falfalaen'* was when I was a child, six or seven years old. At that time I had yet to go to elementary school and I was sent to stay with my grandparents. My parents and siblings were not there. But I was happy. At that time I was enrolled in the Head Start Program for pre-schoolers. Everyday I would wash and eat by myself before heading up the hill to school. At school I learnt songs and stories, I got to draw with crayons, and play. I was really happy with what I was doing.

Other individuals located experiences of "happiness" in those spaces and places where they were able to find some solitude. This often arose in the context of what seemed to me to be rather depersonalized accounts of individuals' experiences walking along village paths, spending time in gardens, or out at sea alone. For many who spoke of *falfalaen'* in such terms, the emphasis was most often placed on how such spaces provided them with a chance to get away from others, to reflect, be peaceful and calm. For instance, Dammal, a low-caste woman in her early fifties, responded as follows when asked when she was most happy,

> Just sitting somewhere. When I was little I liked going out to sea. I wanted to sit and look around and listen to the waves. I went with my uncle once, that was happiness. People might call other things happiness, like hanging around with a lot of people. Yes, there is happiness in it, but it doesn't last. It will be for only a short while before it is over. But that . . . if I listen to the singing of the birds while gardening or walking through the forest and when I come back home I

can still hear the sound that lingers in my mind. . . . Happiness in my life are the moments I am alone listening to everything around me. If there's nothing to do, I can just sit. I will not get bored. I do like being around people and talking to them, but it is when there's no one around that I'm happy.

Still others voiced experiencing happiness in the context of their work. As Gonop, a village chief in his early sixties, explained to me,

My work, I really enjoy it and I would say that the happiest I have been in my life has been while I was working. That is the thing that brings me the most happiness. It is true that there is a lot of suffering associated with work but my mind does not dwell on it. I try not to think about suffering, the pain, or the things that hurt. It doesn't matter what you do, there is suffering in work, but I think there is also some happiness.

Statements concerning an overall lack of "happiness" in one's life, narratives that restrict "happiness" to the context of experiences that were had in childhood, or claims that "happiness" arises in situations where one is able to find isolated reflective solitude all resonate with the view that *falfalaen'* is a mode of worldly attunement in which moral responsibilities, long-term projects, past debts, and current social obligations are avoided, backgrounded, or ignored (cf. again Walker and Kavedžija's discussion of the axes of "responsibility" and "virtue" in the introduction to this collection). Gonop's characterization brings to light, however, a more complicated articulation in which suffering, pain, hardship, effortful striving, and work are interlaced with experiences of "happiness." In this view, "happiness" is not realized in a pure state. Its horizons are not uniform. *Falfalaen'* does not only exist, in other words, in suffering's absence. It is instead intermixed with other embodied modes of being, most pointedly those associated with work. In this respect, *falfalaen'* was deemed as at times potentially blended with experiences of *magaer*, a local term that designates the effort, fatigue, or feelings of physical exertion that arise from hard work or service (see Throop 2010a: 61–67).

When speaking of work and the effortful suffering associated with it, many individuals explained to me that such forms of work-induced suffering, particularly in the case of collective work projects, played a significant role in fostering strong bonds of attachment in the family, the village, and the broader community. The phrase used to describe such forms of attachment when speaking at the level of the village was *amiithuun ea binaw*, literally, "pain of the village" or "the village's pain" (Throop 2008, 2010a). Having participated in my share of village work projects over the years, I understood quite well the bodily aches, soreness, and pains associated with the demands of physical labor associated with them. That mutual suffering that arose from working together could foster shared horizons of purpose, attachment, accomplishment, and social belonging seemed rather reasonable to me in light of such experiences. The way that "happiness" could arise within such efforts took a bit longer to sink in.

As far as my own embodied understanding of possibilities of a "happiness" born of, and interlaced with, collective work was concerned, it was not until the summer of 2005, when I spent the better part of my visit helping the men in my village reconstruct a community meeting house (*p'eebaay*), that I came to understand the possibility of happiness arising in the midst of backbreaking labor. Particularly salient to me at the time was the fact that the activity of working itself seemed to play a role in mollifying building tensions in the village. These had arisen in the wake of a heated meeting that had occurred a few days prior wherein the chiefs had vocally chastised some villagers for failing to show up regularly to help out with village work. This concern was voiced, as Tamag's had been, in the register of a selfish striving for "happiness" on the part of those who had been absent. I reflected on the experience in my fieldnotes in the following terms,

> As far as I could tell, there was no discernible tension and the work continued with the same vigor as it had the previous days. In fact, I would say that this was the first time that I really understood from a firsthand perspective how the power of collective work, effort, and exertion could foster a sense of connectedness within the community. At the time this insight occurred to me, we were all working to pull the large carved mahogany trunks that are to be the main weight-bearing posts for the *p'eebaay*—posts that will hopefully last for the next thirty to forty years and that will have been put in place through the collective effort of all of the men of the village. As we pulled on ropes affixed to the end of the logs, we chanted in a call and response fashion, first *Iy gamow!* ["We together"], then *Ke bowchuw!*, ["A little more"]. Straining with all of our collective power, we managed to slowly move the logs, a few feet at a time, into position. Amidst grunts and groans were laughter and smiles. The feeling of sore, tightening, tiring, and later aching muscles was intermixed with feelings of happiness, amusement, and belonging. (August 11, 2005)

Again the specific goal was not to experience *falfalaen'* through work. Nor was "happiness" understood to be that which sediments social belonging in such contexts. Collective suffering and pain were instead thought to be at the root of such forms of social intimacy. While not deemed to be a specific goal or outcome of collective effortful work, "happiness" remained, however, a possibility as an aspect, layering, or lamination of it. In this way, *falfalaen'* is part of a more complex attunement that also includes horizons established in and through *suffering-for* and *-with* others.

CONCLUSION

In this article, I have tried to make the case that "happiness" should not be understood strictly as either a generalized capacity for flourishing or as an interiorized state. It is instead a form of intermediary experience: an existential orientation that brings into being certain possibilities for articulating relations between self, other, and world. If we are to think of happiness as a felicitous mode of attunement, attachment, and attention that configures the contours of the horizons of our experience, then it might well be true that there are aspects of happiness that mark it as an existential possibility of our shared human condition. As such, happiness, like hope or empathy, might evidence an existential structure that is somehow traceable across individuals, contexts, historical time periods, and cultures. That happiness may manifest in the intensity and contextual specificity of an emotion or may diffusely permeate one's perspective on the world in the form of an intermediary experience like a mood seems to suggest, however, that whatever its existential structure might entail, happiness is not, and can never be, a singular or static phenomenon. Furthermore, the complexity of happiness may be amplified by its combinatorial laminations with other affective and embodied forms. Even in its "purer" realizations, however, happiness is always a dynamic affective formation that shifts, intensifies, diminishes, and transmutes through time. While it seems clear that the contents or objects made relevant by happiness may also vary from one individual to the next and one community or historical period to another, the experiential horizons defined by happiness may further differ, and be differently valued, in significant ways (see Walker and Kavedžija, this collection). For instance, while the precariousness of happiness might in one context give rise to a generative opening up of possibilities, in yet another it may be deemed to foreclose them.

In the case of Yapese communities, orientations to "happiness" are ambivalent. In the lives of the people I got to know best, it was certainly true that subtle, often unmarked and unremarkable, felicitous moods arose in the context of everyday moments of being together, talking, or eating with family and friends. It was also true that experiences that might be recognized as "happiness" further arose, in somewhat more complex ways, in the context of effortful striving to collectively endure the pain and suffering associated with community work obligations. And yet, in the Yapese context, "happiness" is still largely understood to be an experience that narrowly focuses attention to the self's cares and concerns, in the process making less prominent the struggles and suffering of others.

The experience of *suffering-for* others, in contrast, is taken to define a rather different horizon of experience in which there is a distinct foregrounding of attunements to past suffering, compassion for present suffering, and effortful work to better one's family's and one's community's wellbeing in the future. As such, we can understand "happiness" in the context of this particular configuration to be a mode of attunement, attachment, and attention that narrowly defines horizons, in the process excluding others, object, events, and acts from the self's purview. The trouble with "happiness," in this account, is that it takes our attention away from the unhappiness of others (including spirits), the unhappiness of previous generations, and the precariousness of our own happiness, which is in the end always fleeting and fragile.

As is evident in the case of Ahmed's and Berlant's writings, local framings are not the only accounts that trouble the horizons established by happiness. For Ahmed, happiness is characterized as entailing normative assumptions and values that take our attention away from the unhappiness of others. For Berlant, happiness is an affective modulation of optimistic attachment that may in fact be considered cruel to the extent that its very pursuit directly limits possibilities for its actual attainment. Even the most expansive forms of happiness may have thus a constrictive, and perhaps cruel, side.

To conclude, I think it is worth reflecting briefly again on one of the more compelling arguments made by Ahmed in her efforts to return to the original meaning of happiness, a meaning that foregrounds the "hap" or happenstance of happiness. This is a meaning that arguably shifts us away from the narrow horizons that conventionalized forms of happiness define. When the contingency and precariousness of happiness are foregrounded, Ahmed argues, we open a place for possibility, singularity, and difference to arise in the ways that happiness is articulated for ourselves and for those others who may or may not share our particular horizons of experience. While contingent, such forms of happiness may thus be more expansive than those realized within the parameters of normative visions of the good life. Such an orientation to the "hap" of happiness arguably opens a space to come into contact with ways of being that are not simply replications of our own normative understandings of what happiness entails. It is also an orientation to happiness that does not occlude the realities and possibilities of unhappiness. And yet, while a contingent understanding of happiness resonates well with Yapese framings, the putative virtues of the horizons provided by it do not.

Happiness is not alone in evoking such possibilities, however. As Emmanuel Levinas (1998) argues, suffering may also open and not foreclose our own possibilities for being, being with others, and being morally attuned. According to Levinas, in the presence of another's suffering, suffering that is not and can never be my own, there is a recurrent refusal of my attempts to domesticate another's pain to the self-sameness of my being. The suffering in the other, and the suffering that arises in me as the suffering of compassion for the other's suffering, are foundationally incommensurate experiences that are yet articulated through the call to responsibility that they each evoke.

Meaningful *suffering-for* another in the form of compassion results from our experiencing the asymmetry evidenced so forcefully, so palpably, in the face of the other's pain. In confronting the stark impenetrability of pain, the integrity of another being is revealed against the intimate backdrop of our own self-experience. It is in this primordial orientation "for-the-other" as suffering other and not as an object or thing—that is, as a living being and not a thing to be used—that there exists an ethical obligation, Levinas argues, "prior to the statements of propositions, communicative information and narrative" (ibid.: 166). Such an understanding of the moral worth of suffering resonates with a number of Yapese sensibilities and assumptions.

Some forms of suffering, like some forms of happiness, it seems, hold existential possibilities for opening up orientations to alternate ways of being. The problem remaining to be understood, however, is whether or not the possibilities for being revealed within the horizons of the "hap" of happiness and the unassumability of suffering disclose commensurate excesses and singularities, or if instead, as I suspect, each in its own way defines a distinctive horizon of experience that opens upon a unique region of being.

ACKNOWLEDGMENTS

I would like to thank Iza Kavedžija, Harry Walker, and the rest of the participants at the original London School of Economics and Political Science workshop on "Happiness" for their substantial comments and critiques. Thanks are also due to five anonymous reviewers and to my student Christopher Stephan for providing significant suggestions on how to improve the piece.

REFERENCES

Ahmed, Sara. 2010. *The promise of happiness*. Durham, NC: Duke University Press.

Bashkow, Ira. 1991. "The dynamics of rapport in a colonial situation: David Schneider's fieldwork on the Islands of Yap." In *Colonial situations: Essays on the contextualization of ethnographic knowledge*, edited by George W. Stocking, Jr., 170–242. Madison: University of Wisconsin Press.

Berlant, Lauren. 2011. *Cruel optimism*. Durham, NC: Duke University Press.

Daniel, E. Valentine. 2000. "Mood, moment, and mind." In *Violence and subjectivity*, edited by Veena Das, Arthur Kleinman, Mamphela Ramphele, and Pamela Reynolds, 333–66. Berkeley: University of California Press.

Corsín Jiménez, Alberto. 2008. *Culture and well-being: Anthropological approaches to freedom and political ethics*. London: Pluto.

Desjarlais, Robert, and Jason Throop. 2011. "Phenomenological approaches in anthropology." *Annual Review of Anthropology* 40: 87–102.

Duranti, Alessandro. 2009a. "The relevance of Husserl's theory to language socialization." *Journal of Linguistic Anthropology* 19 (2): 205–26.

———. 2009b. "The force of language and its temporal unfolding." In *Language in life and a life in language: Jacob Mey—a festschrift*, edited by Kenneth Turner and Bruce Fraser, 63–71. Bingley, UK: Emerald Group Publishers.

———. 2010. "Husserl, intersubjectivity and anthropology." *Anthropological Theory* 10 (1): 1–20.

Egan, Jim. 1998. "Taro, fish, and funerals: Transformations in the Yapese cultural topography of wealth." Ph.D. thesis, University of California, Irvine.

Geertz, Clifford. 1973. *The interpretation of cultures*. New York: Basic Books.

Heidegger, Martin. (1929/30) 1995. *The fundamental concepts of metaphysics: World, finitude, solitude*. Translated by William McNeill and Nicholas Walker. Bloomington: Indiana University Press.

Hunt, Edward E., Jr., Nathaniel R. Kidder, and David M. Schneider. 1954. "The depopulation of Yap." *Human Biology* 26: 21–51.

Husserl, Edmund. (1913) 1962. *Ideas: general introduction to a pure phenomenology*. Translated by W. R. Boyce Gibson. New York: Collier Books.

———. (1918–26) 2001. *Analyses concerning passive and active synthesis: Lectures on transcendental logic*. Translated by Anthony J. Steinbock. Dordrecht: Kluwer Academic Press.

Jackson, Michael. 1998. *Minima ethnographica: Intersubjectivity and the anthropological project*. Chicago: University of Chicago Press.

———. 2011. *Life within limits: Well-being in a world of want*. Durham, NC: Duke University Press.

———. 2013. *The wherewithal of life: Ethics, migration, and the question of well-being*. Berkeley: University of California Press.

Labby, David. 1976. *The demystification of Yap: Dialectics of culture on a Micronesian island*. Chicago: University of Chicago Press.

Laidlaw, J. 2008. "The intension and extension of well-being: Transformation in diaspora Jain understandings of non-violence." In *Culture and well-being: Anthropological approaches to freedom and political ethics*, edited by Alberto Corsín Jiménez, 156–79. London: Pluto.

Levinas, Emmanuel. 1998. *Entre nous: On thinking-of-the-other*. Translated by Michael B. Mith and Barbara Harshav. New York: Columbia University Press.

Lutz, Catherine. 1988. *Unnatural emotions: Everyday sentiment on a Micronesian atoll and their challenge to Western Theory*. Chicago: University of Chicago Press.

Mathews, Gordon, and Carolina Izquierdo, eds. 2009. *Pursuits of happiness: Well-being in anthropological perspective*. New York: Berghahn.

Robbins, Joel. 2013. "Beyond the suffering subject: Toward an anthropology of the good." *Journal of the Royal Anthropological Institute* (N.S.) 19 (3): 447–62.

Rose, Nikolas. 2006. *The politics of life itself*. Princeton, NJ: Princeton University Press.

Schneider, David M. 1955. "Abortion and depopulation on a Pacific island." In *Health, culture, and community*, edited by Benjamin D. Paul, 211–35. New York: Russell Sage Foundation.

————. 1967. "Foreword." In *The curse of the Souw*, Roy Wagner, vii–viii. Chicago: University of Chicago Press.

————. 1984. *A critique of the study of kinship*. Ann Arbor: University of Michigan Press.

Thin, Neil. 2012. *Social happiness: Theory into policy and practice*. Bristol: Policy Press.

Throop, C. Jason. 2003. "Articulating experience." *Anthropological Theory* 3 (2): 219–41.

————. 2008. "From pain to virtue: Dysphoric sensations and moral sensibilities in Yap (Waqab), Federated States of Micronesia." *Journal of Transcultural Psychiatry* 45 (2): 253–86.

————. 2009a. "Intermediary varieties of experience." *Ethnos* 74 (4): 535–58.

————. 2009b. "Interpretation and the limits of interpretability: On rethinking Clifford Geertz's semiotics of religious experience." *Journal of North African Studies* 14 (3/4): 369–84.

————. 2010a. *Suffering and sentiment: Exploring the vicissitudes of empathy and pain in Yap*. Berkeley: University of California Press.

————. 2010b. "Latitudes of loss: On the vicissitudes of empathy." *American Ethnologist* 37 (4): 771–82.

————. 2012. "On inaccessibility and vulnerability: Some horizons of compatibility between phenomenology and psychoanalysis." *Ethos* 40 (1): 75–96.

————. 2014. "Moral moods." *Ethos* 42 (1): 65–83.

————. 2015. "Sacred suffering: A phenomenological anthropological perspective." In *Phenomenology in anthropology: A sense of perspective*, edited by Kalpana Ram and Christopher Houston, 68–89. Bloomington: Indiana University Press.

Throop, C. Jason, and Alessandro Duranti. 2014. "Attention, ritual glitches, and attentional pull: The president and the queen." *Phenomenology and Cognitive Sciences*. Online First.

Zigon, Jarrett. 2014. "Attunement and fidelity: Two ontological conditions for morally being-in-the-world." *Ethos* 42 (1): 16–30.

CHAPTER TWO

Being careful what you wish for
The case of happiness in China

CHARLES STAFFORD

Let me start by drawing a contrast between happiness as a motive (something I want) and happiness as an outcome (something I get). I may be motivated to do certain things—for example, buy chocolates or ask someone out on a date—because I believe or hope that these actions will lead to me being happy in some sense; but whether I really *will* be happy as a result of them is another matter, of course. I could accidentally buy what for me is the wrong kind of chocolate, the kind with pieces of orange in it, in which case I will be disappointed. As for asking someone on a date: even if things go well—that is, it's not that I end up on the wrong kind of date—the experience may not bring me the happiness I had hoped for. The former case is about life going wrong. The latter (and perhaps more interesting) case is about life going right but still failing to live up to expectations.

This possible disconnect between what we aim for and what we get—emotionally speaking—has been the focus of sustained research by psychologists, economists, and others in recent years. The findings suggest, in brief, that our "affective forecasting" skills are very imperfect (see, e.g., Wilson and Gilbert 2005; Gilbert and Wilson 2009). We tend to overestimate the extent to which supposedly wonderful life events will make us happy *and* the extent to which supposedly catastrophic life events will make us unhappy; the same holds true, it seems, for more everyday kinds of good and bad experiences. There are different explanations for this phenomenon, including the fact that people do not generally know much about things they have not yet lived through. Moreover, cognitive biases may lead them to *focus* on particular aspects of (prospective) experiences while downplaying others: for example, to focus on how much their friends will admire a new pair of shoes while ignoring what it will feel like to wear them.[1]

Such findings, whatever else they may do, raise interesting questions about the psychological foundations of classic utilitarianism and thus of standard economics. It may be rational for us to pursue happiness or more generally whatever it is that we want —"utility"—through the means we have. But what if our predictions of what will make us happy (or more generally satisfied) are unreliable? In that case, the risk is that our actions will misfire: we may well end up with things—including emotions—we were *not* actually wishing for.

One especially consequential version of this forecasting problem relates to the pursuit of wealth. When the developed Western economies in the post-World War II era are taken as an example, there is some truly striking evidence, assuming one accepts it. Per capita income has gone up dramatically, leading to sharp improvements in living standards. It seems, however, that people are no happier on average than they were back in the 1950s (for an overview, see Layard 2005). Why, one might ask, have they worked so hard to get rich if the end result is no more happiness than they had when they started? Richard Easterlin suggests that, among other things, they fail to grasp how short-lived the psychological benefits of extra wealth will be and thus "allocate an excessive amount of time" to trying to get it (2003: 11176; see also Easterlin 2001). They would be better off following the advice of Richard Layard, an economist who embraces a version of old-school utilitarianism. Summing up the evidence, he concludes that happiness/wellbeing is a function not of wealth per se but of having strong and stable families; solid communities and friendships; secure employment and income; good health; personal freedoms (including holding significant rights vis-à-vis government); and religious beliefs, or at least a

---

1.   For an accessible introduction to the psychology of happiness, see Gilbert 2007. A
      very thought-provoking commentary on some of the analytical and methodological
      issues surrounding research by psychologists and economists on happiness can be
      found in Kahneman 2011: 375–407.

guiding system of personal morality.[2] He argues that we should allocate collective time/energy/public funds to sorting out such matters rather than increasing GDP. Indeed, as noted in the introduction as well as other contributions to this collection, policies along these lines have gained significant traction in places as diverse as Bhutan and the United Kingdom (see Cook's article for a detailed discussion of the latter case).

* * *

And yet most anthropologists reading this snapshot of interdisciplinary work on happiness are likely to have serious reservations about it, and not without reason (again, see the introduction, as well as the article by Freeman; see also the recent commentaries in Barbara Rose Johnston et al. 2012). Aside from the challenge of defining and measuring "happiness" in a way that will work across cultures— good luck with that—anthropologists will surely object to the idea that happiness can be assumed to be the priority for humans everywhere that it was for Jeremy Bentham. As the arch anti-utilitarian Marshall Sahlins once remarked, "A people"—by which he means irrational Westerners, and especially irrational Americans—"who conceive life to be the pursuit of happiness must be chronically unhappy" (2002: 17). His broader point is that desires, the things we are motivated to aim for in the first place, are always culturally and historically constituted.

Take the case of happiness in rural China and Taiwan. In fact, the people I have met there during fieldwork *do* indeed seem highly motivated to pursue happiness, pleasure, and wellbeing, and there are many Chinese terms, notions, folk sayings, and practices that relate explicitly to happiness in one form or another.[3] Chinese weddings, for example, are redundantly organized around the

---

2. Framing this in quantitative terms, Layard suggests that six variables "can explain 80% of the variation in happiness" between the fifty countries in the World Values Survey in four different years: the divorce rate, the unemployment rate, the level of trust, the rate of membership in non-religious organizations, the quality of the government, and the fraction of people "believing in God" (2005: 70–71).

3. Note that I have never started fieldwork with the specific aim of studying happiness or wellbeing, per se, nor have I asked my informants to speak directly to the question of happiness. Nevertheless, more general questions related to life aspirations, wellbeing, and personal fulfillment have been central to all of my fieldwork projects, as a result of which I have collected a good deal of data about what actually makes people happy/satisfied, what they appear to enjoy in the course of life, and (to frame

ideal of "double happiness" (*shuangxi*) and the "sweetness" (*tianmi*) that should accompany a "joyous event" (*xishi*) of this kind. Nowadays a whole industry surrounds this. And yet, in traditional Chinese weddings, a *lack* of joy was also meant to be part of the proceedings. As Throop (this collection) says of Yap, the idea that suffering and *un*happiness, in certain circumstances, are especially virtuous is one that has a definite traction in China. Chinese brides (being filial daughters) were expected to be at least superficially miserable about separation from their natal kin via marriage, and thus to sit grim-faced through the accompanying rituals. In some parts of China, they even sang wedding laments in which their marriages were portrayed as a kind of death (Blake 1978; Johnson 2003). Speaking more broadly, the primary focus of weddings (and of the marriages they ritually instituted) was not the happiness or other emotional state of the bride—nor, for that matter, that of the groom. As Freedman explains, "The chief parties to a [traditional] marriage [were] the most senior direct agnatic ascendants of the boy and the girl [to be married]" (1979: 263). For these elders, the emphasis was on sorting out a new affinal connection, one that would benefit all concerned. In short, marriage sealed a relationship between families, not individuals, and *responsibilities* to elders and ancestors lay at its core. This does not mean that happiness was a matter of indifference; but nobody imagined that the emotional fulfillment of the bride and groom was what it was all about—at least not in the traditional system.

As is well known, however, the landscape of Chinese family life and kinship has changed in recent decades along with ideas concerning the emotions surrounding it. The best account is provided by Yunxiang Yan, who documents an increased focus on "private life," and more specifically on the emotional bond between wives and husbands. This is reflected, for example, in the creation of private spaces, such as separate bedrooms in rural homes, where intimacy and marital happiness can be nurtured (Yan 2003: 112–39). In short, people *do* now appear to care about the bride (and the groom) being happy.

Much more could be said about all of this, but here I simply underline two relatively straightforward points, uncontroversial ones for anthropologists. Yes, one can say that the pursuit of happiness exists in China, but, first, many social/

---

things negatively) what it is that makes them notably unhappy, anxious, and so on. For an excellent (historically informed) discussion of Chinese happiness/pleasure, see Farquhar 2002. For recent discussions that seek to bring Chinese folk models of happiness/wellbeing into direct dialogue with quantitative research, see Ip 2011 and 2013.

cultural particularities surround this, and these are bound to deeply shape the actual experience of happiness. Indeed, the general understanding of "being happy," for Chinese people through history, must presumably have been closely linked (albeit often in complex and even paradoxical ways) to whatever one was meant to be doing with one's life. As Sangren has shown, for example, in the traditional Chinese family/kinship system there was a particular cultural logic to the (constructed) desires of individual agents, for example as when daughters sought "recognition" from the parents who would inevitably send them away to another family; in this context, happiness for married-out daughters was surely hard work (Sangren 2003). Moreover, second, the social/cultural particularities of Chinese emotional life do not exist in a historical vacuum: some of the most important of them have been seriously transformed in recent decades (again, as shown by Yan).

Beyond these two points, however, I want to make a third one, and this takes me back to the question of affective forecasting. The examples I began this chapter with are about *me* forecasting *my* emotions, and possibly getting it wrong. In the case of Chinese weddings, however, a great deal of attention is paid to what *other* people might feel if this or that thing were to happen. (Of course, I am not suggesting this is unique to China: that happiness is often conceived as relational, and that it routinely entails moral responsibilities, are among the key points made by the editors for this collection as a whole. Note that Gardner's article, with its discussion of the relational *and* temporal aspects of migration trajectories between Bangladesh and the United Kingdom, is directly relevant to the points I am raising here.) Suppose, for example, that a young Chinese woman ends up marrying a particular man—not the one she would have chosen herself. Her decision to do so and/or her acquiescence in it happening are likely to have been premised, at least in part, on affective forecasting. The elders around her may have told her what they thought and felt, or even just instructed her what to do. But she may also have let the unwanted marriage take place based on her *own* guess or assumption about *what her parents will feel* if prospective fiancé *x* (the one she likes) is chosen instead of prospective fiancé *y* (the one they prefer). Conversely, her mother and father may disapprove of a particular match for their daughter on the grounds that they expect it *will not lead to her being happy* in the long term, whatever she herself may think in advance of it. In such cases, to reiterate, affective forecasting—which, by definition, may be mistaken—is relational rather than being contained within individuals; more specifically, it is intergenerational. As soon as one frames the business in this way, it becomes clear just how complicated it must be in practice, and thus how inadequate simple models of rational maximizing are for capturing real world decision making by socially embedded agents.[4] For not only do we predict what people around us might feel about given outcomes; we also, in many cases, explicitly manipulate each other on the basis of such predictions. The parents who want their daughter to avoid a given outcome—an unhappy marriage to the good-looking but unreliable x—may try to persuade her directly to do what they want, or they may threaten her, or they may work behind her back to undermine the love match. What they hope to achieve via these manipulations is a degree of intergenerational coordination: of attitudes, intentions, decisions, and actions. Simply put, they want her to want, or at to least to accept enough to act upon, what *they* want. And their own preferences for the future are based in part on their (reliable or unreliable) predictions of *her* future emotions. But what if they are wrong?

* * *

Now let us return to the pursuit not of love but of wealth. As already noted, research broadly suggests that "money does not make people happy," but the detailed findings are naturally more subtle than this. It turns out that—with some important qualifications—people of limited means *are* generally made happier by moving beyond the strains and uncertainties imposed by poverty. In this sense, someone who is poor and desires money as a route to happiness is not being irrational. What is surprising (assuming one accepts the premises and findings of the research) is the point at which the link between wealth and happiness begins to tail off. There is much discussion of this cut-off point; but summing up the state of the field back in 2005, Layard concluded that above about US\$20,000 per year (to be more specific, once a country has achieved

---

4.   In this article I do not have space to engage fully with the psychological critique of standard economic modeling; for a very interesting cognitive anthropological contribution to this critique, see Quinn 1978. Note that Quinn's point—an absolutely crucial one—is that the people she studied often use relatively simple heuristics to take decisions about economic life rather than engaging in probability calculations, and so on. Similarly, although I am noting here how "complicated" affective forecasting is in practice, it might also be argued that people often break through this complexity by using simple heuristics (e.g., for selecting husbands) that are readily available in their social environments.

this figure for annual income per head), "higher average income is no guarantee of greater happiness" (2005: 34). Obviously, in many places around the world, this would even today be considered a very high income; but in the United Kingdom, for instance, it is only slightly above the annual pay for someone on the national minimum wage. In other words, most people living in developed Western economies would, I think, find a happiness cut-off point of US$20,000 surprisingly—even astonishingly—low.

So how does this translate to the rural Chinese and Taiwanese cases that I know through fieldwork? Before turning to ethnography, a few things must be noted by way of background. The people I have met during fieldwork have almost all had relatively low incomes, not only by comparison with Western-ers, but also by comparison with their urban compatriots. If the economists of happiness are broadly correct, then these people might reasonably anticipate some years of increased happiness, assuming their incomes continue to rise as they have (on average) done in recent decades.[5] It is also important to stress that the pursuit of wealth is a highly salient topic of public discourse in both China and Taiwan—although the background to the two cases is different. In China, people are keenly aware that chasing money (and also power in various forms, because the two are closely interlinked) is a pervasive social fact at this particular historical moment and something that everyone must engage with in one form or another. Ordinary people routinely debate the moral and ethical implications of this reality (see, e.g., Zhang 2013). The situation in Taiwan is different. One could say that it too is a place where money chasing is pervasive; however, the "economic miracle" happened there some time back—basically, a generation or more ago. Nowadays, people in Taiwan are, if anything, anxious that the economy has stalled and may well stall further owing to a range of politico-economic factors beyond their control. Moreover, whereas Taiwan used to be a capitalist success story posed against the economic failings of China's communism, the mainland's "socialist market economy" now appears to be leav-ing Taiwan in its wake. Folk discourses surrounding the pursuit of wealth have been heavily shaped by these historical considerations.

The final point to note by way of background corresponds to what I have noted above with respect to marriage. Individuals in China/Taiwan may ponder

---

5.   As I note at the end of this article, however, recent findings about levels of Chinese happiness/wellbeing, and more broadly about happiness in developing economies, present a decidedly mixed, arguably "paradoxical," picture in relation to this.

what kinds of economic outcomes would bring them—as individuals—happiness, wellbeing, and so on. But the ebb and flow of life is explicitly framed, much of the time, in relation to what *other* people think and feel. Crucial decisions about education, career paths, investments, major purchases, and so on, are routinely taken collectively in some sense. And it should be noted here that collective family success or happiness may, of course, be *invoked* in ways that ultimately benefit some members of families over others (e.g., elder over younger generations, men over women), just as invoking "brotherhood" within lineages may benefit some lineage members over others (see Watson 1985). This links back to a general Chinese ethos in which individuals are presumed to be morally committed to, and prepared to work hard for, long-term projects of advancing *family* prosperity, regardless of short-term (or even long-term) personal cost (see Harrell 1985).[6] But how durable is this commitment in practice? Is it transmitted across generations without difficulty? Would it survive, for example, the kind of disillusionment that might come to younger generations as they learn that prosperity and material wealth do not (always) equate to happiness? And what if the affective forecasts on which long-term projects of advancement are based turn out to be mistaken?

In considering such questions, I want to draw a broad contrast between two ideal types of families that I will label respectively as "progressive" and "declining." By the former, I simply mean families that are optimistic when it comes to economic life, and more specifically optimistic that the quality of life for younger generations is going to keep improving. This gives individuals a psychological incentive to work hard—that is, because by working hard, and making short-term sacrifices, they assume that things can and will get better financially: that progress can be made. Moreover, they collectively *want* things to get better because they assume or hope (at least at the level of the collective) that this will be a good thing—that is, that more wealth will, indeed, bring them a better quality of life and—in general terms—more happiness overall. A declining

---

6. In his thought-provoking discussion, Harrell accepts that in comparative terms Chinese people appear to work incredibly hard. This may relate to a "work ethic" into which they are socialized, as well as to the existence (under particular historical circumstances) of material incentives that encourage work. But Harrell concludes that basically "Chinese will work hard when they see possible long-term benefits, in terms of improved material conditions and/or security, for a group with which they identify" (1985: 217). When this is lacking, the reality is that they often *don't* work that hard.

family, by contrast, is one that has to some extent given up on this desire to pursue wealth per se as a route to happiness, as I will elaborate below.

* * *

So what does a progressive family actually look like? From my fieldwork over the years, I could cite many examples. For instance, there is the Chen family, who live in the rural Taiwanese town of South Bridge.[7] The husband and wife at the head of this family grew up in relative poverty, and received basic levels of schooling. After marriage, they both worked hard at various jobs before eventually setting up their own small business in a market stall. They made a decent amount of money from this and lived frugally in the countryside. As a result, they were able to save, to invest, and eventually to provide their only son with a first-rate university education in law. At the time of my initial fieldwork, he was just starting out on his professional career. By Taiwanese standards, this family would not have counted as wealthy by any means, but things were getting better. And, I might add, they seemed very happy. Why? In terms of Layard's happiness criteria (cited above), the Chens appeared to be set: the marital/family relationships were solid, they had many friends, they had reasonably secure and nonstressful employment (which, moreover, they seemed to enjoy), their health was good, and they were religious. Furthermore, the narrative arc of their lives was basically an optimistic and, again, "progressive" one. Mrs. Chen's health, which used to be problematic, had improved. They had always been religious, to some extent, but had become even more so, having found a cult to which they were deeply devoted and which (they said) brought them true peace of mind. They had an only son who was obedient and loyal, and whose advancing career they followed with pride. My sense is that their concern was not for him to succeed, as such: they wanted him to have a good life and to be happy, and assumed (i.e., predicted) that some degree of success was a prerequisite for this. Meanwhile, his assumption (i.e., prediction) was that his parents would be made happy if he were to succeed in school and work, and so he set about doing so. His plan was to provide for them in the future even though, in fact, they

---

7.   See Stafford 2006 for a discussion of this family. For the sake of the privacy of my informants, personal and place names, and some other details, have been changed in this and all other illustrations.

almost certainly would not need any help. The Chens' main aspiration for him, they told me, was that he would end up living nearby.

This, then, looks like a family in which the intergenerational coordination of goals and intentions is smooth, and life is basically headed in a progressive direction. The parents, by means of steady work, have constructed a future for their son that they believe will be in his interests, and the son—also by means of steady work—seems determined to make his parents happy by not derailing their imagined future for him (and them). I should add, however, that when I met them there were a few cracks in this narrative. The son, although a good student, did not actually pass the examinations that would have allowed him entry to an especially lucrative career. Furthermore, he had shown no signs of getting married (something his parents considered essential for a good life), or even of thinking about it any time soon. During my fieldwork, there were some tense moments: at one point the son stormed off and left for a few days as a way of letting off steam. It could also be said that by praising and encouraging his educational successes, his parents had risked some of the negative consequences that can follow from this: that is, that their son would become burned out by the pressure (cf. Kipnis 2011), that he would move further and further away as he became more and more successful (cf. James Johnston 2013), and/or that schooling itself would effectively turn him into a different type of person than they themselves were (cf. Stafford 1995). More broadly, I would note that the Chens had a rather ambivalent relationship to the ideals of Taiwanese capitalism. When I met them, they were classic small entrepreneurs: they worked incredibly hard, appeared to enjoy making money, seldom spent much of it, and invested their savings carefully. But they prioritized spiritual fulfillment over material success, and had passed up opportunities to make more money—including, in one case they described to me, out of ethical concern for the impact it would have on a fellow villager in a similar business (someone who was not a close friend). So although they certainly count as a progressive family in my terms, this does not mean that they were unthinkingly and/or unproblematically on the track of pursuing wealth as a route to happiness.

To cite another example, consider the Zhangs from rural northeast China.[8] Like the Chens, Mr. and Mrs. Zhang (both of whom lost parents during childhood) grew up in relative poverty. As children and young adults living

---

8.   See Stafford 2007 for an extended discussion of this family. Again, personal and
     place names have been changed.

during the collectivist era of the 1950s, 1960s, and 1970s, their lives were extremely difficult in many respects. Nor were they able to have any children of their own after they married. However, Mr. and Mrs. Zhang adopted a daughter, and this daughter eventually married a *yanglaoxu*—that is, a son-in-law who formally agreed to look after the Zhangs in old age. (I know little about the background to this match, but bear in mind that it might not have been the adopted daughter's first choice: as a matter of definition, a son-in-law who will agree to care for his parents-in-law, as opposed to caring for his own parents, has a low status.) Neither the daughter nor the son-in-law were highly educated, but they were both working extremely hard when I met them, and in the context of China's post-Mao economic boom they were doing rather well for themselves as construction day-laborers in the nearest city. So the elder Zhangs had a hard-working daughter and her husband living in their home, plus two lovely grandchildren. The future was looking much better than the past, and everyone seemed committed to the collective goal of family improvement.

Again, however, there are a few complications in the narrative arc. In common with many other young couples in modern China, the adopted daughter and her husband felt a tension between the need to provide for the elder Zhangs and the need to provide for their children. To frame this well-known problem in somewhat unfamiliar terms: Exactly whom did they want to make happy? Her parents, their children, or themselves? Generally speaking, they were investing in the future rather then repaying her adoptive parents for support received, thus leading to family tensions. The adopted daughter knew very well that she was *not* complying fully with what her elders wanted, and there was a constant negotiation around this. Meanwhile, the fact of their frantic work schedules meant that (in spite of working nearby) they were increasingly "leaving their children behind" in the countryside: a well-known phenomenon in contemporary China. Was this a reasonable tradeoff: that is, pursuing wealth for the whole family's future while—in effect—leaving the children in the village to be raised by others? Would this increase their happiness and wellbeing in the long term? Would it lead to the children having a happy/fulfilled life? Moreover, I would note that the elder Zhangs had a somewhat ambivalent relationship to the ideals of China's socialist market economy, however much they may have encouraged their daughter and son-in-law to succeed in it. Mr. Zhang was a committed Communist and someone who was seriously troubled by the changes he saw around him as market forces intruded on rural life. In short, as with the Chen family, the Zhangs were not just unthinkingly or unproblematically on the track of pursuing wealth as a route to happiness.

And were they happy? In another article, I have discussed Mr. Zhang's chronic insomnia and his general anxiety about life, which derives from a number of sources (Stafford 2007). Compared to the Chens from Taiwan, he and his wife have more concerns about money, their network of friends and relatives is more fragile, their health is worse, and (significantly in terms of Layard's happiness criteria) they are not actively religious. But Mr. Zhang would be the first to admit that his standard of living is much better now than it was in the past, and that he and his wife are fortunate to have ended up with such a hard-working daughter and son-in-law. I have even heard him, with the help of a small glass of strong northern *baijiu*, become rather at peace with his life, and make glowing statements about the good friends, neighbors, and relatives on whom he relies—not to mention the Communist Party.

Of course, the general emotional fulfillment (or otherwise) of the Chens from Taiwan and the Zhangs from China is not something that can easily be captured in routine ethnographic observations. Their "happiness," to the extent they have it, must be a complex phenomenon: shaped not only by their underlying material circumstances but also by a long list of conflated variables, only a few of which I have mentioned. Moreover, their attempts to make money cannot be assumed to follow from an explicit theory that wealth will bring happiness. Notably, in many cultures/societies, including China, some people work hard because work *itself* is valued—that is, it is not just a way of producing things, or of increasing wealth for oneself or for others; it may also be its own kind of "good" (cf. Potter and Potter 1990: 180–95; Harris 2007).[9] Also, as we might predict for families such as the Chens and the Zhangs, one of the most compelling motivations for intense economic activity is the possibility of slipping back into poverty. The elder Chens and Zhangs have an observable

9.   As Harris notes, work is conceived of differently in different times and places, and its value is not necessarily linked to material rewards. The conceptualization of work/labor may entail the "celebration of human energy, creativity, and [the] capacity to make and expand relationships through work". For example, in the particular Andean case that Harris addresses in her paper, "work is sacralised, seen as an obligation, both because it is part of a continuous mutual nurturance between humans and deities, and because rights to land are articulated through collective work" (Harris 2007: 148). For their part, Potter and Potter (1990) stress the role of work as one of the most important ways of expressing emotion in Chinese culture.

retrospective anxiety about their difficult pasts, something that modulates their optimism about the future. Whatever else they might want out of life (spiritual fulfillment, etc.), they certainly want security: both security of income, and the security of living in strong families and communities that will provide support when difficulties arise.[10] But what I primarily want to draw attention to in these examples is the fact of familial optimism, and a preparedness to try to succeed, whatever may be the contributing factors to this. In particular, I am interested in the outlook of the second generation—that is, of the Chens' son and the Zhangs' adopted daughter—and in the apparent willingness of this generation to study and/or work incredibly hard in order to have, among other things, more wealth. And yet, of course, actually *having* more wealth might be disappointing in the end: that is, it might not bring these individuals and their families what they are hoping for, and in some cases it might even bring them some things they definitely do not want.

* * *

In order to reflect on this possibility, I now turn to a different fieldwork setting, in southwest China near the Burmese border. From my research there in the community of Protected Mountain, I could provide examples of progressive families whose situations are not unlike those of the Zhangs or the Chens.[11] But what is especially interesting about Protected Mountain is its long narrative of economic rise *and fall*. Briefly, in the nineteenth and early twentieth centuries, local people went to Burma as laborers, and not a few of them eventually accumulated wealth as traders. Many of the more successful "sojourners" later returned to Protected Mountain to build beautiful courtyard houses in which to retire. However, history soon intervened. The Japanese occupation dramatically interrupted the Burma trade routes, and after the Communist victory in the Chinese civil war, the border was eventually shut down altogether. After 1949,

---

10. Interestingly, as incomes have gone up in rural China, so too has expenditure on the rituals of gift exchange and reciprocity, which, in effect, produce and sustain relatedness and networks of social support (Yan 1996; Stafford 2000). Although this expenditure on reciprocity could be interpreted as "consumption" (consisting as it does of expenditure on banqueting, gift giving, gambling, etc.), most ordinary people, in my experience, see it as akin to buying insurance: it is a protection against the effects of things going wrong in the future.

11. See Stafford 2004 for a discussion of two cases from this fieldsite.

the explicitly Confucian orientation of Protected Mountain created problems for local people, and during the Cultural Revolution the beautiful traditional detailing of many of the old houses and buildings was either destroyed or hidden behind mud. Today, things have improved. But there is still an air of decline about the place, a sense that things were better in the past than they will ever be again.

Given the circumstances, the fall of the grand families of Protected Mountain must be seen as a historical phenomenon, and as something brought by *outside* and largely uncontrollable forces: the Japanese occupation, the Chinese civil war, Maoist antitraditionalism, and so on. From this perspective, it's not that the families (or the individuals in them) lost the will or motivation to work hard in an attempt to succeed and improve themselves, or that they lost faith in progress and the advantages of wealth; it's more that they had the misfortune to exist at a particular historical moment when everything conspired against them—no matter how hard they tried. But the decline of such families is also, in some cases, portrayed as an *internal* phenomenon, and perhaps even as something that *naturally* happens to families once a certain degree of wealth has been achieved. This may, in turn, set up tensions inside families as hopes and aspirations stop being coordinated across generations, for example as children become disenchanted with the actual state of living with plenty.

In considering the phenomenon of "declining" families in Protected Mountain, however, I need to draw attention to two variants, both of which can be found there. On the one hand, people who accumulate wealth may positively decide to turn their efforts to *higher* things, and perhaps give up the chase for money along the way. Note also that this might be coordinated across generations: for example, a father could decide, having made money, that his children deserve something better than mere money making, and he could push them away from it. This could, in turn, be based on his assumptions about what will give them a good life, and what will make them happy and/or fulfilled. In the case of Protected Mountain, which, as noted above, was explicitly Confucian in outlook, the higher things in question were primarily scholarly and artistic. Drawing on the tradition of valuing "learning" (*xuewen*) over commerce, some families—at least as they tell the story today—began to invest their wealth in education; to cite the Chinese idiom, they "attained Confucianism by way of doing business" (*you shang er ru*). Obviously, a good deal more could be said about this phenomenon. Using the critical terminology of Pierre Bourdieu, one might say that these families grew to value the *symbolic* capital of learning more than the merely *economic* capital of wealth—thus investing the latter in accumulating the former. And in some cases, as Bourdieu would predict, the accumulation of "culture" actually turned out to be a good basis for making yet more money in the future. This analytical framing partly echoes Veblen's stinging critique of the "leisure class" in human history ([1899] 1984). In brief, he claims that *not* working, while applying oneself to noble but ultimately unproductive pursuits, is just another way of competing for status within society. Conspicuous consumption and conspicuous leisure—however nobly construed—are signs of unproductive decadence, and of the human desire to be seen to be better than others, regardless of the ultimate (personal or social) cost.

Veblen notwithstanding, the turn toward culture was largely construed in positive terms by people in Protected Mountain, as I have already said. But there are also instances in which the lack of focus on wealth production was seen negatively—not as a moral renunciation of money chasing but rather as an immoral descent into laziness and/or decay. This, then, is the second variant of a declining family. To borrow the economists' way of putting things, the sons and daughters of the rich (including those in Protected Mountain) sometimes decide to allocate more of their time to, for example, gambling and drinking and vice in general than to wealth production—perhaps in part because of their disillusionment with having had it. Or instead of pursuing proper Confucian learning, while upholding and enhancing family virtue, they might involve themselves in decadent artistic pursuits, or just do nothing at all. They may want to spend without earning, no matter what the consequences. Somewhere along the way, they seem to have lost the incentive—wherever it came from—to work hard for the sake of increasing family wealth. To frame this in relation to emotion and affective forecasting: they have given up striving to get what other people (e.g., their elders) want them to want, perhaps in the pursuit of what might seem (e.g., from the vantage point of their elders) selfish indulgence.

But what does a declining family actually look like in contemporary China and Taiwan? In Shanghai, Taipei, and other cities, there is now conspicuous consumption on an industrial scale, of course, and the rise of a generation gap between apparently hedonistic young people and their elders. In the rural places where I have carried out fieldwork, such tendencies have not been so obvious, in part because the families I worked with were mostly living on relatively low incomes. But the tendencies do still exist, albeit in modified form, the key point being that these are generally cases *not* of wealthy families turning away from wealth but rather of ordinary rural families finding their progressive narrative

going off track. One common issue, for example, is the existence of problem
gamblers or drinkers or drug takers, or those who end up spending more than
they should on household goods or other things simply in order to show off.
Predictably, hard-working elders are bitterly disappointed to find themselves
with descendants who seem determined to destroy their progressive economic
narrative. In some circumstances, this is bad enough to bring a family into serious decline, as in the case of one younger couple I met during fieldwork in
northeast China who were at risk of financial destruction thanks to the husband's gambling problem. Interestingly, his daughter, still a young child, had a
progressive attitude—instilled through a combination of her mother's influence
and the influence of her schoolteachers—and she was harshly critical of her father for the chronic gambling that was, in her view, harming her family. I do not
have enough evidence to know for sure, but I would guess that his behavior was
partly a function of bitterness and cynicism concerning his own life prospects:
What hope was there that a poor guy from rural China would ever make serious money in such a corrupt system? His rejection of the chase after money, his
descent into drinking and, in particular, gambling, was thus very different from
that of elite Protected Mountain families who, in the past, decided to focus their
time and energy on calligraphic skills.

    In any case, the kind of familial "decline" or "decadence" I have observed
during fieldwork has more often been of a relatively low-key and subtle kind:
that is, neither a turning to higher things nor a cynical rejection of life as it is.
For example, the first family I lived with in rural Taiwan, the Lins, were among
the wealthiest in the township (although, in Taiwanese terms, not unusually
so). Mr. and Mrs. Lin lived with their three children in a large house facing the
ocean, and spent more than most local people on food, entertainment, travel,
and so on. Their wealth derived from hard—sometimes truly backbreaking—
work in construction. At the time of my fieldwork, however, I spotted a tension, diffuse but observable, between the outlook of the parents and that of
the children. In brief, the children (still young at the time) were inclined to
avoid schoolwork or chores wherever possible, and to be a little self-indulgent,
for example to eat as many sweets as they could. The parents did not like, and
wished to change, these attitudes, and so there were many fights about it being
time to study, and so on. I also sometimes felt that I observed in the children
a mild—and largely inchoate—contempt for their hard-working parents, who
were so obviously of rural Taiwanese stock. The children, products of high-
quality "modern" schooling as much as of family life, spent most of their free

time watching television programs about urban elites and seemed on track to be more sophisticated and "advanced" than their own parents ... and possibly also much less hard working. One irony about this, already alluded to above, is that the advancement/sophistication of these children—which is precisely what most parents aspire to for their offspring (and certainly it is what they help pay for)—is also something that arguably turns them into fundamentally different kinds of persons than their parents (Stafford 1995). It was hard to picture these Taiwanese children eventually working, as their parents some- times did, in muddy construction sites day and night. Were they themselves aiming for higher things? Did their parents assume that by providing comforts to their children, of one kind or another, they would be making them happy?

Notably, questions of these kinds could also be asked in relation to the Chens and the Zhangs, that is, in relation to the progressive families I have mentioned above. Might the Chens' son become, via education, more interested in pursuing art than in pursuing law? Might that path somehow lead him to abandon his (generally) Confucian outlook, his willingness to work hard just to please his parents? Might the ambitiousness of the Zhangs' daughter-in-law get the best of her, leading her to neglect the happiness not only of her adoptive parents but also of her own children? Through various experiences and interactions in the city, might she and her husband, at some point, lose their willingness to sacrifice so much for a common family purpose?

* * *

At this stage, let me briefly recapitulate the discussion so far. Some economists and psychologists argue that, beyond a certain level of income, wealth does not make us happy. The difficulty is that we sometimes behave as if it *will* make us happy—a potentially disastrous case of affective mis-forecasting. Of course, there is significant variation in definitions and valuations of happiness across cultures, and in the case of China and Taiwan the significance of happiness (and of emotional life in general) has changed over time. Furthermore, when we look at examples of real Chinese and Taiwanese families, we are reminded not only that happiness is a complex psychological phenomenon, but also that the link between the willingness to work and the desire for wealth and/or happiness, as such, is not always obvious. One complication is that people are motivated not only by what they want but also often—and sometimes more importantly—by what the people around them want. In what I have called

progressive families (such as the Chens and the Zhangs), the second generation *does* seem very highly motivated to work in order to have an improved life.
This may be partly, even largely, because they are responding to their own as-
sumptions/predictions about what will make older generations happy. And the
older generations may be pushing them because of their assumptions/predic-
tions about what will make younger generations happy. I have drawn a contrast
between this and the situation in declining families, where the younger generations appear to be losing—or even actively resisting—the motivation for work
and, perhaps, the general belief in progress. There are different scenarios for
this, but some such people may come across as lazy, or self-indulgent. In terms
of China's cultural tradition, they may also come across as strikingly *individualistic* in orientation, that is, as focused on their own happiness, pleasure, or
utility rather than on family goals and family progress. The affective forecasting
they care about, one might say, is of the purely personal kind rather than being
intergenerational.

In his Malinowski Lecture for 2003, Yunxiang Yan explored this issue with
reference to material from long-term fieldwork in Heilongjiang (Yan 2005).
What he describes, however, is *not* a situation in which people are giving up on
progress or rejecting material comfort. On the contrary, Yan describes a situation in which young people in the countryside appear to be chasing utility—
basically in the form of money and material goods—at all costs. Among other
things, some of them attempt to extract maximum bridewealth from their elders
for their own personal benefit. They justify this partly on pragmatic grounds,
but also with reference to a rather dimly comprehended, and deeply utilitarian, notion of "Western individualism."[12] This is not something that Yan finds
it in himself to like, but he does clearly show some of the complex motivations
behind the (individualistic and seemingly unfilial) actions of the young people
he met during fieldwork. As he explains, they are motivated not just by a desire
to be happy, but also by a growing sense that personal happiness and success is
something they actually deserve. While this can be seen as selfish, some people
in the local community do admire young women and men for the strength of

---

12. Yan suggests that while Western individualism is normally assumed to centrally
    involve elements both of self-reliance and of duty to others, the version adopted
    by his informants in Heilongjiang is premised on a good deal of reliance on others
    (especially one's parents and siblings), and very limited duties.

character they show in standing up to elders and extracting what they need, or think they need, in order to face the future (Yan 2005: 644).

By contrast, who has a good word to say for the truly decadent? That is, who has a good word to say for young people who, unlike their parents, are not prepared to work hard in order to improve their standard of living? For those who turn their backs altogether on the idea of wealth or financial security as the ultimate value? It is worth noting, again, that "decadent" young people of this kind might, in fact, be possessed of a kind of worldly wisdom. That is, having grown up in relative affluence—or at least in the absence of poverty—some of them may no longer believe that having money, as such, is a guarantee of happiness or fulfillment. Having observed the lives of the relatively affluent people around them, they may have decided that "progress" is not what they want or expect from their brief existences. What some would interpret as a lack of morality could therefore well be seen as a consistent (if arguably decadent, and potentially radical) ethical stance.

Interestingly, this stance also has a scientific basis, if one believes the recent findings of economists about happiness and wellbeing in post-Mao China. Here the evidence suggests that, "paradoxically," the huge increase in wealth has *not* produced a growth in happiness—that is, in spite of the fact that the uplift from relatively low levels of income should normally have done so. (In other words, this is not a case of a rich country getting richer.) As Richard Easterlin and his colleagues succinctly put it: "There is no evidence of an increase in life satisfaction [in China] of the magnitude that might have been expected to result from the fourfold improvement in the level of per capita consumption that has occurred"—in fact, there is probably a decline in life satisfaction, some would say a very steep one (Easterlin et al. 2012: 9775; for background see also Easterlin 2008 and Easterlin et al. 2010). And why should this be? The most plausible explanation, it seems, is that in spite of rising incomes, people have been made unhappy by a rise in unemployment, by the dissolution of China's (formerly strong) social safety net, by rising material aspirations (which, in effect, can never be satisfied), and by growing economic inequality (Easterlin et al. 2012; see also Brockmann et al. 2008). Note that although the case she discusses is radically different in many of its particulars, the article by Freeman on the Gamo people of Ethiopia (this collection) has definite resonances with the Chinese experience: for example, they seem to be made unhappy by rising inequality. Even for relatively poor people, then, it seems that money is not the route to happiness in all circumstances.

* * *

Of course, the idea that "money does not make you happy" is an element in folk philosophies in many parts of the world, along with the notion that moral perils attach to economic activity in general (Parry and Bloch 1989). In contemporary China, one certainly encounters nostalgia for the Maoist era, when wealth was trumped by higher (collectivist) values, and a regret that today all of social life appears to have been reduced to a chase after money. However, this has to be set against the overwhelming evidence of what people actually prioritize in their own actions—that is, the pursuit of wealth—and the countervailing folk philosophies which encourage them to do so. The proportion of people in China and Taiwan who truly opt out of chasing money, as things stand, is surely very small. One reason for this is that every individual is a locus of affective predictions (reliable or not); to seriously challenge such predictions, for example by adopting a life-course that loved ones see as doomed to failure, is not an easy task.

The economist John Kenneth Galbraith, while not exactly extolling the virtues of decadence, as such, has put in a good word for idleness. As Veblen explained back in the late nineteenth century, idleness is sometimes simply another "good" which is there to impress others—especially those who still have to work for a living. But in a book which interestingly prefigures the conclusions of Richard Layard, and written almost half a century earlier, Galbraith argues (with considerably less cynicism than Veblen) that the modern capitalist system is built to address problems which are simply no longer relevant for those of us living in developed, affluent societies (Galbraith [1958] 1999). Everything is still oriented toward the production of goods, whereas in fact the last thing we need in the affluent world is more material goods. Like Layard, Galbraith thinks that sorting out inequality, unhappiness, and so on, would be a nobler goal than increasing productivity and generating wealth.[13] So why should we still find the failure to be productive so offensive? Why do we condemn it? As

---

13. He says: "The Benthamite test of public policy was 'what serves the greatest happiness of the greatest number', and happiness was more or less implicitly identified with productivity. This is still the official test. In modern times, the test has not been very rigorously applied. We have somewhat sensed though we have not recognized the declining importance of goods. Yet even in its deteriorated form we cling to this criterion. It is so much simpler than to substitute the other tests—compassion, individual happiness and well-being, the minimization of community or other social tensions—which now become relevant" (ibid.: 214).

he observes: "The idle man may still be an enemy of himself. But it is hard to say that the loss of his effort is damaging to society" (ibid.: 215). An argument of this kind, not to mention a fully fledged defense of decadence, will probably not find much purchase in the China of today, nor in Taiwan. But as these societies become increasingly affluent, it seems inevitable that more and more people will find themselves working hard in the pursuit of money that is not, in fact, making them any happier. At least a few of them are bound to catch on.

ACKNOWLEDGMENTS

The research discussed in this article has been funded by grants from the Wenner-Gren Foundation, the Luce Foundation, the British Academy, and the UK Economic and Social Research Council (ESRC).

REFERENCES

Blake, C. Fred. 1978. "Death and abuse in marriage laments: The curse of Chinese brides." *Asian Folklore Studies* 37 (1): 13–33.

Brockmann, Hilke, Jan Delhey, Christian Welzel, and Hao Yuan. 2008. "The China puzzle: Falling happiness in a rising economy." *Journal of Happiness Studies* 10: 387–405

Easterlin, Richard A. 2001. "Income and happiness: Towards a unified theory." *The Economic Journal* 111: 465–84.

———. 2003. "Explaining happiness." *Proceedings of the National Academy of Sciences* 100 (19): 11176–83.

———. 2008. "Lost in transition: Life satisfaction on the road to capitalism." *Discussion Paper Series, Institute for Labor* 3409.

Easterlin, Richard A., Laura Angelescu McVey, Malgorzata Switek, Onnicha Sawangfa, and Jacqueline Smith Zweig. 2010. "The happiness–income paradox revisited". *Proceedings of the National Academy of Sciences* 107 (52): 22463–68.

Easterlin, Richard A., Robson Morgan, Malgorzata Switek, and Fei Wang. 2012. "China's life satisfaction, 1990–2010." *Proceedings of the National Academy of Sciences* 109 (25): 9775–80.

Farquhar, Judith. 2002. *Appetites: Food and sex in post-socialist China*. Durham, NC: Duke University Press.

Freedman, Maurice. 1979. *The study of Chinese society: Essays by Maurice Freedman*. Selected and introduced by G. William Skinner. Stanford: Stanford University Press.

Galbraith, John Kenneth. (1958) 1999. *The affluent society*. London: Penguin.

Gilbert, Daniel T. 2007. *Stumbling on happiness*. New York: Vintage Books.

Gilbert, Daniel T., and Timothy D. Wilson. 2009. "Why the brain talks to itself: sources of error in emotional prediction." *Philosophical transactions of the Royal Society*, Series B, 364: 1335–41.

Harrell, Stevan. 1985. "Why do the Chinese work so hard: Reflections on an entrepreneurial ethic." *Modern China* 11 (2): 203–26.

Harris, Olivia. 2007. "What makes people work?" In *Questions of anthropology*, edited by Rita Astuti, Jonathan Parry, and Charles Stafford, 137–66. Oxford: Berg.

Ip, Po Keung. 2011. "Concepts of Chinese folk happiness." *Social Indicator Research* 104: 459–74.

———. 2013. "Misrepresenting Chinese folk happiness: A critique of a study." *Social Indicators Research* 110: 695–702.

Johnson, Elizabeth Lominska. 2003. "Singing of separation, lamenting loss: Hakka women's expressions of separation and reunion." In *Living with separation in China: Anthropological accounts*, edited by Charles Stafford, 27–45. London: RoutledgeCurzon.

Johnston, Barbara Rose, Elizabeth Colson, Dean Falk, et al. 2012. "On happiness." *American Anthropologist* 114 (1): 6–18.

Johnston, James. 2013. "Filial paths and the ordinary ethics of movement." In *Ordinary ethics in China*, edited by Charles Stafford, 45–65. London: Bloomsbury.

Kahneman, Daniel. 2011. *Thinking fast and slow*. London: Allen Lane.

Kipnis, Andrew, 2011. *Governing educational desire*. Chicago: University of Chicago Press.

Layard, Richard. 2005. *Happiness: Lessons from a new science*. London: Allen Lane.

Parry, Jonathan, and Maurice Bloch, eds. 1989. *Money and the morality of exchange*. Cambridge: Cambridge University Press.

Potter, Heins Sulamith, and Jack M. Potter. 1990. *China's peasants: The anthropology of a revolution*. Cambridge: Cambridge University Press.

Quinn, Naamoi. 1978. "Do MFantse fish sellers estimate probability in their heads?" *American Ethnologist* 5 (2): 206–26.

Sahlins, Marshall. 2002. *Waiting for Foucault, still.* Fourth edition. Chicago: Prickly Paradigm Press.

Sangren, P. Steven. 2003. "Separation, autonomy and recognition in the production of gender differences: Reflections from considerations of myths and laments." In *Living with separation in China: Anthropological accounts*, edited by Charles Stafford, 53–84. London: RoutledgeCurzon.

Stafford, Charles. 1995. *The roads of Chinese childhood: Learning and identification in Angang.* Cambridge: Cambridge University Press.

———. 2000. *Separation and reunion in modern China.* Cambridge: Cambridge University Press.

———. 2004. "Two stories of learning and economic agency in Yunnan." *Taiwan Journal of Anthropology* 2 (1): 171–94. (Special edition, "Learning and economic agency in China and Taiwan," edited by Charles Stafford.)

———. 2006. "Scales of economy: some lessons from a case-study in Taiwan." *China Studies* 3: 20–37.

———. 2007. "What is going to happen next?" In *Questions of anthropology*, edited by Rita Astuti, Jonathan Parry, and Charles Stafford, 55–76. Oxford: Berg.

Veblen, Thorstein. (1899) 1994. *The theory of the leisure class.* New York: Dover.

Watson, Rubie. 1985. *Inequality among brothers: Class and kinship in South China.* Cambridge: Cambridge University Press.

Wilson, Timothy D., and Daniel T. Gilbert. 2005. "Affective forecasting: knowing what to want." *Current Directions in Psychological Science* 14 (3): 131–34.

Yan, Yunxiang. 1996. *The flow of gifts: Reciprocity and social networks in a Chinese village.* Stanford: Stanford University Press.

———. 2003. *Private life under socialism: Love, intimacy, and family change in a Chinese village, 1949–1999.* Stanford: Stanford University Press.

———. 2005. "The individual and transformation of bridewealth in rural North China." *Journal of the Royal Anthropological Institute* (N.S.) 11 (4): 637–58.

Zhang, Hui. 2013. "The ethics of envy avoidance in contemporary China." In *Ordinary ethics in China*, edited by Charles Stafford, 115–32. London: Bloomsbury.

CHAPTER THREE

The good life in balance
Insights from aging Japan

Iza Kavedžija

Seeking respite from the sweltering summer heat, a small crowd of elderly people gathered in the Shimoichi salon, a small, warmly lit space nestled away in a busy, old-fashioned shopping arcade in downtown South Osaka. Oku-san, a wiry man in his late seventies and a gleeful storyteller, ordered a cup of black coffee and launched into a tirade. "I'm used to him leaving the aircon on even when he leaves the house, but this time he left the fridge door open! I wish my grandson would just return home to his mother, he's such a nuisance. He leaves his things lying about and I have to do so much more shopping and cleaning when he's around. . . . He even dries up my beer supply!" This last remark elicited some mirthful laughter from the audience, but Oku-san continued: "My daughter thinks it's easier if he lives closer to his university, and that it's a help for me to have a young person around. She thought he'd give me a hand with housework, but I have more to do this way. I miss having my own space!" Two ladies in their late eighties nodded in understanding. Kondo-san, a calm, broad-faced lady in her late seventies, agreed vigorously: "I live on my own, and it's heaven (*gokuraku*)! I had many hard times in life and now I'm finally free, everything is so easy, I don't have to look after anybody." She went on to explain that her son had invited her to live with him and his family in another prefecture but that she didn't get along with her daughter-in-law, who encouraged her to leave. So she moved in with her daughter, only to realize that to live harmoniously with her daughter's family, she had to be the one to adapt. In order not to be a burden she had to endure many things, all kinds of small annoyances. She eventually decided to make do on her own and now enjoys living independently, despite her limited means. Some of the other salon-goers voiced their agreement with Kondo-san's decision, and she cheerfully continued: "I really enjoy singing these days . . . since I'm "single" again my voice has become quite strong! I love choir practice." On many other occasions, Kondo-san would describe the joys of growing vegetables in rows of pots lined up alongside her house in the narrow street she lives in. She was known in the neighborhood as the "vegetable expert" and she divided her time evenly between her quiet pottering, weeding and watering in her improvised urban garden, and socializing in the Shimoichi salon, exchanging stories and news with others in the cheerful and sometimes raucous atmosphere that Japanese people so often associate with Osaka.

In contrast to the stereotype of the elderly as dependent and frail, many of the older Japanese people I got to know during fieldwork frequently spoke of the sense of freedom they enjoyed in their later years, their enjoyment of hobbies, and the importance of self-cultivation. They were, on the whole, a calm, content, and cheerful crowd.[1] That said, they rarely spoke directly of "happiness"; stating such things about oneself could be perceived as bragging, and it is customary in Japan to represent oneself and one's associates in a modest, self-deprecatory manner. Indeed, if asked directly whether they were happy, or even contented, many would have been reluctant to say that they were. Nevertheless, in their daily conversations among themselves, they often expressed gratitude for what they have, or for what others have done for them, or their joy for certain events, and their deep appreciation of positive, interesting, or beautiful objects or moments. They stated their contentment or dissatisfaction in a variety of ways, and by following their interactions and daily behaviors, and later discussing my

---

1. Overall, the salon-goers were mostly in their seventies or eighties with some in their early nineties. While far from affluent (many were receiving modest state pensions), most owned their own houses, in which they typically lived alone. I deliberately chose to focus my research on relatively healthy older people who lived in their own homes in an urban context, since most previous studies were about the elderly in institutional settings (Hashimoto 1996; Wu 2004; Thang 2001), disembedded from their communities and many of their previous social relations, or alternatively set in rural Japan (Traphagan 2000, 2004).

observations with them directly, I was able to discern certain a range of issues that were considered to be of some importance in relation to leading a good life, or living well and finding contentment in everyday life. As a group, they especially enjoyed telling stories, both as a social activity and as a way to make sense of events in their lives. At the same time, they valued quiet moments of contemplation in everyday activities, like Kondo-san with her vegetables. While they strived for warm social relationships, they attempted to avoid burdening others with their worries or imposing obligations.

These efforts to maintain a meaningful and contented existence, as I hope to show in this article, led them to strive to hold a number of factors in balance, to negotiate a tension between autonomy and dependence, as well as between isolation and burdensome social relationships. On a broader level, they strove to navigate a tension between two contrastive orientations or modes of being in the world: one involving meaning-making activities connecting the past with the present, and pointing to desirable futures; and another focused on the experience and appreciation of the present moment. In tracing through these balances, this article approaches happiness, in the sense of life satisfaction and a sense of purpose, as it is envisaged and crafted through practice—including narrative practice—among this group of older Japanese. To be clear, I have not sought to approach happiness through direct questioning or self-reporting. While my interlocutors seemed generally quite content with their lives, finding much pleasure and enjoyment in the everyday, the question of "how happy they are" was never a central concern. Of greater interest was how they envisaged what it meant to live well, to be happy, and the efforts they made to lead a life they found both pleasant and satisfying.

LIVING WELL IN JAPAN: BALANCING ACTS

In Japan, the literature on happiness is abundant.[2] The shelves of bookshops are populated by a range of popular titles, such as *The mechanism of happiness* (Maeno 2013), by a neuroscientist and robotics expert who argues that happiness can be "controlled" and who proposes four "factors' of happiness" ("let's give it a go," "thank you," "things will turn out somehow," "true to yourself");

---

2.   A comprehensive analysis of this extensive literature is well beyond the scope of the present article, though it would comprise a very valuable study in its own right.

Five things you need to know about happiness (Hakunetsu Kyōshitsu 2014), based
on a popular program aired on the national television network NHK, entitled
Happiness studies; and *"Happiness treatise" for businessmen* (Egami 2015), to mention but a few—along with a wide range of books by foreign authors. In addition to these more practically oriented, "self-help"-style books, there are also
numerous scholarly writings by sociologists, psychologists, and philosophers,
some of which are also read widely.[3] Some of these have a critical orientation:
for example, philosopher Gen Kida (2001) analyzes the reasons for the apparent lack of interest in happiness in historic Japan, as evidenced by the lack of
explicit terms. Happiness (*kōfuku*[4]), he argues, denotes the state of mind of an
individual, and increased interest in it reveals an egotistical tendency in society
(see also Coulmas 2008).

Two of the most common terms for expressing happiness in Japan are *shiawase*, which might be translated as "happiness, good fortune, blessing," and *ureshii*, "happy, glad, pleased." Thus one of my elderly interlocutors explained to me
that she joined a sports club after turning fifty, and as a consequence became
much more active and outgoing, expanding her social circle. "You know, as I
told you, I was already over fifty when I joined the sports club. I made many
friends and become more outgoing. Now I'm really happy" (*honto ni shiawase*).
Nevertheless, most of my friends were not inclined to describe themselves or
their own lives (or the lives of those close to them) as *shiawase*; doing so would
be considered immodest. The term was perhaps more commonly used in the
context of advice, or in the form of an endorsement: for example, a kind, ninety-
year-old lady who came to know me well after many months of meetings, concluded her life story with something she really wanted me to know: "In life, if
you look after your husband's parents, you will be most happy (*jinsei tte, shujinno
oya daiji shitara ne, ichiban shiawase ni ikimasu*). Then your children will follow
suit and you will live well. Yes, if you live like a good couple and look after his
parents, always kindly and with care, then the children will turn out well." Here
as in many other accounts I was given, happiness (*shiawase*) is closely related

---

3.   While my interlocutors did not read such books, they were not entirely unaffected
     by these larger discourses, most notably those involving the term *ikigai*, referring
     to purpose in life, or "that what makes life worth living" (Mathews 1996). For a
     detailed discussion of discourses of *ikigai*, including their role in these peoples' lives,
     see Kavedžija (2013).

4.   This abstract notion of happiness as *kōfuku*, used mostly in writing, overlaps with
     well-being and to that extent it is close to the Western concept.

to care and to close, warm relationships with others. It is to be found in the hope that one will be cared for, as much as in the very process of caring for others. The term *ureshii*[5] was used rather more frequently, and it often punctuated everyday communications, including emails or text messages: "I was happy to receive your postcard, thank you"; "If you could stay a bit longer we would be glad"; "I was pleased you came to visit." In fact, when young children visited the salon on several occasions some of the older ladies remarked how glad (*ureshii*) they were: "How good of you to come, *yo'u kite kurehatta ne.*" As these examples suggest, *ureshii* also has a strong social and relational component but was often used to convey a happy feeling arising from something done for you by another, thus expressing a sense of gratitude.

Despite the relative affluence and stability of Japanese society, reported levels of happiness appear to be rather low (see, for example, Diener, Diener, and Diener 1995). How should we interpret this? The Japanese case suggests that one can be relatively healthy and materially well off, with reasonably good social relationships, and yet nevertheless feel something is missing in one's life. For this reason, as Gordon Mathews (2009: 167–68) suggests, a study of well-being must also focus on sources of meaning in life. Some explanations of this discrepancy of results and predictions focus on terminology and the process of self-reporting, pointing out that Japanese may find it inappropriate to describe themselves as particularly happy, or in any way above average and thus different from the majority. Nevertheless, not all studies have relied on self-reporting (Kan, Karasawa, and Kitayama 2009), and yet they have come up with similar results. Chiemi Kan and colleagues acknowledge that some of this may be a consequence of a constraining social structure, but choose to focus on the cultural conceptualizations of happiness used as a basis for the measurement. They argue that the conceptualizations that had been used may be biased and overly narrow, focusing mainly on personal achievement and positive feelings and assuming that happiness is itself evaluated positively. They show that Japanese people rate much higher in surveys based on a more holistic and culturally appropriate

---

5.   These two terms, *shiawase* and *ureshii,* have some similarities but they are not interchangeable, as the examples above indicate. Ureshii seems to more often to indicate something immediate, while shiawase(na) can have a more evaluative dimension, as in "*shiawase na jinsei*"—a happy life. Another term, *koufuku,* written with characters *kō* (lucky) and *fuku* (fortune, good luck), is more formal and more frequently used in written language and denotes contentedness. For a discussion of other relevant terms and historical changes in meaning see Coulmas (2008: 11).

conceptualization of happiness, and argue that happiness in Japan can often be seen as transient, and the social world as fluid (a place where much depends on others and not just on one's own actions and achievements). Feelings that result from successfully removing oneself for a while from the flow of social life, or associated with a sense of distance or dissociation—such as peacefulness and calm—are therefore an important aspect of wellbeing in Japan, as well as some other Eastern cultures (Kan, Karasawa, and Kitayama 2009).

Similarly, Yukiko Uchida and Shigehiro Kitayama[6] (2009) suggest that in contrast to American conceptions of happiness as an enduring positive state frequently associated with excitement (or high arousal) and personal achievement, in Japan attitudes that might be seen as negative in some ways (for instance, avoiding or withdrawing from reality) and low arousal positive states (such as calmness) were deemed to be relevant aspects of happiness (Uchida and Ogihara 2012: 395). In short, their research indicates that Japanese conceptualizations of happiness not only are less focused on independence and personal achievement than some of the Western equivalents but are also less focused on positive attitudes and often include both poles of an emotion. For example, they may include social support as contributing to a sense of well-being, while calm and quiet relaxation without the pressures of the social world remain equally important. While methodologically and conceptually quite distinct from ethnographic research, these findings resonated with some of my own observations in the field. These conceptualizations of happiness specific to Japanese, and perhaps other East Asian contexts described by psychologists as "holistic," can be seen as incorporating opposite poles of an emotion, or even, I would argue, seemingly opposed values. In this sense they can be described as a series of balances between opposites. In other words, the sense of happiness is derived from a series of balancing acts between extremes and different modes of being.

The tendency of my interlocutors to pay careful attention to achieving this balance is not one that is unique to the elderly, or in any way restricted to the Japanese context. As a way of describing and understanding the good life, it

---

6.   These authors also draw attention to the difference in emphasis on independence in individualistic societies, such as America, and social harmony and dependence in East Asian societies, such as Japan. In the latter, incorporation of the negative experiences into conceptualization of happiness has a social aspect to it, according to this viewpoint: for instance, one may feel happy and grateful for sympathy of others, which resulted from a negative experience that brought one misery and suffering (see Uchida and Kitayama 2009: 442).

bears a certain resemblance to Aristotelian ethics, in which happiness is defined in terms of virtuous activity, and every virtue is a middle state between conditions of deficiency and excess (Kraut 2012). A similar tension, and its relevance for well-being, is described by Michael Jackson: "well-being is . . . dependent on an adjustment or balance between our sense of what we owe others and what we owe ourselves" (Jackson 2011: 195). While the Kuranko of Sierra Leone with whom Jackson worked place their demands on others loudly and explicitly, in contrast to the more formalized interactions and internalized expectations experienced by the inhabitants of Shimoichi, they share the concern with finding a difficult yet valuable balance. I would like to suggest that formulating the elements of the good life in the form of tensions or priorities that need to be kept in balance allows for a certain degree of abstraction, which in turn facilitates comparison with other cultural contexts,[7] as well as other life stages.

Among my older interlocutors these balancing acts included attempts at harmonizing rich social ties and avoiding over-closeness, including the burden that such close relationships can bring with them in the form of social obligations and complex gift exchanges. Similarly, a related balancing act regarding family ties—in which autonomy and freedom must be balanced against dependence and reliance on others—emerged as central for older people I spoke with.[8] In other words, the balances that are required for living well are those that embody the tensions between the values held in high regard by my interlocutors. At the same time, happiness itself is seen as valued positively only to the extent that it encompasses both of these poles, and can otherwise be seen as a fleeting state, or an antisocial one. It can be argued, therefore, that happiness among older Japanese, in practice, is a matter of balancing particular social and moral values. These kinds of values, unlike exchange values, are not simply interchangeable or commensurable, and their conflict cannot be resolved through simple choice, but only through moral judgment (Lambek 2008). In this sense, I argue, happiness is approached as a form of practical moral judgment.

---

7. Such an abstraction maintains a degree of nuance and at the same time may provide useful conceptual tools (if not quite hypotheses to be tested) to crosscultural psychologists, policy makers, and others concerned with happiness research.

8. A number of other balancing acts seemed relevant for the pursuit of the good life, including the navigation of a tension between fate and agency, or life choices and opportunism, though limitations of space preclude a fuller description here.

HAPPINESS IN OLDER AGE

The relationship between happiness and age (or life course) has been the focus of much recent research by psychologists and economists. Some of the most widely reported studies in the media[9] suggest that older people are on average happier than their younger, middle-aged counterparts. The data collected as a part of a large-scale 2008 Gallup survey, for example, examines how psychological well-being varies with age in the United States (Stone et al. 2010), and suggests that older people generally tend to experience positive emotions (or positive affect) more frequently, and that their overall appraisals of their life tend to be more positive than those of younger people. The trend, as described by psychological researchers, seems to follow a much-discussed, U-shaped curve: a gradual decrease in levels of psychological well-being from early youth onward, followed by a movement upward from around the fifties and into the later years. Negative affect, or the prevalence of negative emotions such as stress, worry, and anger, seems to decrease with age (see, for example, Rossi and Rossi 1990; Mroczek and Kolarz 1998).

Based on my own experiences with older Japanese, one explanation for this tendency would be that older people tend to focus more on the things they consider worthwhile, and avoid situations that cause them discomfort. This is not always perceived as something positive, however, and in Japan one would sometimes hear it said that the elderly are "selfish" (*wagamama*). For example, Takahashi-san, a quiet, smiling lady in her mid-seventies who moved to Osaka some years before and had few friends in the area, told me how making friends when you are older can be difficult: "It's easy to have acquaintances, but it's hard to make close friendships (*shitashii*). Older people seek comfort and they withdraw when they don't feel like doing something." Nevertheless, in many other situations, this attitude had positive consequences, as people tended to focus on those aspects of things that they perceived as good.[10]

---

9.   For example, Carstensen (2011); *The Economist* (2010); Bakalar (2010).

10. Recent psychological research on older adults in the United States indicates that older people's perception of time changes, and with realization that time is limited people tend to consider their priorities more carefully. They therefore focus more on positive emotions and things they consider to be worthwhile (Carstensen 2006).

SOCIALITY AND OVER-CLOSENESS

Shimoichi community salon,[11] where I spent much of my fieldwork,[12] is an inviting, warmly lit space in a small, refurbished townhouse located in an old shopping arcade. This arcade was once the vibrant center of Shimoichi, an old merchant neighborhood in downtown South Osaka, but was progressively overshadowed by large supermarkets and convenience stores. With a high proportion of elderly residents, some of whom have lived in the area for several generations, the neighborhood was changing—small, wooden buildings in the inner streets were now surrounded by large high-rise apartment blocks lining the main arteries outlining the boundaries of the neighborhood. The salon was well known to most residents of the neighborhood, as it offered affordable tea and coffee and a space to meet others. It offered a range of activities such as weekly music sessions, weaving workshops, and monthly concerts with an aim of reaching out to the people in the neighborhood. Most of the daily visitors were older people, relatively healthy and independent, mostly living on their own or with their families.

For the most part, the older people who regularly stopped by the salon did not necessarily think of each other as close friends but they expressed concern for each other in various ways, by sharing information and checking up on their neighbors, albeit in a casual manner. For example, one afternoon in late March, Okuma-san came in for the first time in two weeks. Upon greeting everyone she apologized for her long absence and explained that she had been very busy over the cherry blossom viewing season. She had a couple of house guests, and complained how exhausted she was from all the cooking and serving of elaborate, Japanese-style meals, though she'd also had a lot of fun, going to interesting places while showing her guests around. Her explanation was listened

---

11. This kind of community salon, resembling a café but often staffed by volunteers and offering a small selection of affordable hot drinks and sometimes activities or cultural events, can be found in many urban neighborhoods in Japan. Many of the salons are attended mostly by the elderly and are open only on designated days of the week. Shimoichi salon was run by a small not-for-profit organization (NPO) providing various support services for the elderly in the neighborhood, some of which created a small financial surplus used for the maintenance of the salon and its activities, which attracted not only older local residents but also a significant number of young families.

12. The fieldwork on which this article is based was conducted over the course of fourteen months in 2009, with follow-up visits in 2013.

to attentively, and her story attracted the attention of most people gathered around the table. They were very happy to hear she was well, having grown a little worried about her, wondering whether she might have fallen ill. Kato-san had even walked to her place but was baffled at what to do, as Okuma-san lived in a massive apartment block (*manshon*) with hundreds of apartments and a securely locked front door. She realized she couldn't just knock and check on her, so she left. Okuma-san thanked her for her concern and took out a big box of biscuits from Nara, which she had brought as an *omiyage* (a present or souvenir) from the trip she'd made with her friends during their stay, and offered them to everyone.

Most of the salon-goers were concerned about the possibility of appearing thoughtless and were very cautious in their dealings with others, paying particular attention not to burden them, for example, with unpleasant or overly intimate details of their lives, or with their worries, or by giving inappropriately large gifts that would then have to be reciprocated. Gift giving in Japan is a formalized affair, involving exchanges of set value on specific occasions, each meticulously accounted for and reciprocated (Rupp 2003). The kinds of gifts brought to the salon were small packages of food, which were shared and consumed together, and not taken back home. Often these were in the form of *omiyage* (souvenirs) brought back from places people had traveled, or gifts people received from family or neighbors that they wanted to share, such as the small crate of mandarins that one lady received from her granddaughter, too much for her to eat on her own. This act of redistribution allowed for confirming social ties and provided an opportunity to tell a story about her granddaughter to the others in the salon, who praised the latter's caring gesture.

In an attempt to minimize the burden on the salon-goers, the NPO staff and founders explicitly discouraged formal exchanges, stating firmly that, for example, New Year gifts were unnecessary, and politely declined them, referring to such exchanges as "*ki wo tsukau*" (literally, "using one's spirit"). Kuroki-san, one of the NPO staff, explained that this tendency to politely reciprocate probably contributed to the weakening of old-style neighborhood support networks. Now, both when offering and requesting help people are aware of the burden and they started feeling reticent and restrained (*enryo*). Such statements imply a realization that extending too much help and making formal gift exchanges places a burden of obligation on others, such that people became less inclined to ask for help.

The sentiment of not causing trouble (*meiwaku*) to others is a very widespread one in Japan (on the train, for instance, reminders are issued to switch off

mobile phones lest one cause *meiwaku* to others). Many of my older interlocutors were worried about becoming a burden on their children and causing them
meiwaku if they became frail, so they were grateful for the introduction of the
Long Term Care Insurance, on which they could rely to get help and support in
their own homes. In the salon, while the visitors would sometimes share their
worries, they were careful not to impose an overly heavy tone and often made
light of their troubles, in an attempt not to burden others with their problems.
In short, in order to create and maintain social ties and networks of support,
people were cautious not to impose, balancing a tension between sociality and
stifling social relationships, or between supportive friendly relationships and
excessive closeness.

INTIMACY AND INDEPENDENCE

Many of my interlocutors mentioned that the "three-generational household"—
sharing a house with one's children and grandchildren—was widely seen as an
"ideal" way to live. Nevertheless, when it came to their own life choices, they
were clear that this would not suit them in practice for one reason or another.
Kondo-san and Oku-san were not alone in their preference for living on their
own; perhaps around half of the salon-goers lived alone, and most of them
spoke of their feeling of freedom and of their comfortable way of life. Such
examples require us to rethink the link between coresidence and intimacy as
represented in the ideal of the three-generational household. Although intimacy almost everywhere in the world, and perhaps especially in Japan, can be
created through embodied practices such as sharing food or bathing together
(Clark 2009),[13] coresidence is a balancing act between familial involvement and
private, individual comfort. According to Inge Daniels (2010: 47), happy homes
are those that achieve both the intimacy and shared enjoyment of the family
and satisfy the needs of the individual for peace and relaxation, for an escape
from the outside world. This dynamic is further complicated by the fact that the
well-being of individual family members also to a significant extent depends on
the links with people outside the household, something that the ideal of a three-
generational household rarely takes into account. Many salon-goers mentioned

---

13. Importantly, this kind of embodied intimacy achieved through communal bathing,
    for instance, is not connected to privacy (Daniels 2010: 47).

ties to the area in which they lived as one of the main reasons for not wanting to move to their children's house. Of course, in situations of tensions within the home or even just restricted space and conflicting daily routines of older and younger generations, this balance may be disturbed and the effort to maintain harmonious relationships can feel overwhelming. As noted earlier, Kondo-san found living with her daughter too difficult because she always had to adjust and keep out of everyone's way; she eventually decided to move back to Osaka to live on her own, precisely in order to keep the relationship healthy. She enjoyed the company of her neighbors and felt that she could rely on her support networks in the area.

These examples illustrate a tension between intimacy (and dependence on others for various kinds of support, including emotional), and maintaining a degree of autonomy[14] and a sense of freedom. These two were sometimes in tension but, as pointed out by my interlocutors, at times it was precisely by maintaining a degree of independence that warm, intimate relationships were thought to be preserved. In addition, older people in Shimoichi were intent on cultivating various sources of support—like Kikuchi-san, who had no children and made an effort to help out her friends whenever she could, in order to have more people she could rely in times of need. In this context, state resources (including the pension and Long-Term Care Insurance [LTCI], which covers care and home-help for everyone above the age of 65) were understood as one among many possible sources of support, alongside family and neighborhood relationships, including those established through the salon. On various occasions people commented on the limited nature of these resources; a couple of ladies who attended a seminar for volunteers interested in giving older people in the neighborhood a hand, told me one cannot expect that one will be able to get all the support covered by the LTCI (especially in times when the increase in number of older people meant an increasing pressure on the limited funds). Similarly, one man who was reluctant to rely on his family as his only source of support, lest he become a burden on them, was looking for accommodation in a serviced apartment with some support funded by LTCI. In short, in order to lead a good life one needs to strike a balance between maintaining intimacy

---

14. This tension, or more precisely its specific form, is likely to be a recent phenomenon. A historical analysis is, regrettably, beyond the scope of this article. For a discussion of living with others and independently in the Japanese context see also Suzuki (2013).

and a degree of independence. Cultivating multiple sources of support, a varied "dependability" (Lebra 2004: 20), permits one to live independently, so to speak.

"DOING THINGS PROPERLY" AND SELF-CULTIVATION

While not strictly speaking a balancing act in itself, two tendencies seemed very important for my older friends in Shimoichi: self-cultivation, for instance by practicing an art form or dedicating oneself to a hobby; and "doing things properly," with dedication and attention to detail. These tendencies are closely related to each other and provide important background for understanding the immediate orientation, which I describe further in the following section. Kondo-san cheerfully described to me her enjoyment in singing and her choir practice and, on another occasion, the sense of achievement she feels when her singing improves. This tendency to take up a new hobby and focus on developing a skill in later life is sometimes termed *rokujū no tenarai*, or "study in one's sixties." Another man in his late sixties told me about his own new hobbies and those of his friends: he started a drawing course and joined a choir, while his wife attended a hula dancing class with her friends, and his neighbor enjoyed photography classes. I eventually spoke to all of them, and they explained how they enjoyed group learning, as it gave them an opportunity to make new acquaintances, beyond their work colleagues and neighbors. They explained that one's sixties were the ideal time for studying something new, as one was finally free of many obligations, the children having grown up, and being retired one finally had more free time. They also spoke of their fear of becoming too dependent on the routine that their work, care for the family, and housework provided, so learning something new was a way for them to move away from their earlier roles.

Some of my older interlocutors in Shimoichi rarely referred to pastimes as hobbies. Often in their seventies and eighties, they talked about them less in terms of pastimes and more in terms of practice, or the importance of being in the moment, or becoming immersed in the task (*muchū ni naru*). They emphasized the importance of dedication for doing things properly but also for feeling a sense of achievement, and relaxing by not thinking about anything else. Pastimes and daily activities, whether artistic or mundane, were often guided by the principle of "doing things properly" (*chanto suru*), the way they should be done, not sloppily. While this principle may seem constraining in its formality—especially in its more mundane forms, such as being mindful of the proper way of serving tea or coffee to customers—knowledge of the rules and mastery of the pleasing form of an action may bring genuine pleasure. Doing things properly need not be restricted to mastering new skills but when it is, it can further be linked to a notion of self-development, or self-cultivation.

This striving for self-development should nevertheless not be understood as a merely individualistic pursuit, aiming at one's own pleasure. On the contrary, self-cultivation can be understood as equally important for the advancement of the community, and indeed may even be presented as an obligation to the group. For example, older people in Japan who are involved in various societies and groups in order to pursue their hobbies show the commitment to the group they belong to by being involved in projects of "self-development." Furthermore, by cultivating themselves they show their commitment to the wider society and their family, in an attempt to maintain vitality and avoiding becoming a burden (Traphagan 2004: 58). The very engagement in hobbies or pastimes indicates an individual's focus on self-cultivation and discipline, which as such benefits the community, and which in the case of elderly people means showing an effort to maintain mental and physical health in order to avoid burdening the family and community (Traphagan 2004: 74). The well-being of group and individual are, therefore, conceived as closely linked through the idea of the "good person."

"I DON'T NEED SUCH A THING"

Another important aspect of "study at sixty" is the age itself—while the phrase "study in one's sixties" (*rokujū no tenarai*) certainly implies a sentiment that it is never too late to learn, the age of those who took up new hobbies and dedicated their time to self-development was indeed usually the sixties, and less often early seventies. Some people above this age explicitly expressed a lack of interest in learning something new or taking up a hobby, dismissing it as fanciful or frivolous. This need not mean that this generation, many now in their nineties, has no interest in pastimes, but rather that they usually cultivate those they were already involved in, such as origami or growing vegetables. While they happily participated in singing classes organized in the salon, composed of singing traditional or old popular songs, several of the ladies in their nineties or late eighties flatly refused invitations to participate in workshops that involved mastering new skills, such as weaving. When one such lady, Kato-san, was presented with a leaflet advertising "fun classes" designed to improve mental ability, she just giggled and waved her hand saying she has no need of such things (*sonna koto iranai ne*). This was not simply because she thought of herself as sufficiently mentally agile but also because she felt no need to maintain her abilities for a future far ahead. In another conversation this sentiment was made even clearer. When one of the ladies in her late eighties expressed concern about her memory, noting the need to socialize and talk to other people as a form of mental practice, the reaction was positive and encouraging. Ikeda-san and other ladies in their eighties and nineties confirmed the importance of conversations and keeping active but they also agreed with Kato-san, who suggested that if you get to the age of ninety or thereabouts without becoming senile (*boke*), there was really no more reason for concern, as one is most likely to stay bright enough until the end of one's life. In many ways, I think, this positive outlook seemed related to an attitude of appreciation and enjoyment of the moment. While the future is not necessarily foreclosed to older people, as it is nevertheless not available as a place where delayed gratification will occur.[15] As such, they are led to focus on the present moment.

Many older salon-goers had clearly cultivated an attitude of quiet enjoyment and contemplation of everyday things, such as preparing meals or growing vegetables. The sense of enjoyment to be derived from focused, immediate experience was reflected in the idea of "doing things properly," something everyone clearly considered to be especially important. While the insistence that things should be done "the proper way" might be experienced by some as constraining, my hosts showed me how doing things according to a set of rules or customs can lead to sense of control and joy that comes from immersion in the activity. The pleasing feeling that stems from it, even when the activity in question is as mundane as preparing a small origami rubbish box for the coffee tables in the

---

15. While the future does not always seem open in older age, as people approach the end of their lives it is not seen as entirely closed off either. The approaching death is not invariably seen as an end, and many older people dedicate some of their attention to cultivating links with the ancestors (see Traphagan 2000; Danely 2014), and even prepare for death by organizing "living funerals" (Kawano 2004). Nevertheless, precisely because delayed gratification does not seem always available, the sense of one's life as being set on a trajectory relieves one from some of the pressures and responsibilities of youth, as I discuss in more detail elsewhere (Kavedžija 2013).

salon, or cutting spring onions for soup, can be a form of aesthetic enjoyment. This aesthetic disposition, which implies a tendency to observe beauty in everyday things and activities, is certainly not a uniquely Japanese trait, and seems similar to what Joanna Overing (2003) describes as a propensity of Amazonian peoples to appreciate beauty within the flow of social life: an "aesthetics of everyday life" (Overing 2003). Besides skillful activities, taking a moment to observe the changes in weather, a flower arrangement, or the color of tea is something that my older companions would tell me they enjoyed, and as they thought less about what they can expect in the future, this gradually became an increasingly important source of enjoyment in their lives. Such moments, less verbal and thus less often discussed within conversations in the salon, were seen as no less important for leading a good life.

The tendency to do the things one enjoys was further related to a certain sense of freedom arising from having fulfilled one's duty. The stories about their lives that salon-goers gladly shared with each other often detailed the everyday work they did, in employment and for their families. Tokuda-san, a dark-haired bespectacled lady, spoke of her early mornings in the years when her husband worked as a newspaper delivery man, how she would get up at four to prepare his breakfast in time. Ono-san told stories of his work as a graphic designer, the late nights and deadlines and the many drinking parties with workmates that were sometimes a pleasure but also often impossible to decline—a reason, he thought, for his poor health now. Kato-san[16] spoke of her many days spent caring for her four children, how she devoted herself to making them healthy and nutritious meals. Such stories allowed these people to represent themselves in a certain light but also to view themselves in relation to dominant life models, thus contributing to a certain kind of self-understanding, to a manner of making sense of the events in their lives (see Kavedžija 2013). Other mundane and everyday stories were no less important. For instance, one afternoon Kato-san and her friend returned for a cup of tea after an outing to an okonomiyaki[17] restaurant. She told us of the different kinds they had and this soon led to a heated discussion of regional varieties

---

16. For an elaborate analysis of life stories of Kato-san and many others see Kavedžija 2013.

17. *Okonomiyaki* (literally, "what you like") is sometimes described as Japanese-style pancake, mostly made with flour and cabbage, with additions according to taste—pork and shrimps being among the favorites.

of this omelette-like specialty. Most people had a story to contribute to the conversation, about food and regional specialties—Kan-san, for example, told us of a time when he visited Hiroshima for the first time. Eventually, this led to a discussion of meals from their youth. "Do you remember hot cakes? After the war my father made them, baked them on the fire. We lived in a shelter.... There was no rice, so we ate hot cakes, made from flour..." Memories of those pancakes had a trace of melancholy, despite the hardship; many nodded, and soon told their own stories of the Second World War, of shortages, and of the food of their youth.

In the process of retelling stories such as these, especially those pertaining to everyday matters, people reassemble their own lives and the groups of which they are a part. This retelling puts their lives together, reaffirms their groups but also, as implied in the term "reassembling," changes them gradually and imperceptibly in each act of retelling[18] (Frank 2010: 83). Each narrative act then both preserves things (memories, stories, groups, evaluations) and changes them gradually. This sense-making activity is part of the attitude, or mode of attunement, that I call the narrative orientation. To the extent that such activities help to create a sense of meaning or purpose in life, and to evaluate one's actions in relation to other events in one's life, to other people's actions and to their expectations, they are an important element in striving for a good life. Nevertheless, as revealed by the countervailing tendency to focus on the present, on what is immediately in front of one's senses, on doing things in the right way in a dedicated manner, the narrative orientation is not the only attitude contributing to leading a good life, and under certain circumstances, can even jeopardize it (see also Cook, this volume and Stafford, this volume). My own interlocutors acknowledged the perils of too much reflection—as one seventy-five-year-old man said, "It is no good to think about [your life] too much. If I stay on my own too long, I think too much (*kangaesugi*)."

---

18. "Lives and groups require constant reassembling, which is Bruno Latour's general descriptor, and stories reassemble, both individually and collectively. But reassembling is as much about change as continuity; the act of reassembling does not mean keeping things, including memories, as they are. Reassembly enacts what Norbert Elias called process: what is reassembled is never exactly what was, but always a slightly changed version. Most of the time these changes are imperceptible, and the process proceeds unnoticed. Mundane stories—kitchen table stories—imperceptibly reassemble" (Frank 2010: 83).

MAKING SENSE AND BEING IN THE MOMENT—NARRATIVE AND IMMEDIATE ORIENTATION

Leading a good life seems to involve balancing these two distinct orientations. I present them here as a contrastive pair, a dichotomy, but they are so only in the sense that the more one is engaged in the one, the less one can simultaneously be engaged in the other.[19] In this sense, everyday storytelling and other forms of narrative activity can be seen as a part of the narrative orientation, whereas attention to detail and "doing things properly" can be seen as part of the immediate orientation. The former can involve narration but more broadly encompasses sense-making and analytical activities; it is a mode in which one attempts to make sense of a situation, for example, by comparing the existing state of affairs to that desired, and by problem solving. The immediate orientation, by contrast, is oriented toward direct experience. Attention is focused on the present and on one's immediate sensations and surroundings, without comparing these to what is expected or to some ideal, or relating them to memories, and without trying to order them into a sequence. The distinction between these in everyday life is not rigid or absolute[20]; they simply refer to different states that can be experienced by anyone at different times, though some people may naturally incline toward one or the other.

---

19. In the words of Robert Desjarlais and Jason Throop: "From a phenomenological perspective, then, distinctions between subjective and objective aspects of reality, between what is of the mind and of the world, are shaped by the attitude that a social actor takes up toward the world, as well as by the historical and cultural conditions" (2011: 89). The world cannot be grasped in its totality and we always turn our attention to particular aspects of the world and reality that surrounds us and as we do that, other aspects fall out of focus—our changing perspective, our shifting attitude influences our perception, or experience and ultimately, our actions (ibid.: 90).

20. The distinction between these is not clear-cut, so I separate them for heuristic purposes only. They might be best thought of as tendencies, as these states in their pure forms may be impossible. For instance, the example of experienced meditators who manage to achieve a state of focus on the here and now, in which they barely react to distractions in the outside world by trying to understand them, is an extreme case as close as possible to the state of pure immediacy. Most people can rarely expect to experience this kind of state for more than a few seconds (see Williams and Penman 2012). Furthermore, not every form of narrative activity is necessarily part of this reflexive orientation; in fact, some of the sociable storytelling can anchor one in a moment.

What are the implications of these two attitudes or orientations for happiness[21] or leading a good life? The stories we know of others and from others teach us about how to lead a good life, sometimes directly or by example, and at other times by making us aware of what we would rather avoid. The capacity of stories and the storytelling process to create a meaningful sequence from apparently disconnected events makes them an important part of the sense-making process (Ochs and Capps 1996). The narrative orientation, then, promotes a good life to the extent that it helps to transform daily events and happenings, including traumatic or difficult ones, into a meaningful sequence, thereby creating a sense of a meaningful existence. By allowing a comparison with other stories we know, this orientation can facilitate the assessment of what we want and where we would like to go, guiding our choices and (moral) actions. Yet to the extent that reflection and comparison with others can make one's life more miserable and increase a feeling of isolation, the narrative mode can also have negative consequences for leading a good life. Tokuda-san, for example, faced a fear of loneliness as her husband was hospitalized with a serious heart condition. The stories of other ladies in the salon who were living on their own and praised their freedom made her upset and feel even more alienated and lonely. The comparison of her own story with the stories of others kept her in a state of discontent. It is apparent than that while narrative orientation can contribute to a sense of leading a good life, it can also have a detrimental effect. Furthermore, it is important not to overstate the importance of narrativity and reflexivity in the lives of others.

Since the narrative orientation is closely related to meaning-making processes and thus of crucial importance for understanding the relationship of a meaningful life to a good life, I wish briefly to explore some of the problems with which a narrative orientation may be associated. The importance of narrativity

---

21. While beyond the scope of the present article, it would be worth discussing the temporal aspect of happiness with reference to these two modes, and the older age. Happiness is very often seen as oriented toward the future, in a form of some receding temporal horizon, or a promise (Ahmed 2010). In the Aristotelian sense, the assessment of (eudaimonic) happiness has to take into account an entire life, and to this extent it connects the present with the past, somewhat like the narrative orientation. Balancing the narrative orientation as a way of relating past to the present and pointing to possible futures, with an immediate orientation on the present moment, reveals a very different temporal frame for happiness than merely situated in an indeterminate future, a retreating and elusive image of something to come.

for leading a good life has been resolutely criticized by the philosopher Galen Strawson. In his article "Against narrativity" (2004), he formulates two versions of the so-called narrative claim: the psychological narrativity thesis, which states that human beings experience their life as a narrative or story, or collection of stories; and the ethical narrativity thesis, which states that perceiving one's life as a narrative is good, and that narrative awareness is positive. Strawson argues against both of these claims, asserting that some people do not experience themselves in terms of a continuity between past and present. This gives rise to a distinction between what he terms "Diachronic" and "Episodic" self-experience–Diachronics tend naturally to conceive themselves, their own "self," as something that extends in the past and future, whereas Episodics do not have this tendency to see themselves as something that was there in the remote past and will continue in the remote future (Strawson 2004: 430). Strawson first describes these as distinct types of experience and then uses them to characterize two distinct types of person. He argues that people who are Episodic are unlikely to perceive their lives in narrative terms. Based on his own experience as an Episodic, he argues against the position that narrativity is necessary for leading a good life, and asserts that "the best lives almost never involve this kind of self-telling" (437). He speculates that narrativity can, in fact, stand in the way of self-understanding, because every time we recall something from our past, our memory of it changes, and every retelling alters the facts: "The implication is plain; the more you recall, retell, narrate yourself, the further you risk moving away from accurate self-understanding, from the truth of your being" (447). In contrast to Strawson's conception of Episodics and Diachronics as distinct types of person,[22] I would maintain that the immediate and narrative orientations are states, or modes of being in the world, that anyone can experience, even if some are slightly predisposed toward one or the other.

While there are several points of Strawson's argument that I find problematic[23] his warnings against narrative self-refection raise some important issues. First of all, it makes a strong point about the fact that not everyone leads their

---

22. My understanding is somewhat closer to Maurice Bloch's (2011) reinterpretation of Strawson, in which he distinguishes the "core," "minimal," and "narrative" self, and argues that Strawson's distinction between types of person is only valid at the phenomenological level. All people have a narrative self, though some—Strawson's Diachronics—have an "extra," a deep feeling of having a meaningful biography.

23. For instance, I am not certain that it is useful to think of "the truth of your being" as something separate from the process of understanding.

life narratively, construing their experiences in a narrative form. The narrative claim in this strong form, implying that all people live their lives as protagonists in a story, seems implausible to me, and if it presupposes a constant activity, certainly is not supported by my ethnographic evidence, which points to a number of occasions where being in the moment is preferred. In a more general sense, Strawson cautions against judging nonreflexivity to be some sort of morally deficient mode of being in the world. In this light, the resistance to narrativization exhibited by some of my interlocutors should not be seen as problematic, but on the contrary, as a potentially equally fulfilling way of leading one's life, and in some cases, even, as an achievement: successfully living in the present free from the resentment or distress arising from comparison to what could be. Nevertheless, this does not mean that some forms of narrative activity are not considered important by my interlocutors nor that narrative does not have an important role in constructing a meaningful existence. While most of my hosts probably did not narratively conceive their self on a daily basis, various narratives, including a diverse range of stories they heard and recounted, and encountered in the media, played a major role in their everyday lives. It is also worth pointing out that narrative activity conceived broadly need not imply a "diachronic" disposition, and can be "episodic" in the sense that the story can relate to particular episodes or events, without a claim for an overarching unity of life experience. It is thus important to distinguish Strawson's strong narrative claim, which hinges on people conceiving their own selves narratively, and the many other forms of narrative activity.

The importance of stories in people's lives makes it virtually impossible to dismiss the importance of narrative activity for living well. I nevertheless agree with Strawson to the effect that narrativity, to the extent that it involves a self-reflexive construction of self, may present a threat to one's ability to lead a good life, though not necessarily for the reasons he mentions. To the extent that viewing one's life in narrative terms likens it to a biographical project in the making, as theorists of late modernity have suggested, one may feel an increased sense of responsibility for one's life choices and decisions (for example, Giddens 1991). While this means that one is increasingly liberated from traditional social institutions, the process is accompanied by a rise in risks and personal insecurities (Beck 1992). Shaping one's life, just like a story, is cast as one's own responsibility, and this may lead to anxiety—ultimately an existential anxiety that links freedom and responsibility (Yalom 1980). The interest in "mindfulness" as a mode of therapy for depression, helping people to find "peace in a frantic world"

(Williams and Penman 2012), is indicative of the type of problem created by the late modern condition. Mindfulness in this sense refers to a type of meditation practice that focuses on the flow of one's own breath. The intention is to focus on immediate experience and to assume an attitude of observing what is transpiring in one's mind and body, as a way of countering the tendency to compare one's current state to an ideal and to treat the disjuncture as a problem to be solved, leading to the questioning and restlessness that characterize depressive thinking (Williams and Penman 2012). It remains to be seen whether the recent marked increase in cases of depression in Japan (Kitanaka 2011) can be related to the tendencies associated with late modernity, to take responsibility for one's own life and life trajectory, and to internalize blame and dissatisfaction. Yet this seems like a question worth serious exploration.

VALUES IN BALANCE

The construction of meaning in life may contribute to a sense of leading one's life well, but the good life cannot be reduced to a meaningful life. A focus on the meaning of one's own life can have a negative influence on one's general sense of well-being, and can lead to a focus on one's own life as an individual, thus exacerbating a sense of personal responsibility and separation from others, which can also be anxiety inducing. This is illustrated by the fact that a range of local psychotherapies in Japan focus on recognition of one's relationships to others, and feelings of dependence (Doi 1973; Reynolds 1980; Ozawa-de Silva 2006). A good life nevertheless requires a sense of meaning in life, even if the orientation that allows for its creation must be tempered, or kept in check. A good life is also effectively a moral project, involving more than merely a life that is coherent and makes sense (as opposed to a collection of events that follow one after another). In short, the narrative quest for coherence and meaning, and mindful presence in the moment, each have their benefits but also their dangers. The ability to lead a good and fulfilling life would appear to rely on maintaining the right kind of balance between the two.

For my Japanese hosts, happiness was constructed more specifically through a series of balancing acts: between sociality and the burden of over-closeness, or intimacy and a sense of freedom, dependence and autonomy, among others. The poles of these tensions encapsulate important social values: intimacy and sociality and dependability on others on the one hand, freedom and a sense of autonomy on the other. My older Japanese friends often spoke of the importance of either or both of these, and did not believe that one could choose between them and still feel content. Navigation between the opposed poles described above involved a more complex form of moral judgment. In this sense, as noted earlier, such values are unlike exchange values, which are commensurable and between which one can chose. As Michael Lambek (2008) points out, while anthropologists have often seen obligation as the opposite of choice in weighing up nonexchange values, it is more useful to think of judgment as the opposite: "Such evaluation or judgment is grounded in more general, culturally mediated, understandings of the human condition and the ends of human life as well as those internal to the practice at hand" (Lambek 2008: 137). Furthermore, happiness (which can otherwise be seen as fleeting and overly selfish, or self-centered) is only evaluated positively when it involves just such a balance between both poles, both social and moral values. To the extent that its achievement takes place through a balancing of moral values, happiness can be understood as a form of practical moral judgment.

ACKNOWLEDGMENTS

The research that formed the basis for this article was supported by the Japan Foundation, the Japan Society for the Promotion of Science, the Clarendon Trust, and a Wadsworth International Fellowship from the Wenner-Gren Foundation. For useful discussions and suggestions I am grateful to Harry Walker, Charles Stafford, Susan Long, Scott North, and five anonymous reviewers.

REFERENCES

Ahmed, Sara. 2010. *The promise of happiness*. Durham, NC: Duke University Press.

Bakalar, Nicholas. 2010. "Happiness may come with age, Study Says." *New York Times*, May 31, 2010. Accessed on December 1, 2012. http://www.nytimes.com/2010/06/01/health/research/01happy.html?_r=1&.

Beck, Ulrich. 1992. *Risk society: Towards a new modernity*. London, Sage.

Bloch, Maurice. 2011. "The blob." *Anthropology of this century* (1). Accessed December 1, 2012. http://aotcpress.com/articles/blob/.

Carstensen, Laura L. 2006. "The influence of a sense of time on human development." *Science* 312 (5782): 1913–15.

———. 2011. "Older people are happier." *TEDx Women.* Accessed December 1, 2012. http://www.ted.com/talks/laura_carstensen_older_people_are_happier.html.

Clark, Scott. 2009. "Pleasure experienced. Well-Being in the Japanese Bath." In *Pursuits of happiness: Well-being in anthropological perspective,* edited by Gordon Mathews and Carolina Izquierdo, 189–210. New York: Berghahn.

Coulmas, Florian. 2008. "The quest for happiness in Japan." *German Institute for Japanese Studies Working Paper* 09/1. Accessed July 23, 2015. http://www.dijtokyo.org/publications/WP0901_Coulmas.pdf.

Danely, Jason. 2014. *Aging and loss: Mourning and maturity in contemporary Japan* (Global perspectives on aging series).

Daniels, Inge. 2010. *The Japanese house: Material culture in the modern home.* Oxford: Berg Publishers.

Desjarlais Robert, and C. Jason Throop. 2011. "Phenomenological approaches in anthropology." *Annual Review of Anthropology* 40: 87–102.

Diener, Ed, Marissa Diener, and Carol Diener. 1995. "Factors predicting the subjective well-being of nations." *Journal of Personality and Social Psychology* 69: 851–64.

Doi, Takeo. 1973. *The Anatomy Of Dependence.* Translated by John Bester. Tokyo: Kodansha International Ltd.

Frank, Arthur W. 2010. *Letting stories breathe: A socio-narratology.* Chicago: University of Chicago Press.

Giddens, Anthony. 1991. *Modernity and self-identity: Self and society in the late modern age.* Cambridge: Polity.

Hakunetsu Kyoushitsu Production Team, Elizabeth Dunn, and Robert Biswas-Diener. 2014. *"Shiawase' ni tsuite shitte okitai itsutsu no koto NHK'Shiawasegaku"* (Five things you should know about happiness. NHK "Happiness studies"). Tokyo: Kodokawa.

Hashimoto, Akiko. 1996. *The gift of generations: Japanese and American perspectives on aging and the social contract.* Cambridge: Cambridge University Press.

Egami, Go. 2015. *Bijinesuman no tame no "shiawaseron."* ("Happiness treatise" for businessmen). Tokyo: Shōdensha.

Jackson, Michael. 2011. *Life within limits: Well-being in a world of want.* Durham, NC: Duke University Press.

Kan, Chiemi, Mayumi Karasawa, and Shinobu Kitayama. 2009. "Minimalist in style: Self, identity, and well-being in Japan." *Self and Identity* 8: 2–3, 300–317.

Kavedžija, Iza. 2013. "Meaning in life: Tales from aging Japan." DPhil. diss. Institute for Social and Cultural Anthropology, University of Oxford.

Kawano, Satsuki. 2004. "Pre-funerals in contemporary Japan: The making of a new ceremony of a later life among aging Japanese." *Ethnology* 43 (2): 155–65.

Kida, Gen. 2001. "Nihonjin no 'Kofukuron' (The happiness treatise of the Japanese)." *Bungeishunju* 79 (10): 28–31.

Kitanaka, Junko. 2011. *Depression in Japan: Psychiatric cures for a society in distress.* Princeton, NJ: Princeton University Press.

Kraut, Richard. 2012. "Aristotle's Ethics." *The Stanford Encyclopedia of Philosophy*, edited by Edward N. Zalta. Accessed December 1, 2012. http://plato. stanford.edu/archives/win2012/entries/aristotle-ethics.

Lambek, Michael. 2008. "Value and virtue." *Anthropological Theory* 8 (2): 133–57.

Lebra, Takie S. 2004. *The Japanese self in cultural logic.* Honolulu: University of Hawaii Press.

Maeno, Takashi. 2013. *Shiawase no mekanizumu. Jissen koufukugaku nyoumon* (Mechanism of Happiness. A practical introduction to happiness studies). Tokyo: Kōdansha.

Mathews, Gordon. 1996. *What makes life worth living?: How Japanese and Americans make sense of their worlds.* Berkeley: University of California Press.

———. 2009. "Finding and keeping a purpose in life. Wellbeing and Ikigai in Japan and elsewhere." In *Pursuits of happiness: Well-being in anthropological perspective*, edited by Gordon Mathews and Carolina Izquierdo, 167–86. New York: Berghahn.

Mroczek, Dan K., and Christian M. Kolarz. 1998. "The effect of age on positive and negative affect: A developmental perspective on happiness." *Journal of personality and social psychology* 75 (5): 1333.

Ochs, Elinor, and Lisa Capps. 1996. "Narrating the self." *Annual Review of Anthropology*: 19–43.

Overing, Joanna. 2003. "In praise of the everyday: Trust and the art of social living in an Amazonian community." *Ethnos* 68 (3): 293–316.

Ozawa-de Silva, Chikako. 2006. *Psychotherapy and religion in Japan: The Japanese introspection practice of Naikan.* Oxford: Routledge.

Reynolds, David K. 1980. *The quiet therapies: Japanese pathways to personal growth.* Honolulu: University of Hawaii Press.

Rossi, Alice S., and Peter H. Rossi. 1990. *Of human bonding: Parent-child relations across the life course.* New York: Aldine de Gruyter.

Rupp, Katherine. 2003. *Gift-giving in Japan: Cash, connections, cosmologies.* Stanford, CA: Stanford University Press.

Sawada, Janine A. 2004. *Practical pursuits: Religion, politics, and personal cultivation in nineteenth-century Japan.* Honolulu: University of Hawaii Press.

Stone, Arthur A., Joseph E. Schwartz, Joan Broderick, and Angus Deaton. 2010. "A snapshot of the age distribution of psychological well-being in the United States." *Proceedings of the National Academy of Sciences USA* 107 (22): 9985–90.

Strawson, Galen. 2004. "Against narrativity." *Ratio* 17 (4): 428–52.

Suzuki, Nanami, ed. 2013. *The anthropology of aging and well-being: Searching for the space and time to cultivate life together.* Senri Ethnological Studies, No 80. Osaka: National Museum of Ethnology.

Thang, Leng Leng. 2001. *Generations in touch: Linking the old and young in a Tokyo neighbourhood.* New York: Cornell University Press.

The Economist. 2010. "The U-bend of life. Why, beyond middle age, people get happier as they get older." December 16, 2010. Accessed December 1, 2012. http://www.economist.com/node/17722567.

Traphagan, John W. 2000. *Taming oblivion: Aging bodies and the fear of senility in Japan.* New York: State University of New York Press.

———. 2004. *The practice of concern: Ritual, well-being, and aging in rural Japan.* Durham, NC: Carolina Academic Press.

Uchida, Yukiko, and Shigehiro Kitayama. 2009. "Happiness and unhappiness in east and west: Themes and variations." *Emotion* 9: 441–56.

Uchida, Yukiko, and Yukiko Ogihara. 2012. "Personal or interpersonal construal of happiness: A cultural psychological approach." *International Journal of Wellbeing* 2 (4): 354–69.

Williams, Mark, and Danny Penman. 2012. *Mindfulness: A practical guide to peace in a frantic world.* Hachette Digital.

Wu, Yongmei. 2004. *The care of the elderly in Japan.* London: Routledge Curzon.

Yalom, Irvine D. 1980. *Existential psychotherapy.* New York: Basic Books.

CHAPTER FOUR

Techniques of happiness
Moving toward and away from the good life in a rural Ethiopian community

Dena Freeman

Scholars from many different disciplines have written about happiness and well-being in recent years. Psychologists and economists have dominated the field (see, for example, Frey and Stutzer 2002; Kahneman, Diener, and Schwarz 1999; Lane 2000; Seligman 2003), but contributions have also been made by sociologists, neuroscientists, philosophers, historians, and evolutionary scientists (see Davidson 2004; Inglehart et al. 2008; Nesse 2004; Veenhoven 1991; White 2006). Anthropologists, however, have been fairly resistant to the notion of studying happiness (for notable exceptions see Adelson 2000; Jiminez 2008; Mathews 1996; Mathews and Izquierdo 2008; Thin 2005). Part of the reason that anthropologists have been slow to engage with happiness research head-on has been the terms in which this research has been framed by the other disciplines. By far the majority of existing happiness research is based on assumptions about the self, emotions, and experience that anthropologists find questionable, and methodologies that anthropologists find shallow and uncontextualized. People are assumed to be like *homo economicus*, rational, transparent, and universal, and insights into their well-being are garnered by asking them how happy they are on a scale of 1 to 10, and then finding correlations between these scores and various other factors. Research in this vein has generated a huge amount of data about happiness levels in different countries, how happiness correlates—or doesn't—with wealth, or with marriage, or with living in a city, and so on, and has led to much interest in developing happiness indicators and designing policy in order to improve people's happiness. This is all rather alien to the way that anthropologists approach questions of experience and has led to a situation in which anthropology is perhaps the only social or behavioral science discipline that has virtually nothing to say about happiness or the foundations of the "good life."

So, then, how might anthropologists contribute to the study of happiness and well-being? What might we add to the debate? This collection shows many ways that anthropologists can add depth and richness to the study of happiness. In this article I will focus on two key ways that anthropologists can contribute to the debate. Most obviously, anthropologists can provide detailed ethnographic accounts of how people in different places and in different cultural contexts conceptualize happiness, how they talk about it, how they strive for it, and how they experience it. Rich ethnographic descriptions of happy lives in different cultural contexts are as yet few and far between and such accounts of socially and culturally contextualized happiness could do much to broaden the very narrow accounts and assumptions that dominate much contemporary happiness research.

A second contribution that anthropologists can make, and the main focus of this article, is to begin to tease apart the different factors that lead to either happiness or unhappiness in a particular social and cultural context. We can look at specific social and cultural practices that appear to enhance happiness—what I will call *cultural techniques of happiness*—and analyze how they function and how they are intertwined with certain forms of social organization and cultural ideation. In this way we can begin to bring into focus ways that happiness is socially and culturally constituted in different settings and how the nature of happiness, as both concept and lived experience, can change over time.

Tolstoy claimed that "Happy families are all alike; every unhappy family is unhappy in its own way." Is the same true of communities? Is there an ideal form of happiness that all communities can aspire to or do forms of happiness vary in different places and different times? How do we take into account the simultaneous presence of happiness-increasing and happiness-decreasing factors? When happiness researchers tell us that the people of X and the people of Y both score 7 on a happiness scale of 1 to 10, is there is a difference in the nature of this 7, to put it rather glibly, for those that arrived at it by combining, say, a happiness of 8 with an unhappiness of -1, and those that combined a happiness of 9 with an unhappiness of -2?

Ethnographies of happiness as experienced in different historical and cultural settings can offer some insights into these questions and begin to deepen our understanding of happiness as it is experienced by real people, embedded in particular communities, at specific points in time. In the rest of this article I will consider happiness in a community in rural Ethiopia at two different points in time. By comparing the factors and practices leading toward and away from happiness in these two contexts I will try to open up and complexify the notion of happiness and to show how both the concept and the lived experience of happiness can and do change quite radically over time.

TRADITIONAL GAMO IDEAS ABOUT HAPPINESS

The people of the Gamo Highlands in Southern Ethiopia don't talk much about happiness, or about any kinds of feelings or emotions for that matter. But, at least on a cursory surface level, my impression when I first arrived in the mid-1990s and walked through the lush green fields and saw people working together, talking, laughing, and smiling, was that generally they seemed to be very happy. As I stayed longer in the village of Masho, I began to get a clearer picture of what ideals Gamo people held about the good life and how the lived experience of their daily lives engendered a certain feeling of contentment. Gamo ideals of the good life, what they strive for and what they wish for their community, can most clearly be seen in the blessings made at the beginning of any local or communal assembly. Local and community discussions are a regular feature of Gamo life, often taking place several times a week, and they are always preceded by a series of blessings made by the senior men. These blessings always take the same general form and call for two essential elements: peace and fertility. Peace encompasses the values of togetherness, mutuality, and smooth social relations, while fertility includes crops that grow well, women that give birth, and children and animals that grow strong and healthy. In the mid-1990s, and for a long time before, these could be considered to be the Gamo recipe for a good and happy life. And indeed, in their patterns of thought these two ingredients for the good life were interconnected, such that peaceful social relations were actually thought to be part of the cause of biological fertility (Freeman 2002a, 2002b). So, quickly solving conflicts and restoring peace was seen as a sacred as well as a political act, and something that would keep the community and its members healthy and fertile. Thus, when, in 1996, I asked people why they were going to an assembly, they did not reply that they were going to discuss a case about some stolen sheep, or that they were going to decide what to do about a certain community problem, but instead they would say something like, "We are going to the assembly to bring reconciliation to the community. For the grain, for the milk, to make the community well" (Freeman 2002b: 134).

The importance of smooth social relations was emphasized again and again in daily life. Conflicts happened but they were relatively rare. And when they did occur, it was generally on a quiet level—more a case of cold silences or fake smiles than shouting or screaming. And kin and neighbors always made sure to involve themselves in others' conflicts and to help resolve them as soon as possible. Anyone who had an argument with someone else during the day could expect to find the neighbors gathering in his house in the evening, where in a gentle and friendly way, they would ask to hear both sides of the story and steer the two parties to a resolution. It was always stressed that one had to get right to the bottom of things so that there would be no grudge to hold and genuine good relations could be restored. This process of reconciliation is an important technique of happiness in Gamo. I was party to many of these reconciliations during my two years in the village of Masho, and I was always impressed at how people came to a resolution and then left their hurt and anger behind. Anthropologist Judith Olmstead, whose work on the Gamo Highlands was cut short in 1974 by the Ethiopian Revolution, was so impressed by the Gamo techniques of conflict resolution and reconciliation that she later went on to become a professional mediator.

The people of the Gamo Highlands do not value suffering. While there are numerous accounts in the anthropological literature of suffering being considered as important for character formation or for moral purity, the people of Gamo simply see suffering as a miserable state that should be remedied as soon as possible. It is seen as a sign that something is wrong, that things are not in balance, or that a taboo has been broken. If someone is suffering from an ongoing misfortune the response is to look for the cause of this misfortune so that the situation can be rectified and the suffering relieved. If someone is suffering from a known misfortune, such as the death of a relative, people will come to cheer them up, to laugh and joke with them and try to ease them back into the smooth flow of happy social relations.

So while there is no one word for "happiness" and it is not overtly theorized or discussed, it is clear that happiness is seen as the default state that everyone should seek to attain in their social lives. Gamo people do not strive for it, in the sense that they might strive for wealth or political power, but rather it is a way of being that is valued and appreciated. Gamo concepts such as "joy" (*uffaisi*), "smiling" (*michidi*), "peace" (*salame*), and "reconciliation" (*makaino*) are the integral elements of happiness as sought for and experienced in the Gamo Highlands. It is a fundamentally social conceptualization of happiness and it is inherently bound up with the lived experience of peaceful sociality.

HAPPINESS AS LIVED EXPERIENCE

In general day-to-day life it was indeed smooth social relations that did seem to bring about feelings of happiness and contentment. Life in Masho in the mid-1990s was intensely social. People were always with people—farming the land together with family or in work groups, cooking food together with other household women, walking together to market, sitting in community assemblies. There were very few occasions that someone would do something alone. Even if a man might occasionally farm his land alone, other people passing by on footpaths or working in adjacent fields would call out greetings, wish him strength, and perhaps stop to chat about some communal affair or to tease or joke with him. Walking anywhere always took twice as long as it could have, because it was always necessary to stop and greet everyone you passed on the way, to wish them a good day, and again to joke around with them.

Psychologists have suggested that both dyadic social connections and the feeling of being part of a community are important for well-being (see, for example, Baumeister and Leary 1995; Haidt, Seder, and Kesebir 2008) and both of these experiences were available in abundance in Masho in the 1990s. As an outsider-anthropologist I was perhaps aware of these dynamics more acutely than those who had always lived this way. I was overwhelmed with the number of people that I had to relate to and the constant stream of friendly social interaction. At times I would try and hide away for an hour or so in my room, to find some time to be quiet and think, and I would always be sought out after about five minutes with calls to come and talk/eat/play. If I resisted for more than about ten minutes people would become genuinely concerned and start asking if I was feeling ill. When I tried to reply that I was fine and that I just wanted some time to think, I found that such a concept could not be expressed in the Gamo language. The verb that best translates as "to think" also means "to worry" and so I found myself saying "I'm just worrying." People were quick to respond that I shouldn't "think/worry" and to pull me out of my aloneness and back into sociality. Eventually I stopped resisting and surrendered. I remember noticing some months later how different I felt living like that and how much calmer and happier I was—how I felt safe, connected, embedded.

Gamo sociality is emphasized and intensified by two more cultural techniques of happiness. The first of these is the act of "playing" or *ka'o*. The same verb is used to describe children's play, or playing football, but when applied to adult "playing" it refers to the joking, teasing, and banter that characterize much of Gamo social interaction. It would probably not be an exaggeration to say that most day-to-day social interaction in 1990s Masho was "playing." Seventy-year-old Shato,[1] in whose house I lived, was a master at playing. Here are some examples:

> Murunesh, a neighbor, comes into our courtyard. Shato, with a sparkle in his eye and a mischievous smile, shouts, "What are you doing in my house? Did I call you?" Murunesh, laughing, says, "I came because I missed you. I wanted to see your handsome face." Shato: "Nonsense! You've come to eat my food, I know it! And who is this child you have brought with you? Give her to me and get out!" Murunesh, pushing her three-year-old granddaughter in Shato's direction: "Here, take her, she will make you a second wife. . ."

Shato is hoeing one of his fields near the house of Abera, a second cousin. Abera walks past and calls out: "Good morning! Strength to you!" Shato replies, "It's not a good morning, come and help me with this work!" Abera has to quickly find an answer: "Bring me a second hoe and I will hoe with you." Shato: "No, no, take this one. Here, you scoundrel, why are you running in the other direction?" Abera: "Strength to you, strength to you! I must go to the town." Shato, laughing: "Go, go, return in peace."

These types of exchange took place literally all the time, several per hour, and generally left both parties smiling and laughing.

I was forever being told to marry people, to take children back to England, to come and cook dinner, or hoe the fields, or cause the rain to start or stop.

---

1.   All names have been changed.

These invitations to play did more than make me laugh. They kept me on my toes—they forced me to keep sharp and focused, to quickly find witty replies or rebuffs, and to warmly engage with my interlocutors. Rather like a mindfulness meditation, these exchanges kept me constantly "present" and "in the moment." With the constant calls to play there was no time for daydreaming, thinking about something else, or otherwise sinking into one's own world—activities I was rather prone to in my previous life in London. Recent research by psychologists suggests that people—European and American students, that is—who daydream more and have more so-called "stimulus-independent and task-unrelated thoughts," or SITUTs, and are therefore not fully aware and attentive to the present moment, report increased negative affect and lower psychological well-being (Stawarczyk et al. 2012).

The Gamo focus on adult playing encouraged a state of nonreflexivity. It pulled people out of their own thoughts and their own concerns and served to train their attention on the immediate experience of the present moment and the other people in that moment (cf. Kavedžija, this issue). Michael Jackson has suggested that the dance between "being part of and being apart from the world" is a universal feature of human consciousness (Jackson 2012: 2). We all constantly oscillate between states of engagement and detachment, relationship and aloneness. In the Gamo Highlands, the cultural practice of playing serves to continually push people toward the pole of engagement and relationship and to encourage them to be "part of" rather than "apart from" the world. Much more than just a mere backdrop to social life, the Gamo cultural activity of playing is thus an important technique to increase happiness—by making people laugh, by fostering warm social relations, and by training peoples' attention to the present moment.

The second technique of happiness that intensifies sociality in the 1990s was the drinking of coffee. As in many parts of Ethiopia, it was common in Masho for women to prepare coffee and invite friends and neighbors round to drink. Starting with raw coffee beans, the actual preparation of the coffee would take about an hour and a half, and guests would be invited soon after the process started. Guests would straggle in over the next hour or so, and sit in the house and play while the coffee was being prepared. Then the actual coffee drinking would generally take between 30 and 50 minutes, as the pot was boiled three times and guests drank three cups. Coffee drinking was an occasion to down tools, have a rest, and most of all, to play. Groups of neighbors would invite each other on the basis of a loose reciprocity, while passers-by and others would get added to the mix when they were around. During my fieldwork in the 1990s it was typical to partake in coffee like this at least once or twice a day, sometimes more. These occasions were pleasant, relaxed, and sociable. And they were so central to life that even on the occasion when Abebech, the wife of Shato's son, Wendu, happened to give birth one morning—round behind the back of the house—when the house itself was full of guests for coffee, no one thought to leave or stop the coffee drinking. They simply put some straw on the floor for Abebech to lie on, wrapped the baby up and gave it to one of the guests, and carried on with the second cup of coffee.

Thus through three main techniques of happiness—playing, drinking coffee with neighbors, and quickly resolving any interpersonal conflicts—the ideal of smooth and friendly social relations were to a very great extent maintained in Masho in the 1990s, and contributed greatly to people's happiness and life enjoyment.

SOCIO-ECONOMIC CHANGE IN MASHO AND ITS EFFECTS ON HAPPINESS

I have returned to Masho on average once or twice a year since I completed my doctoral fieldwork in 1997 and have witnessed many changes over that time. One of the most important changes has been in the area of production and economic relations. In the 1990s most people in Masho were engaged in subsistence agriculture, growing barley, wheat, potatoes, beans, and *enset*, the false banana plant. Most men would spend much of their time working in the fields, often with household members or with local work-groups, with frequent breaks to stop and play with passers-by and with each other. The work was physically hard but relatively unpressured, and would generally generate enough food to feed the family, plus a small amount of surplus that could be used in various ritual exchanges at marriage, initiation, and the birth of a child, and to contribute to offerings made to the spirits by clan and lineage elders.

However, in 1998, an NGO started a development project in the area and selected Masho as one of its target villages. This was the first NGO project in Masho and it led to great changes in many aspects of life. As I have discussed elsewhere (Freeman 2009, 2012a, 2013a, 2013b), one of the main aspects of this project was to get people to grow a cash crop, in this case apples, and to become more involved in the national market economy. By 2010 over two-thirds of the households in Masho were successfully growing apples, a number of apple cooperatives had been established in conjunction with neighboring communities, and many apple farmers were making a lot of money from the sale of apple fruits and apple saplings.

While still agricultural, working with apples was very different from growing barley, wheat, and the other subsistence crops. Apples, and particularly apple saplings, could bring in big money. Thus, in the decade or so since apples were first introduced, there have been significant changes in working patterns and social relations, which I believe have seriously impacted on people's experience of happiness and well-being.

First, men who produce apple saplings have started to work much longer hours. Since there is a fairly direct link between the number of apple saplings you produce and the money you earn, people have begun to produce apple saplings in the spirit of maximization. Grafting apple saplings is quite labor intensive and thus apple farmers find themselves investing many hours in this work. They have generally been reluctant use family labor or to hire workers to do this for them, both because of the training and skill required and because of the fear of theft, as I will discuss below. So instead they have become more conscious about when they are working and when they are not working, and the previous relaxed experience where work was fairly embedded in the flow of social life has started to fracture (cf. papers by Walker, Lambek). Apple farmers are less keen to take breaks or to stop for coffee. In fact, when I visited Masho in 2008, 2009, and 2010, the number of coffee invitations was noticeably smaller. When I asked Wendu about this he said, " We are busy now. Before we were lazy. Now people are growing apples and they don't want to sit around drinking coffee."

Similarly, while people did still greet each other on the paths, it was becoming much more common for people to simply wish each other well and walk on. The occasions of long conversations and elaborate playing sessions in these chance encounters seemed much fewer. While people in Masho do still play with each other and do still drink coffee, they do it much less than they used to. And thus the joy, connection, and "present moment consciousness" that these forms of sociality used to engender, now do so rather less.

Second, the apple boom brought with it a massive increase in theft. Never much of a problem before, from around 2003 onward theft—primarily of apple saplings—became a major social problem. People would creep into open fields at night, uproot apple saplings, and sell them for a quick profit to the traders that arrived in the local town. The extent of this theft was so great that most apple producers moved their saplings from the fields into their home compounds and started to stay up all night to guard them. As people quipped at the time, referring to the grafting of male and female in apple propagation, and finding the funny side to their unpleasant situation, "the apple sleeps with his wife, while we sleep outside."

Wendu was one of the apple farmers who slept outside for a year or so to guard his apple saplings. During that period he often looked tired and stressed. He also bought a dog to keep in the compound to deter would-be thieves. Starting from this period, people started visiting each other's houses less. No one was sure who was a thief and who wasn't. People had been caught stealing from neighbors and close relatives, so everyone was under suspicion. In this situation, Wendu would keep an eye on visitors who came to the compound. He would get particularly uneasy if they spent too much time looking at his apple seedlings or the fence in that area. Perhaps they were plotting to come back at night and try and steal them? Likewise Wendu and Abebech stopped visiting other compounds so frequently—maybe people would think they were plotting to steal this person's apples? The fear and distrust that developed during this period had a dramatic effect on social relations and how people thought about others. Whereas previously people had related to others in a light and easy way, now the boundaries between one household and the next became psychologically firmer.

In 2005 the local government managed to solve much of the theft problem by closing the route to market for apple saplings and requiring all apple saplings to be sold via cooperatives to licensed traders with appropriate receipts and paperwork. This made it much harder to sell stolen saplings and the intense period of theft came to an end, and apple farmers returned to sleep with their wives (Freeman 2013). However, the changes to local social relations could not be so easily repaired. While visiting has become more frequent again, it is not as easy and frequent as it was before.

Other changes in social relations have also come about due to involvement in the apple business. Instead of working together, farmers now increasingly compete with each other. Neighbors have become competitors, competing to producing the best apples, to sell the most saplings, to get the highest price. Staff at the NGO that implemented the apple project were aware, and rather dismayed, at this situation. The Agriculture and Food Security Program Facilitator told me:

> Our strategy was to build a caring, interdependent society, not a competitive
> society. But a competitive society has come about. Farmers compete with each

other over apple production and access to market, they say that their variety of apple is good while that of others is bad, they argue about everything. There has been a lot of fighting since the apples came. . . . While the project is good because people are getting more money and can send their children to school and wear clean clothes, it is true that it is also making people more separate. People here used to help each other, but now they compete. It's not good what is happening.

As well as being potential thieves and potential competitors, "other people" have also become potential customers. Now that more people have more cash, a number of households have set up little tea shops, particularly those situated on the road into the local town. These houses will typically be new style rectangular mud houses with several rooms. A large room at the front will act as the tea shop, while household members will live in the other rooms at the back. Small benches typically line the walls and a kettle of tea sits on a charcoal stove, ready to serve those wanting a rest on their way into town. Very often customers include kin and neighbors, and thus the line between social visiting and market transaction has become uncomfortably blurred. I recall one time in 2008 when Wendu and I went to visit Adanech, a young neighbor who we saw often, who was at the time ill in bed with flu. We walked in through Adanech's tea shop, where one or two people were sitting drinking, being served by Adanech's husband's younger sister, and into her bedroom. Adanech lay there in bed, wrapped in blankets and sneezing. We sat on small stools opposite her and she propped herself up to talk to us. Wendu immediately started to play, telling her to get out of bed at once and go to work, and soon we were all laughing together. She then offered us some tea and three small cups of tea were bought into her bedroom and we all drank together. We carried on laughing and joking some more, and then when we saw she looked tired we got up to leave. As we wished her a speedy recovery and she thanked us for coming, Wendu put a few coins on the table to pay for the tea. It was an awkward moment, but Adanech didn't refuse. . .

A third change caused by the shift to market-based apple production has been a massive increase in inequality. While there have always been differences in wealth and land-holdings in Masho, these have become much more significant since the arrival of apples. Those farmers with lots of apple saplings have made lots of money very fast—in some cases thousands of US dollars per year, while those with few or no saplings have remained at the same subsistence level as they were before. The differences have become huge. And furthermore, while previous wealth differences used to translate into status differences, as wealthier farmers used their surplus to throw big initiation feasts and in the process redistribute their surplus food around the community (Freeman 2002a, 2002b), today's wealth differences translate directly into differences of consumption. Wealthy apple farmers have built new, modern-style houses, wear nice clothes, own smart bags and cassette players, and in some cases even have televisions and DVD players. Their poorer neighbors continue to live in traditional bamboo houses, wear old clothes, and struggle even to send their children to school.

An interesting finding from the existing happiness research is that happiness and well-being are inversely correlated with inequality. High levels of inequality have been shown to lead to poor health, social conflict, and violence, particularly in those at the bottom of the hierarchy (Wilkinson 1996, 2005), all of which lead away from happiness and well-being. It has also been demonstrated that *relative* wealth is much more important than absolute wealth (above a certain level of poverty) in leading toward happiness (Layard 2005: 43–48). It is a universal feature of human psychology for people to compare themselves to their reference group—if everyone is doing about the same, or they are doing better than others, people tend to feel happy. So an increase in inequality such as we have seen in Masho will have led to an increase in happiness for the few people that have made a lot of money and changed their consumption patterns, and a rather larger decrease in happiness for the many people that have been less successful in the apple business or have failed to enter it at all. This polarization of happiness between the successful and the less successful is a well-known facet of market societies (Lane 2000).

These changes in Masho have led to a further weakening of the social fabric and an increase in resentment and jealousy. In fact, I only learned the Gamo word for jealousy during a visit in 2010. In my two year's intensive fieldwork and all the subsequent trips that I had made I had never come across a situation when the word was used. But in 2010 it came up in a conversation with Wendu and his twenty-year-old daughter, Muna. We were discussing some problems Wendu was having with the Pentecostal Church in Masho. Wendu was in fact one of the longest standing members of the church and had been one of the earliest converts. He had done much to bring in other believers and had been a preacher and a member of the church committee for several years. So I was surprised to learn that the current church committee was accusing him of being involved in inappropriate, un-Christian activities. I asked Wendu what this was all about and he struggled to explain. None of the accusations made any sense. Then Muna, who was also active in the church, leaned forward and said:

> It's because they're jealous. Wendu has done well with apples and they don't like it. They cause him all these problems and make all these accusations, but really they are just jealous that we are doing well. We have done well through working hard, not by doing anything bad, so we know we are in the right. So we will continue to work hard and pray to God and just ignore all these accusations.

Wendu concurred that this was the case. "It's been a headache since the apples came," he told me, "there has been so much fighting and arguing." As well as the arguments with the church, he is always being asked for help by poorer neighbors, and he feels uncomfortable in these situations. He told me about Lembo, just one of the many people that keeps coming to his house to ask for food, money, or work. According to Wendu, Lembo sold all his land some years ago and quickly "ate" the money. He now goes around begging for help and often turns up at Wendu's door. Faced with a direct request, Wendu finds it hard to say no, but he also believes that their different fortunes are due to their own personal decisions and that it is not his responsibility to look after Lembo. Even though Wendu has been one of the "winners" of the apple revolution and now sits toward the higher echelons of Masho society, he has also found that the changes have both decreased as well as increased his happiness.

So, to sum up so far, there seems to be quite a case for thinking that most people's happiness has decreased since the apple boom and increasing involvement in market-based economic activity. The culturally valued state of smooth and peaceful social relations has diminished and the techniques of happiness that previously facilitated warm sociality and "present moment consciousness" have receded into the background. If these are the things that make Gamo people happy, then it would seem safe to say that they are less happy now than they were ten years ago. But . . .

But there is a caveat. Alongside these changes that I do believe have led to a decrease in happiness, there has been another change that I believe has led to an increase in happiness. This is not the increased consumption of goods, which I don't believe has led to any sustained increase in happiness, but a change of religion and, in particular, the engagement in a new form of religious ritual. Alongside the change in production and market activity, there has also been a major religious shift in the same ten years, during which time by far the majority of the people of Masho have converted to Pentecostal Christianity (Freeman 2012a, 2013b). I have suggested elsewhere that there are some quite Weberian links between the move toward market capitalism and the move toward Pentecostalism (Freeman 2012b), but that is not my concern here. Instead, I want to focus on the change in religious and ritual life that people are experiencing and to consider, perhaps, how it affects their happiness.

RELIGION, RITUAL, AND HAPPINESS

For most people in Masho, direct personal engagement with Pentecostal Christianity is very new, something that has only started in the past 2–7 years. Before that the vast majority of the community participated in traditional rituals centered on animal sacrifices and an elaborate series of initiations (see Freeman 2002). These rituals and associated practices structured social and political life and appeased the spirits so that they did not cause illness or misfortune. I have not discussed these traditional beliefs and practices in the foregoing sections because I do not think that they function as cultural techniques of happiness. Like many traditional rituals, they focus on formalized speech patterns and conventions and function to insert persons in the public order and to legitimize the redistribution of surplus wealth. As many classic anthropological analyses of ritual have argued, this formalism renders the intentions or experiences of the participants largely irrelevant (see Bloch 1974; Tambiah 1979; Rappaport 1999). The purpose of these rituals is not to do something to the inner emotional states of individuals; it is to do something to the social order. Their focus is not on the happiness of people but on the happiness of the spirits.

Pentecostalism, however, is a completely different thing. One of its very main objectives is the reconfiguration of the self of the believer. While it is probably true that all of the major world religions seek to effect structured transitions in the inner world of the subject (Shulman and Stroumsa 2002), Pentecostalism puts a particular emphasis on this and is extraordinarily effective in its methods and outcomes. Scholars of Pentecostalism have talked about its ability to bring about a "revision of consciousness" (Martin 1990: 287), a "remaking of the individual" (Maxwell 1998: 352), a "reorientation of persons" (Barbalet 2008: 75). In the context of Gamo, and indeed more generally, the key subjective transformation is to turn the person into a "believer." What this means, though, deserves a little unpacking.

Joel Robbins has pointed out that the verb "to believe" can have two different meanings—"to believe in" and "to believe that" (Robbins 2007). "To believe
in God," for example, means to trust God and to commit yourself to Him. It is
an act, more than a statement, and it signifies a relationship between the believer
and God. "To believe that God exists," however, is something very different. It is
a propositional statement and it implies a state of uncertainty about the propo-
sition. "To believe," in this second sense, is in contrast to "to know." "Believing"
in Gamo is very much *believing in*. It is not about believing that something
(e.g., the Bible) is true, or believing that something (e.g., God) exists. It is more
about trusting and believing in a God that can and will help you, and is only
waiting for you to enter into relationship with Him in order to start bestowing
His magnificent power and goodwill on to you.

For people in Gamo this is a radically new concept. When I asked if they believed in the spirits, people laughed at the absurdity of the question. For them it
is clear both that (a) the spirits exist—there is no question about that—and (b)
you can't "believe in" them because they do not have anything good to give you,
they do not relate to people in that way, they do not care about people and are
not able to protect them. *Believing in* God or Jesus, for Gamo Pentecostals, is
about opening yourself to a new kind of relationship with a new kind of benevo-
lent power. As such, it is a radically transformative process and leads a person to
begin to experience him or herself in a profoundly new way, as someone that is
both loved and empowered.

The process by which this transformation of the self takes place is long and
complex, and can only be briefly touched upon in this paper. The main techniques used are Christian study and experiential ritual. The church's head office
in Addis Abeba produces study materials that are distributed to all the local
churches. The book currently used has ten chapters on topics ranging from "revelation" to "man and sin" to "salvation" and "Holy Spirit." All those visiting the
church are soon invited to participate in a series of small group classes with the
preacher or some of the other church elders that slowly works through the book.
The initial series of classes can last over a year and people then often continue
in other classes or group learning activities. Slowly, gradually, people learn a new
way to view themselves and the world, a new narrative, and a new set of values.

The second technique, and the one on which I will focus a bit more here, is
experiential ritual in the Pentecostal church service. In contrast to traditional
rituals that focus on the social order, Pentecostal ritual focuses almost exclusively on the inner emotional world of the participant. For this reason it has

proved difficult to study with classical anthropological theories of ritual and most scholars have tended to lean to a more phenomenological approach, focusing on bodily experience and meaning-making (see, for example, Coleman and Collins 2000; Lindhardt 2011; Luhrmann 2004, 2012; Steven 2002). As Martin Lindhardt has commented, this approach sees Pentecostal ritual as "an arena of practice through which new dispositions and new senses of self, agency, community and mission are cultivated" (Lindhardt 2011: 8).

Going to a Pentecostal church service in Ethiopia is like going on an emotional rollercoaster. There is no way to sit at the back, remain a neutral observer, and not get swept up in the collective emotional journey. At least I couldn't find a way. Church services generally last around three hours and have a fairly standard emotional shape. After some warm-up with quiet reflection and singing, participants are led to feel first guilt and suffering. The preacher will harangue them, bemoaning the sinfulness of the community, the things that they have done wrong, how they haven't helped others enough, haven't been doing God's word, how there are problems in the community, and so on. During this time it is common to see people with tears in their eyes, looking down at the floor. I would find myself with a heavy heart and somehow absorbing the feelings of sadness and remorse that emanated all around me.

Then the tone would shift, and through stories of God's forgiveness and awe-inspiring good deeds, arousing singing and the use of call-and-response that pulled you into praising God, the mood shifted to awe and gratitude.

"Who put us here in this world?"

"God did."

"Who?"

"God!"

"Why did he do it? Because he loves us! Hallelujah!"

"Hallelujah!"

"And he cares for us! Hallelujah!"

"Hallelujah!"

"Turn to your neighbor, look into their eyes, and tell them that God cares for them!"

In this way, at high volume, and interdispersed with vibrant singing, people's emotions are manipulated from state to state. By the end many people are standing up, arms spread upward, with huge smiles on their faces. The energy causes others to run around the church and occasionally someone will speak in tongues. Most times that I have attended these services, I have found myself swept up in this emotional frenzy and by the time I come out I am feeling somewhat exhausted, and full of gratitude and love and warm feelings toward everyone. Facial expressions and movements suggest that many other people are feeling the same way.

Anthropologists have long noticed that rituals very often make people feel good—they are a prime example of a cultural technique of happiness. From Durkheim's notion of "collective effervescence" through Victor Turner's "communitas" to many more recent studies, we have many ethnographic descriptions of rituals generating feelings of joy, ecstasy, and exuberance during the ritual itself and then leaving people with a sense of peace and calm afterward (see Csordas 2002, 1994; Eliade 1964; Goodman 1988; Katz 1982). There is even a small body of literature seeking to find the causal physiological mechanisms for this generation of positive emotion. Earlier studies looked at the release of endorphins during various ritual activities (e.g., Prince 1982), while more recent work has suggested that various bodily techniques, such as singing together or moving together in synchrony can lead to the experience of positive emotions (Csordas 1997, 1990; McNeill 1995; Williams 1981; Wiltermuth and Heath 2009). Radcliffe-Brown talked about the experience of the dancer losing himself in the dance—a notion very similar to psychologist Mihaly Csikszentmihalyi's concept of "flow" (1991)—and recent work by psychologist Jonathan Haidt has suggested that experiences of transcending the self, feeling part of something that is greater than the self, can generate very positive emotions of awe and elevation (Haidt 2000, 2003, 2008).

The point that I want to make here is that Pentecostal church services in Masho are phenomenally effective techniques of happiness, in more than one way. First, they regularly generate bursts of positive emotions in their participants, a weekly "fix" of love and gratitude, if you like. In fact, many people attend church services 4–5 times per week, so for these devout followers the emotional fix is even more frequent. The regular experience of these heart-overwhelming bursts of positive emotion considerably changes people's lived experience of themselves and the world. Psychologist Barbara Fredrickson, working in a very different context, has suggested that experiences of positive emotion such as gratitude can lead to a broadening of people's attention, more creative thinking, and the cultivation of more social connections, thus leading people to shape their lives so that they experience more well-being (Fredrickson 2001). I have not yet been able to investigate this in Masho, but it is an interesting avenue to explore.

Second, Pentecostals change their subjectivity by deepening their interiority as they develop the process of looking inside. This "opening of inner space" seems crucial to the process of self-transformation (Handelman 2002). All prayer meetings start with a few minutes of silent, personal prayer where people articulate their hopes and desires and also scrutinize themselves and their activities for sins and wrong-doing. This process of introspection is developed through other programs, confessions, and prayer meetings, and is very different to traditional notions that what is inside is best kept there, hidden and out of sight. Through the emotional journey that they then traverse during the church service—through shame, guilt, and sadness to joy, love, and gratitude—Pentecostals are able to understand and experience their emotional lives in new ways that has lasting effects beyond the ritual itself.

Thus the various practices of Pentecostal Christianity, particularly its rituals, act as new cultural techniques of happiness. They provide believers with a new sense of self that is loved and empowered, a new set of values, new forms of community and togetherness, and a new emotional landscape. While I would not go so far as to suggest that all major religions are "ways to happiness," as theologian Don Cupitt has recently claimed (Cupitt 2005), I am sympathetic to the arguments of Paul Heelas and his associates that the focus on "spirituality" and "inner experience" that has emerged in many contemporary religions and spiritual movements does indeed lead participants toward increased happiness and well-being in an increasingly complex world (Heelas 2008; Heelas and Woodhead 2005).

CONCLUSION

It is clear that the changes in Masho over the last ten years have led to both decreases and increases in peoples' happiness. For most people the day-to-day lived experience of happiness in peaceful sociality and nonreflexive present-time consciousness has decreased with the move toward a more market-based socioeconomic reality. The increase in inequality and the broadening of the differences in peoples' consumption habits has decreased the happiness of most people, rich and poor alike. And yet, over the same period, as people have converted to Pentecostal Christianity, they have come to access a new form of happiness, one built on a transformation of their sense of self and a deepening and reconfiguring of their emotional lives.

Are the people of Masho happier now or before? It's hard to say. But what is quite clear is that they are happy in a different way. The integration of Masho into the market economy through apple production has transformed happiness from being imbued in the social fabric of the community to being more about cultivating deep interior spaces. While happiness was once grounded in the experience of peaceful sociality it is now to be found in the experience of a more empowered and liberated self in relationship with God/Jesus. As exchange has become increasingly commoditized, so happiness appears to have become increasingly privatized.

There are two key theoretical points that emerge from this ethnography, one more particularizing and one more universalizing. The first point is that the experience of happiness is fundamentally linked to the cultural sense of self. When the self is transformed, new avenues of happiness (and unhappiness) become manifest as more and different interior spaces are opened up. This point should be taken more seriously by happiness researchers from other disciplines who routinely assume a modern, rational, straightforward self. The ethnographic approach used in this essay makes it clear that such assumptions are not warranted when studying "non-Western" peoples. Cultural senses of self are varied and shifting and need to be taken into account particularly when doing comparative studies of happiness across different countries or populations. It is also extremely likely that the modern rational self is also somewhat of a fiction among "Western" subjects, among whom different interior spaces have developed in response to widely differing childhood experiences. A more nuanced, experience-based account of happiness among these subjects would also unveil richer shades of meaning and deeper understandings of the many and diverse ways that happiness is and can be experienced.

The second point is more universalizing. Despite the differences in the experiences of happiness in the two different cultural-historical contexts in Masho, there is nonetheless one major feature that is shared in both of the different routes to happiness—both of them involve the experience of transcending the self. In the earlier historical period the self is transcended by being subsumed in the social fabric. Cultural techniques of happiness encourage this by constantly directing (mental/psychological) attention away from the self and toward the other, whether by playing, by drinking coffee together, or by generally spending time constantly with other people. In the later historical period the transformed self is transcended in its new relation with the all-encompassing God/Jesus. New cultural techniques of happiness encourage this, particularly in the highly emotional Pentecostal church services and in new narratives of meaning. While in the first context transcending the self is part of everyday life and is very much a way of being, in the second context it is more punctuated, taking place in particular contexts such as church ritual, and is much more intense. Nonetheless the structural similarities are there. This suggests that the experience of transcending the self may possibly be a universal feature of the human experience of happiness.

ACKNOWLEDGMENTS

This article is based on twenty-one months of field research in the Gamo Highlands of Ethiopia between 1995 and 1997, plus subsequent visits in 2005, 2006, 2007, 2009, and 2011. I am truly grateful for the continued warmth and hospitality shown to me by the Masho community over the years. The initial research was generously funded by the Leverhulme Trust, the ESRC, and a grant from the London School of Economics. Later periods of fieldwork were funded by a Research Grant from the Hebrew University of Jerusalem. I was a Visiting Fellow at the Institute of Ethiopian Studies at Addis Abeba University between 1995 and 1997 and between 2005 and 2006 and I am most grateful for their continued support for my research.

REFERENCES

Adelson, Naomi. 2000. *"Being alive well": Health and the politics of Cree well-being.* Toronto: University of Toronto Press.

Barbalet, Jack. 2008. *Weber, passion and profits: "The Protestant ethic and the spirit of capitalism" in context.* Cambridge: Cambridge University Press.

Baumeister, Roy, and Mark Leary. 1995. "The need to belong: Desire for interpersonal attachments as a fundamental human motivation." *Psychological Bulletin* 117: 497–529.

Bloch, Maurice. 1974. "Symbols, song, dance and features of articulation: Is religion an extreme form of traditional authority?" *European Journal of Sociology* 15 (1): 54–81.

Coleman, Simon, and Peter Collins. 2000. "The 'plain' and the 'positive': Ritual, experience and aesthetics in Quakerism and charismatic Christianity." *Journal of Contemporary Religion* 15 (3): 317–29.

Csikszentmihalyi, Mihaly. 1991. *Flow: The psychology of optimal experience.* New York: HarperCollins.

Csordas, Thomas. 1990. "Embodiment as a paradigm for anthropology." *Ethnos* 18 (1): 5–47.

———. 1994. *The sacred self: A cultural phenomenology of charismatic healing.* Berkeley: University of California Press.

———. 1997. *Language, charisma and creativity: The ritual life of a religious movement.* Berkeley: University of California Press.

———. 2002. *Body/meaning/healing.* Basingstoke: Palgrave Macmillan.

Cupitt, Don. 2005. *The way to happiness: A theory of religion.* Salem, MA: Polebridge.

Davidson, Richard. 2004. "Well-being and affective style: Neural substrates and biobehavioural correlates." *Philosophical Transactions of the Royal Society (London)* 359: 1395–411.

Eliade, Mircea. 1964. *Shamanism: Archaic techniques of ecstasy.* Translated by W. R. Trask. New York: Pantheon Books.

Fredrickson, Barbara. 2001. "The role of positive emotions in positive psychology: The broaden-and-build theory of positive emotions." *American Psychologist* 56 (3): 218–26.

Freeman, Dena. 2002a. "From warrior to wife: Cultural transformation in the Gamo highlands of Ethiopia." *Journal of the Royal Anthropological Institute* 8: 34–44.

———. 2002b. *Initiating change in highland Ethiopia: Causes and consequences of cultural transformation.* Cambridge: Cambridge University Press.

———. 2009. "Development and (un)happiness: A case study from rural Ethiopia." *Gross national happiness: Practice and measurement,* edited by Dasho Karma Ura and Dorji Penjore. Thimpu: Centre for Bhutan Studies.

———. 2012a. "Development and the rural entrepreneur: Pentecostals, NGOs and the market in the Gamo Highlands, Ethiopia." In *Pentecostalism and development: Churches, NGOs and social change in Africa,* edited by Dena Freeman, 159–80. London: Palgrave Macmillan.

———. 2012b. "The Pentecostal ethic and the spirit of development." In *Pentecostalism and development: Churches, NGOs and social change in Africa,* edited by Dena Freeman, 1–39. London: Palgrave Macmillan.

———. 2013a. "Pentecostalism in a rural context: Dynamics of religion and development in southwest Ethiopia." *PentecoStudies* 12 (2): 231–49.

———. 2013b. "Value chains for development: An ethnography of pro-poor market interventions in Ethiopia." *Anthropology of This Century* Issue 6. http://aotcpress.com/articles/chains-development-ethnography-propoor-market-interventions-ethiopia/.

———. 2015. "Pentecostalism and economic development in sub-saharan Africa." In *Handbook on religions and development*, edited by Emma Tomalin, 114–26. London: Routledge.

Frey, Bruno, and Alois Stutzer. 2002. "The economics of happiness." *World Economics* 3 (1): 1–17.

Goodman, Felicitas. 1988. *Ecstasy, ritual and alternate reality: Religion in a pluralistic world*. Bloomington: Indiana University Press.

Haidt, Jonathan. 2000. "The positive emotion of elevation." *Prevention and Treatment* 3 (3): 1–5.

———. 2003. "The moral emotions." In *Handbook of affective sciences,* edited by Richard Davidson, Klaus Scherer, and H. Hill Goldsmith, 852–70. Oxford: Oxford University Press.

———. 2008. "Moral elevation can induce nursing." *Emotion* 8 (2): 291–95.

Haidt, Jonathan, J. Patrick Seder, and Selin Kesebir. 2008. "Hive psychology, happiness and public policy." *Journal of Legal Studies* 37: S133–S156.

Handelman, Don. 2002. "The interior sociality of self-transformation." In *Self and self-transformation in the history of religions*, edited by David Shulman and Guy. Stroumsa: Oxford University Press.

Heelas, Paul. 2008. *Spiritualities of life: New age romanticism and consumptive capitalism*. Oxford: Blackwell.

Heelas, Paul, and Linda Woodhead, with Benjamin Seel, Bronislaw Szerszynski, and Karin Tusting. 2005. *The spiritual revolution: Why religion is giving way to spirituality*. Oxford: Blackwell.

Inglehart, Ronald, Roberto Foa, Christopher Peterson, and Christian Welzel. 2008. "Development, freedom and rising happiness: A global perspective (1981–2007)." *Perspectives of Psychological Science* 3 (4): 264–85.

Jackson, Michael. 2012. *Between one and one another*. Berkeley: University of California Press.

Jiminez, A. Corsin, ed. 2008. *Culture and the politics of freedom: The anthropology of wellbeing*. London: Pluto Press.

Kahneman, Daniel, Ed Diener, and Norbert Schwarz, eds. 1999. *Well-being: The foundations of hedonic psychology.* New York: Russell Sage Foundation.

Katz, Richard. 1982. *Boiling energy: Community healing among the Kalahari Kung.* Cambridge, MA: Harvard University Press.

Lane, Robert. 2000. *The loss of happiness in market democracies.* New Haven, CT: Yale University Press.

Layard, Richard. 2005. *Happiness: Lessons from a new science.* London: Penguin.

Lindhardt, Martin. 2011. "Introduction." In *Practicing the faith: The ritual life of Pentecostal-charismatic Christians,* edited by Martin Lindhardt, 1–48. Oxford: Berghahn.

Luhrmann, Tanya. 2004. "Metakinesis: How god becomes intimate in contemporary US Christianity." *American Anthropologist* 106 (3): 518–28.

———. 2012. *When god talks back: Understanding the American evangelical relationship with god.* New York: Knopf.

Martin, David. 1990. *Tongues of fire: The explosion of Protestantism in Latin America.* Oxford: Blackwell.

Mathews, Gordon. 1996. *What makes life worth living? How Japanese and Americans make sense of their worlds.* Berkeley: University of California Press.

Mathews, Gordon and Carolina Izquierdo, eds. 2008. *Pursuits of happiness: Well-being in anthropological perspective.* New York: Berghahn.

Maxwell, David. 1998. "'Delivered from the spirit of poverty': Pentecostalism, prosperity and modernity in Zimbabwe." *Journal of Religion in Africa* 28 (3): 350–373.

McNeill, William. 1995. *Keeping together in time: Dance and drill in human history.* Cambridge, MA: Harvard University Press.

Nesse, Randolph. 2004. "Natural selection and the elusiveness of happiness." *Philosophical Transactions of the Royal Society (London)* 359: 1333–47.

Prince, Raymond. 1982. "The endorphins: A review for psychological anthropologists." *Ethos* 10 (4): 303–16.

Rappaport, Roy. 1999. *Ritual and religion in the making of humanity.* Cambridge: Cambridge University Press.

Robbins, Joel. 2007. "Continuity thinking and the problem of Christian culture: Belief, time and the anthropology of Christianity." *Current Anthropology* 48 (1): 5–38.

Seligman, Martin. 2003. *Authentic happiness: Using the new positive psychology to realize your potential for lasting fulfillment.* London: Nicholas Brealey Publishing.

Shulman, David, and Guy Stroumsa, eds. 2002. *Self and self-transformation in the history of religions*. Oxford: Oxford University Press.

Stawarczyk, David, Steve Majerus, Martial Van der Linden, and Arnaud D'Argembeau. 2012. "Using the daydreaming frequency scale to investigate the relationships between mind-wandering, psychological well-being, and present-moment awareness." *Frontiers in Personality Science and Individual Differences* 3: 363.

Steven, James. 2002. *Worship in the spirit: Charismatic worship in the Church of England*. Carlisle: Paternoster Press.

Tambiah, Stanley. 1979. "A performative approach to ritual." *Proceedings of the British Academy* 65: 113–69.

Thin, Neil. 2005. "Happiness and the sad topics of anthropology." WeD Working Paper No. 10. http://www.welldev.org.uk/research/workingpaperpdf/wed10.pdf.

Veenhoven, Ruut. 1991. "Is happiness relative?" *Social Indicators Research* 24 (1): 1–34.

White, Nicholas. 2006. *A brief history of happiness*. Oxford: Blackwell.

Wilkinson, Richard. 1996. *Unhealthy societies: The afflictions of inequality*. London: Routledge.

———. 2005. *The impact of inequality: How to make sick societies healthier*. New York: The New Press.

Williams, Cyril. 1981. *Tongues of the spirit: A study of Pentecostal glossolalia and related phenomena*. Cardiff: University of Wales Press.

Wiltermuth, Scott, and Chip Heath. 2009. "Synchrony and cooperation." *Psychological Science* 20 (1): 1–5.

CHAPTER FIVE

"Good without God"
Happiness and pleasure among the humanists

MATTHEW ENGELKE

In 1965, a competition was held by the British Humanist Association (BHA) to design a logo for the humanist movement, a universal symbol to signify a commitment to "non-religious people who seek to live ethical lives on the basis of reason and humanity."[1] Over 150 entries were received; the winning design, by a humanist from north London, is called "the happy human." This symbol is now used by humanist organizations throughout the globe—from India to Australia to Canada. Members of the BHA can sometimes be found wearing lapel pins with the Happy Human which read "Happy Humanist" or "Good without God."

In 2008, the comedian Ariane Sherine launched the "Atheist Bus Campaign," with the backing of the BHA and one of the association's most prominent members, Richard Dawkins. The campaign was inspired by Sherine's upset over an advertisement by a Christian organization, which she saw on the side of a bus, the upshot of which was that only Jesus can save you from hell. The

---

1. This is how the BHA currently puts it, on the top of its homepage, www.humanism. org.uk, accessed December 1, 2015.

Atheist Bus Campaign's riposte—which raised over £150,000 in support—was: "There's probably no god. Now stop worrying and enjoy your life."

In 2011, I met Andrew West, a humanist, photographer, and computer whiz; he did a lot of photography for the BHA and later that year went on to become the Association's IT officer. Not long before joining the BHA, he completed a degree in photography, the thesis project for which was a series of portraits of humanists accompanied by their answers to the question: *What are you happy about?*

In March 2014, the BHA produced a series of short animations explaining humanist values and principles, narrated by the actor, comedian, and writer, Stephen Fry (another prominent member of the Association). One of these animations addressed the question: "How can I be happy?" The video went viral, and was viewed on YouTube over 750,000 times in the first several days. It was picked up by the *Independent* newspaper and dubbed, on March 25, "the best thing you'll watch today." Shortly after the launch of the video, and this headline, I had dinner with the BHA's chief executive officer. We talked a lot about the video; he was very happy.

Happiness is part and parcel of humanism. Humanism in contemporary Britain is driven by a passion for the pursuit of happiness.[2] But why happiness? What is it about happiness that stands out for humanists, and what does it entail? To answer these questions, we need to pay particular attention to the ways in which British humanists understand happiness as the struggle for, and promise of, enlightenment. Humanists see themselves as children of the Enlightenment, as taking up the mantle of reason, the tools of science, and the potentials of free thought. Being happy and being "good without god" is a commitment both to pleasure and to progress.[3] And for the humanists, happiness is a subjective experience—but also a sign of the secular.

---

2. "Humanism" is a term with many meanings and a long history. In this article, it means secular humanism. The BHA members I got to know called themselves many things, each of which had specific motivations and intentions. But in general, these humanists, secular humanists, atheists, agnostics, freethinkers, materialists, and so on, wanted to emphasize that they admitted no beyond, that they did not "believe" in anything supernatural, miraculous, or divine.

3. The 2014 World Humanist Congress, hosted by the BHA in Oxford, brought together over a thousand delegates from more than sixty countries. The theme was "Freedom of Thought and Expression: Forging a Twenty-First-Century Enlightenment."

At least one distinguished anthropological elder, Elizabeth Colson, has warned the discipline off the idea of studying happiness—and, still more, any attempts to measure it. "Happiness," she writes, "is in the heart and not in the eye of the beholder" (Colson 2012: 8). In line with the points made by Harry Walker and Iza Kavedžija in their introduction to this *HAU* collection, I find it difficult to see how *measuring* happiness could ever be anthropology's proper remit. That doesn't, however, mean that happiness should be a no-go area for anthropology—especially when the people we study make it so central to their lives and social projects. Indeed, as Walker and Kavedžija note, what anthropology can contribute to happiness studies is "how happiness figures as an idea, mood, or motive in people's day-to-day lives." A small number of anthropologists have also recognized this, and have worked to point out that happiness is more than a subjective experience (see, e.g., Corsín Jimenez 2008; Thin 2012; Jackson 2013; Fischer 2014). As Neil Thin would have it, for instance, "happiness is best understood not as a definable entity but as an evaluative kind of 'conversation' (broadly conceived to include internal dialogues) about how well our lives go" (2012: 33). Thin emphasizes the "internal" aspect of such conversations, and in doing so highlights particular models of subjectivity, models which Colson is also clearly drawing upon. So perhaps in this idiom we can say that happiness may well be "in the heart," as Colson puts in, but also that it is "in the head."[4] For the humanists I studied, happiness is very much like this; it is an idea. They have an ideological commitment to happiness, expressed above all as a pursuit of the good life.[5] And for these humanists, what that means is working to articulate, and live out, Enlightenment values.

---

4. This idiom might not work everywhere in the world (see Throop's and Walker's articles in this collection, for example), but it does roughly for such contexts as Britain and the United States (although in her brief reflections Colson extends it to 1950s Zambia, where she made her mark as an anthropologist). The idiom certainly works well enough for the British humanists I studied: such "head/heart" distinctions map well onto their readings of post-Enlightenment models of subjectivity.

5. It is worth noting that the small amount of anthropological work addressing happiness is often framed in relation to questions of wellbeing and pursuit of the good life (see, e.g, Corsín Jiménez 2008; Fischer 2014). These studies also underscore a common thread in the articles of this *HAU* collection, which is a "concern with *values*" (Fischer 2014: 12, his emphasis; see also Corsín Jiménez 2008: 17–19).

THE BRITISH HUMANIST ASSOCIATION

Founded in 1896 as the Union of Ethical Societies, the BHA has existed in its current constitutional form since 1967. During the main period of my research (2011), the BHA had approximately twelve thousand members (who pay annual dues of £35) and another eighteen thousand supporters (who, at a minimum, receive updates of BHA activities via an e-newsletter). (These figures have now risen.) Based on a survey I conducted in June 2011 (midway through a year of fieldwork), 69 percent of members were male; 31 percent female. Seventy-three percent had university degrees, and 80 percent donated monthly or annually to charities (Oxfam, Save the Children, Cancer Research UK, and Amnesty International were some of the most common). The BHA has a number of high-profile members, many of whom are very active in promotion of the association. In addition to Dawkins and Fry, these include the scientists Jim Al-Khalili, Brian Cox, and Alice Roberts (all of whom have significant media careers in the United Kingdom), journalist Polly Toynbee, comedians Tim Minchin and Natalie Haynes, philosopher A. C. Grayling, and fiction writers such as Philip Pullman and the late Terry Pratchett. The actors Patrick Stewart and Ricky Gervais are also distinguished supporters and so, too, is Simon Le Bon, frontman for Duran Duran.

The work of the BHA can be divided into three areas. The first is the promotion of humanism in policy and public debates. Much of this work is classically secularist, such as campaigning for the abolition of state-funded faith schools and the constitutional right of Anglican bishops to sit in the House of Lords. The second is servicing and fostering local humanist groups; there are about sixty of these, ranging in size from six to sixty people. This grassroots work is extremely important to the BHA: the more locally embedded humanists are, forming communities of discussion, debate, and care, the better. The third main area of focus is the provision of ceremonies: weddings, naming ceremonies, and, above all, funerals for BHA members and anyone else who wants to have a rite of passage that is self-consciously humanist or "not religious." Within the BHA, there is a network of approximately three hundred trained celebrants to provide these ceremonies throughout England and Wales.[6] The BHA is increasingly starting to support other forms of social care, piloting programs in prisons and

---

6.   There is a Humanist Society of Scotland, which operates independently of the BHA (although cooperatively).

hospitals to provide humanist chaplains and other forms of pastoral support. (Not all humanists like using these terms—*chaplain*, *pastoral*—to describe the activities, but there is a lot of support for the initiatives, and the BHA itself sees no reason not to draw on the common understandings of such words.)

"THE TIME TO BE HAPPY IS NOW"

I have said that humanists see themselves as children of the Enlightenment. There is, of course, no way to understand the various intellectual movements and social changes in seventeenth- and eighteenth-century Europe and America as part of a single, straightforward story. And these movements and changes built on what came before them. For the humanists, Greek and Roman traditions of thought are also often embraced. Within the BHA, however, it is the language of the Enlightenment that dominates, and one particular version of the Enlightenment story has pride of place: that in which reason snuffs out religion and gives rise to a modern world governed by science. Theirs is a world in which individuals "think for themselves," and refuse to accept as fact or authority anything that is not based on "evidence." "With these brains we have the ability to question," says Robin Ince, a BHA patron and well-known comedian; "if we fail to do that, if we look for a high priest or elder to do our thinking for us, to instruct us and manipulate us, then we are failing to live up to our potential."[7] The echoes of certain pieces of Enlightenment rhetoric here are unmistakable, those in which the Enlightenment serves as "the starting point of secular modernity and rationality" (Sorkin 2008: 1)—the "Radical Enlightenment" (Israel 2001: 11–12), for which religion cannot be rehabilitated and reason must be exercised. As one member reported to me, on joining the BHA, "Finally I found an organized voice of reason that represented my views and acts as a counterpoint to oppressive religion." "Enlightenment," wrote Immanuel Kant, in 1784,

> is man's release from his self-incurred tutelage. Tutelage is man's inability to make use of his understanding without direction from another. Self-incurred is

---

7. This quote is taken from the BHA's website, in the page header; see https:// humanism.org.uk/news/, accessed December 1, 2015. The quote is one of many by prominent humanists that is randomly generated when loading and reloading a BHA webpage.

this tutelage when its cause lies not in lack of reason but in lack of resolution and courage to use it without direction from another. *Sapere aude!* "Have courage to use your own reason!"—that is the motto of enlightenment. (1963: 3)

It is not that all BHA members spend their days reading Kant, or John Locke, or David Hume. Yet the mantle of *Aufklärung* is held tight and proudly worn. Several of the BHA's most prominent champions and contemporary inspirations—the philosopher A. C. Grayling, the late critic Christopher Hitchens— have, however, read Kant and Locke (and others); they have charted, through their popular writings, a genealogy that links the humanist project to such figures. Less prominently, but no less importantly, the BHA coordinates the Humanist Philosophers group, which includes a number of well-respected academics, such as Richard Norman and Peter Cave. In addition to publishing on their specialist interests, and for general readers too, humanists such as Norman and Cave are regularly invited to speak by local humanist groups, where they present overviews of how humanist thought is linked to that of Enlightenment thinkers and those who came after them, especially such nineteenth-century figures as Jeremy Bentham, John Stuart Mill, and Charles Darwin. In other ways, humanist scientists and science writers—Dawkins, Cox, Al-Khalili, and Roberts—emphasize the Enlightenment through their treatments of science, promotion of the scientific method, and critiques of creationism. The BHA's members, supporters, and publics eagerly soak this up, through their reading practices, for instance, and attendance at the BHA's numerous annual lectures, named, tellingly, after Voltaire, Darwin, Bentham, and Shelley.[8] These pack sold-out auditoriums in London, Oxford, and elsewhere. BHA staff are always giving talks—to local groups, to trainee teachers, to trainee nurses, to school students—which include potted histories of humanism, illustrated by slides with quotes on reason, free thought, and the pursuit of happiness by eighteenth- and nineteenth-century philosophers and scientists (Hume, Darwin, Thomas Huxley, Ludwig Feuerbach).

---

8.   In the survey I conducted, 72 percent of BHA members said they had read Dawkins' most well-known critique of religion, *The God delusion*, in which he is very explicit about his commitment to Enlightenment values. Asked which of three books they would want on a desert island, 2 percent of members chose the Bible; 62 percent chose the collected works of Shakespeare; and 36 percent chose Darwin's *On the origin of species*.

Among historians, none has been more insistent than Roy Porter on the fact that "there never was a monolithic 'Enlightenment project'" (2000: xxi). Yet even so, Porter identifies some lowest common denominators of the changes that took place. One of them concerns the understanding of happiness. "The Enlightenment's great historical watershed," he writes, "lay in the validation of pleasure. . . . The Enlightenment's novelty lay in the legitimacy it accorded to pleasure, not as occasional binges, mystical transports or blue-blooded privilege, but as the routine entitlement of people at large to pursue the senses (not just purify the soul) and to seek fulfilment in this world (and not only in the next)" (ibid.: 258; 260).

The temporal framing of Porter's characterization is important. There is indeed what we might call a "temporality of happiness," as Walker and Kavedžija stress (see the introduction to this collection). In Porter's analysis, after the Enlightenment it gets increasingly premised on a shift from what we might gloss as a religious sense of time to a secular sense of time, a shift that a number of other scholars have written about at great length (see Anderson 1991 for one well-known example, drawing on Walter Benjamin). The temporality of here-and-now, immanent being-in-this-world, is certainly central to the humanists I studied. We see hints of this in the Atheist Bus Campaign's riposte to fire-and-brimstone Christianity; it is also expressed in the BHA's motto: "For the one life we have." A popular quotation on happiness among the humanists comes from the nineteenth-century American agnostic Robert Ingersoll. "Happiness is the only good," Ingersoll said. "The time to be happy is now. The place to be happy is here. The way to be happy is to make others so" (see Jacoby 2013: 97). Like a meme, this proclamation of immanence and the immediate circulates among humanist communities, as, for instance, in the BHA's many PowerPoint presentations dedicated to the promotion and spread of humanism. It is all part of the conclusion that being happy is being secular.[9] To say "the time to be happy is now"—to stress what we do "for the one life we have"—is to take a very

---

9. In her history of nineteenth- and twentieth-century atheism and agnosticism in Britain, Susan Budd highlights this kind of view at several points. In her discussion of the British Secular Union, for example, founded in 1877, she cites its constitution, which advocates "the promotion of political, social or religious reform in any wise tending to increase the secular happiness of the people" (1977: 59). Readers of Budd's history will see how the dynamics and arguments behind antireligious sentiment in the nineteenth century have many parallels with those of contemporary Britain.

particular view of history, of human potentiality, and of the fabric of meaning. As another historian puts it, "Happiness, in the Enlightenment view, was less an ideal of godlike perfection than a self-evident truth, to be pursued and obtained in the here and now" (McMahon 2006: 13). "Humanists do not see that there is any obvious purpose to the universe, but that it is a natural phenomenon, with no design behind it. Meaning is not something out there, waiting to be discovered, but something that we create in our own lives," says Stephen Fry, in the BHA video on how to be happy. "The time to be happy is now," he goes on to conclude. "And the way to find meaning in life is to get on and live it, as fully, and as well, as we can."[10]

Colson might eschew it altogether, but in any case no one who studies happiness claims that it is easy to limn or measure. Happiness has to be seen as an admixture of sentiments, affects, demeanor, and declarations, even actions. Andrew West's photography project, for example, which includes portraits of fifty-eight humanists, contains a range of concrete answers to his question: *What are you happy about?* Many of the answers are generic: "I am happy today because my kids have been making me laugh," says Stephen, a philosopher in Oxford. Others are generic yet inflected with humanist particularities: "I'm happy to be alive, happy with my children and grandchildren who are the only immortality I need. I am happy to live in a world with food, drink, flowers and the astonishing abundance that flows from the imagination of other humans, dead and alive," says Polly, a writer in London. (Notice Polly's emphasis on here-and-now, on *the one life we have*.) Several of the answers include similar references to children and grandchildren, or, failing that, other pleasurable things: flowers, birds, and food. Not a few also reference consumption of various kinds: television shows, clothes, a new pair of stilettos—even the purchase of a camper van.[11]

---

10. "How can I be happy?" https://www.youtube.com/watch?v=Tvz0mmF6NW4, accessed December 1, 2015. I might note here that humanists' commitment to here-and-now does not preclude them from thinking of the future. Some of the humanists I got to know were also deeply involved in environmental campaigns and organizations, for instance; they certainly understood climate change as a serious challenge for humanity and the ecosystem (and had no patience for climate-change skeptics). Interestingly, however, they tended to think of these commitments separately, as if humanism and environmentalism had to be discrete.

11. Porter emphasizes the link between the Enlightenment and modern consumerism and consumption: "New lobbies of enlightened economists and progressive social commentators began to argue that market culture, sport, print and leisure were economically productive entities, forces of civilization and social cohesion"

Other replies are highly specific and tailored, humanist plugs. Says Chris, from Bournemouth: "I'm happy during February 2009 to have been invited to talk to North Yorkshire Humanists & Dorset Humanists about 'Darwin, Science & Humanism.' Darwin showed how man & all living species evolved from earlier ancestors. A supernatural creator is not necessary to explain any living creature's existence on earth." And Allison, from London, is happy "about spending an evening with enlightened people." Joanna, from Lansdowne, tells West she is happy because she has "no worries about dying."

West's portraits give us an excellent range of the ways in which humanist happiness can be understood. The small number of examples I've provided are indicative of the range, and we can use them to explore humanist conceptions of happiness yet further, in terms of both "heart" and "head," as I put it above. Indeed, in reading through West's book, and looking at the portraits, I had confirmed much of what I found in my own fieldwork—not only in outline, but often quite specifically. Of the fifty-eight humanists portrayed by Andrew in his book, twenty-four of them figured in my own research.

Happiness for humanists contains both hedonic and eudaimonic components. When Fry says in the BHA video that we should live *fully* and *well*, he is saying we should combine pleasures (wine, gardening) with purposefulness (political commitments, social justice). And for every humanist I met, the two had to be seen as of a piece. Heart and head. Another of Andrew's photographic subjects, Harry, from London, sums this up perfectly in relaying the two things that make him happy: "making love" and "progress in moral philosophy."

Clearly, as we've seen, happiness is recognized by these humanists in the terms of much happiness science today, and more generally the stereotypical understanding of smiles and joy. (Forty-nine out of West's fifty-eight subjects are smiling in the photos, it might be noted.) The emphasis on laughing with one's children, enjoying a curry, loving a new pair of high-heeled shoes, and making love is all about what Richard Layard calls "feeling good—enjoying life and wanting the feeling to be maintained" (2006: 12).

To be happy because you don't need any more "immortality" than that provided by your grandchildren, though, or because you enjoy the company of

---

(2000: 268). Today, of course, this is often further refined with respect to fair trade campaigns, socially responsible investment, and the like; see Fischer's (2014) comparative ethnography of wellbeing and the good life in Guatemala (among Mayan coffee farmers) and Germany (among supermarket shoppers) for an example.

"enlightened people," or because of progress in moral philosophy, or because you're not afraid of dying, or because you have an opportunity to deny the existence of a supernatural creator (and celebrate Darwin's birthday in the process) is not quite the same. It may well make you feel good, but that's in part because you see yourself as doing good, as living up to your values. The happy life is, in this important respect, the good life. In *The conquest of happiness*, Bertrand Russell, one of contemporary humanism's heroes (and a committed member of the BHA-as-then for much of his adult life), puts it in precisely these terms: "The happy life is to an extraordinary extent the same as the good life" (1930: 173). And the good life is not all about smiles, pleasures, and joys per se.

It's here that humanists inject a bit more Hellenism into their Enlightenment sensibilities than we might find in, say, some utilitarian calculation of pleasure. For while the validation of pleasure is crucial to their cause—while the hedonic matters—this pleasure is, I would argue, part and parcel of a larger ethical and social project in which happiness gets defined through "virtuous conduct and philosophic reflection" (Layard 2006: 22). In short, I argue, for the humanists, the hedonic (the pleasurable) has to be seen as serving the eudaimonic (the good). For a humanist to say she loves her new high heels is not, at core, to betray her entrapment by the "hedonic treadmill" (ibid.: 48–49) of consumption. Or, at least, it is not only ever that. For what such embracement of earthly pleasures is also supposed to suggest is that there are only earthly pleasures to be had—that we are each our own makers. Humanists use their stilettos to beat God over the head; they use their camper vans to run him down in the road. They use their chances to explain why they're happy to be happy here and now in a way that underscores its ethical valences. This is what I mean by arguing that we need to approach happiness as an ideological commitment.

CHOCOLATE AND SEX

Andrew Copson is another of the humanists featured in West's book. Andrew is the CEO of the BHA, and he tells us he's happy "because the sun is shining, I have a new book to read and a glass of ice tea."

Andrew is one of the humanists I got to know particularly well through my research. From January to August 2011, I probably spent about twenty-five hours a week with him, either sitting in the corner of his office, or out and about at various events, meetings, and engagements. Since that time I've seen him regularly. I'd like to use Andrew as an extended example of the happy humanist, to fill out in a bit more detail what we've considered thus far, and in particular how the pleasurable aspects of happiness (the hedonic) should be seen as serving the purposeful aspects of happiness (the eudaimonic).[12]

Andrew certainly liked ice tea. And coffee and hot chocolate and cake. Not long before we first met, he had quit smoking and it made his sweet tooth all the worse. In many ways, Andrew's delight in food, especially sweets, was indiscriminate. He'd just as soon have a hot cross bun from the snack trolley on an intercity train (not really very good) as an artisan brioche from the upscale coffee shop around the corner from his office (quite nice). But at core, Andrew actually had a very well thought-out approach to confections. One day at the office, he was particularly happy when a small, nondescript package arrived. He clapped his hands and gave a little jump in his desk chair before opening it to reveal a box of something called Chelsea Whoppers. Chelsea Whoppers are chocolate-like, fudge-like strips of goodness; they're also hard to find in stores, so Andrew would special order them from online retro candy sellers. They were pure nostalgia, a reminder of his childhood and days gone by. He ate the whole box that day, over the course of which I got to hear a lot about growing up in Britain in the late 1980s and early 1990s.

Andrew grew up in Nuneaton in what he described as a very multicultural environment. His family was not religious, but not particularly antireligious either. He first learned of humanism in secondary school, in a book by Barbara Smoker (a legendary member of the BHA and the National Secular Society, another important nonreligious organization in the UK). He never gave much thought to humanists, though, or to religion, until he arrived at Oxford, to read classics at Balliol College. At Oxford, he got "very angry" at an event he attended sponsored by the Christian Union (at which, he mentioned to me, they were handing out free donuts). A man had come to speak, and

---

12. Copson has given his consent to be named in this section; he felt no need for anonymity, and, given his public profile, as well as the specificity of some of the encounters upon which I draw, I use his real name. In the sections to follow, though, and in line with my other publications on the BHA, where I draw on primary ethnographic data, I follow one standard anthropological convention of using pseudonyms. In almost all cases, however, the humanists I worked with saw no need for this. I think this has something to do with their commitment to a certain understanding of the scientific method and transparency; a humanist should have nothing to hide—not when it's in the service of (social) science.

he said that every time people heard more about the gospel, more about the Good News, but still refused to believe it, the more likely it was that they would be damned. And then later on in his talk, he sort of threw his arms up in frustration and said, "Oh, I don't know why I come to these university events, you're all so clever-clever, you're never going to believe." And I put my hand up and said, "Well, if you think that the more people learn about Christianity and refuse it, the more likely they are to be damned, and if you think that people will inevitably refuse it on [university] campuses, why are you going around deliberately making everyone's damnation worse and worse and worse?"

This is classic Andrew. There were many things that came to bother him about religion and religious belief. And he is on the more explicit end of commitment to being an Enlightened modern. Andrew once chided me, only half-jokingly, for not ever having read the New Testament in Greek. He could recite Matthew Arnold's poem "On Dover Beach" by heart and very well. Half way through his degree at Oxford, he switched to reading History. "I studied Europe up to the end of the classical period," he told me,

and [then] from the eighteenth century onwards, and so missed out completely the middle bit, where all these Christian things happened, and I think actually that is genuinely something that has influenced my view of things. . . . And although obviously I'm not thinking of Pericles every day, I'd be much more comfortable with the literature and culture of classical Athens than with church culture or whatever.

But Andrew is not a "new atheist" humanist; he is not as pugnacious as some. He has worked closely with various bodies on faith-based issues, and serves on the board of the Religious Education Council of England and Wales. (Andrew is a strong supporter of religious education in the national curriculum—and of humanism being included in it.) And for him, the BHA's provision of ceremonies is absolutely crucial to a humanist future. It was Andrew who pushed for (and engineered) the expansion of humanist networks of care into the realms of chaplaincy and pastoral support in hospital, prisons, and the military services. These kinds of community provision are central to his understandings of happiness, wellbeing, and a good life.

One area where Andrew could get indignant, though—where he could get annoyed in the manner of the new atheists—was when the pleasures and joys of this life came under attack. Sometimes the indignation played out sarcastically. In January 2015, he appeared on the BBC's Sunday morning discussion show, *The big questions*, to discuss the government's recent decision not to give legal recognition to humanist weddings in England and Wales.[13] (Andrew is regularly on television and the radio, representing a humanist or "nonreligious" point of view.) Taiwo Adewuyi, a conservative Christian and the founder of "Discuss Jesus," was also on the show; in explaining why he opposed humanist marriages, Adewuyi said that "humanism is . . . a first-class ticket to the very hypersexualized culture that we're seeing." Andrew, with an incredulous smile on his face, began his reply by saying, "Well, if you're going to go to wantonness and debauchery, I suppose you might as well travel first class."[14] Another time, in 2012, we were together, speaking to a prominent conservative evangelical Christian after an event. He and Andrew knew each other relatively well (the public square isn't that big), and the three of us were engaged in polite small talk. Somehow the conversation turned to marriage, at which point Andrew said, "Isn't it strange how evangelical Christians spend so much time telling their children that sex is horrible and disgusting and sinful and yet, at the same time, that they should save it for the person they marry?" As with what we see in some of West's portraits, the barbs and jibes have an ethical valence here, all the more so when they pertain to the pleasures that people might rightly enjoy as human beings with one life to live. This isn't about hedonism for hedonism's sake: this is about being good without God.

It is important to stress that Andrew didn't spend all his time eating Chelsea Whoppers, or mocking evangelical Christians about their attitudes to sex. I have only given a focused account of his character and commitments as relevant to the themes of this article. I got to know Andrew as a serious, committed campaigner for the causes he believes in: equality in state school admissions policies; dignity for those suffering with a terminal illness (the BHA strongly supports legislation on assisted dying); the importance of teaching humanism

---

13. Humanist weddings are legal in Scotland; in England and Wales, BHA celebrants do conduct weddings, but the couple have to have a ceremony at the local Registry Office as well in order to be legally married. The BHA's lobbying in Parliament came very close to success, but faced strong opposition from the Anglican Church and others who opposed the move.

14. BBC One, *The big questions*, "Should humanists have equal rights to religions?" available at https://www.youtube.com/watch?v=3j8jQkSydeo, accessed December 1, 2015.

in the school curriculum; campaigning for humanist weddings; and free speech
and its safe exercise (both in the United Kingdom and elsewhere; the murder
of three atheist bloggers in Bangladesh has been a recent major concern). But
chocolate and sex, and the happiness they bring, are an important part of the
overall picture of being good without God.

RELIGION, REASON, AND EMOTION

The critique of religion and the cultivation of humanism go hand in hand. Within the BHA, religion is humanism's opposite and other; religion is, for many of
these humanists, inimical to reason and the kind of flourishing they value.[15] We
have already had a sense of this. In some cases, humanist happiness is defined in
opposition to religious misery, worry, suffering, or delusion. This is where the commitment to a radical version of the Enlightenment becomes especially relevant.
Christianity, in particular, is, as we've seen, heavily criticized. It is not unusual to
see BHA members, or those in affiliated local groups, turn sour at the thought
of Christian approaches to life, approaches which many of them understand as
dominated by a fixation with and even embracement of suffering, asceticism,
and self-denial. There is no equivalent of theodicy in the BHA's articulation of
humanism. Claims that someone's cancer or a flood or other personal or social
misfortune is "God's will," or, even less nefariously, "telling us something," drive
them mad. Religious mores get cast as tools of subjection and shaming, or called
out as hypocritical, as with Andrew's comment to the evangelical back in 2012.
More generally, humanists often express dismay and sometimes disgust at the
thought that the master sign of Christianity is not a happy human but a suffering man. How, they ask, could any community orient themselves by a crucifix?

The point here is that religion, in this humanist view, is inimical to happiness—true happiness, that is: a eudaimonic happiness grounded in the good

---

15. While I have been writing here about members of the BHA, the attitudes,
dispositions, and commitments we've found are not unique to them. Indeed,
while there are some notable differences with the American context (in terms of
organization, and, in particular, the scale of provision of nonreligious ceremonies),
humanist and atheist groups there often define themselves in explicit opposition
to religion, as defenders of reason, and as committed to a similar understanding of
happiness; see the work of Jesse M. Smith (2013) for one qualitative, sociological
case study.

(secular) life. There are equal measures of opprobrium, then, for Christians and other believers who don't dwell on the crucifixion or suffering. The stereotyped "happy-clappy" Christian is considered just as problematic as what some BHA members would gloss as the guilt-laden, crucifix-wearing Catholic. For some, such believers are seen to be not happy so much as deluded into thinking they are happy, or at least are only superficially happy, because their worldviews cannot allow for the good life as humanists conceive of it. For others, this expression of faith is assumed to be a façade. Even humanists who do accept some of the academic research suggesting that religious people are happier (e.g., Stavrova, Fetchenhauer, and Schlösser 2013) argue that the "religion bit" is secondary: if these people are happy, it is because of the human community they share, not its metaphysical aeration.[16] As BHA members regularly told me, there are clearly benefits to voluntary associations: this is why local groups are such an important part in the BHA's work. Increasingly, local groups are doing the kinds of things that religious groups have traditionally done: calling on elderly members in their homes for social visits; volunteering for local charities and programs; participating in community fairs and civic life; even, in some cases, forming choirs and other corporate activities, such as parkland walking clubs (during which, in some of the more well-developed cases, botanists or geologists might be invited along to explain the local flora, fauna, and landscape). It is this, they said, that fosters happiness and well-being. God has nothing to do with it. (We might compare the similarities and differences with Ethiopian Pentecostal "techniques of happiness" discussed by Dena Freeman, in her article for this collection.) Alongside such arguments, humanists also often point to levels of happiness and well-being in Scandinavian nations, which are regularly referred to as the "least religious" in the world.[17]

---

16. See also Amy C. Wilkins' (2008) qualitative study of the way in which a particular evangelical Christian group in the United States worked to foster happiness and a happy demeanor among its members; what she shows so well is how happiness is not necessarily epiphenomenal, but a normative demand. In this group, at least, "one cannot be a real Christian and *not* be happy" (ibid.: 294, emphasis in original). One point to keep in mind, then, is how happiness can become a demand of authenticity within certain communities of practice. Wherever we find that happiness has an ethical valence, then, it can present something of a catch-22: be happy, or else.

17. The sociologist Phil Zuckerman (2008) has written about these issues in his informative study of Denmark and Sweden. Zuckerman's work is largely qualitative, but he points to quantitative research as well, including that of Ronald Inglehart, Miguel Basáñez, and Alejandro Menéndez Moreno (1998), to support the argument

Another problem with religion, when it comes to the realization of this particular good life, is its disregard for "evidence." This is part of what I mean by saying that in this humanist project, "true happiness" can't be realized except in secular form. Religion frustrates eudaimonia. For these humanists, evidence is a precondition for eudaimonia, because the good life can only be lived with due regard for science. And "evidence" does mean scientific evidence: objective, verifiable, and replicable. Evidence means knowledge rather than belief: fact rather than feeling. If immortality or the supernatural could be "proved" in the same way as the value of the antioxidants in blueberries, then humanists would alter their positions. Striving after truth in such terms, according to strict and well-defined evidentiary protocols, is a central aspect of humanist virtue. "I care passionately about the truth because it is a beautiful thing and enables us to lead a better life," says Dawkins, in a promotional statement on the BHA's homepage.[18] As one member told me, she joined the BHA "to work towards a more rational society." "I had to do something," said another woman. "I had to understand more about religion and how to make Britain a secular society . . . the BHA['s] values are my values."

Logic is another key element here, and was often used by humanists I met to explain why they weren't religious, and why religion itself is a dead end. They are simply not willing to accept that the Son of God, for instance, can defy the laws of nature. As one BHA staffer told me, his mildly active Anglicanism started to unravel from the age of twelve, when he realized that what his Religious Education teacher at school was saying simply wasn't plausible. He began looking up things in the family encyclopedia—archaeological records, geological records. "I think you'll find this with a lot of atheists," he told me. "It's the little things that get you into it [investigating religious claims], because, if there's no evidence . . . a lot falls down in Christianity."

---

that there is no necessary correlation between religiosity and happiness. Notably, too, Zuckerman's qualitative work (see 2008: 57–75) picks up on Scandinavian attitudes toward death, and a strong sense in which the finality of death means that we should seek pleasures and progress in, and for, this world—very much akin to what we find in the BHA's invocations of Ingersoll's saying "the time to be happy is now."

18. It is important not to overstate Dawkins' seeming dourness; while it doesn't get picked up on nearly as often, most of his work—not least his recent memoir (Dawkins 2013)—is threaded through with appreciations of beauty, wonder, and enjoyment: the thrill of science and the majesty of nature.

The dangers of emotionalism are also regularly emphasized. For humanists, a "happy-clappy" Christian is, in this sense, more prone to deny reality and common sense. Edward, who ran a local group in London, gave me an example. For a time he worked at a software company, and one of the women he worked with was a Born-Again Christian. Edward once asked her whether, if her church suggested as much, she would say white is black and black is white. When she suggested she would—if that's what her pastor told her—he concluded that further discussion was pointless. This Christian, he told me, was letting subjective relationships upend reality. "An awful lot of religious people are in that situation," he said. "Having emotional reasons for accepting anything." Among humanists, the first reaction to anything, or the first articulation of a position or a view, was normally made in relation to the primacy of reason and a skepticism toward and wariness of emotion.

Yet the humanist commitment to happiness makes it clear that emotion and sentiment are not necessarily antithetical to reason, or a humanist vision of the world. Secular humanism has often come up against versions of this claim—that it drains the passions, or, in a related set of arguments, "disenchants" the world. Indeed, the extent to which secular humanism has been cast as a bloodless, passionless rendering of modernity has even prompted one academic and secular humanist to make a case for "the joy of secularism" (Levine 2011). A new grouping of popular humanist authors has emerged as well, including a chaplain at Harvard University whose book *Good without God: What a billion nonreligious people do believe* is much more focused on the cultivation of community, joy, and happiness as both a pleasure and a purpose (Epstein 2009).[19]

Certainly, within the BHA, Max Weber's key indices of disenchantment—rationalization, calculation, and intellectualization (Weber 1946: 139–40)—are not uncritically lauded. To be sure, humanists do not go in for what Weber called the "intellectual sacrifice" (ibid.: 156) of the believer; this is, as we have seen, precisely what they want to end. It's what Edward understood his colleague to be admitting—deferring, as Ince puts it, to what the high priest or elder says. Yet "thinking for yourself" and "daring to know" do not demand the surrender of the emotional or, even, certain understandings of wonder. In the funerals that BHA celebrants conducted, for instance, or in local group activities and

---

19. See Paul Dolan (2014) for a popular recent argument on the need to understand happiness in relation both to "pleasure and purpose."

discussions, I often found strong appeals to, and endorsements of, emotion and sentiment. BHA celebrants are a small yet important grouping of association members who consciously stop short of the lauding of reason that often marks, or is seen to mark, the secular-humanist disposition. BHA funeral officiants are called "celebrants" for a reason.[20] A BHA funeral is supposed to "celebrate" the life of the deceased. It is not that sadness and mournfulness are denied or discouraged; of course, humanist funerals can be gut wrenching for family and friends. But BHA funerals are often joyful and irreverent in ways which, for the celebrants at least, are part of their ethical and ideological commitments to "the one life we have." Within the funeral industry more generally, there is increasing talk of "the happy funeral," which is juxtaposed to the "solemn" nature of the traditional church counterpart.[21] These days, jocular and ironic Monty Python and Frank Sinatra tunes are more likely to be heard than Anglican hymns or live organ music. BHA celebrants see themselves at the vanguard of this shift, of helping effect a more general transformation away from suffering, sin, and the horizon of happiness being set in an afterlife.

All the same, celebrants had concerns about emotionalism and, because of it, the dangers of irrationality. One of the most common was with respect to what I've called "the coffin question" (see Engelke 2015): many celebrants saw the presence of the coffin at the funeral as a potential rent in the immanent order, an object that could be imbued by the mourners with an agency or animate presence, and prompt emotional breakdowns (the figure of the widow who refuses to let go of the coffin, drowning in tears). Even among the celebrants, then, the ultimate ordering of things was usually clear. Sentiment should be the servant of reason.

It is in the course of explicitly ethical deliberations that the links between happiness, sentiment, and reason can be seen to matter most. Let me illustrate this by turning to an extended example of a collective exercise in which a group of humanists saw themselves as instantiating their commitment to being good without God.

---

20. I did know one celebrant who wouldn't use the label. He insisted on "officiant." As he put it to me: "I'm not going to use 'celebrant' when I phone up a father whose eight-year-old child's just been killed in a car crash and say, 'Hey, we're here to celebrate her life.' I'm not going to say that."

21. See "Happy funerals: a celebration of life?" http://www.bbc.co.uk/news/magazine-31940529, accessed December 1, 2015.

GRAN'S CAT

When I met Edward—the man who couldn't believe his Born-Again Christian colleague's "emotional reasons for accepting anything"—he ran the Green Vale Humanists and Secularists out of a Friends House (Quaker meeting house) on a pleasant, late-Victorian side street in London. Green Vale was not a large local group; it only had about a dozen regular attendees. In Edward, though, they had an enthusiastic and committed chair. He would organize not only the twice-monthly meetings (one at the Friends House for a semiformal discussion with a guest speaker; the other, less formal, for socializing at a pub), but also occasional trips into central London to see a prominent humanist speak at Conway Hall or a university. In the spring, he would organize bluebell walks through a local nature preserve, followed by a pub lunch. Socializing was important to him, and when I last saw him, in July 2014, just as he was in the process of stepping down as chair of the group (in anticipation of a move abroad), he lamented that if he had had more time, he would have worked on building up "practical involvement in the community," visiting more local schools, for instance, and ramping up a mentoring program with which the group had become involved at the nearby prison.

Edward's primary passion as a humanist was for developing what he called "secular morality." He summed this up in three imperatives: be honest with yourself; be kind; be courageous. When I asked him what makes a morality secular, he said: "Self-honesty, because it is incompatible with religion." But self-honesty is not a term he liked; it involves integrity and courage, as well as self-esteem. "It is a source of frustration to me that there is no English word meaning self-honesty," he wrote to me, in an e-mail, when reading a draft of this article. "So far I have not been able to find one in any other language and can't help thinking it could be because our species would rather avoid the subject. If you find such a word in any language, please let me know." Back when we conducted an informal interview, in summer 2014, he said: "I see virtually all religious people as compromising their integrity, their honesty. They're desperate for comfort. If you're not being honest with yourself, you're not living your own life—you're living someone else's." *Sapere aude!*

Ethics and morality were a major focus of all local groups.[22] At Green Vale, they were even more so than usual. This was partly down to the fact that Edward

---

22. As with reason and rationality, most of the humanists I knew used these terms—ethics and morality—interchangeably. For a discussion of how anthropologists can

staged a series of "ethical juries" at the monthly meetings at the Friends House. Between 2010 and 2014, Green Vale hosted five such events. Edward got the idea of running them from Michael Imison, a trustee of the BHA during the course of my research, who came from a career in television and drama (Michael was a director on an early series of *Doctor Who*). Michael is someone who had also been involved in the Society for the Furtherance of Critical Philosophy (SFCP), which recognizes in particular the importance of Immanuel Kant's work. One of the core activities of the SFCP is to facilitate "Socratic dialogues," a key aim of which is to help "people develop capacity to live as independently-thinking rational ethical agents."[23]

I attended an ethical jury at Green Vale in September 2012. It was a Thursday evening and people were slowly arriving at the Friends House. The rented room was small and looked out onto a garden; it was painted that shade of green that only churches and schools seem to have to suffer. We gathered in a circle of chairs around the evening's facilitator, Ralph, who was visiting from elsewhere in the greater London area, and who had experience of running ethical juries. James, the local group treasurer, was chairing the evening in Edward's absence. In addition to the facilitator, treasurer, and me, four women and eight men attended. This included a woman who was a member of the Friends House, and a Sikh man (who self-identified as such, and was wearing a turban). Another was Mark, a young man in his early twenties from a university on England's southern coast. He was involved in the national-level governance of student atheist, humanist, and secularist groups and, like me, wanted to learn more about ethical juries. Mark hoped to conduct an ethical jury back at his university.

As the group came to attention, one of the men asked Ralph: "What do you mean by *ethical*? It's so misused that word." Ralph paused for a moment before replying: "I can tell you an answer off the top of my head," he said, "but it's up to you." With no greater steer, Ralph moved on by welcoming everyone, and then putting up a PowerPoint slide. He also had a flip chart, which would see much use over the course of the evening. The PowerPoint read:

---

approach this issue, see Lambek (2010: 9); following Lambek (and others), I opt for ethics over morality as an analytical term because of its "greater association with action than propriety and with 'the good' than 'the right'."

23. See http://www.sfcp.org.uk/education/, accessed December 1, 2015.

- Ethical Juries: original idea
- Gather jury
- Select dilemma from personal experience
- Discuss – protect your example giver
- Use Golden Rule, Least Harm
- Vote

After expanding on these points briefly (including the basics on different moral philosophies), Ralph asked us to offer up some possible dilemmas. "It's definitely best to have *personal* dilemmas," James said, "so someone can share all the details." James offered one about a relative's relative who needed bail for a sex trafficking offense. One of the women wanted to discuss relativism, but she didn't have a specific dilemma in mind. Mark offered another possibility: his grandmother has asthma and it's starting to take its toll, and she has a cat, which makes it worse. How much should her children and grandchildren intervene? In a scattershot way, two more potential cases emerged: a friend of a member who is committing adultery; and, even less personally, the public apology that day by a national-level politician over his party's broken campaign promise. But the facilitator, who offered up this last example, was also wary of it: "How can we discuss this as a moral question without getting sucked into 'yah-boo' politics?"

With this mix of choices on the table, all scribbled up on the flipchart, the facilitator asked us to decide on one. Nine people wanted to discuss the cat; three voted to discuss the politician's apology; and one—the woman who mentioned it—wanted to discuss relativism. So we went with Gran's cat. Ralph asked Mark for all the "key features" of the situation.

Gran is eighty-four and of sound mind. She is a widow and has been for some time. Mark's mother is her daughter. Mark suffers from asthma and it runs in the family. His gran has always had cats. Someone asks if she's always had breathing difficulties; no, Mark says, and she has only been diagnosed with asthma in the last year. She has always been very active: loves bowling and badminton. "I would say she's irrational about the cat," Mark says. "I would never tell her this. But I'd like her to rehome the cat." Gran also has low hemoglobin and an arthritic hip, so her condition is not all down to the asthma and the cat. "She has been living life as an elderly person very, very well. Not too long ago she went to China for three weeks." Mark asks us if we need any more facts. Everyone is satisfied for the moment.

"We need to pinpoint the moral issues," Ralph said. One of them is intervening. But what is intervening? Do you put pressure on her to get rid of the cat? Or do you just say something?

"I think suggesting to the lady that she get rid of the cat is very reasonable," said a man in a blue shirt. "Just saying something: I don't see that as putting any pressure."

The facilitator wrote this up on the flip chart:

Pressure vs. suggestion

Then an elderly man with glasses and a beard said: "I don't see this as an entirely moral question, really. This is a health and welfare issue. The GP [doctor] can give her a simple choice, which isn't moral."

Another elderly man said: "This is a question of trade-offs. Probably over sixty, you say, no, don't change things." He goes on to tell us he had a friend who died recently, aged seventy, from lots of drinking and smoking. But he wouldn't have told him to stop; he was too old. "And the pleasure was worth it." It would have been doing more harm than good.

"If you were to remove the cat, the loneliness would do more harm," said the Sikh man.

"The GP has to tell her she has a choice," said the elderly man with glasses and a beard, again. "Live with the cat and accept the consequences; or get rid of the cat, live longer but perhaps less happily."

The woman interested in relativism, who was a nurse, raised the possibility of Mark kidnapping the cat. Then she went on to tell us about the health issues and dilemmas she's seen with religious people who refuse treatment, before coming around to Mark's gran. "But it's her choice!" she ended by saying.

Ralph tried to focus us. "What are the moral principles? I'm not seeing these here."

At this point, Mark added that one of the considerations had to be that his gran is of sound mind; she has her faculties. The bearded man, seeming to pick up on the nurse's earlier question, wondered what would happen if the cat just "disappeared."

"I think this is more your problem than your gran's," the Quaker woman suggested.

"That's true in a way, yes," admitted Mark. She's the only grandparent he has left, though, and he doesn't want to lose her.

Ralph wondered: "Is the cat issue more a diversion from the issue of how Gran will look after herself as she gets older?"

Mark didn't really focus on Ralph's question. He went on to tell us his family had the opposite scenario with his paternal grandfather, who was of sound body but not sound mind.

"As a nurse," the nurse offered at that point, "I think that after a few months, she would feel better."

There was some shuffling in the seats at this suggestion; not everyone agreed.

"The most moral solution to the problem is to leave her alone," said the bearded man, definitively.

"Yes," replied Mark. "And we're [Mark's family] very much on the 'suggestion' end [of the facilitator's spectrum]. But she says she's getting depressed about being old."

James came in at this point to suggest that at issue are three ethical principles (respect for autonomy; honesty; concern for welfare) and two "skills" (judgment; diplomacy). Ralph said there's another "moral principle": frankness.

"It's all based on quality of life," said a man who had been quiet to that point.

"As she's of sound mind, you have to respect that," said the bearded man.

"Well, any suggestion is pressure," said the nurse. "What for someone is a suggestion is pressure to someone else."

"That's where diplomacy comes in," Ralph offered.

"There's a least-harm-thing end, as well," said Mark, referencing Ralph's flip chart, which by this point was littered with scribbles, Venn diagrams, and various connecting lines, including a split between the "social/psychological" issues involved and the "physical" ones. Pointing to them, Mark said the social/psychological side and the physical side couldn't be neatly separated.

Ralph started to wrap things up. "How have you experienced this discussion?" he asked Mark.

"I think everyone [relates to] the issue of getting old," Mark said, "because this is very emotionally charged. I haven't heard anything that suggests I should be more interventionist. But I didn't think I would. But I feel happy to have been affirmed. And I can look back on this in years and not feel guilty, feel I've approached it in the right way."

We didn't formally vote after this, but it was clear that the group wasn't suggesting a radical course of action. Given how this only confirmed Mark's view, there was not much further ado. Just as we were about to break up, though, and share some biscuits, the bearded man with glasses said he brought up the GP because it's a GP's job to interfere. A woman in a floral-patterned shirt, who had been totally quiet to that point, jumped in quickly: "And he's objective!" Mark admitted he never would have thought of the GP as relevant (he also didn't say if the GP was a man or a woman); surely it was up to the family. And with that we did get to the biscuits, small talk, and our journeys home.

As with events I observed at other local groups, the ethical jury at Green Vale circled around the exercise of reason, here in the pursuit of happiness. The dilemma posed by Gran's cat involved the issue of responsibility—but also balance, and discerning motivations. What must one do for others, and how can such action be recognized? Was this about Mark's happiness, or his grandmother's? How can her pleasure, in spite of its costs, be differentiated from Mark's pain? Turning the matter over to the doctor—making it a scientific rather than a social issue—was, clearly, a nonstarter for most participants, yet not all of them, and it kept recurring until the very end of the session. I was struck by the after-the-fact contribution by the woman in the floral-patterned shirt. It was as if she had to say it—she had to point to what she perceived as a doctor's objectivity. Objectivity really does matter to humanists; where it is perceived, it must be pursued.

For most of the participants, though, such objectivity was, in this instance, not relevant to the discussion. Without it, what mattered most was Mark's gran's ability to decide for herself. The fact that Mark emphasized his gran was of "sound mind" was crucial to the deliberation. Guided by their own compasses of reason, those gathered had to respect her freedom of choice. Despite Mark's concern that she was being "irrational," the group—and even Mark, I would argue—recognized that rationality and reason are, in some instances, not the final appeal—"Because this is very emotionally charged," as Mark said. The cat made Gran happy. That was what mattered in the end. She was getting increasingly depressed about being old, Mark told us, but the cat was clearly a source of comfort, despite any extent to which it might have been exacerbating her physical condition.

CONCLUSION

In August 2014, almost two years after this ethical jury, I spoke to Mark on the phone. "Things are much the same," he told me. Gran still had the cat. "There's unlikely to be, to my mind, any resolution. The cat will likely outlive Grandma, and the cat gives her a lot of comfort." Mark's love for his grandmother struck me as irrepressible. I was surprised by the course of our phone call. This is not someone I got to know in my research; we only met at the ethical jury and I called him out of the blue. Within a minute of being on the phone, though, Mark was filling me in on his grandmother's continuing verve for life, and her independence. Not long before, he explained, Grandma had prepared a big dinner at her house, much to Mark's mother's dismay; Grandma had only recently returned from a spell in hospital. (And it was always *Grandma* or *Gran* with Mark; he never used the possessive to differentiate her identity.) And then there was her plan to go to Vietnam, at the start of 2014. This was "kiboshed" by Mark's mother, Mark said, much to Grandma's frustration.

Had the ethical jury been helpful? It had, he said. In line with what he said at the jury, it was mostly about confirming his sense of things—about knowing he had reached his decision in the right way. Yet the perspectives of others really helped. "I got the inkling that I was undervaluing the comfort this creature was providing to Grandma. It was well meaning [to think of getting rid of the cat] but perhaps unfounded. . . . The opinions that people give [in ethical juries] are fairly well informed, and I appreciated how these should be taken seriously." He was appreciative of the reasoned deliberation. "It's a funny situation to be in a group where [reason] guides discussion so strongly," he said, but very valuable. Reason, he said, is "an overarching principle. It definitely does guide conversation. But I think there's a self-awareness of it being an unobtainable goal. Part of the human condition is that we want to be reasonable and rational. But we're not."

In his masterly book on Britain and the Enlightenment, Roy Porter has occasion to cite a saturnine remark of William Hazlitt's: "Reason, with most people, means their own opinion" (in 2000: xxiii). Hazlitt is another of the humanists' predecessors and inspirations (he is the subject of a recent biography by A. C. Grayling [2013]), someone for whom reason is *not* one's own opinion. Not entirely.

It is in the tension between the objective and the subjective understandings of reason, and how this relates to happiness as both a pleasure and a purpose, heart and head, that we find Britain's humanists today—people like Mark, for whom "true" reason is an overarching principle, yet one we can never live up to. Mark was "happy," he told the group at Green Vale, to have been confirmed in his thinking. The issue here, though, wasn't about living up to some categorical imperative (à la Kant). Nor was it a straightforward utilitarian calculus (à la Bentham). Humanist ethics are, in the terms of moral philosophy, a virtue ethics, what James Laidlaw has recently described, after Alasdair McIntyre, as "the pursuit of ideals through socially instituted and habituated practices, the importance of narrative understanding and reasoning, and the idea of ethical traditions being constituted in part through ongoing argument" (2014: 79). As one of the BHA's trustees once put it to me, reason "applies when you would have a serious decision to make about *how* to do something, more than *what* to do."[24] Mark was happy to be confirmed in what he did (or didn't do) about his gran and her cat, but the process of deliberation itself, of judgment, was equally central to the character and quality of his happiness.

In *Man a machine*, a mid-eighteenth-century text that was scandalous even by radical Enlightenment standards (see Israel 2001: 704–9), Julien Offray de la Mettrie offered a withering attack on metaphysics and the soul, on the existence of anything beyond the material and here-and-now. His work was offered in praise of science—and of pleasure. "The world will never be happy until it is atheist," he wrote. In such a world, "deaf to all other voices, tranquil mortals would follow only their own spontaneous inner council . . . the only one that can guide us to happiness along the happy paths of virtue" (cited in McMahon 2006: 227).

According to Darrin McMahon, such talk of virtue—and the classically inspired understandings of reason that accompanied it—is misleading in La Mettrie. Virtue was vice: he was a hedonist for hedonism's sake. In his extremism, indeed, he was "snipping the suture that had held Western intellectual life together since the time of Socrates: the link between virtue and happiness; the link between happiness, reason, and truth" (ibid.: 229).

Humanists in Britain might well cheer at La Mettrie's remark: being good without God is, in the final analysis, for them, the only authentic option. The world will never be happy until it is atheist. But humanists are not snipping at the suture of Western intellectual life. As I have tried to show throughout this article, they work to reinforce the link between virtue and happiness—to make

---

24. See also Lambek's (2010: 19–25) discussion of Aristotelian virtues, in which "a practice is ethical insofar as the goal is not instrumental but reaching for excellence within the particular practice—and for human good or happiness overall in the practice of practices" (ibid.: 21). This is precisely what was at stake in the deliberation on Gran's cat.

happiness about the heart, but also the head. Socrates still matters in their view, alongside the watershed validation of pleasure.

Maybe we could say humanists want to have their cake and eat it too—or their Chelsea Whoppers, as the case may be. Pleasure is part and parcel of the humanist vision of the world; it is something we deserve to have. But pleasure for humanists comes not solely in the act of consumption or consummation, for any such act must be seen as part of an overarching commitment to the idea of happiness, to what it means to be good without God—to strive for the values of Enlightenment and "the one life we have."

ACKNOWLEDGMENTS

Research for this article was funded by the Economic and Social Research Council (RES-000-22-4157). I would like to thank the many humanists—named and anonymous—who gave so generously of their time for this work; some also read drafts of this article and provided helpful feedback. Parts of the paper were presented to the "Green Vale" group in October 2015. Harry Walker and Iza Kavedžija deserve special mention, as well, for their thoughtful comments at several stages and for organizing the workshop at the London School of Economics and Political Science at which the first draft was delivered; I also benefited a lot from a writing workshop luncheon with my departmental colleagues at the LSE. Other drafts were presented in seminars at Duke University, the University of Michigan at Ann Arbor, the University of Cambridge, and King's College London; my thanks to the organizers and audiences on those occasions.

REFERENCES

Anderson, Benedict. 1991. *Imagined communities: Reflections on the origins and spread of nationalism.* Second edition. London: Verso.

Budd, Susan. 1977. *The varieties of unbelief: Atheists and agnostics in English society, 1850–1960.* London: Heinemann.

Colson, Elizabeth. 2012. "Happiness," in Vital Topics Forum: "On happiness," 7–8. *American Anthropologist* 114 (4): 6–18.

Corsín Jiménez, Alberto, ed. 2008. *Culture and well-being: Anthropological approaches to freedom and political ethics*. London: Pluto.

Dawkins, Richard. 2013. *An appetite for wonder: The making of a scientist*. London: Black Swan.

Dolan, Paul. 2014. *Happiness by design: Finding pleasure and purpose in everyday life*. London: Penguin.

Engelke, Matthew. 2015. "The coffin question: Death and materiality in humanist funerals." *Material Religion* 11 (1): 26–49.

Epstein, Greg. 2009. *Good without God: What a billion nonreligious people do believe*. New York: William Morrow.

Fischer, Edward F. 2014. *The good life: Aspiration, dignity, and the anthropology of wellbeing*. Palo Alto, CA: Stanford University Press.

Grayling, A. C. 2013. *The quarrel of the age: The life and times of William Hazlitt*. London: Phoenix.

Inglehart, Ronald, Miguel Basáñez, and Alejandro Menéndez Moreno. 1998. *Human values and beliefs: A cross-cultural sourcebook*. Ann Arbor: University of Michigan Press.

Israel, Jonathan. 2001. *Radical Enlightenment: Philosophy and the making of modernity, 1650–1750*. Oxford: Oxford University Press.

Jackson, Michael. 2013. *The wherewithal of Life: Ethics, migration and the question of well-being*. Berkeley: University of California Press.

Jacoby, Susan. 2013. *The great agnostic: Robert Ingersoll and American freethought*. New Haven, CT: Yale University Press.

Kant, Immanuel. 1963. "What is Enlightenment?" In *On history*. Edited and translated by Lewis White Beck, 3–10. Indianapolis: Bobbs-Merrill.

Laidlaw, James. 2014. *The subject of virtue: An anthropology of ethics and freedom*. Cambridge: Cambridge University Press.

Lambek, Michael. 2010. "Introduction." In *Ordinary ethics: Anthropology, language, and action*, edited by Michael Lambek, 1–36. New York: Fordham University Press.

Layard, Richard. 2006. *Happiness: Lessons from a new science*. London: Penguin.

Levine, George, ed. 2011. *The joy of secularism: 11 essays for how we live now*. Princeton, NJ: Princeton University Press.

McMahon, Darrin. 2006. *Happiness: A history*. New York: Grove Press.

Porter, Roy. 2000. *Enlightenment: Britain and the creation of the modern world*. London: Penguin.

Russell, Bertrand. 1930. *The conquest of happiness*. London: Allen & Unwin.

Smith, Jesse M. 2013. "Creating a godless community: The collective identity work of contemporary American atheists." *Journal for the Scientific Study of Religion* 52 (1): 80–99.

Sorkin, David. 2008. *The religious enlightenment: Protestants, Catholics and Jews from London to Vienna.* Princeton, NJ: Princeton University Press.

Stavrova, Olga, Detlef Fetchenhauer, and Thomas Schlösser. 2013. "Why are religious people happy? The effect of the social norm of religiosity across countries." *Social Science Research* 42: 90–105.

Thin, Neil. 2012. *Social happiness: Theory into policy and practice.* Bristol: Policy Press.

Weber, Max. 1946. "Science as a vocation." In *From Max Weber: Essays in sociology.* Edited and translated by H. H. Gerth and C. Wright Mills, 129–57. Oxford: Oxford University Press.

Wilkins, Amy C. 2008. "'Happier than non-Christians': Collective emotions and symbolic boundaries among evangelical Christians." *Social Psychology Quarterly* 71 (3): 281–301.

Zuckerman, Phil. 2008. *Society without god: What the least religious nations can tell us about contentment.* New York: NYU Press.

CHAPTER SIX

Mindful in Westminster
The politics of meditation and the limits of neoliberal critique

Joanna Cook

HAPPINESS AND NEOLIBERALISM

The in-depth ethnographic approach to happiness taken in this volume reveals the concern people take to live well. The essays collected here explore the temporalities of happiness, as well as the self-making, evaluative judgments and shared values that lead to and constitute happiness in both the short and the long term. These are variously considered with reference to the incorporation of ambivalence (Throop), finding balance between immediacy and narrative location (Kavedžija), or the integration of good character, social justice, and self-realization (Lambek), for example.

Such an anthropological contribution to contemporary discussion about happiness is welcome. It provides a timely redress to the relative lack of anthropological intervention in current debates on the subject elsewhere. This silence is in part the result of an association drawn by social scientists between political interest in emotional wellbeing and forms of neoliberal governance. As the editors of this collection note, "There is a certain suspicion of happiness as an essentially bourgeois preoccupation, increasingly associated with a neoliberal agenda, and potentially at odds with emancipatory politics." In such a framework, happiness becomes a personal responsibility divorced from broader structural conditions, and its pursuit becomes a self-conscious project of self-improvement, irrespective of the social or political contexts in which such projects are found. As such, is it little wonder that, in a volume that reveals the multiple values and temporalities of happiness, political interest in the emotions remains "a little disappointing" (see Robbins' Afterword, this volume), framed as it is as the atrophying embrace of "the purveyors of neoliberalism" (see the Introduction, this volume)?

Political interest in happiness is located at the "very busy crossroads of psychology, economics, and policy discourse" (Robbins, this volume). I take one such crossroads as my ethnographic focus in order to examine the analytic framework of neoliberalism itself. I focus on an All-Party Parliamentary Group in Westminster convened to investigate the policy potential for mindfulness in the UK in order to ask whether political interest in mindfulness renders individuals solely responsible for their own wellbeing. What social and moral values inform the process of political inquiry and are they accounted for by the analytic framework of neoliberalism?

I argue that an interpretation of political interest in wellbeing as "neoliberalism" is too narrow to account for the multiplicity of interests and values incorporated in the process of political inquiry. For all that it can be analytically useful to theorise neoliberalism as the colonization of the emotions, against which social scientists rail, in practice that colonization is rarely total. I argue that subjectification practices, even those critiqued as "neoliberal," are rarely totalizing, that self-governance is not divorced from broader structural or politico-economic concerns, and that subjectification practices may hold diverse or multiple meanings. To reduce political interest in happiness and wellbeing to "neoliberal responsibilization" inhibits us from accounting for the multiplicity of values and motivations involved in political inquiry. By remaining anchored in ethnography it becomes possible to identify the limits of neoliberalism. In so doing we are able to account for the multiplicity of values with which the political inquiry process is invested. Furthermore, I argue that once we recognize the multiplicity of values, which lies beyond the scope of an analytic framework of neoliberalism, we are able to examine the ways in which the maintenance of this multiplicity provides a motor for political processes. If, following Joel Robbins (this volume), we assume that all social formations contain a plurality of values, then we ought to be cautious of dismissing political interest in wellbeing as unitary neoliberalism: here too, ethnographic inquiry reveals complex, socially embedded concerns with happiness and wellbeing that cannot be contained within the narrow analytic framework of "neoliberal responsibilization."

IDENTIFYING THE LIMITS OF NEOLIBERALISM

The concept of neoliberalism has been central to social scientific analyses of the relationship between changing forms of state responsibility, socioeconomic organization, and forms of reflexive self-governance. "Neoliberalism" is used to account for the development of a more technocratic and managerial role for the state (Gledhill 2004; Ferguson 2006) based on a belief in the justice of the market leading to deregulation, flexible working, the liberalization of capital, the reduction of the state, and restrictions on public spending. This is sometimes characterized as a move away from a theory of social welfare as the responsibility of government through a reinterpretation of the governability of subjects (Rose 1999a, 1999b). Risk and uncertainty increase as a result of changing socioeconomic structures at the same time as technologies of "responsibilization" proliferate (Rose 1996a, 2001, 2007; Shamir 2008), by which state involvement in social welfare is reduced and replaced with groups and individuals who are encouraged to "take responsibility" for self-governance and decision making (Bennett 2008). Sennett suggests that under such conditions individuals must dwell "in a continual state of vulnerability" (1998: 83; see also 2006). Writing of flexible corporate practice, he argues that people are driven to achieve, but the institutional structures by which this might occur are left open and flexible. The economic necessity to pursue multiple possibilities and the capacity to adapt to volatile and changeable demands requires a particular strength of character, "that of someone who has the confidence to dwell in disorder, someone who flourishes in the midst of dislocation" (Sennett 1998: 62). Sennett argues that the freedom of the flexible capitalist is amoral, and that the demands of spontaneity and flexibility can be self-destructive.[1] The individual is responsible for maximizing her emotional capital, and needs to protect herself in a condition of endemic uncertainty. The management of risk, engagement, and response

---

1.   Similarly, Bauman (2007) has argued that social forms and institutions no longer act as frames of reference, and individuals learn to be flexible and adaptable under conditions of unending precarity.

becomes the responsibility of the individual (Beck 1992). With the diminution of the events and conditions that influence experience (the "happ" of happiness), experience must be privately created. Resilience and flexibility are required in an environment of uncertainty and risk, in which institutional supports have been rescinded to the capricious demands of consumer capitalism.

Drawing on Foucauldian theory, Rose has analyzed neoliberalism as a practice of governance for the minimization of costs and maximization of profits, as "a 'way of doing' directed towards objectives and regulating itself through continuous reflection" (Foucault 2008: 318). He argues that neoliberal governance is achieved through techniques that encourage subjects to take responsibility for their decision making and subject formation (Rose 1999a). Neoliberal governance is understood to be based on processes of "subjectivation"—identity-forming processes by which the subject is constituted. The state and professional organizations assume the role of managing populations for optimal productivity, while subjects take responsibility for their own self-governance. These processes of self-governance lead subjects to act in ways that reinforce their subjection (Rose 1996b). Under this transformed understanding of governance and responsibility, the subject is "free" to make choices concerning her own welfare, guided by the management of an "empowering" state. Such responsibility is meted out to all subjects irrespective of the structural or socioeconomic factors that might impinge on any form of decision making (Rose 1999b; Ferguson and Gupta 2002; Ong 2006). The neoliberal subject becomes "an entrepreneur of himself" (Foucault 2010: 226), and work upon the self becomes an investment in capital. Gershon characterizes this as "a self that is a flexible bundle of skills that reflexively manages oneself as though the self was a business" (2011: 537).[2] Governing individual dispositions, emotions, and motivations then becomes an individual responsibility and the site of governmental focus, structured by economic interests and market logic (Rose 1996a, 1996b). Individuals become productive members of society, not only through their labour, but also through the labour to shape themselves as such. The subject has to be educated ("made up," in Rose and Miller's terms [1992]) through techniques that enable her to take herself as a project, as if she were her own entrepreneur.

Analytically, the concept of neoliberalism helps to account for the relationship between forms of governance, self-governance, and capitalist market

---

2.   For Gershon, neoliberal agency creates relationships that are morally lacking and overlooks differences in scale.

forces. But how do we decipher its limits? Are there forms of governance and reflexive self-governance that are not accounted for by a focus on neoliberal "entrepreneurialism"? As Hilgers asks, "Should we regard any mode of government that adopts a principle of optimisation, sometimes in a single domain, as neoliberal?" (2010: 360). In this contribution, I consider the limits of neoliberalism through an ethnographic focus on political interest in mindfulness-based interventions in civil society. In the United Kingdom, mindfulness is a political concern. Mindfulness meditation, an awareness practice which originated in Buddhism, is being interpreted as a positive intervention for societal problems as wide ranging as depressive relapse, criminal recidivism, children's academic performance, and worker burnout. It is believed to help practitioners cope with life (from stress, anxiety, and depression to impulse control, emotional regulation, and intellectual flexibility) and is now taught in major civil society institutions in the United Kingdom, including hospitals, prisons, schools, and private businesses. In 2014, an All-Party Parliamentary Group (APPG) was established in Westminster, committed to investigating the ways in which public policy might incorporate mindfulness-based practices. From May–December 2014, eight parliamentary hearings of the Mindfulness All-Party Parliamentary Group (MAPPG) were held in Westminster, each focusing on a different area of public life. An inquiry report was drafted by the supporting secretariat outlining key policy recommendations for funding, implementation, and research, and this was launched in Parliament in October 2015.

As a focus of public policy, is mindfulness training placed in the service of neoliberal governance? Through an ethnographic consideration of parliamentary hearings on mindfulness, participant observation with the secretariat (the Mindfulness Initiative), interviews with members, and analysis of the final policy document, *Mindful Nation UK*, I examine the ways in which issues of self-governance and responsibility were motivated, debated, and framed. In the following, I argue that an analysis of political interest in mindfulness as "neoliberalism" frames subjectification as making people totally responsible for their mental health, detached from a broader socioeconomic and structural context. This is not borne out ethnographically. Furthermore, I argue that an analysis of self-governance as neoliberalism assumes that practices of subjectification are always already in the service of neoliberalism. Rather than offering either a critique of, or an apology for, mindfulness, I take political interest in mindfulness as my ethnographic focus in order to examine the multiple meanings and values invested in subjectification practices, and the ways in which diversity is maintained through the structure of political inquiry. Mindfulness as a political focus is being framed in multiple ways simultaneously, many of which lie beyond the limits of the analytic framework of neoliberalism. I argue that the political value of the inquiry process rested on the maintenance of multiplicity in the meanings and values of self-governance.

MINDFULNESS IN PARLIAMENT AND THE ESTABLISHMENT OF THE APPG

Mindfulness, as it is now found in British workplaces, education, healthcare, and criminal justice, originated in Buddhist meditation. It gained legitimacy as a secular and therapeutic practice following the development of mindfulness-based stress reduction in the 1970s and mindfulness-based cognitive therapy in the 1990s, and subsequent scientific research into their efficacy. Beginning in the 1950s in Southeast Asia, reformist monks developed, reinvigorated, and propagated a form of meditation, *vipassanā*, based on a Buddhist text, *The Mahāsatipaṭṭhāna Sutta* (see Jordt 2007; Cook 2010; Braun 2013). The propagation of *vipassanā* was presented as a move away from "esoteric" meditative practices toward a more "rational" and "authentic" practice for salvation, available to monastics and laity (Van Esterik 1977). Mindfulness (Pali: *sati*) was understood to be an ethically positive perspectival awareness, which could be cultivated through meditative discipline, requiring morality, concentration, and wisdom. In the 1970s, Jon Kabat-Zinn developed mindfulness-based stress reduction (MBSR), at the University of Massachusetts Medical Center, originally to address chronic pain and a range of conditions that were difficult to treat (Kabat-Zinn 1990).[3] He interpreted mindfulness as a universal human capacity that could be developed by patients in order to alleviate suffering. In his foreword to the APPG Inquiry Report, *Mindful Nation UK*, he writes that mindfulness—

being about attention, awareness, relationality, and caring—is a universal capacity, akin to our capacity for language acquisition. While the most systematic

---

3.   Earlier movements had sought to explore the benefits of dialogue between psychology and Buddhist and meditative practice (for a history of the dialogue between Buddhism and psychology in America, see Metcalf 2002; on the relationship between psychology and Zen Buddhism, see Fromm, Suzuki and De Martino 1970; on the psychological framing of Transcendental Meditation, see Williamson 2010).

and comprehensive articulation of mindfulness and its related attributes stems from the Buddhist tradition, mindfulness is not a catechism, an ideology, a belief system, a technique or set of techniques, a religion, or a philosophy. It is best described as "a way of being." (Mindfulness All-Party Parliamentary Group UK 2015: 5)

In his development of MBSR, Kabat-Zinn sought to routinize mindfulness in targeted interventions in order to address the suffering of ill health in pragmatic ways.

Drawing inspiration from MBSR, mindfulness-based cognitive therapy (MBCT) was developed in 1991 by Zindel Segal, Mark Williams, and John Teasdale in Cambridge, England, as a psychosocial intervention for the prevention of depressive relapse (Segal, Williams, and Teasdale 2013). In the cognitive framework for depressive relapse, suffering was interpreted as resulting from the ways in which patients related to experiences, rather than the experiences themselves. As such, if patients could learn to relate to experience differently, they would suffer less. Thus, the cognitive framework of MBCT rests on the premises that there is a cognitive component to depressive relapse and that people have the capacity to learn ways of relating to their thoughts and feelings that will enable them to maintain mental and emotional balance, even in the face of challenging experiences. MBCT was found to reduce depressive relapse in three randomized-controlled trials (RCTs) (Teasdale et al. 2000; Ma and Teasdale 2004; Kuyken et al. 2008), following which it received recommendation from the National Institute for Health and Care Excellence (NICE) and was mandated on the National Health Service (NHS) for people who had experienced three or more depressive episodes, but who were currently well. The contemporary interest in mindfulness results, in part, from an increasing evidence base for mindfulness-based interventions and their subsequent uptake.[4]

Despite the findings of the RCTs and the NICE recommendation, MBCT remained widely inaccessible across the NHS. One of its developers, Mark Williams, proposed the introduction of mindfulness courses for politicians in Westminster in order to bring MBCT to their attention. As one of the chairs

---

4. There is increasing evidence that MBCT might help large numbers of people experiencing depressive affect and patterns of recurring depression (cf. Baer 2003; Coelho, Canter, and Ernst 2007). Kuyken et al. (2008) demonstrate that MBCT is equivalent to maintenance antidepressants for the prevention of depressive relapse but is superior in terms of quality of life and residual depressive symptoms.

of the APPG commented, he "decided the only way to get the policy establish-ment really engaging with mindfulness was to take it to them." Williams col-laborated in an in-Parliament initiative led by Richard Layard, an economist and life peer in the House of Lords, and Chris Ruane, then a Labour MP,[5] to establish mindfulness courses for parliamentarians. To date, 130 parliamentar-ians and 220 staff have completed an adapted MBCT course in Westminster. The course is taught in groups of eight to twelve led by a trained therapist, over an eight-week period. The most commonly used definition of mindful-ness in this context is "the awareness that emerges through paying attention on purpose, in the present moment, and nonjudgementally, to things as they are" (Segal, Williams, and Teasdale 2013: 132). The group meets once a week for two and a half hours. Aspects that are taught in the course include attentional control (mindfulness) cognitive skills (decentering, observational capacity), and behavioral skills (developing active/movement body-based skills) (ibid.). The course is built up of a series of intentional exercises, including mindfulness of breath, mindful movement, a body scan, mindful eating, as well as intentionally bringing an attitude of kindly awareness to everyday activities such as doing the washing up, eating, or bathing. Each session is followed by "homework"—guid-ed mindfulness practices which participants listen to at home, bringing mind-ful awareness to specified routine activities, and pleasant and unpleasant events calendars; in the penultimate week, participants also complete an action plan.

In a presentation to the London Buddhist Society, one of the key nonpar-liamentary members of the APPG commented, "The thing about politicians is once they get the taste of something they want to do something. And this is an important point actually, because the doing has a sort of driving momentum." Politicians who had completed a mindfulness course sought to establish an APPG to identify problematic issues that were being faced in four areas of civil society—the criminal justice system, the national curriculum, the NHS, and the workplace—and the potential for mindfulness-based interventions to address them. APPGs are informal cross-party groups brought together to develop pol-icy recommendations for government on subjects for which there is cross-party interest. Nominally run by members of the Commons and Lords, the secre-tariat is provided by individuals and organizations from outside Parliament. The APPG was supported by the Mindfulness Initiative, an advocacy/"secretariat"

---

5.   Chris Ruane was the member of Parliament for the Vale of Clwyd. He lost his seat in the General Election of May 2015.

group comprised of professionals from a range of areas, drawn together by their professional and personal commitment to mindfulness. These included a senior journalist, the directors of Bangor and Oxford University Mindfulness Centres, the founder of the Mindfulness in Schools Project, the clinical lead for an NHS trust, and a senior economist and peer. Associates of the Mindfulness Initiative included a director of the Royal Society of Arts, a director from the corporate sector, experts in mindfulness and the criminal justice system, clinical psychologists, the chief operating officer of an educational trust, and others. The mission of the APPG was set out as providing a forum for discussion in Parliament about the role of mindfulness in public policy, promoting mindfulness in tackling a range of critical challenges that the government faced, advocating for more research to strengthen the existing evidence base, and showcasing best practice.

In May 2014, the APPG was launched in Parliament in an atmosphere of anticipation. In a large meeting room in Westminster, there was standing room only as approximately three hundred people, including thirty members of Parliament (MPs), crowded in attendance. Professor Willem Kuyken, a cognitive psychologist and the director of the Oxford Mindfulness Centre, described the meeting as "a wow moment," and a palpable sense of excitement filled the room. After the launch, eighteen people came forward to the organizers and asked how they could help. As one of the organizers said later, "They covered such a wide range of skills and backgrounds . . . this is 80 percent volunteer effort." From May–December 2014, eight parliamentary hearings of the APPG were held in Westminster, each focusing on a different area of public life. These were: mindfulness in the workplace; mindfulness and mental health; mindfulness in the criminal justice system; mindfulness and physical pain and mindfulness for NHS staff; mindfulness in education; mindfulness in the workplace II; mindfulness and policing; and mindfulness and gangs. Following the inquiry period, a report was written by the Mindfulness Initiative on behalf of the MPs who had chaired the inquiry. The report was launched in Parliament in October 2015. It outlined the character and scale of the challenges identified in health, education, the workplace, and the criminal justice system, and the existing evidence for mindfulness-based interventions. It called for targeted interventions in each area and funding for further research.[6] Each section of the report was written

---

6. The report can be viewed online (see Mindfulness All-Party Parliamentary Group 2015).

by two or three members of the Mindfulness Initiative, and these sections were then edited into a single document by two editors. The contributions of each of these people were smoothed into a single voice and there are no authors named in the final document.

MINDFUL NEOLIBERALS?

Over the period of the inquiry process, public interest in mindfulness reached unprecedented heights and mindfulness made frequent appearances in the media. The primary academic analysis of the popularity of secular mindfulness practice has been that it is a neoliberal tool: it has been analyzed as reflecting changing frameworks of state responsibility and an increasing emphasis on the "responsibility" of subjects to self-manage at a time of increasing privatization. It has enabled governance at a distance by making people responsible for their own mental health. For example, Purser and Loy (2013) write of recent interest in mindfulness,

> There is a dissociation between one's own personal transformation and the kind of social and organizational transformation that takes into account the causes and conditions of suffering in the broader environment. Such a colonization of mindfulness also has an instrumentalizing effect, reorienting the practice to the needs of the market, rather than to a critical reflection on the causes of our collective suffering.

Žižek (2001) has gone further and proclaimed that "Western Buddhism . . . is establishing itself as the hegemonic ideology of global capitalism." He argues that a "western Buddhism meditative stance" functions as an ideological supplement to the stress of capitalist dynamics, and is "arguably the most efficient way for us to fully participate in capitalist dynamics while retaining the appearance of mental sanity." Such critiques extend into the relationship between "emotional self-optimization" and happiness. For example, Binkley (2014) argues that through self-help books, spiritual mentoring, business management, and relationship counseling, happiness is presented as attainable by everyone, irrespective of their socioeconomic circumstances, dispositions, or life experiences, and this leads to a moral responsibility to be happy. As he writes, "We are all complicit in our own asphyxiation everyday. We do the work of asphyxiation, we call it our freedom, our enterprise, and our happiness. And we should stop" (ibid.: 175). Similarly, Ehrenreich (2009) argues that positive thinking has entered a symbiotic relationship with capitalism in America, with an emphasis on unending consumption and an imperative for growth. She argues that in the United States, happiness is in the service of a rightwing neoliberal agenda in which it becomes a moral and a personal responsibility.

According to such critiques, happiness and wellbeing are psychologized and individualized, such that they become the responsibility of the individual rather than reflective of broader structural, political, or social inequalities that require redress. A search for happiness becomes now a self-conscious project of self-improvement that can be trained and cultivated, and mindfulness is a means by which this might be achieved.[7] In the United Kingdom, Davies has argued that the emotions have become enslaved to neoliberalism:

> Once social relationships can be viewed as medical and biological properties of the human body, they can become dragged into the limitless pursuit of self optimization that counts for happiness in the age of neoliberalism. (2015: 213)

Davies argues that a focus on happiness as a personal responsibility deflects attention from socioeconomic struggle. It is suggested that individualizing and psychologizing wellbeing or mental health does nothing to address the structural inequalities or forms of political disenfranchisement that may lead to the experience of negative feelings in the first place. Stress, anxiety, and depression are reframed as personal, not political, problems. In a consideration of the micromanagement of individuals, he writes:

> If a certain physical context (such as work or poverty) is causing pain, one progressive route would involve changing that context. But another equivalent would be to focus on changing the way in which it is experienced. . . . If lifting

---

7.   In such a reading of mindfulness, the emotionally "fit" are happy. They put their time in on the meditation mat, and the result is hedonic buffness. As Nandy puts it, such a conceptualization rests on "a self-conscious, determined search for happiness from a mental state to an objectified quality of life that can be attained the way an athlete—after training under a specialist and going through a strict regimen of exercises and diet—wins a medal in a track meet" (2012: 45). The implication of this is that unhappiness does not result from external circumstances but is a personal failure.

weights becomes too painful, you're faced with a choice: reduce the size of the weight, or pay less attention to the pain. In the early twenty-first century, there is a growing body of experts in "resilience" training, mindfulness, and cognitive behavioural therapy whose advice is to opt for the latter strategy. (2015: 35)

While this is a poor account of "resilience" training, mindfulness and cognitive behavioral therapy,[8] we might make his argument better. It could be argued that training in mindfulness is creating exactly the forms of reflexive subjectivity on which neoliberalism thrives. Mindfulness is being encouraged in civil society as a technique for cultivating a particular reflexive perspective, which fosters intellectual flexibility and emotional resilience. Through repetitive and ongoing training, practitioners seek to develop a different relationship to thoughts, feelings, and bodily sensations. Thus, developing an analysis of mindfulness as a neoliberal tool, we could argue that mindfulness not only aligns with neoliberalism, but it also provides the motor for it: learning practices of emotional regulation and reflexive awareness "responsibilizes" practitioners, who are simultaneously "resilient" enough to remain unaffected by the emotional and psychological effects of neoliberal uncertainty and individualism. Suffering becomes the responsibility of the individual rather than a result of sociopolitical influences such as class, race, gender, or the happenstance of misfortune. Furthermore, individualizing suffering silences the possibility of addressing it as a social or a political issue. In such a reading, the current political interest in mindfulness is indicative of broader political shifts in which state responsibility for social welfare has been ceded to technocratic managerialism.

THE LIMITS OF NEOLIBERALISM

Is mindfulness in Parliament a neoliberal tool of "responsibilization" at a time when the state is assuming an increasingly managerial role, social welfare

---

8.   For example, mindfulness practitioners learn to pay *more* attention to thoughts, feelings, and bodily sensations, not less. Mindfulness-based interventions that address depression and anxiety are premised on the theory that patterns of emotional avoidance function to reinforce negative emotional states. Learning to pay attention "in a particular way, on purpose, in the present moment and non-judgmentally" may alleviate suffering because aversive patterns that contribute to emotional distress are reduced (Segal, Williams, and Teasdale 2013).

provision is being radically reduced, and significant funding cuts to the NHS are leading some to argue that we are witnessing a process of "stealth privatization" (Lacobucci 2013)? In the following, I will develop an ethnographic argument critiquing such a position by demonstrating that subjectification practices are never totalizing, that politico-economic concerns remain central to professional interest in self-governance, that subjectification practices may hold multiple and/or diverse meanings (cf. Cruickshank 1999), and that the maintenance of this multiplicity is essential in the process of political inquiry.

Mindfulness practice encourages practitioners to "turn toward" difficulty. It is a technique that is explicitly intended to enable a practitioner to relate to herself differently, with an attitude of "friendly curiosity" and compassion (Feldman and Kuyken 2011). This fits comfortably within a framework of subjectification and reflexive self-governance. But, as I will argue, to theorize this as a practice of neoliberal "responsibilization" by which the practitioner is made totally responsible for her own mental health detached from her socioeconomic and structural context is not borne out ethnographically. In part, this theorization rests on an assumption that neoliberalism has achieved what is feared, that the subject who learns to "take responsibility" for her own wellbeing and happiness does so totally: if we are not there yet, then we are on the verge of a Huxleyan dystopia in which "happiness" is achieved though the soma of mindfulness. Recognizing the limits of neoliberalism moves us away from a conceptualization of neoliberalism as a totalizing ideology and allows us to explore the practices of people who recognize collective and structural causes of suffering at the same time as seeking practices of subjectification for improving wellbeing.

Throughout the inquiry process, participants worried over the unhappiness reported in large-scale surveys and the prevalence of mental health issues presented in epidemiological statistics, basing their discussions on professional and personal experience. In contexts of limited institutional and financial support, many had introduced mindfulness courses into their work in an effort to address suffering. Speaking with a mental health nurse from Devon, I asked him how he had developed a mindfulness course at work.

Well the real challenge is the practical stuff . . . and the culture. At work there's no time and no money. I'm working with patients all day, under pressure, there's never enough time. And I had to work hard to set it up. I couldn't have done it without my supervisor's support . . . finding a room was a nightmare.

Outside of the hearings, discussion oriented around governmental cuts to funding, the increasing prevalence of mental health issues presented in epidemiological statistics, and the challenges that speakers had experienced in establishing mindfulness courses. For the people involved, mindfulness was not understood as a mask for austerity. They understood mindfulness as an intervention that might help people deal with stress, anxiety, and depression in contexts of social and political disenfranchisement. This came as a response to the immediate challenges of working with people who face mental health issues during a time of privatization and a shrinking state mandate for social welfare. Mental health was framed as a major problem in the United Kingdom, and this was, in part, because of the increasing risk, inequality, and hardship that people in different populations in the country were thought to face. Rather than looking at the macro-level of neoliberal forces, which can appear totalizing in their colonization of wellbeing and the responsibility to self-manage, by exploring the ethnography of political process we can account for the concerns and interests of people working in different sectors of civil society. The promotion of mindfulness in public policy was an effort to do something about the tangible struggles that professionals describe witnessing in each of their sectors, given that each sector is undergoing transformation.

The relationship between self-governance and political economy is an important one. Governmental emphasis on patient empowerment emerges from changing relationships between state and citizens, and the role that the state plays in the welfare of citizens. It is not a coincidence that austerity and a discourse of "patient empowerment" are developing simultaneously. But not taking this seriously enough casts it as merely a smokescreen for austerity (cf. Howell 2015).[9] Encouraging subjects to take responsibility for their mental health is understood as a form of governance that "tricks" them into self-governance and effaces political-economic relations. Practices of self-governance are interpreted

---

9.   In Howell's research on psychological resilience in military settings, resilience training is understood to optimize military force, and to reduce healthcare costs by preempting mental distress in soldiers at a time of shrinking defense expenditure. It is possible to interpret this as a form of training by which soldiers are made responsible for their own mental health, which has the effect of effacing a politics of austerity in which welfare entitlements are shrinking. But Howell argues that this is an insufficient analysis of the aims of military resilience programs, which are to enhance (not just to responsibilize) soldiers, "a more ambitious aim than responsibilisation" (2015: 69).

as only individualizing and psychologizing suffering, and thereby obfuscating the social or political causes of mental health issues at a time of increasing social welfare cuts. Patient empowerment, then, becomes a mask for austerity.

While anthropologists have theorized neoliberalism as a mode of governance based on an entrepreneurial model that emphasizes individual risk and responsibility (Gupta and Ferguson 1992), they have noted that it is rarely, if ever, totalizing in practice. Kingfisher and Maskovsky (2008) consider the limits and challenges to theories of neoliberalism highlighted by the implementation of neoliberal policies. They point to the unevenness of neoliberalism's spread and the ways in which it articulates and intersects with other political-cultural formations and governing projects. Their aim is "to treat neoliberalism as a process rather than a fait accompli" (ibid.: 115; see also Maskovsky and Kingfisher 2001), thereby highlighting the production and reproduction of patterns of inequality, and questioning the totalizing nature of neoliberalism. In so doing, they are able to provide analytical space to consider the limits of neoliberalism. Elsewhere, anthropologists have demonstrated that local manifestations reveal the limits of neoliberalism and its articulation with other cultural, political, and economic forms (see Gledhill 2004; Freeman 2007).

Healthcare policy provides fertile ground for thinking about these limits. Patients are increasingly encouraged to make decisions for themselves, which are simultaneously embedded in broader networks of responsibility and care (Zignon 2010; Fordyce 2012). Trnka and Trundle (2014) suggest that ideologies of patient "empowerment" in which the citizen is imagined as independent and responsible, self-managing, and acting in a way that promotes her own health and wellbeing may in practice be neither realized nor desired. Forms of identity, collectivity, and interpersonal connections may intersect with and contest neoliberal frames. Trnka and Trundle argue that "social actors . . . move between different moral, ethical, and affective valences of what it means to be 'responsible' subjects without necessarily feeling conflicted, in need of resolution, or necessitating 'moral breakdown'" (ibid.: 141; see also Zigon 2010). Social relations incorporate multiple framings of responsibility, sometimes accounted for through neoliberal logics of self-responsibility and care of the self, and sometimes interpreted in terms of interpersonal responsibility and obligation. As Trnka and Trundle argue, "Despite its flexibility, neoliberalism cannot encompass the breadth of subjectivities and collective relations that constitute contemporary enactments of responsibility" (2014: 141) Furthermore, guidelines promoting self-managed care may be interpreted in multiple ways, informed by preexisting understandings of responsibility and accountability in healthcare (Scheldeman 2008; Trnka 2014). Responsibility has been central to a range of anthropological concerns, including: political justice and an equitable system (Rawls [1971] 1999; Corsín Jiménez 2008); national identity and kinship (Gammeltoff 2007); personal and professional ethics (Brodwin 2013); agency and moral blame (Davis 2012); and self-care and decision making (see Mol 2008; Premkumar 2015). A theory of neoliberal "responsibilization" helps to account for the ways in which the subject becomes responsible for emotional self-regulation. But if the category of "responsiblization" remains limited to the neoliberal framework, it becomes hard to account for other forms of responsibility or responsiblization that might be in play, or the multiple effects of reflexive self-governance.

THE MEANINGS OF MINDFULNESS: MAINTAINING MULTIPLICITY

A danger of theorizing practices of subjectification as neoliberal is that they come to be read as always already in the service of a neoliberal agenda. If neoliberalism has permeated the regulation of the emotions, then there is no room to understand attempts to address what are identified as the dehumanizing effects of neoliberalism through practices of subjectification as anything other than more neoliberalism. The way in which the subject relates to herself is both the symptom and the cause of neoliberalism: the symptom because anxiety and depression result from the uncertainty and individualism of neoliberal structure; and the cause because reflexivity and emotional regulation are necessary for neoliberalism to flourish. Not only is neoliberalism a totalizing reality, but also any response to it that entails subjectification tightens its colonization of emotional life. As Reveley writes, subjectification is interpreted as "producing a wholly negative, disempowering form of strangulating self-entrapment" (2015: 88).

The political authority of the APPG rested, in part, on the orchestration of participants from different social worlds without reducing the diversity of their interests and perspectives. Evidence was presented which suggested that mindfulness-based interventions might be of benefit for a range of different problems (e.g., criminal recidivism, impulse control, emotional regulation, and depressive relapse) without reducing them to the same problem, or supposing that mindfulness might be helpful for addressing all or some of them for the same reasons. Throughout the inquiry process, mindfulness was understood to help practitioners cope with life in different ways. Divergent emphases on the meaning of mindfulness reflected the heterogeneity of those involved and the diversity of issues under consideration. While they were understood to share some characteristics, the differences between them remained present. The eight parliamentary hearings focused on a different area of civil society, which co-alesced beneath four broad headings: health, education, criminal justice, and the workplace. In the hearing on mental health, it was reported that up to 10 percent of the UK adult population will experience symptoms of depression in any given week and that depression is two to three times more common in people with long-term physical health problems. In the hearing on education, emphasis was placed on the value of "character building" and "resilience" in the promotion of nonacademic skills and capabilities for students. In the hearing on mindfulness and the workplace, the meeting was told that the leading cause of workplace sickness absence in the United Kingdom is mental ill health. Interest also oriented around the use of mindfulness in the development of higher cognitive skills such as working memory functioning and decision making. Executive control and emotional regulation were also of central concern in the hearing on mindfulness and the criminal justice system. Violence in prisons and rates of reoffense were linked to, but not reduced to, problems in psychological processes and states. In the description below, I will draw on events from the hearings on criminal justice, the workplace, long-term physical health conditions, and NHS staff. Each parliamentary hearing was specifically targeted to address an area in which high levels of mental health diagnoses, stress, or anxiety had been identified. Each followed a similar structure incorporating: participation in a mindfulness practice; presentation of statistics on the scale and form of a particular societal problem and its economic implications; personal testimonies from people for whom mindfulness practice had been radically transformative; the existing evidence for the efficacy for mindfulness-based interventions in each area; and reports on the implementation of small-scale mindfulness interventions.

Hearings were held in large wood-paneled committee rooms in the Houses of Parliament, overlooking the Thames. Each of the hearings was full, and I was told that it was unusual to have so many ministers present at APPG meetings, and even more unusual for them to stay for any length of time. Over the course of the hearings, upward of eighty people presented statistics on challenges being faced by populations in different areas of UK life, accounts of research on mindfulness, their experiences of implementing mindfulness-based courses, and their personal experiences of practice. These people were drawn from different areas of expertise and work, and included but were not limited to researchers, civil servants, MPs, ex-offenders, probation managers, patients, school children, third-sector officers, private sector workers, NHS service commissioners, healthcare professionals, psychologists, and teachers. The orchestration of such a broad and specialist group of people was made possible by a clear agenda for the running order and tight time keeping by the chair of each meeting (usually a politician). Speakers were encouraged to keep to time, usually no more than five to ten minutes. This, and the range and volume of information being presented, gave a clear pace to the proceedings. Each meeting followed a similar running order: a welcome from the chair; a short mindfulness practice; statistics on the range, scale, and character of a problem; an overview of research evidence for mindfulness; testimonials from people who had benefited from mindfulness; accounts from professionals who had implemented mindfulness-based initiatives in their area; discussion around the barriers to adoption of mindfulness in a given area; and an open discussion on coordination and next steps.

At the start of each hearing, assembled professionals, MPs, and peers were invited to settle into a short mindfulness practice led by a respected mindfulness teacher. As one of the cochairs commented at the hearing on mental health, the short mindfulness practice was important because we were there to discuss mindfulness, and this ought to be done mindfully. At the APPG on long-term physical health conditions and NHS staff, the practice was led by a consultant clinical psychologist and mindfulness teacher from the NHS:

> So, bringing awareness into the body and perhaps noticing the contact of the feet on the floor. . . . Feelings of touch, pressure between the body and the chair. Now, taking our position in a way that has a quality of wakefulness. . . . A sense of dignity. . . . Being present with our experience. Choosing whether to close the eyes now or keep them open but with a downward gaze. . . . Guiding the attention inward. . . . Noticing the thoughts or images running through the mind. . . . What feelings are around for you? What's the emotional tone, if you will? . . . What sensations are presenting themselves in the body? . . . Not trying to change anything here, just tuning in to what's here for you. . . . And now, narrowing the focus of attention to the sensations of the breath in the body. . . . Noticing the movement of the breath, coming up close to these sensations and recognizing them. . . . Noticing the breath moving in the abdomen. . . . Stretching and relaxing back the muscles of the abdomen as you breathe. . . . Following the in-breath

for its full duration. . . . And the out-breath for its full duration. . . . Allowing the breath to be natural, not trying to change it or control it. . . . Being with these breath sensations. . . . Noticing how the mind moves off into thinking, guiding it back to find the breath once again. . . . And now expanding awareness around the breath to include a sense of the body as a whole. . . . Noticing subtle movements throughout the whole body. . . . Opening up to felt experience in the whole of the body right now. . . . Noticing the shape of the body and the space it takes up. . . . The boundary of the body in the environment. . . . Noticing sensations of clothes against the skin. . . . Expanding awareness beyond the body now to include a sense of the environment, perhaps noticing the temperature, the feeling of air against the skin. . . . Noticing sounds. . . . Being aware of the room. And if eyes are closed, beginning to open them, bringing awareness to what is seen. . . . Being in this room, sitting together. . . . And carrying this awareness into the next moments of our being together.

Participation in the mindfulness practice changed the feeling of the hearing significantly. Each time, the bustle of arrival gave way to a quieter and more focused sense of engagement. Each hearing then continued with the presentation of statistics identifying the character and scale of the problem that was to be considered that day. For example, at the hearing on criminal justice, statistics collected by the prison reform trust revealed that nearly half the prison population suffer from depression or anxiety (Ministry of Justice 2013) and the suicide rate is almost fifteen times higher than in the general population (Department of Health 2004; Samaritans resource pack 2004). At the hearing on mindfulness and the workplace, it was reported that since 2009 the number of sick days lost to stress, depression, and anxiety has increased by 24 percent (Annual Report of the Chief Medical Officer 2013).

An autobiographical narrative then followed from someone for whom the problems identified in the hearing were personally relevant and who had benefited from mindfulness. Here, the value of mindfulness extended much further than the problems presented statistically (such as absenteeism, recidivism, burnout, chronic pain, etc.). Mindfulness was presented as having had a profound and transformative effect on the speaker. For example, an ex-offender told the hearing on criminal justice of his previously troubled life, his discovery of mindfulness, and how much he had been affected by this. Preventing reoffense was implicit in his account, but he placed emphasis on his overall experience of life and his relationships with others:

I was diagnosed with PTSD [posttraumatic stress disorder] when I was five. My carers were violent. I didn't know what was happening. If you grow up in a war zone, you become a warrior. I got into alcohol and drugs. I ended up in prison. I had regret for the past and fear for the future. I was robbed of the present, and mindfulness gave that back. It's revolutionized my way of seeing the world and myself. My kids have never seen me violent and I'm trying to teach them through mindfulness. You have to try it. As they say in Glasgow, "Better felt than telt." I could tell you about all the miracles in my life, but you have to go out and taste it for yourself. Five years ago I was in a homeless shelter and now I'm sitting in Parliament.

Similarly, at the hearing on mindfulness and the NHS, an Accident & Emergency mental health nurse who works nights and has two teenage sons reported that she joined a mindfulness course at work out of curiosity and that it had a radical impact on her life:

It's been quite life changing for me. I found quite quickly that my thought processes changed and I hadn't realized that maybe I had got quite bogged down in things; I just thought it was the passage of life and it takes its toll on everyone. You know, we all have bereavements, we all have losses, things go wrong in our lives. During the course, I was just like my old self, just like when I was a lot younger. I was happy, I was feeling joy in things, and I hadn't realized that that part of my life had gone.

Testimonials were then followed by econometric data on the forecasted cost of mental health problems to the state, and a presentation of the quantitative evidence for the efficacy of mindfulness as a targeted intervention to address specific problems. This was followed by accounts from professionals who had introduced mindfulness-based interventions in their given field and the challenges that they had encountered. At the hearing on criminal justice, a senior representative for the Welsh probation service presented her experience of running a mindfulness pilot project in a probation hospital in Cardiff. This was conducted with two high-risk sexual offenders and one high-risk violent offender, all of whom had spent at least five years in prison. Simultaneously highlighting economic efficiency and personal transformation, she presented a case study of a violent offender who had used mindfulness to control his impulse to commit a violent act. He had witnessed a young man being disrespectful to an older lady at a bus stop and was immediately awash with powerful fantasies of violence. He vividly imagined putting the young man's head through the screen of the bus shelter, to the extent that he heard the glass breaking and smelt the blood. At the same time, however, he heard his mindfulness teacher's voice in his head, saying, "Notice what is happening right now. Move towards the positive." The probation executive told the hearing, "He was able to witness the thoughts in a nonjudgmental way, and allow them to pass without reacting to them and being violent. We costed up that scenario and found that it would have cost £100,000 in services if he had followed through on that impulse."

By collecting together sets of evidence the breadth and character of different problems were represented at different scales (personal, societal, epidemiological, and professional). Mental health issues were framed as sharing a common identity *and* as being unique to each domain. This enabled the range and character of challenges experienced by different groups of people to be discussed without the differences between them being elided. Maintaining this multiplicity of meaning and the breadth and specialism of the contributors was understood to mark the success of the inquiry process and the drafting of the inquiry report. Participants identified diverse societal problems, and the inquiry process was intended to explore the evidence and potential for mindfulness-based interventions in addressing them. In the course of this process, mindfulness was understood through different frameworks. This shifting ground—the meaning of mindfulness, and the range of problems that were under consideration—was held together through the structure of the inquiry process itself. That is, while the "meaning" of mindfulness was multiple and the populations and problems were diverse, the pattern and sequence of the process created coherence between seemingly very different scales and orders of issues. This did not flatten diversity but, rather, enabled it.

CONCLUSION

In her ethnography of UN-sponsored international conferences, Riles (1998) explores the challenge that negotiators face in holding multiple levels of action in view at once. She asks, how does institutional knowledge achieve its effects, and what effects does it achieve? She argues that the production and ratification of intergovernmental agreements involve nonrepresentational patterning. In focusing on the aesthetic form to which information in documents adheres, rather than the meaning of information, she is able to consider "the way that the form of the documents made manifest a reality of levels and levels of realities" (ibid.: 379). Similarly, standardization in the inquiry process brought together multiple levels of reality—the scale changing of statistics and personal testimonies, for example—and also multiple realities—the experiences of people in diverse parts of civil society dealing with different problems. The overall aesthetic of the process enabled multiple meanings of mindfulness and societal problems to be considered in one coherent endeavor.

The inquiry process was constituted through the orchestrated dialogue of a diverse and professionalized group of people rather than a "top-down" implementation of "big policy." Throughout the inquiry process and the drafting of the report, social problems from disparate areas of civil society were collected together. This multiplicity of meaning was maintained through the development and enforcement of a clear pattern of procedures, which enabled the representation of multiple levels of reality within and across each focus. This ensured integrity of approach in the presence of diversity of meaning. The narrower focuses of each hearing (such as preventing depressive relapse or improving students' attentional control) were contained within the standardization of the proceedings. The development of the inquiry process required methods for creating reliability of information across domains, agreed methods of gathering information, and some sense of integrity (of data, evidence, and recommendations) that stretched across local contingencies, interpretations, and meanings. Both scales of information and the framing of mental health issues remained multiple throughout the process. The aesthetic of the inquiry acted as a container allowing for multiple meanings of mindfulness without demanding consensus.

I have argued that an analysis of self-governance as a neoliberal tool risks interpreting "responsibilization" through a totalizing framework: practices of self-governance are read as individualizing and psychologizing suffering, and thereby obfuscating the social and political causes of mental health issues at a time of increasing social welfare cuts. But this leaves analysis of governance limited to a framework of top-down intervention and does not account for diversity in the motivations, experiences, and efforts of people practicing self-governance and the collaborative nature of the political processes by which it is promoted. Self-governance, then, becomes a mask for austerity. I have suggested that it is possible to identify the limits of neoliberalism by resisting the temptation to move beyond the ethnographic movement. In so doing, the motor of political process is revealed to be the maintenance of a diversity of meanings of self-governance.

ACKNOWLEDGMENTS

I am very grateful to Harry Walker and Iza Kavedžija for their feedback and encouragement throughout the process of writing this article. I would like to thank the two anonymous reviewers at *Hau* for their careful reading, engagement, and encouraging provocations in response to earlier drafts. I would also like to thank Giovanni da Col for his insightful comments and suggestions, and Justin Dyer and Sean Dowdy for their skillful editing.

REFERENCES

Annual Report of the Chief Medical Officer. 2013. *Public mental halth priorities: Investing in the evidence.*
https://www.gov.uk/government/uploads/system/uploads/attachment_data/file/413196/CMO_web_doc.pdf (accessed June 9, 2016).

Baer, Ruth A. 2003. "Mindfulness training as a clinical intervention: A conceptual and empirical review." *Clinical Psychology-Science and Practice* 10: 125–43.

Bauman, Zygmunt 2007. *Liquid times: Living in an age of uncertainty.* Cambridge: Polity Press.

Beck, Ulrich. 1992. *Risk society: Towards a new modernity.* London: Sage.

Bennett, Jamie. 2008. "They hug hoodies, don't they? Responsibility, irresponsibility and responsibilisation in Conservative crime policy." *The Howard Journal* 47 (5): 451–69.

Binkley, Sam. 2014. *Happiness as enterprise: An essay on neoliberal life.* Albany: State University of New York Press.

Braun, Erik. 2013. *The birth of insight: Meditation, modern Buddhism and the Burmese monk Ledi Sayadaw.* Chicago: University of Chicago Press.

Brodwin, Paul. 2013 *Everyday ethics: Voices from the front line of community psychiatry.* Berkeley: University of California Press.

Coelho, Helen F., Peter H. Canter, and Edzard Ernst. 2007. "Mindfulness-based cognitive therapy: Evaluating current evidence and informing future research." *Journal of Consulting and Clinical Psychology* 75: 1000–1005.

Cook, Joanna. 2010 *Meditation in modern Buddhism: Renunciation and change in Thai monastic life.* Cambridge: Cambridge University Press.

Corsín Jiménez, Alberto. 2008. "Introduction: Well-being's re-proportioning of social thought." In *Culture and well-being: Anthropological approaches to freedom and political ethics*, edited by Alberto Corsín Jiménez, 1–32. London: Pluto Press.

Cruikshank, Barbara. 1999. *The will to empower: Democratic citizens and other subjects*. Ithaca, NY: Cornell University Press.

Davies, William. 2015. *The happiness industry: How the government and big business sold us well-being*. London: Verso.

Davis, Elizabeth Anne. 2012. *Bad souls: Madness and responsibility in modern Greece*. Durham, NC: Duke University Press.

Department of Health. 2004. *The National Service Framework for mental health—Five years on*. December. http://webarchive.nationalarchives.gov.uk/20130107105354/. http://www.dh.gov.uk/prod_consum_dh/groups/dh_digitalassets/@dh/@en/documents/digitalasset/dh_4099122.pdf (accessed June 9, 2016).

Ehrenreich, Barbara. 2009. *Bright-sided: How the relentless promotion of positive thinking has undermined America*. New York: Henry Holt and Company.

Feldman, Christina, and Willem Kuyken. 2011. "Compassion in the landscape of suffering." *Contemporary Buddhism* 12 (1): 143–55.

Ferguson, James. 2006. *Global shadows: Africa in the neoliberal world order*. Durham, NC: Duke University Press.

Ferguson, James, and Akhil Gupta. 2002. "Spatializing states: Toward an ethnography of neoliberal governmentality." *American Ethnologist* 29 (4): 981–1002.

Fordyce, Lauren. 2012. "Responsible choices: Situating pregnancy intention among Haitians in South Florida." *Medical Anthropology Quarterly* 26 (1): 116–35.

Foucault, Michel. 2008. *The birth of biopolitics: Lectures at the Collège de France, 1978–79* Translated by Graham Burchell. New York: Palgrave Macmillan.

Freeman, Carla. 2007. "The 'reputation' of neoliberalism." *American Ethnologist* 34 (2): 252–67.

Fromm, Erich, D. T. Suzuki, and Richard De Martino. 1970. *Zen Buddhism and psychoanalysis*. London: HarperCollins.

Gammeltoft, Tine M. 2007. "Prenatal diagnosis in postwar Vietnam: Power, subjectivity, and citizenship." *American Anthropologist* 109 (1): 153–63.

Gershon, Ilana. 2011. "Neoliberal agency." *Current Anthropology* 52 (4): 537–55.

Gledhill, John. 2004. "Neoliberalism." In *A companion to the anthropology of politics*, edited by David Nugent and Joan Vincent, 332–48. Malden, MA: Blackwell.

Gupta, Akhil, and James Ferguson 1992. "Beyond culture: Space, identity and the politics of difference." *Cultural Anthropology* 7 (1): 6–23.

Hilgers, Mathieu. 2010. "The three anthropological approaches to neoliberalism." *International Social Science Journal* 61 (202): 351–64.

Howell, Alison. 2015. "Resilience as enhancement: Governmentality and political economy beyond 'responsibilisation'." *Politics* 35 (1): 67–71.

Jordt, Ingrid. 2007. *Burma's mass lay meditation movement: Buddhism and the cultural construction of power*. Athens: Ohio University Press.

Kabat-Zinn, Jon. 1990. *Full catastrophe living: How to cope with stress, pain and illness using mindfulness meditation*. New York: Delacorte.

Kingfisher, Catherine, and Jeff Maskovsky 2008. "The limits of neoliberalism." *Critique of Anthropology* 28 (2): 115–26.

Kuyken, Willem, Sarah Byford, Rod S. Taylor, Ed Watkins, Emily Holden, Kat White, Barbara Barrett, Richard Byng, Alison Evans, Eugene Mullan, and John D. Teasdale. 2008. "Mindfulness-based cognitive therapy to prevent relapse in recurrent depression." *Journal of Consulting and Clinical Psychology* 76: 966–78.

Lacobucci, Gareth. 2013. "Leading doctors condemn NHS tendering processes." *BMJ* 346: fl 476.

Ma, S. Helen, and John D. Teasdale. 2004. "Mindfulness-based cognitive therapy for depression: Replication and exploration of differential relapse prevention effects." *Journal of Consulting and Clinical Psychology* 72 (1): 31– 40.

Maskovsky, Jeff, and Catherine Kingfisher. 2001. "Introduction." *Urban Anthropology and Studies of Cultural Systems and World Economic Development* 30(2–3): 105–21. (Special issue, "Global capitalism, neoliberal policy and poverty.")

Metcalf, Franz Aubrey. 2002 "The encounter of Buddhism and psychology." In *Westward dharma: Buddhism beyond Asia*, edited by Charles S. Prebish and Martin Bauman, 348–64. Berkeley: University of California Press.

Mindfulness All-Party Parliamentary Group. 2015. *Mindful Nation UK*. The Mindfulness Initiative, October. http://themindfulnessinitiative.org.uk/images/reports/Mindfulness-APPG-Report_Mindful-Nation-UK_Oct2015.pdf (accessed June 8, 2016)

Ministry of Justice. 2013. *Gender differences in substance misuse and mental health amongst prisoners*. London: Ministry of Justice.

Mol, Annemarie. 2008. *The logic of care: Health and the problem of patient choice*. London: Routledge.

Nandy, Ashis. 2012. "The idea of happiness." *Economic and Political Weekly* XLVII (2): 45–48.

Ong, Aihwa. 2006. *Neoliberalism as exception: Mutations in citizenship and sovereignty*. London: Duke University Press.

Premkumar, Ashish. 2015 "'The opposite of a history': What substance use in pregnancy can lend to an ethics of accompaniment." *Medicine Anthropology Theory* 2 (2): 28–53.

Purser, Ron, and David Loy. 2013. "Beyond McMindfulness." *Huffington Post*. http://www.huffingtonpost.com/ron-purser/beyond-mcmindfulness_b_3519289.html (accessed June 9, 2016).

Rawls, John. (1971) 1999. *A theory of justice*. Cambridge, MA: The Belknap Press of Harvard University Press.

Reveley, James. 2015 "Foucauldian critique of Positive Education and related self-technologies: Some problems and new directions." *Open Review of Educational Research* 2 (1): 78–93.

Riles, Annelise. 1998 "Infinity within the brackets." *American Ethnologist* 25 (3): 378–98.

Rose, Nikolas. 1996a. "The death of the social? Re-figuring the territory of government." *Economy and Society* 25 (3): 327–56.

———. 1996b. *Inventing our selves: Psychology, power and personhood*. New York: Cambridge University Press.

———. 1999a. "Inventiveness in politics." *Economy and Society* 28 (3): 467–93.

———. 1999b. *Powers of freedom: Reframing political thought*. Cambridge: Cambridge University Press.

———. 2001. "The politics of life itself." *Theory, Culture & Society* 18 (6): 1–30.

———. 2007. *The politics of life itself: Biomedicine, power and subjectivity in the twenty-first century*. Princeton, NJ: Princeton University Press.

Rose, Nikolas, and Peter Miller. 1992. "Political power beyond the state: Problematics of government." *British Journal of Sociology* 43 (2): 172–205.

Scheldeman, Griet. 2008. "Primed for well-being? Young people, diabetes and insulin pumps." In *Culture and well-being: Anthropological approaches to freedom and political ethics*, edited by Alberto Corsín Jiménez, 80–94. London: Pluto Press.

Segal, Zindel V., J. Mark G. Williams, and John D. Teasdale. 2013. *Mindfulness-based cognitive therapy for depression.* Second edition. New York: Guilford Press.

Sennett, Richard. 1998. *The corrosion of character: The personal consequences of work in the new capitalism.* New York: Norton.

———. 2006. *The culture of the new capitalism.* New Haven, CT: Yale University Press.

Shamir, Ronen. 2008. "The age of responsibilization: On market-embedded morality." *Economy and Society* 37 (1): 1–19.

Teasdale, John D., Zindel V. Segal, J. Mark G. Williams, Valerie A. Ridgeway, Judith M. Soulsby, and Mark A. Lau. 2000, "Prevention of relapse/recurrence in major depression by mindfulness-based cognitive therapy." *Journal of Consulting and Clinical Psychology* 68: 615–23.

Trnka, Susanna. 2014. "Domestic experiments: Familial regimes of coping with childhood asthma in New Zealand." *Medical Anthropology: Cross-Cultural Studies in Health and Illness* 33 (6): 546–60.

Trnka, Susanna, and Catherine Trundle. 2014. "Competing responsibilities: Moving beyond neoliberal responsibilisation." *Anthropological Forum* 24 (2): 136–53.

Van Esterik, John L. 1977. "Cultural interpretation of canonical paradox: Lay meditation in a central Thai village." Ph.D. dissertation, University of Illinois.

Williamson, Lola. 2010. *Transcendent in America: Hindu-inspired meditation movements as new religion.* New York: New York University Press.

Zigon, Jarrett. 2010. *"HIV is God's blessing": Rehabilitating morality in neoliberal Russia.* Berkeley: University of California Press.

Žižek, Slavoj. 2001. "From Western Marxism to Western Buddhism." *Cabinet* 2. http://www.cabinetmagazine.org/issues/2/western.php (accessed June 9, 2016).

CHAPTER SEVEN

The path to happiness?
Prosperity, suffering, and transnational migration in Britain and Sylhet

KATY GARDNER

> *People between two countries always feel sorrow. Mothers and fathers worry about how their child is doing in another country. The child sometimes finds happiness. From the Bangladeshi point of view they are sleeping in a big bed, eating chicken and wearing expensive saris. But some only feel pain, like when a chilli is rubbed into your flesh: a burning pain like that.*
>
> – Mrs. Khatun, London, 1996 (cited in Katy Gardner, *Age, narrative and migration*)

While it is axiomatic that migrants move in order to improve their lives, attracted by "pull factors" such as economic opportunities, modernity, freedom, and so forth, research drawing upon metrics of well-being implies that it does not lead to happiness for those who leave (Bartram 2010, 2011; Nowok et al. 2011; Graham and Markowitz 2011), those left behind (Borraz, Pozo, and Rossi 2008), or those who return (Bartram 2013). Ethnographic accounts point to similar conclusions: migration is associated with upheaval, rupture, and longing.[1] Popular stereotypes support these findings, presenting a picture of sorrow, separation, and loss, or what Sara Ahmed calls "the melancholic migrant" (Ahmed 2010: 121–59). In this article I shall explore these contradictions, drawing upon my research among transnational migrants in Britain and Bangladesh, which I have been carrying out since the late 1980s (Gardner 1995, 2002, 2008, 2012a). Rather than to seek definitive answers concerning whether or not migration makes people happy—as we shall see, the answers to this are highly subjective and ever changing—my intention is to ask what we might learn about migration in particular and the human condition in general by considering how journeys purportedly undertaken in order to find happiness so often lead instead to grief, longing, and dislocation.

Within Sylhet, Bangladesh and its transnational fields in Britain, migration's contradictions are palpable. That the majority of migrants to Britain, or *Londonis* as they are known, have been successful in achieving a better life for their families appears to nonmigrants to be obvious. Their large houses, well-fed bodies and consumer goods are testimony to the local dictum that if one wishes to prosper, migration is the only way forward. But does this prosperity lead to the contentment that the nonmigrants imagine? In my research *Londonis'* accounts of their lives are filled with loss and conflict. Since my doctoral fieldwork in Sylhet in the late 1980s I have revisited my research village many times, as well as conducting research in London with British Bengali elders and children (Gardner 1995, 2002; Gardner and Mand 2012; Gardner 2012a) and have been privileged to see these contradictions play out over peoples' lives. Although migration is passionately desired and imagined as *the* route to a better life, the reality is more ambivalent, both for those who go and for those who stay behind (Gardner 2002, 2006, 2008). So what goes wrong? Is it that people are inherently bad at predicting what will make them happy, as suggested by some psychological research (Gilbert 2009); is migration is simply a *bad choice?* Or are more complex processes at work?

One way to answer this is to think of migration as a "happiness project" (Ahmed 2010). By doing this we shift attention from the ways in which migration leads to material prosperity to its emotional implications. This discursive shift is also made in Sylhet, where as I describe below, people talk about

---

1. See, for example, Rytter (2013); Salih (2003); Hondagneu-Sotelo and Avila (1997); Baldassar (2008); Parrenas (2005); Charsley (2013).

migration in terms of the happiness it is assumed it will bring (*kushi*) rather than in strictly economic terms. This is not simply because for the very poor happiness and contentment are not possible without material security but also because *bidesh* (foreign countries) have assumed an almost mythical status in Sylhet, which transcend mere economic success. Combined with this, as Ahmed argues, happiness can be understood less as a measurable emotion and more as "a wish, a will, a want" (Ahmed 2010: 2). Rather than seeking to describe what is at best a fluid and elusive state of being, Ahmed suggests, social scientists might profitably think of happiness in terms of what it *does*. By becoming associated with certain objects or projects, "happiness shapes what coheres as a world" (Ahmed 2010: 2); it is a state that is anticipated rather than actual, "a question of following rather than finding" (2010: 32). As individuals, we therefore face choices or paths that we believe will lead to happiness, the promised end point of our journey. Such perspectives chime with work in the growing field of "happiness studies" (Thin 2012), which stress how happiness is often imagined as a future state, rather one experienced "in the *now*." As Daniel Gilbert wittily puts it, "our brains were made for nexting, and that's just what they'll do" (2009: 191/4847 kindle). Thus, while a vast literature addresses immediate and practical ways to become happy (for example, Paul Dolan's 2014 book *Happiness by design*) the human tendency is to imagine happiness as something that will take place in the future.

From this, the relationship between migration and happiness becomes more complex than the simplistic causality inferred by economics and metrics. After all, the difficulties of working out what factors cause happiness in happiness research are legion (Thin 2012: 110). We also face the problem of how to evaluate emotions and well-being as reported by interlocutors, both in the present and in the past, for as we shall see, people have a tendency to forget or misreport how they feel or felt. A related difficulty is what is meant by "happiness," a question that continues to dog philosophers, theologians, and psychologists, not to say anthropologists (Thin 2012; Johnston et al. 2012). What exactly is happiness, and how do we know if others have it, or *are* it? As Andrew Beatty has argued, anthropologists struggle with interpreting and conveying emotion across cultures (Beatty 2010, 2005).

Although I cannot solve such problems here, in what follows I take Ahmed's concept of happiness as a promise and project as my starting point, considering how the project of happiness via migration is worked on, experienced, and lived by different people, in different locations across transnational space and at different stages in their life course. The question then becomes not so much "what are the outcomes?" but "what does this particular happiness project *do*?" By treating happiness as a project—an enterprise that projects people into the future—we focus on how it is imagined and the routes taken in order to reach it, both over the life course and over space. Migration is particularly interesting in this context for the project is not only spread over time ("I will meet the man of my dreams" or "I will lose weight") but also over geography ("If I go to that place I will be happy"). It is, literally, a mapping of the future, in which particular states of well-being and affect are like contours on the map: *here* are the lows, and *there* are the highs. Or are they? As we shall see, while the project of geographical movement brings my interlocutors closer to prosperity, economic opportunities, security, and improved social status, these do not necessarily lead to long-term contentment or happiness.

So how to unravel the contradictions? And what about the tricky relationship between well-being (the promise of migration) and emotion? As Joel Robbins suggests in this volume, these may be quite different. One way forward is to focus not only on what is promised by migration but to interrogate the values that underlie the project and then link these to associated emotional states. After all, not all happiness projects are the same; they depend on cultural and historical context and are underpinned by specific values (romantic love, aesthetic ideals of bodily perfection, for example). Returning us to classical theory, Robbins asks how commonly held values are associated with human flourishing and the relationship between the quest for a good life and the emotions it produces. As he reminds us, Durkheim argued that effervescence is produced when social values are collectively performed. If family togetherness is an important value, for example, then a meal or family party will produce effervescence. But since in any society there are plural values we are left with the thorny problem of what happens if and when these clash or contradict each other (Robbins, this volume).

By considering the values of happiness, I suggest that some of the difficulties faced by Bangladeshi migrants and their families result from the fundamental contraction of a happiness project aimed at the flourishing of the group (migration) and based around the core value of prosperity, which clashes with another core value: familial togetherness. In what follows, I refer to states of being that Bangladeshis call *kusi* (happy), *santi* (peaceful), or *bhalo jiebon* (good life). These are discursively opposed to *kostor* (suffering) and *chinta* (worries). As we shall see, while core values are deeply implicated in what people report causes happiness—familial togetherness and economic prosperity are both central—these states, and the degree to which particular values are enacted are also influenced by where people are in their life courses as well as their gender, not to say where they are geographically (Gardner 2002). It is not simply that values that are successfully enacted produce eudaimonia and at times effervescence (analytically separate states of being that are both encompassed by the emic use of the term "happiness" or *kushi*). It is that, as Ahmed stresses, the process is temporal: to get to the promised happiness takes time and may involve other emotions and states of being. As others have noted, migration can involve considerable hardship but is aimed at a payoff at the end (Jackson 2013: 131; Lucht 2013). We must also distinguish between the supposed beneficiaries of the project: is it the individual or the group? In what follows we see how individuals pay for the good of the group by their suffering. Here, the primary objective is the longer-term well-being and prosperity of the family mapped onto a real and imagined geography of good places and good things. As we also see, the suffering of individuals is temporal; a migrant to Britain may face loss and yearnings for home, but over time these feelings subside. Similarly, his mother might weep for him but feel great satisfaction at the improvements to her farm that his remittances have brought. As always, ambivalence lies at the heart of the migrant experience.

In order to illustrate these processes I discuss a Sylheti family who, like many of their neighbors and relatives, has relentlessly pursued migration as a path toward familial prosperity. Through consideration of their stories, I hope that we might learn not only of the deep tensions and contradictions that transnational migration brings but also how "the promise of happiness" helps order peoples' relationships to places and their movements across the world.

TRANSNATIONAL MIGRATION AND THE PROMISE OF HAPPINESS

While happiness per se is rarely evoked, the literature on transnational migration is animated by plenty of hope, ingenuity, and innovation, as well as melancholia and nostalgia. While originally much work in the 1990s interrogated political processes, nation building, and citizenship,[2] other research has examined the

---

2.   For example, Basch, Glick Schiller, and Szanton-Blanc (1994); Glick Schiller, Basch, and Szanton-Blanc (1992); Fitzgerald (2000); Ong and Nonini (1996); Georges (1990); for an overview see Vertovec (2010).

processes of kinship across transnational space, pointing not only to how relationships are ruptured but also how they enable transnational movement, are remade across space, and the narrative and ritual work involved (see, for example, Bryceson and Vuorela 2002; Chamberlain 1997, 2011; Olwig 2007; Shaw and Charsley 2006; Gardner and Grillo 2002; Gardner 1993; Abranches 2014). A growing body of work focuses on questions of care, both for elders (see Gardner 2002; Baldassar 2008) and children (see Parrenas 2005; Schmalzbauer, Verghese, and Vadera 2007; Olwig 1999; Coe at al. 2011; Gardner 2012b). Here, the stress tends to be on separation and loss, the difficulties of long distance intimacy, or its lack. Rhacel Parrenas, for example, has charted the damage done to children left in the Philippines by their migrant mothers (2005), while in *Global woman* Barbara Ehrenreich and Arlie Russell Hochschild describe a global economy of emotion in which love and care are drained from the South to the North, to the benefit of privileged children and their families in the metropole and to the detriment to those left behind in the now emotionally impoverished South (Ehrenreich and Hochschild 2003).

If so much is put at peril and so much emotional work is required in threading together geographically distant lives and papering over the cracks in intimacy, care, and love, why migrate? While the primary reason is usually economic—people from poorer countries migrate in order to find work—evidence from around the world indicates that once a pattern of movement between two or more countries has been established, locations on the transnational map can assume symbolic roles, signifying relative success or failure, happiness or despondency, onto which aspirations concerning a better life, modernity, or progress might be mapped (cf. Vertovec 2010). People also move between the different locations in order to create and recreate family relationships, provide care, or charity, (Bryceson and Vuorela 2002) or to educate their children (Zeitlyn 2012, 2015; Gardner and Mand 2012). To understand these complex motivations more fully, let us turn to Sylhet, where the role of *bidesh* (foreign countries; overseas migration) in shaping peoples' life chances as well as their emotional horizons cannot be understated.

THE PROMISE OF MIGRATION IN SYLHET

Although within Bangladesh as a whole the role of international migration has become increasingly important to the economy, Sylhet has a special history of connection to foreign countries, in particular Britain. Indeed, whether or not one is a *Londoni* has become the main arbiter of wealth and status (Gardner 1995, 2008). From the beginning of the twentieth century, men from Sylhet traveled to Calcutta, where they found work as seamen, or *lascars*. Chain migration meant that soon particular villages and areas within Sylhet had established networks of migration. Most of the ships went to the London Docklands, where some of the men jumped ship. By the 1940s, a small group of pioneering Sylhetis was working in the kitchens of London's hotels and restaurants. These men formed a bridge head for the much larger group, who were to arrive from the 1950s onward as industrial workers, hired to assist in the postwar reconstruction of Britain. The connection between Sylhet and Britain was so well established that by the 1960s a section of the British High Commission was established there.

By the time I did my fieldwork in the late 1980s the signs of successful migration were ubiquitous. *Londonis* had bought up most of the local land and were building big houses. Chain migration meant that new geographies of *Londoni* villages had arisen: particular *gustis* (lineages) as well as villages had high numbers of *Londonis,* and were far wealthier. By the time of my fieldwork, patterns of landholding in Talukpur, the village where I worked, showed that those who originally migrated to the United Kingdom had risen to the top of the socio-economic hierarchy, while those who hadn't tended to lose land (Gardner 1995). Over the intervening twenty-five years the inequalities have become increasingly explicit (Gardner 2009, 2012a). While large and dominant lineages capitalized on the opportunities and have irregular donations (or both) by UK relatives in times of need (Gardner 2012a). Although agriculture remains important to the local economy, those that work the land are usually nonmigrants from low-income households. As has been reported elsewhere in Asia, more prosperous or middle income households have tended to withdraw from agriculture, leaving it to laborers or sharecroppers (Hall 2012; Jeffery 2010). This leaves few options available for young men from prosperous rural households. Like their counterparts studied by Craig Jeffery in India, they spend their days in "time pass," hanging around and waiting for their futures to materialize (Jeffery 2010). Some become "business men," running shops funded by their *Londoni* relatives (Gardner 2008; Gardner and Ahmed 2009). A minority aims for higher education and a profession. The majority aim to migrate.

Nowadays migration to the United Kingdom is largely only possible via the marriage migration of sons and daughters (Gardner 2006, 2008). Failing that, there are other destinations. Within the local culture of migration places are arranged hierarchically, with the old and established at the top: the United Kingdom, the United States, and occasionally destinations in Northern Europe, and other destinations in the Middle East, South East Asia, or South Africa beneath. The possibilities for long-term settlement and the degree of economic opportunity are the main factors that make different destinations more or less attractive. While it is relatively easy to gain a contract for the Middle East, for example, settlement is out of the question, and however hard one might work, the economic opportunities are limited by legal restrictions on foreigners owning businesses or property. For others, illegal migration is the only possibility: either to the Middle East, or taking one's chance and facing the huge risks of arduous and dangerous journeys West or East. The risks are substantial. Indeed, it is not unusual for households to sell all their land in order to fund a member to migrate only to find that the *dalal* (agent) has cheated them, providing false papers or in some cases providing nothing after disappearing with their money (Gardner 1995, 2012a).

Within this context migration seems to be the only way to get on in life. While translated literally as "foreign countries," *bidesh* has become laden with implications not only of economic prosperity but also long-term happiness. "Take me to London!" people exclaim when they meet me. Women proffer their children, men their services as drivers or housekeepers. "Why do you want to go there?" I ask. "Because it is beautiful (*shondur*)," they say, or "I will be happy (*kushi hobe*)," or "It's peaceful (*santi*)." In what Steven Vertovec has termed a "transnational habitus" (Vertovec 2010: 69) it seems hard to imagine paths to happiness or well-being that don't involve traveling abroad. "This place is full of suffering," (*anek kustor*) they tell me, "people are poor" (*manoosh garib*). In contrast, *bidesh* is good, and getting oneself or a family member there, by hook or by crook, is deeply desirable: the path to happiness is, quite literally, the path to *bidesh*.

There is more to the adulation of *bidesh* than money. Aspirations and the desire for status figure large. Returning *Londonis* and their British-born children and grandchildren arrive in their home villages in the role of patrons, their bags filled with gifts not only for their immediate relatives but also the many people who they help to support. Their modern consumer goods, whether electronic gadgets and smart phones, nappies, ground spices, televisions, or globally branded clothes and cosmetics, all indicate a life of ease and style. They are people on the move, sophisticated and educated, with lifestyles that those left behind can only dream of. Their houses exemplify the dream. Two- or even three-story mansions, with palatial pillars, large walls, bathrooms with showers, and Western toilets, they could not be more different from the houses of most nonmigrants: mud and thatch dwellings without sanitation. Paradoxically, while for those in the *desh* (home), *Londoni* houses signify all that is good about *bidesh* and are sites for dreaming of the good life, many of their owners live in far less glamorous homes in the United Kingdom. British Bangladeshi children on visits to the *desh* find themselves treated as high status visitors, living in palaces and playing in swimming pools (referring to the large ponds that are shared among households in family compounds) a far cry from the cramped council flats where they live in (Gardner and Mand 2012; Mand 2010; Zeitlyn 2012). Indeed, as we shall see, the reality of life in Britain is often very far from how it is imagined from the vantage point of Bangladesh. South Asian migrants to Britain experience the paradox of upward mobility in Bangladesh at the cost of downwards mobility in the United Kingdom, working multiple shifts in restaurants and taking up a lowly social position in British society, with its embedded racisms and exclusions (Charsley 2005).

Migration is thus more than an economic project. It is seen as a pathway to long-term well-being and status, a happiness project par excellence. The promise of migration is everywhere in Bangladesh: images of Tower Bridge, airplanes, and Big Ben depicted on the sides of CNG scooter taxis and rickshaws, English language schools going by the name of "Oxford" promoted on walls and hoardings, or fast food outlets named "London Fried Chicken." The promises are so vivid for young men with few other opportunities: go abroad, preferably to Britain, find work, and make money; reach a state of understanding and knowledge and become cosmopolitan, wealthy, and sophisticated. Put simply: while losers stay put, winners move.

CONTRADICTORY VALUES OF HAPPINESS

Bidesh and *London* are therefore not simply places, they are also projects that give a geographical expression to a core value in Sylhet: prosperity and profit (*laab*). To be enterprising, to profit in one's dealings and speculations—whether in migration or business—is a key aspiration for men. Indeed, as others have also noted, migration is closely tied to projects of masculinity in South Asia (Osella and Osella 2000). According to the narratives of older Bangladeshi men living in London in the late 1990s, for example, a successful man provides for his family, accumulates wealth, and is cosmopolitan (Gardner 2002). In my research with Bangladeshi elders in East London in the late 1990s the men's stories were organized around particular tropes, which pointed to migration as the route for becoming fully adult, worldly, and wise. Their stories often emphasized how they got lost during their first days in the United Kingdom, but then found their way, moving from ignorance to "understanding," how their lives were dominated by work and how important it was for them to provide for their families (Gardner 2002: 77–81).

Wealth (*doni*) and prosperity is materialized not just in business ventures or money but also the fertility of the land, vividly described as golden (*shonar*). Women as well as men take great pride in familial prosperity, materialized in by beautiful and expensive (foreign) saris and jewelry at weddings, but also by the fecundity and flourishing of their homestead land. In a fifteen-minute long video, taken on my phone to show to her sons in Britain, Amma walked me around her *bari* (homestead) pointing out the improvements that had been made with remittances from the United Kingdom: a large pond stocked with fish and surrounded by bean plants, a new cow, a much improved water pump that was noisily supplying water to an area of *iri* rice, and the new broiler farm.

If prosperity is a key value then its performative enactment, the event in which effervescence is generated, is the cooking and serving of huge meals, using homegrown ingredients. As I have described in earlier work, food from the *desh* is strongly valued by British transnationals for its spiritual and emotional connotations (Gardner 1993; see also Abranches 2014). Social media is used today to transmit images of the riches of the land. For example, I frequently receive pictures of fish, jackfruit, and rice fields, sent to me on the messaging app Wassup by family members in the *desh*. Likewise, photos are posted on Facebook by the British contingent of the elaborate dishes they have prepared for special occasions in the United Kingdom. But rather than simply displaying these riches, it is the entertaining of guests, and their consumption of the food in both *desh* and *bidesh* that causes real pleasure. A visit to family in the North of England will involve a huge meal, attended by as many members of the family network who can fit around the table and prepared all day by the family women, who watch with approval as men, guests, and children tuck into piles of rice, Bangladeshi fish, chicken and lamb biriyani, shabji, and so on (the women will eat later). The same is true for the village: when guests come, no holds are barred in the preparation of the feast.

If meals enact the value of prosperity they also enact the value of togetherness and connection (*Shompoko*). When are you happy? I asked my friends in both Bangladesh and Britain; "when everyone is together," I was told. A large and busy household embodies the value of togetherness. Even if women sometimes complain of things being *too* busy, being alone is to be warded off at all costs. Here we arrive at the contradiction that exists at the heart of migration's promised happiness: to become prosperous one must migrate. But this means leaving people behind. Moreover, since families were reunited in the United Kingdom in the 1980s, the extended family is spread over both places. Complete togetherness is thus never feasible. Rather than the dichotomy of "home" and "away" in which migrants leave their families to go abroad, transnational Bangladeshis face the contradiction of "home" and "away" being in both places at once; despite the dreams of elders in Britain, who fantasize about returning "home" only to find themselves alienated and missing their UK-based relatives (Gardner 2002), there can be no return to a place where everyone is together.

Let us now turn to my stories. Based on my observations of and conversations with a transnational family who I have known since the late-1980s and see every few years, these illustrate both the inherent ambivalence of migration as well as how peoples' accounts shift over time. There is no clear ending: during one meeting someone might appear to regret the migration, manifesting signs of remorse and unhappiness; a few years later they have forgotten (or do not want to remember) the earlier unhappiness. The researcher's wish of clear outcomes is constantly confounded.

I shall start with Khaled[3] and his older brothers. Khaled left for the United Kingdom as a young man, for according to the local "happiness script" this was the place where he would find fulfillment and the right path in life rather than lazing around in the *desh*, getting into trouble, and achieving very little. As a newly arrived groom facing the disjuncture between places and roles in Britain, including the downward social mobility of becoming a *ghar jamai* (husband living in wife's home; cf. Charsley 2013) he became despondent and depressed. Later, however, all this was to change. After Khaled and his brothers, I shall turn to their sisters and mother.

---

3. All names have been changed and some details scrambled to maintain the anonymity of my informants.

THE PATH TO HAPPINESS: KHALED AND HIS FAMILY

I first met Khaled in 1987, a cheeky, gap-toothed lad, aged about five. His family lived in what was known as "*sareng bari*" (family compound of ship foreman). The patriarch, Abdul Syed (Khaled's grandfather) had gone to Calcutta in the 1930s; as a *sareng* he was a key figure in establishing local migration networks. After his death in the 1960s, the *bari* was divided between his sons into four separate households. By 1987, only two of these households remained. Two of Abdul Syed's sons, who had gone to the United Kingdom in the 1970s, had relocated their families to Burnley. The third, UK-based brother had died, with his widow remaining in the *bari* with her three sons. By the end of my fieldwork this family had relocated to the United States.

Toward the end of my fieldwork, as I was preparing to go home, something surprising happened. During a visit to a neighbor I was told that Khaled didn't have two older brothers, but *three*. "Ask Khaled's mum about Samsun," the neighbor urged, somewhat spitefully. "See what she tells you!" When I broached the subject, Khaled's mother burst into tears. It was true, she said. She had not seen her eldest son since he was nine—nearly ten years ago—when he left for Burnley with his uncle. It was *good*, she added, dabbing at her tears. He would be happier there. I was aghast, not only at the collective effort of keeping such a secret for over a year, but at what it must have meant to have sent such a young son abroad. Only now did I begin to grasp the emotional implications of migration. It promised regular remittances for those who stayed behind and improved the life chances for those who left, true. But it also meant rupture and heartache: the separations of husbands, siblings, and—tragically—parents and children. Women whose husbands or children are abroad often spoke of the pain caused by these separations. As Mrs. Khatun tells us in the introductory quote to this article, it is "like having chilli rubbed into your skin" (Gardner 2002).

This pain is ongoing for Khaled's mother (his father died in 2004), not to say Samsun. Though she insists that he was sent to the United Kingdom for his own good, according to his older sisters he believes that it was only to earn money to support his family, not for *his* happiness at all but for the happiness of those remaining at home. As one of the sisters told me, while his parents were "senseless" with grief at his departure, today he accuses them of not loving him sufficiently and prioritizing the family needs over his, and is rarely in touch. Here, we see how the "happiness script" both plays into decisions concerning movement and is used to contest it. Though his parents justified the movement of their son to Britain in terms of "happiness" ("*tumi kushi hobe*": you will be happy), thirty years later Samsun throws it back at them. This is *not* to suggest that Samsun was "trafficked" by his parents—i.e., sent *only* to earn money for them—but rather that in their evaluation of possible futures, having a son in the United Kingdom with his uncle would bring longer-term benefits for all of them, the value of prosperity. As Jeffery has observed in India, the emerging rural middle class often prioritizes long-term future goals over short-term gains (Jeffery 2010: 4), shifting the temporal horizons as in the context of rapid global and local change. Migration is one such strategy.

Meanwhile, Khaled's family continued their quest for *bidesh*, with its promises of happiness. By 2002, more members had migrated. Khaled's older brother, Taj, had married his Burnley cousin and was running an Indian take away. He was getting bored and unruly, Taj tells me in 2013. He needed to have his energies poured into work and business, enterprises that could not be pursued in the *desh*. His US cousins had also left by 2002 and now manage restaurants in California. Technology changes the nature and content of transnationalism. These days everyone owns a mobile phone and the youngest generation are all on Facebook, via their smart phones. Whereas in 1987 people painstakingly wrote (or got others to write) letters to their relatives, sometimes waiting for months for a reply, now Britain and Bangladesh are routinely connected for hours. Sylheti London and *Londoni* Sylhet have become transnational communities par excellence; people are constantly moving between the nodes, marriages are arranged, money transferred, deals over property and businesses brokered.

There have been other changes. One of Khaled's sisters, married to her paternal cousin (himself the son of a *Londoni*) has married off her oldest daughter to a professional man in Bethnal Green; by 2014, her oldest son had also married a British Bangladeshi. When I return, every two or three years, there are new babies and toddlers, aunties on visits from the United Kingdom, a different family of poor relatives living in the rooms vacated by the *Londoni* cousins. In 2004, however, Khaled was still in Talukpur. His older brother Taller was busy looking after the land, but while he seemed relatively settled and content, Khaled, like Taj before him, was kicking around, stuck in "time pass" (Jeffery 2010). It was around this time that the family decided he should go to the United Kingdom for a "visit." Why? I asked. "Because it will make him happy." At the time Khaled seemed to believe this; indeed, he spoke enthusiastically of his plans. I was enlisted as a sponsor and official letters were written. The application was refused. More years passed and the quest continued. Khaled had no future in Bangladesh, the family declared; it was in Britain where he would find fulfillment. Then finally his British cousin Mumtaz agreed to marriage and after a lavish village ceremony followed by a wait for the papers, Khaled was off.

A year later I visit Burnley. Khaled has been there for six months, and I'm expecting to see him at Taj's house. He is, however, notably absent. I meet Mumtaz, who has lived in Burnley since she was three. She's warm and chatty but at mention of Khaled's name she rolls her eyes. "Still in bed," she sighs. Eventually he turns up, silent and thin. He doesn't want to chat. As Mumtaz drives me to the station, she opens up. It is so difficult for Khaled, she tells me. The work is too hard, involving long shifts in the take-away; after a lifetime of ease in the village he is not used to it. Worse, he's not bothering to learn English, which he will need for the citizenship test. He can't adapt, she confides; coming to Britain was a shock, compounded by this new style of marriage to a British girl, who speaks the language fluently and knows the ropes. In sum, he's depressed, refusing, in Mumtaz's interpretation, to adapt and fulfill the role of successful migrant man.

Katharine Charsley described such husbands in detail in her research among British Pakistanis in Bristol. Charsley has identified men who have come to Britain to marry British Pakistani women as particularly vulnerable to depression and dejection and she has shown how the quest for migration leads in Britain to many to assuming the position of *Ghar Jamai*, (husband living in his wife's family home; an emasculated figure in popular culture). As Charsley argues, the loss of status and perceived emasculation of being a *ghar jamai*, plus the downward mobility of migration to Britain, can lead to violence and separation in the marriages, risking the happiness of men as well as their wives (Charsley 2005, 2013).

But when I next visit Burnley, in 2013, things are very different: reminding me, once again, of how as ethnographers we must not rush to conclusions, for life continues to unfold. In the four years since my last visit, Khaled has had two children and seems much happier. Mumtaz still rolls her eyes at him, but there is little sign of his earlier dejection. Meanwhile his brother, Taj, who has been energetically building his restaurant businesses and has assumed considerable local stature tells me how coming to Britain saved him from his hot temper. He had too much energy, he says. In Bangladesh there was no good place for it to go. He is much happier here.

A few months later in Bangladesh I am told a different story by Khaled and Taj's sisters. Neither of their brothers originally wanted to go to Britain, they say. In fact, they were pressured by their parents and extended family, who were worried at the way they were drifting and getting into trouble in the *desh*. Here, it seems, concern for the long-term well-being of these young men led to a family decision in which places were measured in terms of the relative opportunities they might provide; in the geography of well-being and life purpose, Britain was seen as a better option. To my bewilderment these new accounts contradicted my memories of what I was told at the time. I originally believed that Khaled was excited by the prospect of migration but now it seems his arm was twisted. Given the ambiguities of migration and the mixed feelings it evokes, not to say the human tendency to misremember or even misread the feelings of others (had I assumed that Khaled wanted to migrate? Or had his sisters assumed that he hadn't?), on reflection this is perhaps not so surprising.

Let us now turn to the family women: Khaled's mother and older sisters. As my conversations with these women over the years reveal, the pain of migration is often experienced very acutely by those who stay, especially women (Gardner 1995, 2006, 2002). Combined with this, suffering in order to promote the greater good of the family is expected and even embraced as part of being a mother and wife. Indeed, it is made bearable by the promise of eventual happiness, to be experienced at an unspecified point in the future. Khaled's mother weeps every time she speaks to her sons on the phone. She worries about them continuously. Yet despite this, she still insists that migration is "good." She, after all, had wanted them to migrate; she was "senseless with grief" when Samsun departed when he was aged nine, but had agreed that this was the best long-term strategy. Indeed, although migration has caused heartache it does not mean that the family strategy of continuing settlement in Britain has failed; after all, it was she who so proudly urged me to film the *bari* with all its projects and improvements. Rather, within the transnational habitus of the British-Sylheti social field it is hard to envisage a good life *without* migration. The quest remains for happiness—for the larger group as well as the individual—via economic security and the opportunities for a better life that Britain offers. But the journey to the end point—the happiness that should be found once the migrant has successfully reached and adapted to Britain—is strewn with difficulty.

As the weeping of Khaled's mother implies, suffering on behalf of the good of others is gendered. Here, worries and stress (*chinta*) are the price paid by individual women for the longer-term well-being of their children and family, but also identify them as morally good and it is hoped that this will lead to rewards later on in this, or the after life. This distinction between happiness as a long-term project (or promise) that one journeys toward over the life course and happiness as an emotion, experienced in the present, was made to me by one of Khaled's sisters, Tulsama, in a conversation about her own life. Having left an unhappy marriage in her mid-twenties, Tulsama lives in her natal home, and is without children. In discussing another sister, who has three children, now at universities and colleges in Bangladesh and abroad, Tulsama commented how much her sister had suffered on their behalf, with *anek chinta* (lots of stress and worries) as she and her husband struggled to fund them through school, university, and so on. Tulsama, in contrast, was at peace, she told me. Indeed, over the years I have seen how she has reconciled what at first seemed to be a disaster—the breakdown of her marriage and return to her father's home—with increasing acceptance, gained partly through regular prayer and working hard within the family home. Here, the lack of a long-term future-orientated project of promised happiness, embodied in having her own husband and children, has meant she has fewer worries and is arguably, on a day to day basis, *happier* than her stressed out sister. Once again, her story is unstable, because like most people she doesn't always know exactly how she feels and her moods shift. Though she had laughingly declared that she didn't care about diabetes (which her mother has, causing a rethink of the family diet) since she has no husband or children so might as well eat herself silly and die, a day later she told me that these days she was happy, saying that "I don't have any children to worry about, so I'm at peace. I have learned how to be patient."

Meanwhile, migration's promise of happiness continues to allure, despite its known capacity for pain. Handing me a letter from the US government, Khaled's mother and her aging brother asked me to translate. The letter informed them that they had been placed in a queue for a visa number, and may have to wait many years before their application could be processed. Apparently their "American" brother had sent for them both. I was aghast: what on earth was Khaled's mother thinking? In her 70s, with adult children and grandchildren at home, sons in the United Kingdom, failing health, and most of her time spent praying and reading Quranic texts, why would she want to go to the United States? She didn't, she said. Her brother nodded sagely. They didn't want to go, but if the opportunity arose they would take it, for migration was *bhalo* (good), the way forward for the family. After all, despite the heartache, Khaled and his brothers were leading prosperous lives in the United Kingdom and their remittances have helped pay for the broiler farm, fish pond, and new trees that

I had been commissioned to film. Again, the family's accounts of how they are doing changes every time I visit and according to who is speaking: like most families, their fortunes ebb and flow.

CONCLUSION: MIGRATION AND THE PROMISE OF HAPPINESS

My objective in writing this article has not been to evaluate in a straightforward way whether migration has led to happiness for Khaled and his family. As we have seen its emotional consequences change over time and according to individual subjectivities and perspectives. Rather, it has been to suggest that by posing the question we might interrogate some of its emotional implications. Transnational migration has led to increased prosperity for those concerned, something that, as the very poor are fully aware, is the basis for well-being. Yet it also involves separation from loved ones, placing conflict and ambivalence at the heart of the transnational experience. As we have also seen, the particular political economy of British Bangladeshi transnationalism intertwines with Ahmed's "happiness scripts" (2010), which plays out around an imagined *bidesh* for those in the *desh*. No matter that the outcomes are often less than happy. The point is that it is hard to imagine future happiness without *bidesh* featuring. As Ahmed suggests, the point of the promise of happiness is to travel, not to arrive. In this sense, it is easier to anticipate happiness than to actually *have* it (Ahmed 2010: 31). This observation is particularly pertinent for migrants who, because their happiness projects involve geographical movement, face inevitable loss and disjuncture: by definition, moving on means leaving people and places behind.

It is here that consideration of the *values* of happiness becomes useful. In the case of British Bangladeshis, the key values of prosperity and togetherness work to produce movement, since migration brings people together across transnational space as well as economic opportunities, and contradict each other, since movement also brings separation. As my brief account of Khaled's family implies, we must also distinguish between the promise of happiness and the more pragmatic project of well-being. While places are imagined via fantasies of happiness (*bidesh* is described, literally, as "*kusi*," happy) they are experienced in terms of actual, measureable well-being, a state that we might usefully distinguish from happiness. As an emotion, happiness is by definition transitory and experienced by individuals rather than the larger group.[4] Thus, while Khaled experiences the jolt of becoming a *ghar jamai*, working long hours in a restaurant, and learning that life in Northern Britain is not how those back in the *desh* imagine, by marrying his cousin and joining his brothers in Burnley he has improved the life chances of his family in Bangladesh who now have another member in the United Kingdom to support them. Those left behind also suffer. In Bangladesh his mother weeps for him but she tells me that it is "good" that he has gone to Britain because life is better there. Here, what we see is how the quest for the long-term well-being and prosperity of the group can involve the temporary unhappiness of individuals. Indeed, living well, whether this involves ensuring physical well-being, providing for one's family, or building a more secure future, does not preclude unhappiness.

In writing of Khaled and his family and attempting to calibrate my knowledge of them against these questions of relative happiness, I face the impossibility of reaching an end-point or conclusion, for their stories remain unfinished. Not only have their own accounts of motivations and emotions shifted as they look back on events but the future remains unknown, both to the anthropologist and her interlocutors (Dalsgaard and Frederiksen 2013). From this, we should take seriously Michael Jackson's plea that the purpose of ethnography should be ethical rather than epistemological. Rather than producing answers (migration makes people happy/unhappy) we should be questioning what is taken for granted (Jackson 2013: 118). Basing his moving account of ethics and well-being on the detailed life histories of three migrants, who have overcome great hardship and adversity in order to ensure lives worth living, Jackson argues that the lives and stories of migrants can understood as analogies for all human experience. As he writes: "rather than implying that people necessarily find fulfillment in being settled in one place or possessing a single core identity, I consider it imperative that we complement this view of a stable self with descriptions of human improvisation, experimentation, opportunism and existential mobility. . . . This capacity for strategic shape shifting, both imaginative and actual, defines our very humanity." (2013: 202). Indeed, as he continues, we *all* have migrant imaginaries because all of us have to cope with change, whether across space, time, or shifting selfhood and relationships to others.

---

4.   Here I depart from Dumont's account of effervescence, which is experienced collectively via performance of collective values, understanding emotion as primarily individual phenomenon.

Migration thus exemplifies the human condition and our universal and ongoing ability to adapt, compromise, and suffer in order to make our lives better. By understanding it as a happiness project rather than a fixed process with measureable outcomes (*does migration make people happy?*) we see how it provides a geographical expression to the dreams and aspirations of Sylhetis, a literal mapping of the future that orders movements over time and space. Yet as with all happiness projects, by focusing on an imagined end point, in this case foreign countries or *bidesh*, migrants and their families are often unprepared for the contradictions, loss, and grief that the journey to arrival at this end point involves. In this sense the contradictions and ambivalences of migration are merely a particularly vivid example of the contradictions and ambivalences that face us all: we believe in the promise of happiness, but the journeys we take to reach the desired end point are inevitably bumpy.

ACKNOWLEDGMENTS

Research for this chapter was funded, in part, by an AHRC (UK) grant.

REFERENCES

Abranches, Maria. 2014. "Remitting wealth, reciprocating health? The 'travel' of the land from Guinea-Bissau to Portugal." *American Ethnologist* 41(2): 261–75.

Ahmed, Sara. 2010. *The promise of happiness*. Durham, NC: Duke University Press.

Baldassar, Loretta. 2008. "Missing kin and longing to be together: emotions and the construction of co-presence in transnational relationships." *Journal of Intercultural Studies* 29 (3): 247–66.

Bartram, David. 2010. "International migration, open borders debates, and happiness." *International Studies Review* 12(3): 339–61.

———. 2011. "Economic migration and happiness: Comparing immigrants' and natives' happiness gains from income." *Social Indicators Research* 103 (1): 57–76.

———. 2013. "Happiness and 'economic migration': A comparison of Eastern European migrants and stayers." *Migration Studies* 1 (2): 156–75.

Beatty, Andrew. 2005. "Feeling your way in Java: An essay on society and emotion." *Ethnos* 70 (1): 53–78.

———. 2010. "How did it feel for you? Emotion, narrative, and the limits of ethnography." *American Anthropologist* 112 (3): 430–43.

Basch, Linda, Nina Glick Schiller, and Cristina Szanton-Blanc. 1994. *Nations unbound: Transnational projects, postcolonial predicaments, and deterritorialized nation-states.* New York: Gordon and Breach.

Borraz, Fernando, Susan Pozo, and Máximo Rossi. 2008. "And what about the family back home? International migration and happiness." International Migration and Happiness. Universidad de la Republica dECON Working Paper (March 3, 2008).

Bryceson, Deborah, and Ulla Vuorela, eds. 2002. *The transnational family: New European frontiers and global networks.* Oxford: Berg.

Chamberlain, Mary. 1997. *Narratives of exile and return.* Piscataway, NJ: Transaction Publishers.

———. 2011. *Family love in the diaspora: Migration and the Anglo-Caribbean experience.* Vol. 1. Piscataway, NJ: Transaction Publishers.

Charsley, Katharine. 2005. "Unhappy husbands: Masculinity and migration in transnational Pakistani marriages." *Journal of the Royal Anthropological Institute* (n.s.) 11: 85–105.

———. 2013. *Transnational Pakistani connections: Marrying "back home."* London: Routledge.

Coe, Cati, Rachel R. Reynolds, Deborah A. Boehm, Julia Meredith Hess, and Heather Rae-Espinoza, eds. 2011. *Everyday ruptures: children, youth, and migration in global perspective.* Nashville, TN: Vanderbilt University Press.

Dalsgaard, Anne Line, and Martin Demant Frederiksen. 2013. "Out of conclusion: On recurrence and open-endedness in life and analysis." *Social Analysis* 57 (1): 50–63.

Dolan, Paul. 2014. *Happiness by design: Change what you do, not how you think.* London: Penguin.

Ehrenreich, Barbara, and Arlie Russell Hochschild, eds. 2003. *Global woman: Nannies, maids and sex workers in the new economy.* London: Macmillan.

Fitzgerald, David. 2000. *Negotiating extra-territorial citizenship: Mexican migration and the transnational community.* San Diego: Centre for Comparative Immigration Studies at the University of California.

Gardner, Katy. 1993. "Desh bidesh: Sylheti images of home and away." *Man* (March): 1–15.

———. 1995. *Global migrants, local lives: Travel and transformation in Bangladesh.* Oxford: Oxford University Press.

———. 2002. *Age, narrative and migration: The life course and life histories of Bengali elders in London.* New York: Berg Publishers.

———. 2006. "The transnational work of kinship and caring: Bengali–British marriages in historical perspective." *Global Networks* 6 (4): 373–87.

———. 2008. "Keeping connected: Security, place and social capital in a Londoni village in Sylhet." *Journal of the Royal Anthropological Institute* (n.s.) 14: 447–95.

———. 2012a. *Discordant development: Global capital and the struggle for survival in Bangladesh.* London: Pluto.

———. 2012b. "Transnational migration and the study of children: An introduction." *Journal of Ethnic and Migration Studies* 38 (6): 889–912.

Gardner, Katy, and Zahir Ahmed. 2009. "Degrees of separation: Informal social protection, relatedness and migration in Biswanath, Bangladesh." *Journal of Development Studies* 45 (1): 124–49.

Gardner, Katy, and Ralph Grillo, eds. 2002. *Transnational migration and ritual,* Special edition, *Global Networks* 2 (3): 179–262.

Gardner, Katy, and Kanwal Mand. 2012. "'My away is here': Place, emplacement and mobility amongst British Bengali children." *Journal of Ethnic and Migration Studies* 38 (6): 969–86.

Georges, Eugina O. 1990. *The making of a transnational community: Migration, development and cultural change in the Dominican Republic.* New York: Columbia University Press.

Gilbert, Daniel. 2009. *Stumbling on happiness.* New York: Random House.

Glick Schiller, Nina, Linda Basch, and Cristina Blanc-Szanton. 1992. *Towards a transnational perspective on migration: Race, class, ethnicity and nationalism reconsidered.* Annals of New York Academy of Science, Vol. 645. New York: New York Academy of Science.

Graham, Carol, and Julie Markowitz. 2011. "Aspirations and happiness of potential Latin American immigrants." *Journal of Social Research and Policy* 2 (2): 9–25.

Hall, Derek. 2012. "Rethinking primitive accumulation: Theoretical tensions and rural Southeast Asian complexities." *Antipode* 44 (4): 1188–1208.

Hondagneu-Sotelo, Pierrette, and Ernestine Avila. 1997. "'I'm here, but I'm there: The meanings of Latina transnational motherhood." *Gender and Society* 11 (5): 548–71.

Jackson, Michael. 2013. *The wherewithal of life: Ethics, migration, and the question of well-being*. Berkeley: University of California Press.

Jeffery, Craig. 2010. *Time pass: Youth, class and the politics of waiting in India*. Stanford, CA: Stanford University Press.

Johnston, Barbara Rose, Elizabeth Colson, Dean Falk, Graham St John, John H. Bodley, Bonnie J. McCay, Alaka Wali, Carolyn Nordstrom, and Susan Slyomovics. 2012. "On happiness." *American Anthropologist* 114 (1): 6–18.

Lucht, Hans. 2013. *Darkness before daybreak: African migrants living on the margins in Southern Italy today*. Berkeley: University of California Press.

Mand, Kanwal. 2010. "'I've got two houses. One in Bangladesh and one in London . . . everybody has': Home, locality and belonging(s)." *Childhood* 17 (2): 273–87.

Nowok, Beata, Maarten Van Ham, Allan Findlay, and Vernon Gayle. 2011. "Does migration make you happy? A longitudinal study of internal migration and subjective well-being." *Environment and Planning A* 45 (4): 986–1002.

Olwig, Karen Fog. 1999. "Narratives of the children left behind: Home and identity in globalised Caribbean families." *Journal of Ethnic and Migration Studies* 25 (2): 267–84.

———. 2007. *Caribbean journeys: An ethnography of migration and home in three family networks*. Durham, NC: Duke University Press.

Ong, Aihwa, and Donald Nonini, eds. 1996. *Ungrounded empires: The cultural politics of modern Chinese transnationalism*. New York: Routledge.

Osella, Filippo, and Caroline Osella. 2000. "Migration, money and masculinity in Kerala." *Journal of the Royal Anthropological Institute* 6 (1): 115–31.

Parrenas, Rhacel S. 2005. *Children of global migration: transnational families and gendered woes*. Stanford, CA: Stanford University Press.

Rytter, Mikkel. 2013. *Family Upheaval, mobility and relatedness among Pakistani migrants in Denmark*. Vol. 21. Oxford: Berghahn Books.

Salih, Ruba. 2003. *Gender in transnationalism: Home, longing and belonging among Moroccan migrant women*. London: Routledge.

Schmalzbauer, Leah, Alice Verghese, and Meena Vadera. 2007. "Caring for survival: Motherwork and sustainable feminisms." *Sonita Sarker* 11: 43–56.

Shaw, Alison, and Katharine Charsley, eds. 2006. "Special Issue: South Asian Transnational Marriages." *Global Networks* 6 (4): 331–44.

Thin, Neil. 2012. *Social happiness: Theory into policy and practice*. Bristol: Policy Press.

Vertovec, Steven. 2010. *Transnationalism*. London: Routledge.

Zeitlyn, Benjamin. 2012. "Maintaining transnational social fields: The role of visits to Bangladesh for British Bangladeshi children." *Journal of Ethnic and Migration Studies* 38 (6): 953–68.

———. 2015. *Transnational childhoods: British Bangladeshies, identities and social change*. London: Palgrave Macmillan.

CHAPTER EIGHT

Militantly well

Henrik E. Vigh

CHAOS PILOT

Raul was lethargic. For the eleven months I had known him he had done little but sit slumped on a chair or the low wall in front of Tio's house. When I would meet up with him, we would hang out as part of a peer group of young urban men in an inner city suburb of Bissau. Yet while the other members of the group at times had things to do and places to go, Raul restricted his movements to re-positioning his body within the few square meters of shade offered by the build-ing and the tree in front of it. Moving only to eat or relieve himself, he became over the months a sort of slothful assemblage, almost inseparably connected to the crumbling structure on which he draped his body.

Truth be told, he could not have done much even if he wanted to. Stuck in a postwar city where economic decline was growing more and more pro-nounced, and in a state where the political situation had moved toward an in-creasingly crippling deadlock, his options were limited. As a consequence, he had succumbed to a state of hibernation, passing slow days in the hope that some kind of positive change would eventually appear on the horizon. At times we would spend almost the entire day together, without saying much, sharing an occasional meal and commenting on the odd event on the street in front of us. We coexisted in a state of boredom that almost suspended the passage of time.

Raul was, like my field assistant, Vitor, who introduced me to him, a former militiaman in the Aguenta militia. When I first came to Bissau in 2000, I sought out the Aguentas in order to look at the demobilization and reintegration of ex-soldiers. I quickly found a field assistant who was himself a former member of the militia, and he led me to a group of them who would gather in a peer group in the *barrio* (neighborhood) in question. During the war in Guinea-Bissau (from 1998 to 1999) the government side of the conflict, led by the late President "Nino" Vieira, mobilized a militia to support its military struggle. Dubbed the Aguentas (i.e., supporters), the militia was primarily mobilized from Bissau, the country's capital—one of the few parts of the country still under government control at the time (Vigh 2006). Though they were haphazardly mobilized, the Aguentas shared a number of characteristics at the time of their constitution. Though ethnically and religiously diverse they were primarily Papel and Catholic-Animist, viz. the 5th largest ethnic group and the largest religious community in the country. Neither religion nor ethnicity seemed, however, to be influential in their constitution or everyday interaction. As urban youth, many were born of mixed marriages and their self-identification centered on being urbanite rather than rural, modern rather than traditional.

As the war progressed, Raul and his fellow Aguentas found themselves on the losing side of the conflict. The Aguentas were eventually defeated and disbanded in late 1999, and left to go back to their *bairros*, to lick their wounds and suffer the embarrassment of returning home as demobilized and ostracized losers. When his side was defeated, Raul lost the network that he had hoped would help him in life after the war, which resulted in a lack of livelihoods and possibilities. Losing the war did not lead to persecution or revenge attacks on the Aguentas in Bissau. But it did result in a disenfranchisement of such magnitude that it appeared to obscure any move into a better social position and future. Raul was lethargic but to a large degree this was because postwar circumstances had closed off his possibilities in life.

This was, however, to change as fighting broke out again on November 23, 2000. The shooting flared up in the afternoon, and as night fell, the skirmish escalated into full-blown battle between different military factions (see Vigh [2006] for a detailed political description of the event). Though Bissau had only recently emerged from a prolonged period of warfare, the tension had been building for months, lingering as a constant and uncanny companion to the proclaimed peace. I was in the city center when the first shots were fired and made it back home as it intensified. The walk home was uneasy and surreal. Within hours groups of women were already on their way out of town, walking silently along the road, carrying their children on their backs and their belongings on their heads. In contrast, the bar down the road was rowdy with a handful of people drinking intensely in what seemed like an act of defiance. Farther up the road, Raul and the group had as usual gathered in the street outside Tio's house, the sound of their discussion traveled down the road leaving fragments of the conversation hanging in the air. As I reached them Raul looked at me and stated, "*es ke no ta kunsi*" ("this is what we know"), painting a picture of the outburst of fighting as expected and habitual. In contrast to the unsettled nature of the situation, he was calm and collected. Having survived the war a few years earlier—first as a young man in a city at war and a later as a militiaman on the front lines—he did actually know war better than many others.

Raul's attitude made him stand out in the small crowd. While most people in the group were negatively affected—some depressed and others enraged— Raul appeared attentive but at ease. Over the next couple of days the fighting moved through Bissau and into the countryside. As it escalated some people hid while others sought to flee the city; in contrast, Raul became revitalized and navigated the uncertain situation as if it were his environment of choice. Moving back and forth between fraction and military formations, he used the conflict to reengage and his skills to liaise and connect. I would see him move swiftly up the street, stop to assess the passability of the road ahead, and continue in a confident flow. As he returned home he would spend a bit of time talking, pass on information about what was happening, and move on again. In the volatile situation, which otherwise halted the movement of the city as most people lost their bearings, Raul seemed to gain his—like a chaos pilot[1] whose capacity lies in maneuvering tumultuous circumstances and acquiring insights in situations that are otherwise conducive to confusion.

The conflict ended in the total rout of the military faction led by the former Army Chief of Staff, ex-Brigadier General Asumané Mané, leaving Bissau to

---

1.   The concept of "chaos pilot" has a tradition in Denmark as both an education and an aspiration. Emerging from the culturally and politically alternative parts of 1980s political movements, it became institutionalized as a school for entrepreneurship and design in 1991.

return to its normal state of agitated stagnancy. In the unreliable calm I managed to ask Raul about the recent development and his view of it. He answered:

> There are those who do not want peace, who want war. When war comes they are okay (*saffa*), you understand? If there is confusion they are the ones who see their path (*caminho*).

What did you do?

> When there is war, there are those who will become frightened (*elis ki panta*). In wartime a lot of people will just be afraid . . . to the point where they hide. That is what war is like, everyone just looks after his own head, you know!? But for those who know war there is a type of path (*typo di caminho*), you see?

Though he was referring to people higher up in the system who, as he saw it, would use conflict to rearrange the landscapes of power, he seemed to fit the description better than most. The conflict allowed him to see *um typo di caminho* ("a type of path"), as he phrased it, which breathed new life into his truncated existence. He maneuvered the situation as "edgework," not as the voluntary risk-taking of those who have other options (Lyng 2005; Lyng and Matthews 2007) but as the action of those who are so marginal that their potential for engagement is limited to the fissures and crack of the dominant order—or the imposition of alternative ones. You must be in motion, *movimenta*, he would say, and for the radically excluded, conflictual disruption indeed provides a space of participation (Richards 1996; Vigh 2006, 2009), making engagement and mobilization a potential, albeit desperate, move toward a better state of being.

HAPPINESS AND HARDSHIP

I first met Raul sixteen years ago. At the time I was not interested in conflict but in its aftermath, yet as it has consistently refused to acquire the suffix "post" in the country, with one coup or attempted coup following another, I have been able to ethnographically follow the militiamen ever since, allowing me to see not just the way that they have been demobilized but the multiple and recurrent nature of their mobilization and demobilization. The longitudinal aspect of the work has allowed me to illuminate the ways that they navigate militant[2] networks and conflictual events. Taking my cue from Raul's story, what I will do in this article is explore conflict and mobilization in relation to ideas of emplacement and the struggle for happiness. In doing so, I will show how the conflict engagement of the Aguentas may shed light on the ways that warfare can open up otherwise closed social environments for the young men that participate in it, and enable movement toward better lives and positive futures. In other words, instead of researching such moves into militant formations by illuminating what people see themselves as having to fight against—the last decades of war in Bissau being remarkably devoid of ideological standpoints and collective visions of dangerous others (Vigh 2009)—the article looks at the visions of well-being that transcend the experience and knowledge of oncoming wartime suffering.

I have written about the Aguenta militia elsewhere and sought to make sense of their conflict engagement by focusing on the concept of "social navigation" (Vigh [2003] 2006, 2006, 2010) and by situating them in contexts of "crises and chronicity" (2008). In contrast, the current article looks specifically at their mobilization through the concept of "emplacement" and relates this to ideas of happiness and well-being in Bissau. Though visions of happiness figure as powerful motivators for the young men I talk to, it remains, as we shall see, illusive and elusive as an experiential state. It figures as an existential goal that avoids capture, making the pursuit of it stand forth as its primary instantiation. In this manner the article takes its inspirations from Michael Jackson "in understanding well-being, not as a settled state but as a field of struggle" (2011: ix). It asks, thus, what happiness might look like seen from a situation of conflict and scarcity, where it may be imagined to be located, and how it may be attained (cf. Jiménez 2008: 181)? Doing so allows me to clarify how mobilizing into a militia in the midst of war may be seen as a way to gain well-being by moving toward positions of social worth and value[3]; a process of emplacement that shows how imaginaries of being well motivate action as both short-term and long-term orientations (cf. Thin 2008: 151).[4]

---

2. "Militant" is used in the traditional meaning of the word signifying "engaged in warfare, warring . . . disposed towards war" (www.oed.com).

3. This is, of course, not as unusual as it may seem. Much mobilization in, for example, the United States and the United Kingdom can be seen as driven by the same dynamics, as the military offers social mobility to those who often struggle to attain it.

4. The concept stands in contrast to "forced" mobilization. I recognize that "voluntary," when caught between a rock and a hard place, may not be a choice per se.

I realize that the Aguenta militia may be seen by some to provide a peculiar point of departure for addressing well-being. As a youth militia in one of the world's poorest and most unstable societies, the logical angle of approach might appear to be a focus on suffering and despair (cf. Robbins 2013).[5] The militia was a haphazardly formed fighting force. Poorly trained and unimpressive in terms of numbers, equipment, and abilities, they fared poorly in warfare and are spoken of in Bissau as *carne di bazooka*, ("bazooka meat") or cannon fodder (Vigh [2003] 2006, 2009, 2011). Yet, while life in the militia may stand in direct contrast to our common understandings of well-being, such hardship and suffering is, as we shall see, shadowed by dreams and ideas of happiness and made endurable as a perceived movement toward better lives and more valued positions of being. Happiness and hardship are in this respect dialectically related as one instantiates an imaginary of the other. Just as the experience of happiness can conjure a fear of its termination, so hardship may be brightened by hopefulness, and suffering by imaginaries of well-being (Jackson 2011).

In Bissau, happiness emerges perhaps less frequently and more fleetingly as its coming into being is quickly surpassed by the reality of everyday social, political, and economic life. Yet though the phenomenon may be experienced as an ephemeral experience rather than a lasting state, happiness is not necessarily ontologically different in Bissau in comparison to elsewhere. The points of departure may be more meager and the aspirations more modest but the concept is similar in use. Just as we in English may differentiate between different shades of happiness and well-being along temporal and contextual parameters, from the situational and fleeting sensation of pleasure to the underlying experience

---

5.   This division between the anthropology of suffering and the anthropology of "the good" has come to the fore within the discipline over the last couple of years. Joel Robbins' article "Beyond the suffering subject," (2013) forcefully argues that the last twenty years of our discipline has been characterized by a focus on such issues, and that we need to redirect anthropology toward a focus on the good. Suffering, Robbins holds, became influential as it offered anthropology an experiential state, which unites humanity and makes the other imaginable as self, as it is seen to define the minimal commonality underlying the human condition. Robbins' article is both acute and timely, and the few works on the anthropology of suffering that he lists as examples appear to fit the critique. The problem is that they are exceptions to the rule, and that the major part of the literature dealing with such experiential states does *not*. On the contrary, they deal with, and may more reasonably be highlighted for their focus on hope, coping, and compassion even if set in situations of distress or suffering. They work, thus, with exactly the dimensions of human life that Robbins criticizes them of overlooking.

of contentment, the intense affective state of joy, and the more lasting condition of well-being, so to, in Bissau, is the concept internally differentiated from pleasure, *sabi* (literally, "sweet"), to *bem estar* ("well-being"), *fica contente* ("being content"), and *alegria* ("happiness" or "joy"). However, despite the differentiated nature of happiness its many shades share a similar trait, namely that it is commonly experienced as a hope and aspiration. It is a condition we strive to move toward, which orientates action and stands as a beacon of our being. The concept seems to have most life while it is being pursued as "people use it to designate what they don't have yet, what they are longing for, that which they have just lost and would like again" (Lear 2000: 23).

DISPLACED WITHOUT MOVING

Focusing on happiness and well-being in relation to the mobilization of the Aguentas in general, and Raul's story more specifically, may in this perspective partly inform us of the motives behind their conflict engagement. Despite the common-sense distance between warfare and happiness a closer look may illuminate how such motivations are socially anchored, and how the well-being people strive toward is informed by relational concerns and obligations. In the Bissauan case this means framing happiness and well-being within a state of prolonged decline and political instability (Vigh 2008; see also McGovern 2011). Guinea-Bissau has been caught in a process of economic and political deterioration for the better part of its existence as an independent country, to the point where political instability and insecurity is perceived as chronic, and where people experience their lives as increasingly difficult to live in agreeable or meaningful ways. However, the consequences of crises and decline affect diverse social groups in different ways, closing down various avenues of possibility and creating specific situated concerns.

One result of the above-mentioned process of decline is that an extraordinarily large part of the younger male population—the unconnected and disenfranchised—have become trapped in a position of persistent economic and political marginality (Vigh [2003] 2006, 2008; see also Cole 2004; Jensen 2008; Pratten 2007; Mainz 2008) where it is increasingly difficult for them to meet gendered and generational norms and obligation. As I have described elsewhere (Vigh 2006, 2015) they are expected to move toward feeding into family networks rather than merely feeding off them, yet as many are incapable of surviving without the help of families that they ideally ought to be supporting, they are caught between the expectations and obligations placed upon them and their meager possibilities of meeting these, leaving them unable to position themselves positively in the relational landscape that their lives are anchored in. It is impossible for them to set up a household, marry, and provide for parents, female relatives, wives, and girlfriends, and their social failings keep them trapped in the category of youth—as untimely dependents—relegating them to the position of, literally, social retards, lacking in worth and attraction (Vigh [2003] 2006).

The result is an experience of enforced presentism (Guyer 2007) as a sociospatial predicament of entrapment "of having nowhere to go" and no way of furthering or consolidating one's life in an acceptable or recognized manner. That is, of existential *im*mobility (Hage 2003: 20; cf. Hage 2005; see also Jansen 2014). They have, we may say, become displaced without moving. As the political and economic conditions have deteriorated around them it has become increasingly impossible for the young men I work with to gain the social position and possibilities expected of them, leaving them detached and distanced from who they "ought" to be.

This experience of social displacement creates a struggle for emplacement, *not* as a question of physical localization (Englund 2002: 263; Jansen & Löfving 2009) but as a striving toward being positively situated in a relational landscape. It results in a longing to attain valued presence in respect to the life-conditions of one's important others. The desire to inhabit a position of relational worth means that emplacement comes to stand as an image of happiness, as conviviality—a satisfying rather than sullen sociality (cf. Overing and Passes 2000: xiv).

OPENINGS

Displacement and emplacement are, in this perspective, questions of sociality rather than locality. Although they constitute multifaceted and open-ended processes, which stretch from the political to the existential (cf. Huttunen 2010; Glick Schiller 2012: 527), they refer to the experienced relational and positional *quality* of our lives.

> Emplacement provides a prism that incorporates . . . subjective sentiments, on
> the one hand, and the structural forces that both contribute to defining the

sociocultural criteria of these sentiments (e.g., through cultural idioms about the good life) and the constraints to achieving such ends (e.g., local social hierarchies, broader socioeconomic structures, etc.), on the other. (Bjarnesen 2013: 40)

As we shall see, for the young men I talk to emplacement is articulated as a desire to move toward a position of social worth from where it is possible to become reciprocally pivotal rather than marginal (Vigh 2015). It is, as such, not an end point of movement but the attainment of a (minor) patrimonial position from where one can distribute resources and futures. Forced to wait for better times, they search for inclusion in economic and political life,[6] and warfare and heightened conflict may provide just that. In this respect Raul and my other informants react to war not just by assessing the dangers of it but also by scrutinizing it for possible subsistence, security, empowerment, mobility, and emplacement (cf. Lubkeman 2008). In a society like Guinea-Bissau, the move from crisis to conflict or warfare becomes a vital conjuncture—an intersection of change and opportunity that opens up otherwise frozen socio-political landscapes, enabling young men to navigate networks and events toward better states of being (cf. Johnson-Hanks 2002).

When I first started my fieldwork with the Aguentas I initially asked rather simplistically why they had joined the militia in the first place. At the time the question was not such an unusual one. The Aguentas had just lost the war and been demobilized, and as they returned home to their neighborhoods from the barracks in town, or the places where they had been keeping their heads down in the aftermath of the war, people would ask *"ke ke bu bai busca la"* ("what were you looking for there")? The young soldiers would often reply pragmatically. *M'bai busca nha vida*, ("I went looking for a life"), they would say, or alternatively *m'bai busca nha futuro* ("I went looking for a future") or *m'bai busca nha caminho* ("I went looking for a path"). The replies direct our attention to the fact that a decent existence, future, or positive life trajectories were not seen as

6. As the logic of patrimonialism is reciprocal rather than transactional people sketch possible trajectories into the future by letting themselves be "exploited" in the present in the hope that it may generate a prospective reciprocal obligation. Thus, despite the fact that it is becoming increasingly clear, following the period of prolonged decline, that the return rate of the tactics of patrimonial alliance is poor (Durham 2000: 113), it is still treasured as the only possible way of escaping the position of marginality and exclusion that characterize the social position of urban youth in the city.

present in the period prior to their mobilization. Nelson, another young Aguenta from Bissau, had willingly mobilized in 1998 in order "to look for a life,"[7] as he termed it. Joining the militia had been an attempt to align himself with a *homi garandi*, a big man, in order to gain entry into a political network and thus secure access to flows of power and resources; an attempt forge the connections and liaisons that would allow him to survive physically and socially. His mobilization was motivated neither by greed or grievance (Berdal and Malone 2000), but merely by the search for a better future than what was imaginable from the impoverished status quo surrounding the position of being a young, urban male in Guinea-Bissau. From Nelson's point of view, envisioning himself as a soldier and as postwar victorious was the only positive prospect in sight.

However, probing ideas of "paths," and "futures" a bit further, and asking into what they actually saw themselves as moving toward, it becomes clear that military life was not just described as a means to attaining social standing but was also articulated (somewhat ironically) as a position of relative safety. Mobilizing could be a way of moving toward emplacement, encompassing the experience of empowerment, as a struggle toward the positive social positioning and embeddedness that might enable one to engage and attain recognition and respect (Bourgois 1996). But it equally offers security, as a very first foundational step toward being well at all. The relative lack or loss of social networks and connections renders young men unprotected in a volatile and impoverished social environment, creating a longing for positions where danger is not a constant and perils less prevalent. In a country without institutionalized authority to protect one's safety; without a working legal system, police force, or impartial judiciary, disenfranchised young men inhabit a position of precarity—a vulnerability beyond poverty (Butler 2012).[8] In this manner, mobilization may come to be treasured as a way of gaining entry into a social or patrimonial network, providing not just access to flows of resources and possibilities but security through mutual dependence and obligations of protection.

What I will do in the remainder of this article is move, empirically and analytically, from empowerment to emplacement. Where the former defines the more immediate experience of gaining a sense of security and the attainment of social standing, the latter describes an imagined movement into a position

---

7.   *M'bai busca nha vida.*

8.   The concept of precarity is interesting in this context as it literally means "obtained by prayer," indicating the level of agentive limitation and power at play.

of positive social embeddedness. Both are related to the struggle for well-being and happiness yet characterized by different temporal stages of the phenomena.

EMPOWERMENT

For the unprotected, Bissau is generally an uncertain place to come of age. The experience of being an unconnected urban youth in the city is not just defined by the poverty and lack of mobility but by insecurity and danger. While this accounts for most of the poorer inhabitants of the city, the lack of protection was particularly prominent for many urban youths during the war when the majority of the Aguentas were mobilized. Luiz, for example, was stuck close to the frontline of the fighting as he tried to protect his family's few belongings. It was, at the time, a common tactic for families, who had the misfortune of having the war encroach upon their neighborhoods, to ask their young men to remain to look after their houses while the rest of the family fled. Escaping the war, most families could take only their most needed or treasured possessions with them and in order to protect the rest from being looted, and their houses from being occupied by soldiers, young men were often singled out to stay behind. As we were talking about how and why he entered the Aguentas, Luiz explained:

> They fled, but I stayed in Bissau in order to take care of the house. I had to stay, but I had nothing, no food, not a thing. . . . When the fighting started again [after a small ceasefire] a man came from the government to call us up [to join the Aguentas] . . . so I thought that if I went to the Aguentas, I would be able to go [at the same times as I] could protect our house.

Luiz stressed later in the interview that joining the militia would both deliver and allow him to provide in material terms. *M'na bin tene tamben* ("but I would also get [something]"), he said, as the militia would supply food enough for people to survive, and many were given half a bag of rice as payment for mobilizing. However, it also offered the muscle necessary to feel safe in a vulnerable situation. In other words, though mobilizing means drawing near to violence in terms of actual battles and fighting, it also offers security and protection in the intermediate periods between hostilities, making the move toward the militant formations a safety issue (Vigh 2011). It can be understood as an attempt to exchange generalized low-intensity uncertainty with momentary high-intensity insecurity, paradoxically providing respite from the chronic lack of safety that defined and defines everyday life for many young, urban men in the city.

The act of gaining security was, however, a first step in a further movement. *M'bai pa m'pudi fica bem* ("I went so that I could be well"), Orlando simply answered as we were talking about his decision to enter the Aguentas. Mobilization was for Orlando a future-bound act aimed at achieving a better life. When I asked what would make him feel "well," he answered:

Food, women, a car, migration, well-being, you understand? You have stability, security, earn a living. . . . Living conditions! . . . That's what fires up the light in your belly.

Sinti ki luz na barriga ("fire up that light in your belly"), is Orlando's way of phrasing hope, as an embodied feeling of optimism and elevation. The quotation is interesting as it shows that mobilization was motivated by ideas of well-being as a nodal point that connects disparate meanings by centering other notions around it (Lacan [1960] 2004). From the concrete substance of food to the abstract dream of migration, Orlando sees mobilization as a chance to improve the situation at hand and gain security (denoted as *stabilidade* and *securidade*)—the lack of uncertainty and insecurity being seen as the primary characteristics of being well.

Yet becoming a member of the Aguenta militia does not just provide safety when not actively engaged in combat, it also generates a positive social position in relation to family, friends, and romantic relations. The most obvious connection between mobilization, happiness, and well-being is, in this perspective, that it offers provisions in a landscape of scarcity. When demobilized, and thus not part of the militia, many young men in the city have to rely on their network of kin in order to feed themselves. You have to "beg for flour," *pedi semoula*, they say, describing the belittling aspect of constantly having to ask for food. While the Aguentas did not receive much in terms of money or goods, joining the militia meant no longer having to worry about everyday survival. The point may seem banal, yet joining not only secures one's physical being but equally effectuates a change in one's social position. Gaining access to regular provisions moves one out of the category of being a poor man toward being a potential provider. Joining the militia reversed then these men's habitual social position and possibilities. From being insecure, marginal, and abject, without power or possibility, they were granted centrality (however momentary and expendable), security, and possibility. In a similar manner, demobilization is conversely experienced as social detachment, not just from the militant formation one was part of but from the secondary social position and possibilities that it offered.

DESTITUTE AND UNDESIRABLE

Mobilization affords, in other words, a move into other and more positive social positions, something that is clear in, for example, the intimate relationships that my interlocutors seek to forge and engage in. When Nino Vieira, the former president who had initially mobilized the Aguentas, was killed in 2009 and the Aguentas lost yet another conflict, many of my interlocutors found themselves, once again, without a patron or the security and backing of a patrimonial political network. They were, ten years after they had first been mobilized, back where they started, unprotected and unconnected. I re-met Latino shortly after the skirmish that caused the death of President Nino. He was sitting on a doorstep in a dark *beco* (alleyway) in Bairro Reina, a deprived neighborhood in Bissau. When I asked him how he was, he laconically replied, "here I am," locating himself as a mere physical presence.

I struggled to get a conversation going, ritually inquiring after the well-being of his various family members. Having asked after what seemed like the majority of his extended family, I started running out of kinship terms and asked about his girlfriend instead. He looked up briefly and answered that he had nothing to offer women. His measly social and economic possibilities meant that he was struggling to survive, and as sex and relationships contain a clear transactional dimension in Bissau, Latino was frank about his unattractiveness as a partner. His awareness of his predicament echoed a common complaint among my interlocutors. Women often expect to receive money from boyfriends, as well as a gift (money or goods) after sex. As a result, many of the young men I talk to bemoan the grasping demands that attractive girls make, and the fact that they themselves have so little to offer in transactional terms. In other words, when not mobilized, their poverty and lack of positive futures make my interlocutors unappealing partners, demoting them to the lower echelons of desirability in romantic and sexual terms. While demobilized, the Aguentas thus share a common complaint as they contrast their current lack of appeal with their time in the Aguentas, idealized as a period when women flocked around them. They hark back to their attractiveness to women while in the Aguentas, the promiscuity made possible by being a militiaman, and frequently engage in hyperexplicit descriptions and performances of their coital exploits—bodily movements and sound effects included.

As I was primarily interested in politics, I found the endless and excessive stories about fucking trivial. I would fold away my notebook when they started and patiently wait for the topic to sway back to something more noteworthy before opening it again. Yet the massive presence of sexual discourse and descriptions might actually be ethnographically interesting in its own right. Their descriptions were mostly told in the past or future tense, as articulations of a time when the narrators had been or would once again become attractive partners. The sex talk, in other words, was a reminiscence of a time when they had social status and worth, which was seen as directly measurable in the ease of access to women. The performative nature of their "sexploits," the explicitness and extreme extent of the stories, were enactments of social worth, referring back to being "somebody" socially substantial rather than immaterial, positioning them as masculine rather than socially emasculated (cf. Dolan 2009, Vigh 2015).

The reminiscence thus relates to situations of receiving social recognition, of being seen as a person of worth with the ability to act and attract. *M'kumelis tudo* ("I *ate* them all"), Iko said about a group of girls in his neighborhood that he had slept with during his time as an Aguenta. To eat is a metaphor for fucking, and in contrast to his demobilized position, the statement narratively redefined him not as someone to whom things are "done" but as someone with the capacity to "do" (Feldman 1991:101; Jackson 2005: 73). The somewhat boring sex talk resolved into rather interesting enactments of figments of past and potential status and a bestowal of social standing, attractiveness, and sex.

The story of the Aguentas can very well be told as a tale of suffering. Yet confining their mobilization to a narrative of anguish and distress would conceal the fact that what motivates and moves people to mobilize. Suffering and hardship are clearly important aspects of the social and political environment that their lives are set in, but spending time with groups of demobilized Aguentas, most often hanging out in Bissau's inner suburbs, what is foregrounded in the stories they tell are feelings of camaraderie and empowerment—not as an ability to exert power over people but as an enabling condition of engagement. Issues of violence and war are, in fact, mentioned very little. At times, conversations will touch upon the hardship of actual warfare and the fear and chaos of the battlefield; however, during my fifteen years of on-and-off fieldwork with Aguentas there has been very little talk about trauma or suffering. They generally do not dwell on the intricate details of violence or the anguish of warfare (cf. Robbins 2013: 455). When they actually mention suffering it is most often in stoic ways, and when addressing combat, violence, and wounds—both those they had suffered and those they had inflicted—they limit themselves to factual accounts of what happened, to whom, and what the consequences were for the present and future. They are, as

Jackson shows in his work on Sierra Leone, focused on social futures rather than "psychic wounds" (2004: 72), on potentials rather than traumatic pasts. I do not want to downplay the devastating experiences of warfare, nor rule out the possibility that posttraumatic stress may be an adequate diagnosis, yet for the young men that joined it, the militia is not seen merely as a formation of suffering but as an opening in an otherwise closed and stagnated social environment.

EMPLACEMENT

Mobilization may as such offer both a possibility to move into a better position in the here and now as well as to move out of poverty and marginality and into a space of future well-being and happiness, moving us from the hedonic to the eudaimonic—that is, from the relief of gaining security and value toward the satisfaction found in meeting cultural norms and social expectations, and, hence, realizing one's potential (Keyes, Shmotkin, and Ryff: 2002). It can, in this respect, be related to a struggle to gain a sense of social fulfillment. This move between well-being in the immediate future and the more distant was made clear to me by Vitór as he was explaining his reasons for mobilizing into the Aguentas:

> Things might get better if I went there [enrolled], well you know, things like . . . things like the military they give you money. Others were [here in Bissau] until they stopped school . . . they said: "Well the day my studies end, and I finish school, I don't have anything to do, you see? If I stay here [in the Aguentas] maybe when the war ends I might have a chance to get money to go abroad and study or to go to military academy or things like that. . ." Others say: "[When] the war ends, I'll have no [living] conditions," or "If I leave it will be worse," because they fled during the war, they fled and things went badly, they didn't have money to buy anything, they didn't have rice, they didn't have a thing. So they had to return to Bissau, to stay here, and maybe get a hold of these things. Others came for that reason and because of food and things like this, you see. . . ?

The quote stretches, once again, from the near future to an imaginary of a more long-term goal of "going abroad," going to "military academy," et cetera, in order to improve one's existence. As regards the latter aspirations, being a militiaman is not seen as a goal in itself but as a means to acquiring social mobility and a better life after the war.

As shown earlier, mobilization is in this manner seen as a navigable connection and a way to embark upon a potential trajectory. It becomes a means by which people can seek to gain the momentum they imagine will enable a move toward a better social position by acquiring the ability to sustain intimate others and gain worth through the distribution of goods and capital within affective circuits (Vigh 2015). "You know," Dario lectured me,

> here if you do not give to your family you are bad (*mau*). If you are a man, even if you only have a little, you must give if someone asks. If you want to be a man, you must find money to put [something] in the mouths of your family, if you do not give you are worthless.

Though articulated as obligation, the ability to provide is experienced as a desire. It is a longing for a position where people are able to fulfill the expectations placed upon them, a desire to be recognized in terms of what you offer others. We seek to "come into our own with others," Jackson states, suggesting, "hope is predicated on the experience of being integral to the lives of others" (2011: 92). Hope and happiness are, from this perspective, not merely inner states but closely related to the satisfaction that emerges from one's *emplacement*, that is, through a positive engagement with one's social environment (Moore 2013: 36). Yet the ability to participate as someone who counts is not equally distributed but experienced in terms of centrality and marginality. "Anxiety and audacity, fear and courage, despair and hope are born together. But the proportion in which they are mixed depends on the resources in one's possession" (Bauman 2002: 122), making the movement toward happiness, in the sense of positive emplacement, a greater journey for some than others. As Amadu explained to me, trying to describe his feeling of inadequacy and his hope for a better life,

> We do not have 100 percent. We only have 50 . . . 50 percent . . . [but] if you are a man then only 50 percent is worthless. To be a man you must be 100 percent. Even if you suffer, you suffer on the inside. You cannot show it. You must be 100 percent. Manliness is secret (*machuandade i secreto*). You do not cry, but if you are 50 [percent] that is no good.

> *How do you become 100%?*

> If you help your family. If you have a job, you have means (*meio*). Like this you are 100 percent. Clearly.

The expectation placed upon you as a young man in Bissau is, I have suggested, one of increasingly coming to provide for and look after your kin. As you progress through life, your sphere of provision is expected to increase, turning you into a "big man" whose merit is relative to the number of people for whom you provide. What Amadu describes is a situation where the parameters of manliness are becoming increasingly unattainable because of the many years of crisis that have marred Guinea-Bissau, leaving him in a state of diminished manhood; as, in his words, half the man that he ought to be.

When I ask young men in Bissau about their imagined futures, and what they envisage themselves becoming, their answers often start with a default "*um align*" ("somebody"), a concept that, in all its vagueness, is defined merely by being a valued and recognized part of a relational landscape. When further clarifying what "being somebody" actually entails, the term is often qualified as being "good" or "respected." The point may be straightforward, but it not only indicates an aspiration that guides my informants' action but equally directs our attention to their current experience of being the opposite: insubstantial and caught in a situation of existential occlusion. In this respect, demobilization entails being reverted into a figure of social incompletion, just as remobilization provides a possibility of fulfillment, creating a willingness to reengage. As Samba explained, seeking to describe the inspiration that ex-President Nino Vieira installed in the urban youth who mobilized into the Aguentas, "it is a thing of influence (*fluencia*). He had this influence [that gave the] possibility of having hope."[9]

CONCLUSION

> "Look at me I am still sitting here.
> When you leave and come back again I will still be sitting here.
> Nothing changes. The only difference is that I am no longer young.
> Now I am just poor."
> – Nelson, 2011

Nelson did not move on in life by joining the Aguenta militia. Though he was repeatedly mobilized, demobilized, and remobilized over a period of ten years,[10]

---

9.   *Possibilidade pa tene esperanca—muito allegria pa.*

10. The last time in spring 2009.

he ended up defeated and demoralized sitting in the same run-down area of Bissau with the same group of friends, waiting once again for better times and brighter futures. With an aptitude for joining the losing side of any battle, he never experienced victory. Instead of moving toward a better life he found himself drifting from the social position of "youth," a position that at least offers the possibility of mobility, into a default position of poverty; a social position of generalized immobility as *um algin coitado* ("a poor man"). Though struggling to gain momentum in life he managed, in other words, only to glide into a generic space of scarcity and to become further caught in a marginal position within a turbulent and volatile political scenario.

This article has sought to illuminate happiness and well-being from within a space of hardship and conflict. Looking at the Aguentas through a prism of emplacement has clarified how mobilization is related to gaining security, provision, and prospects, directed toward a feeling of safety and the relief of being connected and protected. Yet it also shows how, in situations of conflict, the pursuit of happiness may paradoxically produce actions that bring people into a space of suffering. In this respect, happiness can have an ironic presence when sought in conditions that are not generally conducive to it. Not only may the struggle to attain it bring one into harm's way; as Nelson's story indicates happiness may also remain a phantom state of being despite peoples desperate struggles to attain it. It is illusive and elusive, potentially present but presently absent as an experiential state that avoids capture (Gotfredsen 2013).

Yet perhaps happiness actually has most life while it is being pursued. As an existential goal it reveals itself in imaginaries and instantiations that are transitory and contingent. It moves as people move along, shifting elsewhere when approached, making us chase it regardless of the situation we find ourselves in (Jackson 2011: ix). The Aguentas may provide an unusual point of departure for describing and discussing happiness and well-being. Yet they offer a good description of how we struggle to attain it and how it may inform our acts and motives in even the most difficult of circumstances. This becomes terribly clear as urban youth seek to navigate war as a vital conjuncture, a constellation of events that opens up otherwise frozen socio-political landscapes. As we have seen, happiness in such situations becomes a bearing, simultaneously a directionality as well as an awareness of one's position or embeddedness relative to one's surroundings.

REFERENCES

Bauman, Zygmunt. 2002. "In the lowly Nowherevilles of liquid modernity: Comments on and around Agier." *Ethnography* 3 (3): 333–49.

Berdal, Mats R., and David Malone. 2000. *Greed and grievance: Economic agendas in civil wars.* Boulder, CO: Lynne Rienner.

Bjarnesen, Jesper. 2013. "Diaspora at home?: Wartime mobilities in the Burkina Faso-Côte d'Ivoire Transnational Space." PhD thesis, Uppsala Universitet, Institutionen för kulturantropologi och etnologi.

Bourgois, Philippe. 1996. *In search of respect: Selling crack in El Barrio.* Cambridge: Cambridge University Press.

Butler, Judith. 2012. "Precarity talk: A virtual roundtable with Lauren Berlant, Judith Butler, Bojana Cvejić, Isabell Lorey, Jasbir Puar, and Ana Vujanović." *TDR/The Drama Review* 56 (4): 163–77.

Cole, Jennifer. 2004. "Fresh contact in Tamatave, Madagascar: Sex, money, and intergenerational transformation." *American Ethnologist* 31 (4): 573–88.

Dolan, Chris. 2009. *Social torture: The case of northern Uganda, 1986–2006*: Oxford: Berghahn Books.

Durham, Deborah. 2000. "Youth and the social imagination in Africa: Introduction to parts 1 and 2." *Anthropological Quarterly* 73 (3): 113–20.

Englund, Harri. 2002. "Ethnography after globalism: Migration and emplacement in Malawi." *American Ethnologist* 29 (2): 261–86.

Feldman, Allen. 1991. *Formations of violence: The narrative of the body and political terror in Northern Ireland.* Chicago: University of Chicago Press.

Glick Schiller, Nina. 2012. "Situating identities: Towards an identities studies without binaries of difference." *Identities* 19 (4): 520–32.

Gotfredsen, Katrine. 2013. "Evasive politics: Paradoxes of history, nation and everyday communication in the Republic of Georgia." PhD diss. in Social Anthropology, University of Copenhagen.

Guyer, Jane. 2007. "Prophecy and the near future: Thoughts on macroeconomic, evangelical, and punctuated time." *American Ethnologist* 34 (3): 409–21.

Hage, Ghassan. 2003. *Against paranoid nationalism: Searching for hope in a shrinking society.* Annandale, New South Wales: Pluto.

———. 2005. "A not so multi-sited ethnography of a not so imagined community." *Anthropological Theory* 5 (4): 463–75.

Hoffman, Danny. 2011. *The war machines: Young men and violence in Sierra Leone and Liberia.* Durham, NC: Duke University Press.

Huttunen, Laura. 2010. "Emplacement through family life: Transformations of intimate relations." *COMCAD Arbeitspapiere—Working Papers* 87: 236–55.

Jackson, Michael. 2004. *In Sierra Leone*. Durham, NC: Duke University Press.

———. 2005. *Existential anthropology: Events, exigencies and effects*. Oxford: Berghahn Books.

———. 2011. *Life within limits: Well-being in a world of want*. Durham, NC: Duke University Press.

Jansen, Stef. 2014. "On not moving well enough: Temporal reasoning in Sarajevo yearnings for 'normal lives.' " *Current Anthropology* 55 (9): S74–S84.

Jansen, Stef, and Staffan Löfving. 2008. "Introduction: Towards an anthropology of violence, hope and the movement of people." In *Struggles for home: Violence, hope and the movement of people*, edited by Stef Jansen and Staffan Löfving, 1–24. Oxford: Berghahn Books.

Jensen, Steffen. B. 2008. *Gangs, politics, and dignity in Cape Town*. Oxford: James Curey Ltd.

Jiménez, Alberto Corsin. 2008. "Well-being in anthropological balance." In *Culture and well-being: Anthropological approaches to freedom and political ethics*, edited by Alberto Corsin Jiménez, 180–97. London: Pluto Press.

Johnson-Hanks, Jennifer. 2002. "On the limits of life-story in ethnography: Towards a theory of vital conjunctures." *American Anthropologist* 104 (3): 865–80.

Keyes, Corey L. M., Dov Shmotkin, and Carol D. Ryff. 2002. "Optimizing well-being: The empirical encounter of two traditions." *Journal of Personality and Social Psychology* 8 (6): 1007–22.

Lacan, Jacques. (1960) 2004. "The subversion of the subject and the dialectic of desire in the Freudian unconscious." In *Hegel and Continental European philosophy*, edited by Dennis King Keenan, 205–36. Albany: State University of New York.

Lear, Jonathan. 2009. *Happiness, death, and the remainder of life*. Cambridge, MA: Harvard University Press.

Lubkemann, Stephen. C. 2008. "Involuntary immobility: On a theoretical invisibility in forced migration studies." *Journal of Refugee Studies* 21 (4): 454–75.

Lyng, Stephen. 2005. "Edgework and the risk-taking experience." In *Edgework: The sociology of risk-taking*, edited by Stephen Lyng, 17–50. New York: Routledge.

Lyng, Stephen, and Rick Matthews. 2007. "Risk, edgework, and masculinities." In *Gendered risks*, edited by Kelly Hannah-Moffat and Pat O'Malley, 75–98. Milton Park: Routledge-Cavendish.

Mainz, Daniel. 2008. "Neoliberal times: Progress, boredom, and shame among young men in urban Ethiopia." *American Ethnologist* 34 (4): 659–73.

McGovern, Mike. 2011. *Making war in Côte d'Ivoire.* Chicago: University of Chicago Press.

Moore, Bryan. 2013. "Flow theory and the paradox of happiness." In *Positive psychology: Advances in understanding adult motivations,* edited by Jan D. Sinnott, 35–42. New York: Springer New York.

Overing, Joanna, and Alan Passes. 2000. *The anthropology of love and anger: The aesthetics of conviviality in native Amazonia.* London: Routledge.

Pratten, David. 2007. "The 'rugged life': Youth and violence in Southern Nigeria." *Pulse* 4 (1): 1–38.

Richards, Paul. 1996. *Fighting for the rain forest: War, youth, and resources in Sierra Leone.* Portsmouth, NH: Heinemann.

Robbins, Joel. 2013. "Beyond the suffering subject: Toward an anthropology of the good." *Journal of the Royal Anthropological Institute* 19 (3): 447–62.

Thin, Neil. 2008. "'Realising the substance of their happiness': How anthropology forgot about Homo gauius." In *Culture and well-being: Anthropological approaches to freedom and political ethics,* edited by Alberto Corsin Jiménez, 135–55. London: Pluto Press.

Utas, M. 2003. *Sweet battlefields: Youth and the Liberian civil war.* Uppsala: Uppsala University Dissertations in Cultural Anthropology.

Vigh, Henrik. (2003) 2006. *Navigating terrains of war: Youth and soldiering in Guinea-Bissau.* Oxford: Berghahn Books.

———. 2006. "Social death and violent life chances." In *Navigating youth, generating adulthood: Social becoming in an African context,* edited by Catrine Christiansen, Mats Utas, and Henrik Vigh, 31–60. Uppsala: Nordic Africa Institute.

———. 2008. "Crisis and chronicity: Anthropological perspectives on continuous crisis and decline." *Ethnos* 73 (1): 5–21.

———. 2009. "Wayward migration: On imagined futures and technological voids." *Ethnos* 74 (1): 91–109.

———. 2011. "Vigilance: On negative potentiality and social invisibility." *Social Analysis* 55 (3): 93–114.

———. 2015. "Mobile misfortune." *Culture Unbound: Journal of Current Cultural Research* 7 (2): 233–53.

CHAPTER NINE

Le bonheur suisse, again

Michael Lambek

> *Happiness is good activity not amusement.*
>
> – Aristotle, *Ethics* X, 6

Happiness raises serious challenges as a subject; difficult to speak about without sounding either trite or ironic.[1] As Tolstoy famously wrote, happy families are all the same. The absence of happiness is evidently a different matter. Tolstoy's compatriot Akhmatova was led to ask, "Whoever said you were supposed to be happy?" And Kolakowski (2012) takes the question a step further, wondering, "Is God Happy?" It is also difficult to ask people directly about happiness, whereas you can generally hear what makes people unhappy without asking. Unhappiness is perhaps the best diagnostic of happiness. But the larger problem is how to escape from the discourse of happiness to the substance. As we say repeatedly in North America, after swallowing our antidepressants, happy birthday, merry Christmas, and have a nice day. Or as Kolakowski bluntly remarks, "Happiness is something we can imagine but not experience" (2012: 16).

Although Kolakowski was speaking about one's own happiness, this may be a lesson for ethnographers as well—the happiness of others is only something we can imagine, not experience. This is not only because the state or condition is elusive or because we can never fully know another or know exactly how he

---

1.   The title of this chapter is after Luc Boltanski, *Le bonheur suisse*.

or she feels, but also because of a fundamental uncertainty as to what happiness "is" and how we might define or describe it, let alone authoritatively establish its presence. How we perceive the happiness of another is linked to how we conceive of it as a concept. It is naïve to assume that we simply know what it is—or will know it when we see it—before we start to study it.

"Happiness" contains the same difficulty as all words that are located somewhere between, or simultaneously as, an emotion and a moral quality, or a value and a virtue. Work on such "moral sentiments" (Smith [1759] 1976) wavers between being overly linguistic (semantic or pragmatic) in analysis, and overly psychological, without grasping them as broader features of the world.[2] Is happiness (to be) understood as biological, psychological, phenomenological, ethical, cultural, or political (a happy, prosperous nation), and in what ways are these connected? Is it personal, interpersonal, or transpersonal?

There are also existential questions. Is happiness ordinary or extraordinary? Is it characterized by tranquility or intensity, contentment or joy? Is it a limited good or like a love triangle—my happiness at your expense? Can we be happy in knowledge of the misery of others? Can happiness last? Can we really live "happily ever after"?

It is unresolved, perhaps irresolvable, whether happiness is an ideal or a condition, and many complex arguments arise, whether we take one or the other tack. For instance, there is the translation problem: if happiness and wellbeing are more distinct in English than in French, or happiness and luck than in German, imagine the differences between English and Malagasy, or with Greek *eudaimonia*. And the evidence problem: If happiness is a condition, how do we know it when we see it? Should we rely on personal reports or indexical signs?[3] If I am aware that I am happy, does not my self-consciousness already mitigate

---

2.   Although happiness can be seen as the end of ethics by both utilitarian philosophers and virtue ethicists, and could even be called a metavalue (Lambek 2008b), philosophy has not generally treated it directly as an emotion or a subjective state. Anthropological work on ethics, including my own, has largely ignored the emotional quality of ethical states or attributions, while the literature on emotion (e.g., Lutz 1988) does draw attention to the ethical dimension of emotion talk. See also Leys (2007) on guilt and shame, Fassin (2013) on resentment and *ressentiment*, and more generally from philosophy Strawson (2008) and Baker (2010), all of which deal with negative sentiments. For recent attempts to bring emotion into ethical accounts, see Throop (this collection) and Cassaniti (2015).

3.   There is also the measurement problem. Elizabeth Colson quotes herself approvingly from 1962: "We cannot measure or record happiness" (2012: 7).

the condition?[4] Is happiness only a judgment after the fact? Moreover, one can fool others and even oneself. Should one speak, after Harvey Sacks (1984), of "doing being happy"?

I have decided to cut through these difficulties by taking as the unit of happiness not a statement, bodily expression, or feeling, but a life. I treat happiness not as an abstract ideal, value, or attribution, nor as an immediate sensation or emotion, but as what is tacitly affirmed and manifest in the living and recollecting of an actual life. I describe a man who regards his life with contentment. It is a life in which the protagonist has embraced local models, expectations, and criteria and has excelled. Hence it is a life of virtue in the classical sense and in the eyes of his contemporaries. However, I do not say that only this kind of life could be happy; it is one kind of happy life. It is also a Protestant (*Reformiert*) life, characterized by a strong work ethic and a certain sobriety, lived at a period of history when opportunities presented themselves to hard-working and self-directed individuals to fulfill their goals, earn a reasonable livelihood, and participate actively in their community. Like all lives, it is inflected by moral luck (Williams 1981).

It is also a Swiss life. Hence a second aim of the article is to depict a Swiss way of life. This is difficult because Switzerland has been subject to so much popular representation that no one, Swiss included, can approach their lives except through a veil of stereotypes. Happiness is one epithet that has been applied to the Swiss collectively, as they have been imagined, by themselves and by many observers. On the very day I sat down to revise this essay, the BBC carried a headline "Switzerland is 'world's happiest' country in new poll."[5] Indeed, among the factors that led me to Switzerland were, first, that it is a place about which no one speaks without some kind of value judgment, and, second, because I thought it would be interesting to study a society that was prosperous and peaceful (cf. Steinberg 1976). What would the human condition look like in or from such a place? Because so much contemporary anthropology concerns places and people characterized by poverty, submission, or suffering, it could

---

4. This would seem to follow from Dean Falk's suggestion (2012: 8–9) that happiness is a matter of focused attention. Conversely, perhaps self-awareness *is* a constitutive feature of happiness?

5. Interestingly, the survey appeared to say nothing about the psychological state of individuals. "The study . . . takes into account variables such as real GDP per capita, healthy life expectancy, corruption levels and social freedoms" (April 24, 2015, http://www.bbc.com/news/business-32443396).

be of interest to restore some balance. Thus, one of the questions that brought me to Switzerland is rather like the ones that motivated the editors of this collection.[6]

I was heartened to discover that Luc Boltanski addressed very similar issues in *Le bonheur suisse* (1966).[7] Boltanski raises the significant question of how to picture a society already inundated and captivated by portraits of itself. How do you move beyond evident and omnipresent stereotypes without dismissing what may be true in them? He makes an important methodological move, pointing out that he is studying self-definition, the expressed ideology, rather than national character per se; in my earlier language, the ideal rather than the condition. He also observes that while the dominant Swiss virtues appear to be the same across the language borders, the relationships that people bear toward the virtues, notably their ability to live up to them, vary by class and across the urban/rural divide.

Another question that Switzerland and its stereotypes raise is the relationship, conceptually and empirically, between happiness and boredom. Is Switzerland happy or boring? Is happiness distinct from and opposed to boredom, or might happiness itself be boring? Is that not one of the objections intellectuals have made to the bourgeoisie? Is that not one of the objections people make to the *idea* of Switzerland? Does happiness emerge in acts of engagement or struggle, or is it to be found in complacency? These questions are also internal to Switzerland, evident in the polarized ideal types of the hardy mountaineer and the satisfied bourgeois, but also transcended by two significant features, both noted by Boltanski, namely that (a) the work ethic was as characteristic of urban as of rural Swiss and (b) all Swiss citizens are by one definition bourgeois, being identified saliently and in the first instance as having the responsibilities of citizenship of specific municipalities, of whatever size.[8]

---

6. These ideas were developed long before Joel Robbins' provocative article on the subject (2013). Need I add that any study of prosperity, happiness, or wellbeing must transpire with a degree of irony?

7. The book was published one year after Denis de Rougemont's *La Suisse ou l'histoire d'un peuple heureux* (1965). Boltanski's book is curious insofar as it reports on a project led by Isac Chiva, Ariane Deluz, and Nathalie Stern, who first engaged him to statistically analyze survey questionnaires. Nevertheless, Boltanski writes as already a Bourdieusian, beginning many sentences with "*tout se passe comme si . . ./* everything takes place as if . . ." and taking pleasure in exposing forms of deception.

8. In Switzerland, the term "bourgeois" refers to local citizenship rather than class, but

As it turns out, and despite Swiss irony about themselves (which is considerable), I recount the life of a man who conforms somewhat to type and without intentional irony. Willi Preisig is neither a banker, hotelkeeper, nor psychoanalyst, but a retired dairy farmer, a citizen of Appenzell Ausserrhoden[9] and an inhabitant of the "pre-Alps" rather than the high Alps. He is not a stereotype, but a type, a legitimate figure (Barker, Harms, and Lindquist 2013) in the Swiss landscape, and a serious, dignified individual. Switzerland is a country characterized by a quite particular juxtaposition of bureaucracy, conformity, and freedom. Most contemporary farmers in Switzerland are not entirely happy people; they own farms too small to be viable, survive on government subsidies, and are subjected to strict environmental regulations and impracticable bureaucratic controls.[10] Willi is a generation or more older than these people, and his experience speaks more to the freedom side of the story. But many of his generation were also unhappy, largely owing to poverty, and they expressed their unhappiness by emigrating.

I draw on Willi to illustrate a certain form of life (obviously not the only one to be found in Switzerland). I claim neither that every participant in this form of life will be happy, nor that I offer a full life history or an intimate portrait of a unique individual, nor yet that I can provide objective criteria for identifying, let alone measuring, happiness. My subject in this article is Willi's life as he presented it to me; it is not Willi himself, not his subjectivity; it is not a complex personal portrait that takes into account a person's inner doubts or contradictions. The exercise is rather to draw on Willi's life as he described it both for purposes of ethnographic exposition and to think about happiness by means of consideration of a life, that is, as an attribute of a life, and possibly of a way of life, rather than of a person or personality.[11]

---

the implication is also that this is more salient than class; to be bourgeois is to be equal to others. Residents who are not citizens are manifestly unequal. Regarding the work ethic, it is a relative ascription, differently viewed from France than from Germany, perhaps, and subject to stereotypes across internal lines.

9. Appenzell is a small canton subject to its own stereotypes within Switzerland as rural and conservative. It is divided into two half cantons; Appenzell Ausserrhoden is largely Protestant and considered by other Swiss less distinctive and conservative than Appenzell Innerrhoden, which is Roman Catholic.

10. Droz and Forney (2007) argue that agrarian reforms are destroying the farming way of life.

11. Hence, although it draws on only one person, this essay is not conceived as a fully person-centered ethnography in the sense of Levy and Hollan (2015), nor

* * *

I met Willi at the Sonne, the small hotel that served also as restaurant, bar, and café for people of a small *Gemeinde* (municipality) in western Appenzell Ausserrhoden. Willi would roar up dangerously on his motorcycle. Dismounting, he removed his helmet and goggles, adjusted his rucksack, and grasped two canes in order to hobble painfully up the steps. I spoke with him mostly through the help of the waitress, Kathy. Kathy was the girlfriend of the cook; she was unhappy, and indeed the family of her partner was not a happy one, the father and former owner of the Sonne having unexpectedly committed suicide some years prior to my stay. Ostensibly high rates of suicide are the reverse side of Swiss happiness.[12]

The hotel owners were a family of the *Dorf*, the nucleated part of the *Gemeinde*, whereas Willi was a farmer (*Bauer*) and herder (*Senn*), though now living in a flat in the *Dorf*. Appenzeller farms are dispersed; elongated farmhouses with attached barns dot the landscape. The lines between farmers and villagers were not strict, people insisted, but in practice there were some differences, including the fact that most residents of the village were shopkeepers, small business owners, butchers, bakers, mechanics, or white-collar workers. What lay just below the surface of the bucolic countryside, historically and literally, was industrial labor; most farmhouses once had weaving looms in their basements (*Weberkeller*), while the bourgeois owners and suppliers built more substantial houses in the *Dorf* and neighboring town, a few families rising to considerable wealth and political prominence. From the mid-seventeenth to the mid-eighteenth century, Reformed (Protestant) Appenzell Ausserrhoden was perhaps the

---

did I know Willi long enough to produce a full-length, well-rounded, or intimate portrait of the order of Crapanzano (1980) or Shostak (1981). I do not discount or dismiss the study of subjectivity as an ethnographic endeavor, but the subject of this article is a life in its outward forms and achievements (as described by the man who lived it), not a person or a self, or inner experience. Conversely, the article does not claim to offer a full analysis of society in this part of Switzerland, though it uses the discussion of a single life (a key interlocutor) toward that end. Despite some important studies (R. Bendix 1985; J. Bendix 1993; Witschi 1994; Blum, Inauen, and Weishaupt 2003; see also Lambek 2007 for a different individual portrait), there is, to my knowledge, no comprehensive ethnography of Appenzell Ausserrhoden or Innerrhoden.

12. This would not have surprised the Freud of *Civilization and its discontents* ([1929] 1991), who argued that social harmony and peace turn personal aggression inward.

most industrialized and, aside from Malta, the most densely populated part of Europe (Schläpfer 1977: 45).[13] The ascendants of many present-day Ausserrhoders were undernourished child laborers working long hours in dark basements, the difference from Manchester being that their workplaces were within their own homes. Max Weber, or "Weaver," as my research suddenly made clear to me, would have been fascinated by the fact that the adjacent Catholic half-canton of Appenzell Innerrhoden had no weaving industry, providing a laboratory ripe for a historical sociologist. The half-cantons split apart in what they proudly represent today as a peaceful partition (*Landteilung*) in 1597.

In the not distant past, there was also a sharper distinction between the *Bauern* and *Sennen* families. The former owned the hay fields and barns and a few head of cattle. The *Sennen* were vertical transhumants who migrated annually between the relatively low lands of the *Bauern* and the summer pastures up on the mountain, where they milked the herd and made cheese. During the winters, *Bauern* families hosted *Sennen* families, the women cooking side by side. *Sennen* cattle fed on the stubble and on stored hay and deposited their manure to grow the next crop. The annual move to the summer pastures, the *Alpfahrt*, was highly ritualized and remains celebrated today: male *Sennen* wear colorful clothing, with eastern dyes once purchased in the markets in Milan, and carry heavy cowbells over their shoulders. Virtually every Appenzeller I met, whatever his or her age or occupation, maintained an emotional attachment to the mountain, the Alpstein. People gaze at the mountain from their windows or from benches set along the forest edges all over Appenzell and they hike it on weekends and holidays. Some people still graze flocks at the cliff face in the summer months and participate in a cheese cooperative. The mountain makes people happy, or perhaps serves as a mirror to reflect their happiness back to them, helping them to realize their happiness.

* * *

I first met Willi in 2003, when he was eighty-eight. He looked back at his life with considerable satisfaction, rather like the grandfather invoked by Rita Astuti in her essay on Vezo kinship in Madagascar (2000). He spoke with pride

---

13. The population of Appenzell Ausserrhoden reached its peak of 57,973 in 1910, when 50 percent of the work was still in textiles, but by 1941 it had declined sharply to 44,476 (Schläpfer 1977: 48).

about children and grandchildren, but even more about the growth of his farming enterprise and his successful transferral of it to his offspring. What he recalled with most happiness was his youthful trip to the *Sennenball*, the annual midsummer cowherds' ball, an event that through his eyes has become legendary in mine, and one to which I will invite you shortly.

As we talked over glasses of red wine, he told me that he (actually his middle son) looked after ninety cows, distributed over three *Alpen* (highland pastures), with a big barn on one high pasture housing fifty head of cattle and with twenty-six on his farm. Willi had nine children, thirty-three grandchildren, and thirteen great-grandchildren. He had owned an *Alp* as well as a farm and farmhouse. This had not come easily, he said, and he was proud of his success; reflecting on it was certainly one of the things that made him happy in the present. Willi had worked hard on other people's farms in his youth in order to earn the money to purchase his property.

As a child, Willi heard his Sunday school teacher compare herders to the pastoralists of the Old Testament and knew he wanted to be a farmer. However, his father disapproved; the latter worked as a carpenter in a factory in town and also made good money designing embroidery patterns.[14] His mother worked as an office cleaner at the same company. His father asked the company for a job for his son but, to his great anger, Willi refused. This was a time when work was hard to find; many people were unemployed. However, Willi's teacher knew someone who was seeking a farmhand. Willi was able to work on this man's farm during the summer and went to school to learn farming in winter. At the first farm, Willi earned only 20 Swiss francs per month, which, he said, was very little. But the farmer fed, housed, and clothed him, so it was enough. Willi was the youngest child in his family and the only one to become a farmer.[15]

Willi finally saved enough to rent a farm and his enterprise gradually grew. He said people today didn't know that he began with only three cows and a pig. The next day, as we continued the conversation, he explained how hard his wife, Katarina had worked, both on the farm and raising so many children. She had been a servant at the farm where he was hired. He was seeking a girlfriend and a wife; he looked far and wide and didn't recognize that she was right in front of him. Later he thanked God for realizing this. "*She was sent from heaven.*"

14. Neither Willi nor his father worked at weaving or actual embroidery.

15. One sister never married, but served in households her whole life; the other became a nurse. A brother trained as a mechanic and eventually became a salesman.

Willi said he always believed in God, and that God helped him through many problems. In the 1930s, the Catholics and the Protestants (*die Reformierten*) did not get along well. But it is the same God, he affirmed. "God is the same in Switzerland and in Canada. *People make things complicated, but God makes things simple.*" Willi leaned toward me with urgency and said, "It is important to believe. We all have a Maker. And we will all return to our Maker." Willi himself, like virtually all elderly people in Ausserrhoden, was *Reformiert.* He didn't often go to church because he could no longer hear the preacher well, but he had been there on the Sunday prior to our talk.

Willi met his future wife at the age of twenty and married her at twenty-six. They stayed with the farmer, who had hired them for six years. In those days, he explained, you weren't allowed to have a relationship with a fellow farm worker, a girlfriend, not in the same house, so their situation was quite unusual. They married in 1941, but then had to be apart when he was mobilized. However, the war enabled him to earn some money he could put toward the rental and later purchase of his own farm. In 2003, he volunteered that they had been married sixty-two years. Willi always spoke with great numerical precision.

* * *

What Willi recalled from his courtship was the *Sennenball.* This took place (as it still did in 2003) once a year on the first Monday after *Jakobi* (St. Jacob's day), which is July 25.[16] It was held at the Rossfall, a restaurant halfway up to the Schwägalp. The ball was held for herders from the entire western part of Appenzell Ausserrhoden; Catholics of Innerrhoden had their own ball. You could attend only if you had your boss's permission and he agreed to take over your work for those hours. Also, you had to have a girlfriend; you couldn't go alone. Every year, Willi searched for a woman and couldn't find one until God said, *look beside you.* You had to attend as a couple, but, Willi added mischievously, no same-sex ones. You also had to have special clothes. Today many people come to watch; it's become partly a tourist attraction, like a show. You wear the traditional clothes and do special dances with your partner and in a group.[17]

---

16. Willi said there used to be a ball in winter also, but this no longer existed.

17. Here and elsewhere, I am paraphrasing Willi's speech as I recorded it in my notes. Willi is perfectly conscious of the way tradition has become objectified but distinguishes that from the way he has experienced it.

When Willi was young, it was unusual to have a day off. For the *Sennenball* he got only half a day. He had to walk very fast down from the *Alp*, for two and a half hours. "*Only a man in love would do this.*" Katarina joined him there, coming up from the farm. They went to the ball once before they married and once after. Willi said he wanted to show me the Rossfall, and later we made the expedition.

The next day, Willi returned to the Sonne with photos and memorabilia. He showed me a photo of his farm (*Liegenschaft*) located on a hill not far from our windows. The house dates to 1505. It is constructed of wood with flowerboxes and an adjacent flower and vegetable garden and barn.[18] Willi first rented and then bought it. At the age of sixty-eight he passed it on to his youngest son, who has expanded it since.

There were photos of Willi giving a speech to his yodeling club, and many of the *Alpen*—both the one he worked at as a youth and the one he later purchased. There was a dance card from the Rossfall with an image of a man in yellow breeches and several shots of the annual procession to the *Alp*. A girl walks in front, leading the goats. A man walks at the head of the cows, dressed also in yellow breeches. When the path is very steep, Willi explained, the men take the heavy bells off the cows and wear them themselves, walking with a special stride so that they ring musically. Although they went up in a festive group, only one or two of the men stayed the whole summer, looking after the cows and making the cheese. During his youth, Willi spent seven summers on the *Alp* of his employer; he liked the work but said it could get lonely. Willi wore traditional clothes every day on the *Alp*.

There was a photo of Willi surrounded by children and grandchildren on his seventieth birthday and a poem in Swiss German written by a son-in-law. A whole album was devoted to the erection of a new barn on the *Alp*. The barn, belonging to his second son, had two rows of twenty-five stalls, thus room for fifty cows. Willi stained all the wood; he was seventy-five at the time. When the roof beams were finished, they raised a small fir tree decorated with colored ribbons, placed as thanks that no one was injured and also for good luck. The workers drank a glass of wine to celebrate and sang in the local and beloved form of polyphonic yodeling known as *Zäuerli*.[19] In 1991 Willi's middle son made his first *Alpfahrt* wearing the

---

18. See Hermann (2004) on Appenzell farmhouses.

19. Zäuerli is still practiced by young people and is, as a knowledgeable referee pointed out, "an enormous source of happiness and nostalgia." For professional recordings see Zemp (1980); for current ones, search online for Zäuerli. A brief segment surprisingly appears in the recent film *The Grand Budapest Hotel*.

brown vest and breeches signifying ownership of the herd. The back of the photo album had some blank pages; "*left for my funeral*," said Willi dryly.

The barn raising points to the orderliness and precision of pre-mortem inheritance, a subject Willi discussed at length. Willi and his wife had six daughters followed by three sons. When the children were growing, they helped on the farm, and once they reached a certain age, he paid them for the work. It was clear to his children that the first son to marry would inherit the farmhouse and farm. Usually this is the oldest, but in this case the boy was disinclined. From an early age, he indicated that he didn't want goats for Christmas, whereas the other two boys received them as presents and gradually built up their herds and learned to care for the animals. When they got a bit older, they received calves for Christmas and birthdays; the girls received household items. When the youngest of the three boys decided to marry, Willi called his children together to divide the estate. The youngest son purchased the farm, at a price far below market value. Willi then allocated the *Alp* to his second son.[20]

From the payments received from the two sons, Willi gave 10,000 francs to each of the other siblings. He said proudly that while division of the estate is often a big problem, this was not the case in his own family.[21] He planned everything carefully. If something were to go wrong for the son who has the farm, the other brothers have first rights to buy it from him. This point was written up and deposited at the municipality office. It remained a real possibility because the son had only two children of his own, both daughters, and they learned other trades and weren't much interested in farming. So one concern of Willi's remained: Who would inherit the farm after his son? One of Willi's daughters who is a farmer's wife could buy her brother's farm; the point is that it should go to someone who will operate it, that is, to someone who chooses farming as a living.[22] The second son, who inherited the *Alp*, has a farm in a neighboring *Gemeinde*. He married a farmer's daughter where there were no sons, so he and his wife will likely inherit that property. He currently rented it from his wife's parents.

---

20. Willi's farm was thirteen hectares of which ten were cultivated and three forest. Willi's youngest son rented an additional thirteen hectares of *Weide* (grazing meadows) from a retired farmer and did not bring his cattle to an *Alp* in the summer. Willi's middle son had use of fifty-two hectares on the *Alp*, one parcel of which was his own and the rest rented. He spent fifteen weeks a year on the *Alp*.

21. Willi attributed conflict in the family of the hotel owners to the inability of the mother to gracefully hand over control to the next generation.

22. This is in part because of strict zoning laws.

In addition to the farm and the *Alp*, the two sons had to purchase cows from Willi. Because they had received a salary from him all along, they were able to do so. (Kinship and commoditization are not understood as antithetical.) By the time he sold, Willi's herd had grown from three to fifty-eight head of cattle. The money from the sale of the farm didn't go far once he had paid the remaining children, so Willi and his wife needed the money from the cows to live on (they also received a modest pension). The goats had always been the exclusive property of the sons; their milk was taken to the factory to make goat cheese or consumed at home. When Willi was young, families made their own cheese and butter and sold some but consumed most. Now the milk is taken daily to the factories for production.[23]

The oldest son never married and took a job selling agricultural implements in the neighboring town. Willi reiterated that you give to the first son who gets married and wants to farm. A man without a wife has too many problems to run a farm. To this, Kathy the waitress added that single male farmers often took to drink.

* * *

A week later Kathy, Willi, and I drove up to Schwägalp, at the base of the immense rock face of the Säntis peak, and toured the cheese factory, run as a cooperative of fifty-seven farms and with the facility to process 6,100 liters of milk daily. Rounds of *Schwägalpkäse* sold at 22 francs per kilo. Willi expressed his pleasure at visiting the *Alp* and called it the most beautiful place he had ever been to. The whole area is very dramatic, composed of meadows, forest, streams, and rock. The huts, carved partly into the hillsides, are within view of one another and cattle wander between them. The air is fresh and there are trout in the streams to supplement the milk diet.

On the way down, we stopped at the Rossfall. The ballroom was on the second floor. It was a lovely place, square with an uncharacteristically high ceiling and

---

23.   , In nine months, a lactating cow gives around six thousand liters of milk, around twenty-two liters per day. Cows are milked twice daily; an exceptional cow, milked three times, might give between thirty-five and forty liters of milk a day at her best period. Calves are allowed to drink for half a year. Heifers begin to calve at three and Willi let them calve three times before selling. At six they need more food. The purchasers were farmers in lower areas who had better fodder. Steers were sold at one or two years. Farmers differed with respect to the age of the livestock they chose to keep, and Willi's son had fewer calves than he did.

large windows on three sides. The windows contained semicircles with stained glass arranged in star-like geometric patterns. A painted frieze showed scenes from each season of the year: the procession of animals up to the *Alp*; wild animals; harvests; hay pulled in horse-drawn sleds over the snow. The men in the paintings wore yellow breeches, high white socks, white shirts, red vests, and black hats with flowers. Antlers, stuffed birds, and large cowbells also adorn the room.[24]

In Willi's youth, the Rossfall was at the end of the road; once the road was pushed further and new restaurants built higher up, it lost business and was threatened with closure. The citizens of the *Gemeinde* made a special effort and formed a co-op to buy and save it; later it was in private hands.[25] More than one elderly person came to reminisce, the owner told me, and indeed Willi settled with no hesitation at the *Stammtisch* (regulars' table), where he knew several of the other men.

24 04 2004

Figure 1. Gasthaus Rossfall - Urnäsch, AR. Photo taken from website.

24. Most of the stained glass and paintings were done by local workmen after the old building collapsed in 1981. There were two portraits of men smoking pipes, wearing skullcaps and earrings said to be at least a century old. In one corner of the room, there was a small platform for musicians, the *Gigestahl*. The traditional orchestra had two violins, a bass, and a *Hackbrett*, a string instrument hit with hammers. The restoration cost almost three million francs; donor families had their names inscribed on the windows.

25. In fall 2012 it appeared to be for sale over the Internet.

* * *

Another day at the Sonne, we were joined by an elderly gentleman, Hans L, a villager not a farmer. Kathy later explained that the two men loved to talk and argue with each other. They almost never agreed on politics, but they respected and liked each other. The talk would get especially heated before a referendum or election. They each knew lots of people, and their conversation covered details of marriage and kinship in addition to politics.

Willi mentioned the *Stimmbürger*, the voting citizens. "We voters decide." But he added that a lot of people didn't vote. I asked why and he said, "They're not interested." Hans interjected, "If we had more problems, like hunger, perhaps more people would vote. But everything works, people are reasonably satisfied." (*Le bonheur suisse*.) Willi added that citizens are asked to vote too often about seemingly small and trivial things; there are too many referenda. A salient part of Swiss democracy, citizen-initiated referenda to remove unpopular regulations take place when enough signatures are gathered. A *Volksinitiative*, to add text to the Swiss constitution, requires a majority of cantons as well as a popular majority. Willi thought this right, since rural cantons have different interests than urban ones, whereas Hans affirmed that the majority of people was the more important principle. Debating this sort of question is central to the Swiss ethos, their respective positions emphasizing a more conservative and a more liberal outlook, respectively.

Willi was never a member of a political party, preferring to be independent. Yet his civic engagement was extensive. He served on the municipal council (*Gemeinderat*) for seven years. He received 8 francs for each meeting attended, but they would go for dinner after the meeting and spend more than that. As a council member he was appointed *Bürgerpräsident*, a position he held from 1964 to 1972. His responsibility was to prepare the cases of everyone who applied for *Einbürgerung* (naturalization, citizenship) in the citizens' assembly that voted in new citizens.[26] Willi told me about one case, a young Italian man of very good reputation. A lawyer argued they shouldn't grant citizenship to a Catholic. Then Willi took the floor and said, we have freedom of religion in Switzerland. We

---

26. On acquisition of citizenship, see Centlivres (1990). In 2003, the federal high court declared the method of *Einbürgerung* by means of a public citizens' vote unconstitutional and a violation of human rights. It had already been disbanded in Herisau during the 1970s.

can't deny him citizenship on this basis, and even if we did, he could take the case to the high court and win. So the opinion of the assembly was turned and people voted him in.

Willi had not wanted to join the municipal council in the first place, but said he did so to ensure representation from the agricultural faction. In addition to serving as *Bürgerpräsident*, he sat on the agricultural, children's home, building, and health committees, the auction committee to dispense the goods of bankrupt farmers, and the forest, legal guardianship, and young offenders committees. The latter provided work as punishment. Willi said he declined to stand for cantonal representative, because he wanted time with family.

The public office most important to Willi was presidency of the *Viehzuchtgenossenschaft*, the livestock-breeding cooperative. He accepted the position once his children were old enough to take responsibility at the farm and held it for some twenty years, not for the money but because he loved cattle. He evaluated the quality of the cows, judged their value and health, and recorded any signs of illness or weakness. He said proudly that Appenzeller cattle were unequaled, adding jokingly that if they were side by side, he would rather look at a cow than a woman.

Willi was not a vet and didn't doctor cows for the canton, although he treated his own. He gave cows points for their beauty and fitness. He had learned a lot about cows from the time he spent on the *Alp* and had gone to a special agricultural school (*Landwirtschaftschule*) from the age of sixteen to eighteen. This was not usual at the time, he explained, so he knew more than many other people. Attending the school was his choice; he paid for it with his own money, having nothing left over for any kind of enjoyment. The only government subsidy he ever received was to help build a paved road to his farmhouse. "You get support from the *Bund* [Federal government] if you switch to *bio* [organic] agriculture, but the bureaucratic dimension is enormous. There are lots of rules, regulations, and requirements, and if you miss out on even a single one you don't get the money. It's very difficult and cannot really be followed in practice." That's why Swiss farmers emigrated to Canada. "*There are too many rules here!*" He added that Swiss people liked to be autonomous, free of rules, to be able to do what they wanted. I remarked on the paradox that this society was so highly regulated.

Willi did try to preserve the farming way of life, and to this end in 1963 he helped found the *Landjugendgruppe*, an association providing young people from farm families with a chance to meet suitable marriage partners who also wanted to stay on the land. It led to many a marriage, he said, and members still celebrated each other's weddings.

We briefly discussed the expansion of voting in the *Landsgemeinde* to include women. This was the annual public assembly of all cantonal citizens in which votes were taken by a raising of hands (J. Bendix 1993). Women were included in Appenzell Ausserrhoden in 1989, and eight years later the assembly voted itself out of existence; it continues in Appenzell Innerrhoden, where it is also a tourist attraction. Here the men wore bourgeois clothing, not herders' outfits, and carried swords. Willi explained that the men wore dark clothes so that their white hands were visible. He called it the *Urdemokratie*, the original democracy.

Willi originally was uncertain whether giving women the vote was a good thing. He always discussed each issue with his wife before voting and took her opinion into account, but admitted that the man had the final say. Willi reflected that when he was young, women stayed home and looked after the children and so they had little understanding of public affairs. Now that a lot of women either had no children or went to work anyway, they understood them better (and so there was more reason they should have the vote). However, he did not approve of women working: "*They should look after their children!*" He explained that the family was the most important institution. "*If the family isn't happy, the whole of Switzerland could have problems!*"

Willi was president of his *Lesegesellschaft* for four years. These "reading societies" were originally district (*Bezirk*) discussion groups, and some proved the foundation of the modern political parties (and illustrate the Habermasian public sphere). They met monthly over the winter. At first, people were too poor to have their own subscriptions to newspapers and periodicals so they pooled them. The *Lesegesellschaften* bought and then circulated them among the members, functioning rather like libraries, Willi explained. A number of *Lesegesellschaften* still existed.[27] Willi's group had around forty members, including not only farmers but also teachers and others, from all walks of life. Willi explained that the *Lesegesellschaften* were nonpartisan, politically neutral places for thinking things through together. They discussed policy and forthcoming issues, "so we went to the Landsgemeinde well prepared to vote." In his early years, people

---

27. There were five *Lesegesellschaften* in Herisau during the time Willi was active. Although literacy was part of the Protestant tradition, the *Lesegesellschaften* were definitely not religious (Peter Witschi, pers. comm.).

didn't have time to go to read the papers in the restaurants, so, although voices were equal, someone, usually the president, had to come to each meeting well prepared to talk. In any case, Willi never just sat and listened; that was why, he said, they wanted to give him more and more responsibility. They discussed primarily local issues, örtliche Probleme, like the schools, but also external issues, concerning NATO, for example. Willi thought it was good for Switzerland to join the United Nations, but not the European Union.

When I suggested that the reading societies might have been the foundation of democracy, Willi agreed strongly. "Parties today may be larger and stronger, but not necessarily better! Parties are too interested in money. Decisions are better reached within the Lesegesellschaften since politics with conscience is the basis. *Thank God we still have some conscience!*" he concluded, "*even in the Bundesrat.*"

Willi also spoke positively about the cooperatives (*Genossenschaften*) of foresters, cheese makers, and so forth. These, he said, illustrating with his hands, emerged from below, not from the top down. Switzerland, he concluded, was the oldest democracy in the world. To people like Willi, these were not mere words but the product of lived experiences and the model for living.

* * *

On later occasions, I visited Willi in his flat, once alone and the following year together with Bea Schwitter, from the University of Zürich. There I met Willi's wife, Katarina. On the first visit, the couple graciously set aside their Parcheesi game and invited me in for coffee and cake. Since unsuccessful operations to replace her hips a decade earlier, Katarina moved about in a wheelchair. Willi shopped and cooked, following his wife's instructions. He wasn't accustomed to household duties at first, he said, but was very glad to have some work to do. The apartment was large and airy. They were happy to have a beautiful view of the Alpstein from their windows. The rooms were clean and tidy, with adjacent duvets neatly folded on the bed. Katarina had a workroom where she knitted blankets and socks for her grandchildren. "I have the time," she explained.

On the walls were a lovely painting of an *Alp*, in a style Willi called *naïf*, old photos of their parents, and a photo of three generations of men at the *Alp*: Willi, his middle son, and the son's oldest son, who would also become a farmer. There was a framed picture of Willi and Katarina's sixtieth wedding anniversary in front of the Sonne, with all the children and grandchildren.

They turned next to photo albums evoking further details of their lives There was a photo of the young couple at the Rossfall—Katarina in a Toggenburg *Tracht* (outfit)[28]—and photos of their engagement when they were each twenty-five and of their marriage six months later. Willi got two days off army service to get engaged, at Katarina's father's farm. They exchanged gold rings. She still wore hers; Willi's *"got lost inside a cow!"* He was helping the cow give birth, it was very slippery and somehow the ring came off. There was an album devoted to their children's families, with precisely two pages for each, including a wedding photo, a shot of their house, and a photo of their children. They had optimistically left two blank pages blank for the eldest son, who was then fifty. The daughters all married farmers. Willi and Katarina listed the professions of each grandchild. Some were farmers or in farm-related business. One grandson-in-law had a farm too small to live from so he was also a butcher and a driver. The wife worked in a hospital. One daughter had married a farmer in canton Zürich; their daughter in turn was a schoolteacher, married to a Canadian.

There were photos of the houses in which they had lived, and one of the house where Willi grew up, taken much later. Looking at it, he said he had had a good youth. There were pictures of the *Alp* where he first worked and later their own *Alp*. In their wedding photos and those of their children, people wore traditional dress, the husbands in beautiful *Sennen* outfits with shiny gold ornaments and red vests. But when the newest generation married, the brides wore white and the men suits. They ducked under arches of flowers set up outside the churches. The stacks of photos shifted from images of grandchildren, to calves, to udders. Katarina also showed me postcards sent from all over the world by various grandchildren.

When I contacted him again in 2004, Willi pronounced himself happy to hear from me and asked whether I had already published something about him. He received us that same afternoon in his house. Asking whether we planned to take notes, he immediately led us to the kitchen table, which contained two hardback volumes of *Appenzeller Geschichte* and a couple of novels. The Parcheesi board was laid out on another table. Willi wore suspenders, his old-fashioned trousers, and a pale blue lightly embroidered shirt characteristic of local farmers. Katarina moved in and out of the conversation. She inspected the cake we brought and put it away. Willi offered us coffee and opened a bottle of sparkling

---

28. Katarina was from a farm high up in the neighboring Toggenburg valley.

mineral water. He asked Bea her last name and her *Heimatort*, eager to place her and happy to discover her origins were not in a large city.

They showed us more photo albums and reviewed their children and grand-children. Five of the six daughters trained as homecare nurses once their children were grown and they were free to make some money. The latest grand-daughter to wed worked as a *Senn* and married a mountain farmer (*Bergbauer*). Other grandchildren were between twenty-one and thirty and might still marry, they said, hopefully. People married later than before, because women worked now. I suggested that Katarina had worked when she was young, but they said this was just an apprenticeship.

In those days, the late 1930s, Katarina explained, your parents looked after you on their farm so long as you went to school. Then you had to go work on someone else's farm. Her father had a large farm and was quite well off, but she was sent to a different farm to make money directly after confirmation, at the age of sixteen. She'd attended an agricultural housekeeping school. Willi and Katarina worked together on a big farm. Katarina did housework but also cut hay and so forth. Everyone helped; there were horses, no machinery. They were not unhappy. I asked Willi if he had been exploited and he said decisively, "*No.*" I assume this is because he, like Katarina, understood his work there at the farm as an apprenticeship, because he chose the work, because it enabled him to build toward his own enterprise, and, finally, because he worked alongside the owners and relations with them were warm.[29] The farmer attended their twenty-fifth wedding anniversary and later moved in with them at Willi's farm for the last eighteen months of his life.

Katarina was from a big *Sennen* family, one of nine siblings, her father one of thirteen. I asked whether big families were good. "In big families children learn to share, an advantage for the rest of your life. When there are only one or two children, they are not accustomed to do without. One bears one's upbringing throughout life. Things from early life become ingrained."

Willi knew the *Sennenball* had been held the past Monday. One of his grandsons had danced there; they had his picture from the newspaper. One dance is composed of a team of eight young men holding hands in a circle,

---

29. By contrast, there have been recent stories in the Swiss news of "contract children" who in earlier decades were sent by social workers to farms where their labor was exploited (BBC Switzerland: "Stolen childhoods," November 2, 2014: http://www.bbc.co.uk/programmes/p0297188).

with the alternate four held almost horizontal very close to the floor between their upright partners; "It requires a great deal of strength," Willi emphasized. This grandson was currently working as a *Senn* on an *Alp*. In former days, they reflected, there were only a very few times you had free from work. There were no holidays. *"Holidays' meant going on military service, but sometimes that was no holiday!"*

Willi and Katarina showed us a wonderful photo of themselves as a very young couple from 1936. It was color tinted by hand and gave them very rosy cheeks. It was taken at the *Sennenball*, the occasion of their first kiss! Willi laughed. He rented a large farm and people told him he was crazy, because it was such a difficult time for farmers. But he put his faith in God. He quoted Jeremias Gotthelf, an early nineteenth-century Swiss novelist and pastor, who said, "*Im Haus muss beginnen was im Staate leuchten soll*" ("What shines in the state must begin at home"). Like many Swiss, when Willi thought about politics in the public sphere, he understood it as emerging from values rooted in the household.

Willi had had hip operations some years earlier; that was why he walked with sticks. He thought perhaps the hip problems came from working very hard in his youth. In the *Alp*, you often had to carry loads of wood, and he was proud of lifting very heavy weights. When the doctor first examined his hip, he was amazed he'd postponed the operation for so long, as the bones were rubbing against each other. He had lived in pain for several years but hadn't wanted the operation. Afterwards he admitted he should have done it years earlier. "*But one survives.*"

It was getting difficult for them to attend grandchildren's weddings, but they received frequent visits from them and enjoyed staying home. "We don't know how long we can go on living here, so the time here counts. *It is a gift, staying at home at our age.*" Both were eighty-nine.

I asked about the values Willi had lived by. "*Real values,*" he said at once. He started with almost nothing, he continued. Then followed six years of military service (because of the war and when he could otherwise have been accumulating cattle). But they were always healthy, and that was very important. "*Trust in God,*" he added. Even today, this was the foundation of their daily life. I asked why people were leaving the church. "If people leave the church, that is their business. But no one can run away from God, only from the church. No human being can make a decision until they are born and no one can choose his or her death, unless they commit suicide. Even then, many are unsuccessful."

Willi said he hoped he had passed his values on to his children. "But you can't prescribe them. You show by the example of your own life. Nothing else, but I tried my best." He learned his values from his mother and father; they had the same values (although they were not farmers). He was confirmed in the church but never worked for it directly. "One can just as well do things in the background; it doesn't matter whether others see it or not."

Kathy had told me that Willi used pious sayings and written folk wisdom to guide his life, and indeed these are ubiquitous in German-speaking Switzerland, and can be seen, for example, inscribed on signs hung along mountain paths. Before we left, Willi showed Bea the wooden plaque on his wall commemorating the seventy-fifth anniversary of the *Viehzuchtgenossenschaft* (1892–1967) that took place during his presidency. On it was carved a poem that, he affirmed, was very important.

Der Bauer steht auf verlässlichem Grund
Ihn bindet ein alter verschwiegener Bund
Die Arbeit macht seine Hände steif
Die Arbeit macht seine Seele reif
Ein jedes Werk das er vollbringt
Ist das Werk das um ein Wunder ringt
Ist auf Verheissung aufgebaut
Weil'er der eignen Kraft vertraut

The farmer stands on sturdy ground
He maintains an old concealed alliance
Labor makes his hand stiff
Labor makes his soul ripe
Every work that he accomplishes
Is a work that strives for a miracle
It is built on a promise
From confidence in his own strength.[30]

---

30. Written by Huckenberger, a farmer in canton Thurgau. Bea corrected my transcription and translation but told me that she did not fully understand the poem, finding the language old-fashioned and poor. The translation does not fully bring out the distinction between "*Arbeit*" and "*Werk*" (for which, see Arendt [1958] 1998).

* * *

I have used Willi's conversation to illustrate aspects of farming life at a certain period in this part of Switzerland. It may be that I have taken his description of his life at face value, but my aim has not been to understand his inner life so much as to depict his own depiction of contentment. And even if you do not want to be a Swiss farmer yourself, with worn-out hips, a stiff hand, and never a day off, you have to acknowledge that Willi has a "ripe soul."

I draw on Willi's life to illustrate something about the social conditions of his time and place that enabled a good life of a certain kind. I am not interested either in generalizing about men like Willi or in describing happiness in the abstract. Willi is not unduly self-conscious. He did not go out of the way to describe himself as happy, and it is not for me to describe his happiness in an emotional sense (nor was it an explicit object of my questions). But he evidently manifests a happy life, a life well lived. He exemplifies the virtues he describes; he simply has the character he has, *is* the person he is. My concern is not with Willi's subjectivity or the depths of his character but with what he presented of himself to me (and as I received it). His world is one in which both rational calculation and divine will play their part. He has a Protestant work ethic, even a Weberian calling (*Beruf*); without being born into a farming family, he developed the ethos of a self-sufficient farmer and achieved success according to local ideals of the farmer's life and of civic engagement. I take Willi to epitomize a certain liberal ideal of wellbeing and an ideal liberal citizen in a political sense.[31]

Willi was, I conclude, a good and happy man, and I have been describing a good and happy life (without, of course, advocating it as the best or only good life). This is not to deny there may have been periods of conflict or unhappiness in his life or even some concealed regrets, or that one could interrogate his sense of satisfaction. What I offer is an interpretation, based on the evidence I have presented here.

I cannot, of course, either solve the mystery of human happiness or give an original philosophical response to it, and it has not been my intention to do either. With respect to the happiness of *this* life, I would emphasize the way the temporal and the ethical dimensions intertwine. Central is Willi's satisfaction

---

31. Liberalism is part of a general Swiss ethos, but Appenzell Ausserrhoden has considered itself particularly liberal; the word "liberal" recurred frequently in my discussions with citizens and in the historical sources

at accomplishments over time, a sense of direction, fruition, and resolution, as evident in his career and the smooth generational succession he enabled. These are achievements over which many Swiss farmers worry. At least in retrospect, Willi had the sense he always knew where he was going, and when he didn't, he says, God stepped in and showed him the way. Willi also recognizes where he has been. He understands his freedom not as existential but as a matter of faith and of meeting his practical needs and familial and civic responsibilities. His autonomy is never individualistic or isolated but mediated through work, family, and political engagement. Not wealth but work and family. Not just simple labor, daily toil (*Arbeit*), in Arendt's sense ([1958] 1998), but also work in the sense of something produced, something that lasts (*Werk*), and that is framed within the commitment to a calling.[32]

Willi said he felt called to livestock from his first childhood lessons in the Bible. Labor was indeed long, repetitive, arduous, and sometimes lonely, but he showed nostalgia for the *Alp* and its connotations of masculine independence as well as a real interest in cows. There was also the courtship and happy marriage and the settlement of the children, livestock, and land. Willi argues for the primacy of the family over the political sphere, but this is precisely because he sees a direct connection between them. Wellbeing and ethical conduct are simultaneously conditions of family, municipality, and country. Here he exemplifies the Swiss political ethos, which has been one of starting at the local community and placing the most weight on the smallest level of inclusion (in striking contrast to the French model).[33] Willi has been an engaged and active citizen, seeing one duty of citizenship as critically evaluating and discussing the issues before voting, and another as holding office. His life also illustrates the inseparability of the ethical from the aesthetic, evident in the love, appreciation, and care of landscape, tradition, and livestock. His interest in the latter is comparable to ethnographic descriptions of eastern and southern Africa (Evans-Pritchard 1940 and Solway 1998, respectively), albeit the attention of the African livestock holders is turned to the beauty of oxen or bulls, and that of Swiss farmers like Willi to lactating cows.

The values by which men like Willi live have sometimes been described as ascetic. I would protest that this diminishes them and risks parody. My

---

32. It seems to me that for Willi and people like him, *Arbeit* has many of the positive qualities that Arendt somewhat snobbishly reserved for *Werk*.

33. See Weinberg (1975). As one manifestation, municipal tax is higher than federal.

approach in this article has been evidently broadly Aristotelian. To return to Aristotle's words in my epigraph, "Happiness is good activity not amusement." In this tradition, a good human life requires the exercise of the capacities rather than simply the fulfillment of needs (Lambek 2008a, after Macpherson 1973). The availability of the means for, and appreciation of, such exercise—in work, politics, art, music, philosophy, nurture, or love—is salient. Phrased another way, the values intrinsic to the means, or internal to practices, must not be overshadowed by those external to them (MacIntyre 1981).[34] Perhaps most striking in this region, until recently, civic engagement has been a significant field in which a man could exercise his capacities, not unlike male citizenship in the ancient Greek *polis*. Willi took full advantage of the opportunities and has also been lucky. His own view is also Aristotelian in the sense that he advocates discipline over rule following and that his sense of freedom emerges as a judicious but not unthinking or unforceful adherence to social convention.[35]

At the beginning of the article, I addressed a common stereotype of Switzerland and the Swiss as boring. It is one thing to depict the lives of others, from the outside, as boring; it is quite another to experience boredom for oneself. The conditions necessary to preclude boredom are not reducible to objective features, like the number of venues for entertainment, or even more subjective ones, like the edginess of the art scene. Practices through which to exercise the capacities must be available and meaningful. It is hard to be happy when frustrated, undirected, understimulated (or perhaps overstimulated). Stimulation comes from activity—this may be quiet contemplation, intellectual enjoyment, or reading literature; it may be something more vigorous or creative, like writing, hiking, or singing; and it may be something more practical, like raising livestock or children, or deliberating and administering the political life of one's community. And of course practice entails the balancing among such activities.[36]

---

34. I have also argued (Lambek 2008b) that happiness might be considered the metavalue, that is, the value internal to the art of living, understood as the metapractice.

35. For further discussion of the ethics of freedom and judgment, see the contributions to Lambek (2010) as well as Lambek (2015).

36. There is also a balance among the virtues or practices such as piety (Mahmood 2005; Hirschkind 2006) or freedom (Laidlaw 2002) highlighted in recent anthropological work elsewhere.

To answer the earlier provocation, happiness is precisely not boredom, and Swiss citizens like Willi are a far cry from the inhabitants of provincial Russian cities, as described by writers like Chekov or anthropologists like Anna Kruglova (2015), who struggle with and against what Kruglova calls "acedia." Happy people may sometimes appear boring to writers and intellectuals in their midst, but that is not the same as to say that they are bored themselves. One reason, then, for making happiness a focus of ethnographic investigation is precisely to use it as a lens to see what interests people, what engages, and challenges them. "Happiness" in this sense is more an ethnographic means than an ethnographic end, much as happiness in ethnographic practice is to be found in the means of our work rather than in externalized ends. (My happiness comes more in the conduct of fieldwork and the struggle of writing this article than in seeing it in print.)

Of course, this means that we do not experience our work as alienated from our being. Willi's is what I would call an integrated life. Work, property, autonomy, family, God, political conversation and engagement, landscape, and love—all come together in a harmonious whole.[37] To draw from various accounts of ethics, there is a relation between good character, social justice, and self-realization, between virtue and happiness. Willi is justifiably well respected. A feature of his life, characterized by its absence, is abjection; Willi never had to suffer social shame for his origins, citizenship, class, religion, or sexuality. Likewise there is little indication of loneliness.

The life-course is not fully individual, but articulated with consociates and people of alternate generations. To conclude, I want to emphasize, as Willi does, that succession is critical, each generation taking the place of the one previous to it, mutually confirming their actions. Ideally, the young are happy to succeed their parents, the old to see the young doing so. But succession is also fraught with uncertainty and danger—competition, ambivalence, unexpected events, changed circumstances, and difficult choices. It is bittersweet insofar as the arrival of one generation signals the eventual departure of another. Nor does the happiness of one generation confirm the happiness of the next. Social conditions were right for talented, hard-working, and patient people like Willi

---

37. Pieces that don't fit, like the oldest son's divergent interests, are partly acknowledged—he received different kinds of gifts on his birthdays—and partly not—Willi still hopes for his eventual marriage.

to succeed; whether this is still possible for the following cohorts of Swiss farmers is more doubtful.

ACKNOWLEDGMENTS

Research and writing have been supported by the Social Sciences and Humanities Research Council of Canada with a standard research grant and a Canada Research Chair. Thanks to Iris Blum, Eva Keller, Peter Witschi, and especially Bea Schwitter for multiple forms of assistance, and Iza Kavedžija, Harry Walker, Frank Muttenzer, Jeanne Rey-Pellissier, and Giovanni da Col for additional astute comments. Earlier drafts were read by five referees (three of whom read them twice) who provided serious and helpful feedback. Their responses speak directly to the difficulty of portraying happiness. Earlier versions of the article were delivered at the London School of Economics and Political Science workshop on happiness and the Ethnology seminar at the University of Zürich.

REFERENCES

Arendt, Hannah. (1958) 1998. *The human condition.* Chicago: University of Chicago Press.

Astuti, Rita. 2000. "Kindreds and descent groups." In *Cultures of relatedness*, edited by Janet Carsten, 90–103. Cambridge: Cambridge University Press.

Baker, Judith, 2010. "Philosophical comments on Charles Stafford and Francesca Merlan." In *Ordinary ethics: Anthropology, language, and action*, edited by Michael Lambek, 225–31. New York: Fordham University Press.

Barker, Joshua, Erik Harms, and Johan Lindquist, eds. 2013. *Figures of Southeast Asian modernity.* Honolulu: University of Hawai'i Press.

Bendix, John. 1993. *Brauchtum und Politik: Die Landsgemeinde in Appenzell Ausserrhoden.* Urnäsch: Museum fur Appenzeller Brauchtum.

Bendix, Regina. 1985. *Progress and nostalgia: Silvesterklausen in Urnäsch, Switzerland.* Berkeley: University of California Press.

Blum Iris, Roland Inauen, and Matthias Weishaupt, eds. 2003. *Frühe Photographie im Appenzellerland 1860–1950.* Herisau: Verlag Appenzeller Hefte.

Boltanski, Luc. 1966. *Le bonheur suisse: D'après une enquête réalisée par Isac Chiva, Ariane Deluz et Nathalie Stern.* Paris: Les Éditions de Minuit.

Cassaniti, Julia. 2015. *Living Buddhism: Mind, self and emotion in a Thai community.* Ithaca, NY: Cornell University Press.

Centlivres, Pierre, ed. 1990. *Devenir Suisse: Adhésion et diversité culturelle des étrangers en Suisse.* Geneva: Georg Éditeur.

Colson, Elizabeth. 2012. "Happiness." *American Anthropologist* 114 (1): 7–8.

Crapanzano, Vincent. 1980. *Tuhami: Portrait of a Moroccan.* Chicago: University of Chicago Press.

Droz, Yvan, and Jérémie Forney. 2007. *Un métier sans avenir? La grande transformation de l'agriculture suisse romande.* Paris: Karthala-IUED.

Evans-Pritchard, E. E. 1940. *The Nuer: A description of the modes of livelihood and political institutions of a Nilotic people.* Oxford: Clarendon Press.

Falk, Dean. 2012. "Happiness: An evolutionary perspective." *American Anthropologist* 114 (1): 8–9.

Fassin, Didier. 2013. "On resentment and *ressentiment*: The politics and ethics of moral emotions." *Current Anthropology* 54 (3): 249–67.

Freud, Sigmund. (1929) 1991. *Civilization and its discontents.* In *Civilization, society and religion.* Translated by James Strachey, The Freud Penguin Library, Vol. 12, 251–340. Harmondsworth: Penguin.

Hermann, Isabell. 2004. *Die Bauern-häuser beider Appenzell.* Herisau: Schläpfer.

Hirschkind, Charles. 2006. *The ethical soundscape: Cassette sermons and Islamic counterpublics.* New York: Columbia University Press.

Kolakowski, Leszek, 2012. "Is God happy?" Translated by Agnieszka Kolakowska. *New York Review of Books* LIX (20): 16.

Kruglova, Anna. 2015. "Anything can happen: Everyday morality and social theory in Russia." Doctoral dissertation, Department of Anthropology, University of Toronto.

Laidlaw, James. 2002. "For an anthropology of ethics and freedom." *Journal of the Royal Anthropological Institute* (N.S.) 8 (2): 311–32.

Lambek, Michael. 2007. "The cares of Alice Alder: Recuperating kinship and history in Switzerland." In *Ghosts of memory: Essays on remembrance and relatedness,* edited by Janet Carsten, 218–40. Oxford: Blackwell.

———. 2008a. "Measuring—or practising well-being?" In *Culture and well-being: Anthropological approaches to freedom and political ethics,* edited by Alberto Corsín Jiménez, 115–33. London: Pluto.

———. 2008b. "Value and virtue." *Anthropological Theory* 8 (2): 133–57.

———, ed. 2010. *Ordinary ethics: Anthropology, language, and action.* New York: Fordham University Press.

———. 2015. "The ethical condition." In *The ethical condition: Essays on action, person & value*, 1–39. Chicago: University of Chicago Press.

Levy, Robert, and Douglas Hollan. 2015. "Person-centered interviewing and observation." In *Handbook of methods in cultural anthropology*, edited by H. Russell Bernard and Clarence Gravlee, 313–42. Second edition. Lanham, MD: Rowan & Littlefield.

Leys, Ruth. 2007. *From guilt to shame: Auschwitz and after*. Princeton, NJ: Princeton University Press.

Lutz, Catherine. 1988. *Unnatural emotions: Everyday sentiments on a Micronesian atoll and their challenge to Western theory*. Chicago: University of Chicago Press.

MacIntyre, Alasdair, 1981. *After virtue: A study in moral theory*. Notre Dame, IN: University of Notre Dame Press.

Macpherson, C. B. 1973. *Democratic theory: Essays in retrieval*. Oxford: Clarendon Press.

Mahmood, Saba. 2005. *Politics of piety: The Islamic revival and the feminist subject*. Princeton, NJ: Princeton University Press.

Robbins, Joel. 2013. "Beyond the suffering subject: Toward an anthropology of the good." *Journal of the Royal Anthropological Institute* (N.S.) 19 (3): 447–62.

Rougemont, Denis de. 1965. *La Suisse ou l'histoire d'un peuple heureux*. Paris: Hachette.

Sacks, Harvey. 1984. "On doing 'being ordinary'." In *Structures of social action: Studies in conversation analysis*, edited by J. Maxwell Atkinson and John Heritage, 413–29. Cambridge: Cambridge University Press.

Schläpfer, Walter. 1977. "Das Land Appenzell und seine Geschichte." In *Das Land Appenzell*, edited by Herbert Maeder. Olten: Walter Verlag.

Shostak, Marjorie. 1981. *Nisa: The life and words of a !Kung woman*. Cambridge, MA: Harvard University Press.

Smith, Adam. (1759) 1976. *The theory of moral sentiments*. Edited by D. D. Raphael and A. L. Macfie. Oxford: Oxford University Press.

Solway, Jacqueline. 1998. "Taking stock in the Kalahari: Accumulation and resistance on the Southern African periphery." *Journal of Southern African Studies* 24 (2): 425–41.

Steinberg, Jonathan. 1976. *Why Switzerland?* Cambridge: Cambridge University Press.

Strawson, P. F. 2008. *Freedom and resentment and other essays*. London: Routledge.

Weinberg, Daniela. 1975. *Peasant wisdom: Cultural adaptation in a Swiss village.* Berkeley: University of California Press.

Williams, Bernard. 1981. *Moral luck.* Cambridge: Cambridge University Press.

Witschi, Peter. 1994. *Appenzeller in Alle Welt: Auswanderungsgeschichte und Lebensschicksale.* Schläpfere: Herisau.

Zemp, Hugo. 1980. *Switzerland: Zäuerli, Yodel of Appenzell.* CD. Smithsonian Folkways/UNESCO Collection of Traditional Music.

CHAPTER TEN

Joy within tranquility
Amazonian Urarina styles of happiness

HARRY WALKER

> I'm living peacefully now. Nothing happens. . . . We're all living peacefully be-
> cause I have my sons to whom nothing happens because I'm with my husband.
> Even when he's drunk, he doesn't do anything to me, that's why I'm peaceful. . . .
> I'm living contentedly. He works properly, this man, I prepare my manioc beer
> for him, and he invites his neighbors, I also invite my female companions. So I'm
> working peacefully.

Rosa held my gaze as she answered my questions about her new life as a married
woman. She went on to emphasize how difficult it was when her husband traveled far away, leaving her alone with the children, but how she would wait patiently for him until his return. She told me how her husband's peaceful life now
contrasted dramatically with the ongoing problems he had with his previous
wife. The term she used over and over again, *raotojoeein*, meaning loosely "being
calm" or "being tranquil," is one I often heard used by my Urarina companions
when speaking about fond memories of times past, but also when invoking the
ideal style of life they sought to bring about for themselves and their loved ones,
and was closely linked to ideas of satisfying forms of work. As one man put it
succinctly when I inquired about his hopes and dreams for the future: "I hope

to live peacefully." A straightforward aim, I thought at the time, if somewhat unexciting. Only much later did I realize just how sophisticated was this ideal of tranquility, and how it brought into alignment a constellation of ideas ranging from truth and right to sensory pleasure, freedom from anxiety, moral conduct, and the opportunity to pursue one's own good in one's own way.

The Urarina, a group of around four thousand hunter-horticulturalists who inhabit the Chambira river and its tributaries in the Peruvian Amazon, are not alone in their preoccupation with "the good life." Anthropologists of Amazonia have routinely been invoking this and related concepts since well before the recent surge of interest in Western popular discourse—largely, I think, because it is so clearly a central concern of native Amazonian peoples themselves. Philippe Descola (1996), in his meticulous study of the Jivaroan economy and its embeddedness within the social and cosmological order, was able to show how it was the distinctive Jivaroan conception of "the good life," with its emphasis on marital harmony, the provision of ample home-made manioc beer and the like, that effectively prevented the intensification of agriculture where ecological conditions would otherwise have allowed for it, thus keeping production in a condition of homeostasis. Descola's argument ran directly counter to the materialist and ecological determinist theses of the time, which emphasized the so-called "limiting factors" of soil quality, protein scarcity, and so on, while in some ways anticipating the belated "discovery" by some Western economists that maximizing happiness may be a more worthwhile goal than increasing material wealth, and that the two do not always coincide. In a different vein, Joanna Overing (e.g., 1989) pioneered the study of what she termed the "art of living" or the "aesthetics of everyday life," showing how the Western distinction between ethics and aesthetics is irrelevant in a world where people strive for beauty in their social relations with others. In various ways, concepts of "the good life" or "living well" have since pervaded a large number of anthropological accounts of Amazonian sociality (e.g., Overing and Passes 2000a; Belaunde 2001), which often emphasize the ways in which Amazonian social life focuses on emotional comfort and the maintenance of good or harmonious interpersonal relationships, some of which may even extend beyond the human sphere to embrace nonhumans in an expansive social order. This is not to say, however, that violence, hostility, conflict, and danger are absent from Amazonian life; on the contrary, they are ever-present, and indeed they comprise the sociocosmic backdrop against which the ideals of peaceable everyday sociality must inevitably be understood (Overing and Passes 2000b: 6–7). Moreover, as Fernando

Santos Granero (2000) has argued, though peaceful conviviality is more than an unrealizable ideal, its achievement in practice is nevertheless constantly undermined, precisely because it entails such strong feelings of love, trust, and generosity: any rupture in such relations quickly generates equally intense negative emotions, such as anger, hatred, or shame, which end up driving people apart.

Despite this long-standing interest in the conditions of the good life, or the "criteria of good living," to use Descola's expression, there has been relatively little exploration of what it actually feels like to lead a good or virtuous life, or how this correlates with happiness as a positive affective state: the relationship, we might say, between morality and pleasure. While Amazonians clearly enjoy and hold in very high esteem the sensory pleasures associated with food, sex, and meaningful, sociable work, among other things, exactly how short-term, apparently subjective forms of enjoyment relate to broader conceptions of the good (e.g., Robbins 2013), and longer-term goals or aspirations in life, remains an open question. It has been suggested that ideals of happiness and wellbeing may be closely linked to health and productivity (Izquierdo 2009), as well as social relations and success in common subsistence activities (Reyes-Garcia and Tsimane' Amazonian Panel Study [TAPS] 2012). According to one study, among the Bolivian Tsimane (ibid.), the most frequently mentioned reason for happiness was, significantly, "nothing bad happened." Yet, despite widespread recognition among scholars of the general importance of "peacefulness" or "tranquility" in everyday sociality, precisely what this means, in moral or affective terms, has scarcely been investigated.

According to Durkheim, for whom the relationship between the moral and the sensuous was in many ways a key concern, socialization entailed an emancipation from sensory pleasures through the acquisition of a shared moral sensitivity, comprising common rules of conduct directed at a higher end which he equated to the good. Such a conception, which Durkheim drew from Kant, thus seeks sharply to distinguish morality from happiness (or pleasure) and provide a firm grounding for the former. The framing of morality in terms of the obligations incumbent upon people, however, appears ill suited to the Amazonian context, where rule following is not a salient feature of moral life, and where scholars have found greater mileage in approaches drawn from virtue ethics, which emphasize the cultivation of moral character rather than doing one's duty or bringing about good consequences. On the other hand, Durkheim also acknowledged a possible connection between the sensuous and the moral in his notion of collective effervescence, as a kind of exaltation that reaffirms social bonds and imbues shared moral values with powerful affective meanings, thereby enhancing their salience in everyday life. Such a conception suggests that certain moral dispositions or sensibilities may be reinforced precisely in liminal, transitory moments of shared jubilation; and indeed later scholars—most notably Victor Turner (e.g., 1969)—have shown that liminal or liminoid moments may play a crucial role in orienting people to others.

In engaging with these issues, we are soon confronted with a great rift that has run through Western thinking about happiness from ancient times to the present day. Much work in the recent "economics of happiness" movement follows a broadly utilitarian approach whose purest form may be found in Jeremy Bentham's assertion that maximizing the sum total of happiness in society should be everyone's goal, and the explicit aim of governmental policy. In this view, happiness is conceived as a positive affective state, or simply "feeling good," and often associated with a subjective sense of satisfaction with life. An alternative approach follows Aristotle's conception of happiness as a life of virtue, emphasizing ideas of purpose and self-actualization, while stressing that the goals of life are diverse and not always dependent on subjective experience (see, e.g., Ryan and Deci 2001; Tomer 2011; Henderson and Knight 2012: 196). Adherents of the latter approach point out that the conception of happiness as a subjective feeling is a recent development, and that the ancient philosophers who saw happiness as the goal of life were talking about a far broader conception of human flourishing, one which has a certain objective content to it and involves a strong moral or evaluative component. This ongoing debate is sometimes referred to as the tension between hedonic and eudaimonic approaches, and while some have attempted to reconcile these by suggesting that a life rich in both kinds of pursuits is associated with the greatest degree of wellbeing (e.g., Huta and Ryan 2010), the relationship between these two forms of happiness remains unclear, not least in terms of how they might actually interact in practice in a given social context.

In this article, I suggest that Urarina manage two distinct but related concepts of happiness that loosely (though not entirely) map onto this division between hedonism and eudaimonia. Both are ultimately social and relational ideals, attributes of groups rather than individuals, as it were, though one corresponds to short-term, momentary pleasure, and the other to a more enduring sense of a life well lived, rich with meaning and purpose, and centering on a quite distinctive and multifaceted concept of tranquility. I argue that they are not contradictory, but come into alignment in interesting ways; in particular, I suggest, the short-term concept resembles a total social fact, one which condenses the meaning of the long-term, more objective concept of living well, in all its complexity, into an enjoyable subjective experience. Central to both forms of happiness are a particular form of nonalienated labor in which people are free to extend their capacities in satisfying ways, and a sense of harmony or correspondence between people's attitudes, beliefs, and actions, one that endows them with a sense of individuality while contributing to a distinctive and intrinsically enjoyable "style of life."

THE VIRTUES OF TRANQUILITY

The Urarina pursue a generally subsistence lifestyle of hunting, fishing, small-scale horticulture, and gathering wild forest fruits and other produce, interspersed with occasional bouts of extractive activity for passing fluvial traders under the system of *habilitación*, in which goods are advanced on credit in order to incite people to work. They mostly live in small, scattered settlements of around ten or twenty houses, each relatively autonomous both economically and politically. Although few Urarina today would readily be described as Christian, either by outsiders or by themselves, it is quite possible that Christianity—as imparted by Jesuit and Franciscan missionaries in the seventeenth and eighteenth centuries, for instance—has nevertheless shaped present-day moral values, as it may have done elsewhere in the region (see, e.g., Fausto 2007). Over the course of a couple of years spent living with them, I came to appreciate that Urarina people maintain a certain conviction that despite life's many hardships and struggles, their own way of life is the best one possible. They are especially scornful of urban life, where "you can't do anything unless you have money," though they also disparage the ways of their indigenous neighbors, who, they admit, are stronger and richer, but also, they insist, morally inferior. Though they sometimes lament the fact that many of the neighboring Candoshi have entered wage labor or become so-called "professionals," few Urarina, when given the opportunity, were themselves willing to enter wage labor for more than a few days at a time, valuing their flexibility and freedom more than increased income or the ideal of "progress." People would often remark that they want to, or should, "replace [their] forefathers": that is, live their lives in broad accordance with the same general values and aspirations as previous generations.

In seeking to characterize these values and aspirations, a good place to start is the ubiquitous Urarina term *raotojoeein*, which, as noted above, means loosely "being calm" or (as I prefer) "tranquility." Its prevalence in everyday conversation would be difficult to overestimate: someone asked how a recent trip into the forest went, for example, or how a patient recovering from illness was faring, could well be expected to answer, simply, "tranquilly." To begin with, it is clear that *raotojoeein* implies freedom from danger and distress. As such, we are immediately reminded of superficially similar ideas in ancient Greek and Buddhist philosophy, most notably the concept of *ataraxia*, or tranquility, promoted as the goal of life, or *telos*, in both Pyrrhonism and Epicureanism (e.g., Warren 2002). Tranquility in this context may be glossed as freedom from disturbance, or absence of trouble, and for the Skeptics in particular arises from a suspension of judgment concerning the nature or essence of things. Unlike the ancient Greek *ataraxia*, however, the Urarina ideal of tranquility should not be taken to imply an attitude of equanimity, mental composure, or emotional stability in the face of external fluctuations or adverse circumstances (e.g., Striker 1990). Nor does it equate to an absence of passion. For Urarina, as for perhaps most other native Amazonians, certain legitimate forms of violence, especially violent revenge against enemies, may be an important part of the good life, or at least may imbue life with a sense of purpose even as it disrupts the hard-won state of tranquility. On the other hand, it is in many ways the perennial threat of violence, the sense that danger lurks around every corner, that renders its absence so valuable. As Peter Gow (2000) has observed, his initial sense that daily life among the Piro was rather boring gradually gave way to an appreciation of the fact that this apparent boredom was experienced not as a lack, but as a positive achievement—a goal, in fact, of social life. "Doing nothing" was not only essentially an invitation to sociality, it was also necessarily a state carved out against a background of inevitable suffering and helplessness, in a cosmos pervaded by the constant threat of violence in which myriad hostile agents, human and nonhuman, always threaten to disrupt the calm surface of life, bringing illness or misfortune, or worse.

It is very common when among Urarina people to hear someone say, "nothing happened" as a form of praise, to mean that everything went well. In Rosa's account, with which this article began, she repeatedly emphasized that "nothing happened" to express her satisfaction with her husband and with married life in general. Yet this apparent lack of events certainly does not imply boredom. So far as I can tell, the Urarina have no term for boredom, and while it is perfectly possible that the experience of boredom is not unknown to them (especially in the city, as I discuss further below), I think they would be more likely to describe such a feeling as a kind of "sadness," arising from a temporary lack of people with whom to socialize. This indeed is what people would say—"it's sad"— when large numbers of people left the village for a few days to extract timber for sale. When surrounded by one's kin, with ample opportunities for productive labor, it seems more or less impossible to be bored.

Examining more closely the Urarina term for tranquility, *raotojoeein*, would seem to imply a much greater semantic density than obtains in its English equivalent. The stem *rao* or *rau* is found in a number of possible cognates, all associated in one way or another with Urarina conceptions of the good. These include words for calm (*raoti*), peace (*raotono*), taste (*raotono*), right or law (*rauhi*), an honorable person (*raunacaaena*), to be straight (*rauhicha*), truth (*rauhijidi*), to make happy (*rausiaaeca*), to heal (*rautaa*), and to like or enjoy (*rautatoha*). There are echoes here of the Cofán ideal of *opa*, which Michael Cepek (2008) has suggested denotes the paradigmatic Cofán conception of the desirable. *Opa* is used equally to refer to a "satisfying" existence, a "happy" community, and a "good" person, while also (and perhaps above all) referring to a certain quality of collective calmness, and freedom from fear. In the words of one of Cepek's informants: "*Opatssi* means living without being timid or nervous. It means that you'll be happy" (ibid.: 341). In my case, the Urarina word *raotoha*, or "delicious"— which would seem to be part of the same semantic matrix—was in fact the very first Urarina word I ever learned, quite simply because it was the first word my hosts took it upon themselves to teach me, immediately after we shared our first meal. The singular importance of this moment will become clearer below, as we see precisely how the sociable enjoyment of food is integrated into the wider constellation of values that make life rich and worth living.

Beyond the numerous semantic connections to morally worthy conditions and qualities, tranquility is associated with a range of other conditions necessary for living well, free of fear and stress, including good food and an abundance of game animals; good weather, especially sunshine, implying plenty of time remaining until the inevitable apocalypse; harmonious sociality, full of wit and good humor while avoiding heated emotions; and ample opportunities for the free and peaceful exercise of one's skills in carrying out productive chores, especially tasks dedicated toward the satisfaction of the needs or desires of others, such that competence and concentrated exertion become an expression of control and self-mastery. Urarina conceptions of the good life are broader than any straightforward concept of happiness would imply, and it is the former rather than the latter that they typically seem to strive for. Shamanic knowledge and power, for example, are extremely highly valued and widely sought after, but can only be obtained through stringent forms of discipline and self-denial, and often lead to a life full of suspicion and magical violence. There is a widespread sense in which "suffering" is seen as essential for obtaining certain benefits, including especially bodily skills or forms of knowledge (see also High 2010: 758). Ultimately, perhaps we should say that happiness acquires meaning in relation to suffering, but that both may nevertheless figure as valued components of a more overarching conception of a purposeful life (see also the introduction to this collection).

In a similar vein, it is also important to note that Urarina do not live tranquil lives all the time, free from anxiety and fear. On the contrary, their lives are all too often pervaded by hostility and envy, tension and resentment, and ongoing attempts to ward off dangers from all sides. In some cases, tranquility is willfully disrupted through the active pursuit of conflict or danger, the production of enmity, or engagement with a hostile exterior, which may also figure as an important and socially productive dynamic of Amazonian life (see, e.g., Overing 1981; Viveiros de Castro 2001: 37–8). Tranquility is an ideal, a goal, achieved for periods of time, but never permanent, and it cannot be taken for granted. It is, importantly, not a natural state, but a collective achievement of people working well together: an immaterial product of people's labor. It is conducive, in turn, to meaningful involvement in work and love, allowing these to come to the fore of daily experience, giving rise to lasting satisfaction and a sense of purpose. Achieving a state of tranquility opens up new horizons for action and is the condition of possibility of a life of meaning in which one is free to develop one's capacities and to exercise virtues such as generosity, self-control, and respect for others.

THE MASTERY OF WORK

In contemplating our own ideal working lives, leisure time often seems to emerge as a central preoccupation. In his classic paper on "the original affluent society," Marshall Sahlins (1968) claimed that hunter-gatherer societies had achieved an easy form of material wellbeing because their needs were few and easily met by just a few hours of work per day. Descola (1996) and others have pursued similar arguments in an Amazonian context on the basis of meticulous measurements of time spent by both sexes in work as opposed to "leisure" activities. This kind of study arguably reflects a certain concern in the West with increasing leisure time—a laudable goal, by all means, but one that can regrettably come to substitute for that of improving or transforming the work experience itself. It seems to me that Amazonians do not rigidly distinguish between work and free time, nor do they see leisure as the more enjoyable of the two. What better accounts for their "affluence," if that is the right term, is the pleasure and satisfaction they find in their work, arising largely from the ways in which work itself is organized. As Overing has written apropos of the Venezuelan Piaroa, "The affluent community . . . was the one that could take into account on a daily level both flexibility in schedules of work and individual preferences for the specific tasks themselves . . . affluence was a matter of achieving personal comfort in work, and not of productive accumulation" (1989: 166).

Many basic work activities, such as gardening or gathering wild forest produce, are carried out in pairs or small groups. As the composition of these groups differs according to the task, specific social relationships can be activated or nurtured through the choice of activity. Moreover, insofar as Amazonian sociality routinely stretches beyond humankind to implicate a range of nonhuman animals, plants, or spirits, successful engagement in many subsistence tasks can require management of these relationships in some form or another (e.g., through the performance of ritualized songs or chants). Given how interpersonal relationships are consistently singled out as the most important factor in subjective wellbeing, we should perhaps not underestimate the importance of engaging with the living landscape intersubjectively, rather than as objective resources awaiting exploitation (Miles-Watson 2010). Such intersubjective relations with nonhumans are of course often highly unstable, and may be downright anxiety inducing, as noted above, further casting into relief the ideal of tranquility. When managed successfully, however, they may contribute to the sociability of productive life and perhaps even to that sense of immersion in a mesh of immanent mental processes that Gregory Bateson (1972) associates with the idea of grace.

Another reason why people mostly enjoy their work seems to be that opportunities for action remain more or less equal to people's capabilities, allowing them to become immersed in their tasks, exercising their skills in a concentrated but relaxing way. An activity such as extracting timber, for instance, contains within it a universe of technical operations—clearing, felling, cutting,

rolling, tying, floating—each of which requires the mastery of a specific set
of technical operations, thus offering considerable experiential diversity even
within a "single" chore. This opportunity for the exercise of practical mastery is
a key reason why the vast majority of Urarina find city life highly unsatisfac-
tory, even downright frustrating. After one prolonged period of idleness in the
city, during which time he had done little but sit around in the old church in
Iquitos where all Urarina are welcome to stay for free as long as they please,
one man said to me, "I just can't stand it anymore here. I want to go back to
my work. In the city you can't be tranquil." Though it is not always achieved,
people strive for a kind of rhythm while they work, such that even hard labor—sometimes described as "suffering"—can still ultimately be experienced
as satisfying. "Working in the field, you really suffer . . . but we live well," as
one person put it.

This merging of action and awareness within daily activities resembles what
psychologists have described as the experience of flow: "People become so involved in what they are doing that the activity becomes spontaneous, almost
automatic; they stop being aware of themselves as separate from the actions
they are performing" (Csikszentmihályi 1992: 53). There is a sense of total concentration and focus, combined with relaxation and a sense of involvement or
absorption in the task at hand. It is not the sense of *being* in control that people
enjoy, but the sense of *exercising* control in difficult situations (*ibid.:* 61). The
freedom to act on the need to create opens up possibilities of self-realization,
and directs desires toward externalization through creation rather than the acquisition of goods. As Hegel and Marx recognized, such creative work allows
persons to know one another by externalizing themselves in an existence oriented toward others.

For this reason, I think, the prototype of "real work" is not wage labor. Thus
when I once stopped briefly in an Urarina community and asked after the
schoolteacher, who was a friend of mine, I was told simply, "He's at his work."
My interlocutor clearly did not mean the school, which was deserted, despite it
being a weekday. Instead, the implication was that he was out fishing or tending his garden, engaged in productive labor in order to meet the immediate
needs of his loved ones. In engaging in such work, people typically have a wide
range of tasks from which they are free to choose at will, and this "pluriactivity"
(Gasché and Vela Mendoza 2012) is central to one's ability to live well. People
do what they feel like doing on any particular day, do it with whom they wish to
socialize, and (with the partial exception of schoolteachers) rarely engage in the

same activity for more than a couple of days running—which is of course one reason why anything resembling long-term wage labor is steadfastly avoided by the majority. In Marxian terms, people manage to avoid any form of alienation from their labor or its products.

Even short-term paid work is only temporarily attractive: when an oil company once began drilling in the area, for example, the company representative announced that there was work available and that people should turn up at the site each morning, ready to go. For a short while, the company was inundated each day by a sea of willing workers. But the numbers very quickly dwindled to a small trickle, and their performance on the job grew increasingly erratic. One day, I overheard the company representative exclaim in frustration to a colleague, "I can't go on! I just can't work with these people!" In a similar vein, when Urarina today enter temporarily into apparently hierarchical relationships with labor bosses, or *patrones*, they manage to do so largely on their own terms and always for limited periods of time. Indeed, while the system of *habilitación* is sometimes seen as exploitative, both by Urarina and by other outside observers, its intermittent nature allows it to fit in well with the flexible and varied schedules that most people prefer.

INDIVIDUALITY AND STYLE

That there is something resembling a consensus among Urarina on the basic requirements of living well should not be taken to imply a homogeneity of values, or that there is little or no significant individual variation in life choices or goals. For some people, the desire for continuity with the ancestors exists alongside (or is even superseded by) a parallel desire for "progress," to "be civilized," to move away from the ancestors to the extent that the latter lived in what by some standards now appears as a state of savagery, ignorance, and violence. Such people commonly extol the virtues of so-called "civilized" life in sedentary, orderly villages fashioned in accordance with the model of the Native Community set forth by the Peruvian government, complete with elected officials, a primary school, football field, communal first aid kit, and the like. Maintaining a community of this sort requires ongoing "collaboration" from its inhabitants, in various ways, and this pressure can give rise to tensions, usually when those desiring progress seek to impose their vision on others by inducing them to contribute to common community projects.

On the whole, however, differences in values do not give rise to conflicts, because of the pervasive emphasis on individual autonomy. People would rarely if ever dream of telling someone else what to do. Hence the general refusal to "read" or appear to know what is going on in the mind of another—an insistence on mental opacity that appears to reflect people's sensitivity to impinging on others' self-determination (see Stasch 2008). The Urarina are not moralists who seek to impose a single view on all, and within the context of an overarching emphasis on tranquility, they recognize that good lives may take many different forms—at least up to a point—because lives are made good by the possession of many different goods. These can be combined in many different ways, and perhaps even ranked in different orders of importance, depending on people's character and their social context, but because these can differ greatly, there cannot be a single blueprint of how one should live. It is perhaps less a matter of what is done than *how* something is done that leads to enjoyment in life: what Irving Goldman (1963), writing of the Amazonian Cubeo, has referred to as their "style of life." According to Goldman, each social relationship for the Cubeo demanded a specific atmosphere of feelings, sentiments, and emotions: "Nothing of consequence can result from an act divorced from its proper mood" (ibid.: 253). Manufacture itself was a pleasurable recreation, and when the exertion of some particularly strenuous task—such as housebuilding—broke "the spell of good feeling," it was exchanged for another (ibid.: 66). Economic expansion or material advantage was of far less interest than emotional comfort or ease and personal autonomy. In the successful creation of a Cubeo community, Goldman suggested, its members had achieved a "spontaneity of correspondence between emotion and action" (ibid.: 285, see also Overing 1989).

The concept of a style of life is useful in describing how people derive enjoyment. Though the concept of style is most commonly understood as an aesthetic judgment, it can be used to characterize the moral aspect of some lives, as emerges from distinctive ways of acting. As the philosopher John Kekes points out, a good life is made enjoyable by pleasure derived from certain kinds of activities: from "actions done in the right way, from our rightful being, from the possession of a manner that confers merit, and from being the right manner of man. The enjoyments these ingredients of a good life provide are the result of one's style of life, from *how* something is done, not what is done" (2008: 22). Styles of life reflect one's attitude to life in general and to one's own life in particular. Even though the Urarina may easily appear to an outside observer to be quite homogeneous in many ways, with relatively little variation in beliefs, attitudes, and behaviors, there is in fact—as everywhere—considerable scope for individual variation in attitudes and values, within the broader spectrum of possibilities recognized as valuable or legitimate in a particular cultural context. Some men I knew, for example, would seek out a quiet, modest existence at some distance from other households, characterized by heightened levels of self-sufficiency and relatively free of material possessions; others would thrive on being at the center of social and political life in the most densely populated villages. Such life choices are equally good, and seen as such, provided that they accurately reflect what people most deeply care about, and that those leading such lives are in control, rather than at the mercy of necessity and contingency. If so, they exhibit a form of mastery of life that is both virtuous and inherently enjoyable.

Not all Urarina, it should be said, enjoy the privilege of a successful or enjoyable style of life. For example, one man I knew was virtually obsessed with his own political career, and with winning the countless minor feuds in which he constantly found himself embroiled wherever he went. He pursued victory by seeking to expand his power and influence, and for a while was convinced this would come with greater official (governmental) recognition as a citizen and legitimate authority in the community. Yet he was continually frustrated in these endeavors by his inability to negotiate the complex bureaucracy required by the Peruvian state to obtain even the simplest form of identity documents, such as a birth certificate. He did not seem to particularly enjoy his existence, on the whole, because his style of life comprised attitudes that were in some sense unrealistic, together with patterns of action that were not particularly successful, with the result that he was unable to live on his own terms. As another of my collaborators once expressed it: "Wherever he goes, he just can't live tranquilly."

Styles of life make corresponding actions characteristically and identifiably the actions of particular individuals. People do what they do cheerfully, confidently, wholeheartedly, and so on; as Kekes (2008) puts it, it is as if their characteristic actions bear their personal stamp. Independence; wit and good humor; exuberance and wholeheartedness; the pursuit of knowledge; creativity; political achievement; compassion for others: all these and more may feature more or less prominently in Urarina people's attitudes to life, informing their sensibilities, motivating their most important activities, eliciting their deepest emotions, providing a standard of judgment for evaluating what is good or bad and better or worse in their lives. To the extent that people's attitudes, beliefs, and emotions are consistent with each other, and consistently reflected in their actions, no matter what those actions may be, they have a style of life that reduces the extent to which they are at the mercy of necessity or contingency, and thus allows for an enjoyable feeling of control or mastery, similar to that derived from valued forms of labor.

Free from fear and anxiety, in good health, people are thus encouraged to pursue their own conception of the good in their own way. This is a central component of Amazonian individualism, where self-determination is highly valued, but remains resolutely social at the same time, and, far from coming into conflict with the needs of a wider social group, often directly supports them. If the mastery of work allows for a feeling of autonomy and control, the practice of these techniques is nevertheless always aimed at satisfying the needs and desires of others, at improving their wellbeing. Thus, men master the art of hunting so that their wives and children can eat meat; women master the art of weaving so that their husbands and children can sleep well at night; and so on. Total self-sufficiency is never the aim; instead, balancing autonomy and desirable forms of dependency is always a central concern and a source of deep satisfaction.

Tranquility (*raotojoeein*), then, as an enduring (though not permanent) attribute of a group of intimates, usually close kin, would seem to be the outcome or product of certain kinds of action in the world, or work conducted in the right kind of way. As an achieved state of being that enriches lives and makes them valuable, it might usefully be construed in terms of Urarina conceptions of the common good. As Michael Hardt and Antonio Negri (2009) point out, the notion of the commons refers to such environmental resources as land and water, but equally (and, in the modern West, increasingly) to the results of human labor and creativity, in the form of ideas, languages, knowledge, codes, affects, and so on. Refusing any rigid distinction between the "natural" and "artificial" commons, these authors argue that under what they term biopolitical production, what is ultimately produced is not simply objects for subjects, but subjects for objects, or forms of subjectivity itself: the object of production, in other words, is a subject defined by a social relationship or a form of life. Tranquility, I suggest, might be considered as precisely such a form of life. Such a construal does not imply homogeneity, nor is it at odds with the emphasis on individuality as revealed through a style of life. As Hardt and Negri make clear, far from negating difference, the common brings with it an affirmation of singularities.

THE RETURNED HUNTER

I now want to turn from these long-term senses of tranquility, as part of the commons and an aspect of people's lives as a whole, to a more short-term sense of "feeling good." To refer to this latter state, Urarina may use the expression *rachojoiha*, "to be happy," which can refer to any scenario of momentary joy: As one man told me once: "When my son Jorge was born, I was so happy (*rachojoiano*). Before that I only had daughters. But you know, sometimes fathers want to have sons, to accompany them and help them with their work. And son-in-law isn't the same." Another man said: "I'm happy when my family arrives, when my son comes to visit, and sleep in the house, and stays here a while." Other moments of joy would include the baptism of a child, or drunken dancing at a party (or, better still, both at once: "Baptizing a child makes people dance with enthusiasm!"). We may note that such moments, pregnant with possibility, imply a state of arousal or excitement, and are also best shared with others, or held in common, in which the positive affect is not easily reducible to individual experience. Yet when I began asking a range of different people to give me an example of a time in their own lives when they felt "happy," I was curious to find that many independently offered, by way of example, the moment of seeing someone returning to the community having just slain a large game animal, knowing that they would soon all eat together. In fact, for many people, this apparently straightforward scenario seemed to epitomize or exemplify the Urarina conception of happiness. As such, I wish to spend a moment exploring it further, elucidating its components.

To begin with, it is noteworthy that the experience singled out as happy is not the straightforward gratification of the senses through the process of eating, or even the sight of one's children taking pleasure in this way. It is instead an *anticipation* of that moment, while it still exists in the future as something to look forward to. The reasons for this, I think, will soon become apparent. Secondly, given the enjoyment that comes from practical mastery in general and from hunting in particular, it is of interest that no one, not even men who were accomplished hunters, gave as an example of happiness their own returning to the village with an animal. There can be no doubt that hunting is considered great fun, and I have seen little among Urarina to compare with the adrenalin and excitement that comes from spotting and pursuing potential prey. Similarly, though they always make efforts to appear low key and implacable, and would never dream of boasting, returning hunters must feel a real surge of pride at their success and the happiness they bring to others. But active excitement, the rush of blood and the frenzy of pursuit—like immediate sensory gratification—did not seem to encapsulate real happiness as well or as fully as the more passive but morally loaded state of anticipation of a pleasurable moment shared with others in which need is alleviated.

The importance of food—or, more specifically, the importance of satisfying people's desires for food—has been demonstrated by Gow (1991) to be central to the functioning of the subsistence economy. Piro people find the sight of a child eating earth, and thus satisfying its own desires, to be intensely disturbing. Yet there is a broader context to the scene of the returned hunter, in the sense that Urarina believe that game animals were placed on the earth by the divine Creator (*Cana Coaaunera*), for their nourishment. Animals are divine gifts that manifest the Creator's concern for humankind, and His pity for those in His care: proof of His active, caring presence. While a scarcity of game is a sign that all is not well—that humans have been forsaken or the apocalypse is near—finding and killing an animal conversely implies that the Creator is looking kindly upon His children, who live "under His watchful eye" (*notaracae*), as people sometimes put it. At these times, not only those humans who will eat feel happy: I often heard it said that pet birds, for example, know in advance when a hunter will return to the village, knowledge they communicate to their human owners by "dancing" and "jumping for joy," throwing dry grass up into the air.

Yet to overemphasize the cosmological dimensions of this moment would risk obscuring its phenomenological aspects, the importance of which become clear when one has lived in this way for a period of time and experienced firsthand this very moment. One of the greatest difficulties I faced in adjusting to life in the jungle was adapting to the highly erratic food supply. I generally made an effort to eat as and when others did, and this often meant long periods of time, sometimes a day or more, subsisting on little more than warm banana drink, which, as Urarina say, "deceives the stomach" but never really satiates. Hunger for meat would begin to dominate my thoughts, even as my belly was kept full by watery banana, and I began to devote more and more time to thinking about my next meal and where it might come from. I suspect others were often in a similar situation, which is why a hunter would usually set out into the forest on the stated grounds that his wife or children were desperate to eat meat. It is in this context, too, that we must place the sight of his successful return, animal in hand: an immediate relief from anxiety about the food supply, and an anticipated relief from hunger. This sense of relief brings with it a feeling of lightness, an easing of burdens, and a sense that one is being taken care of, looked after. In such moments, life is truly good.

It is worth spending some time on what happens next, for while sharing food has very often been discussed by anthropologists from a conceptual standpoint in terms of the creation of kinship through shared bodily substance, very few have explored it from the point of view of what it actually feels like for one doing the eating. In Amazonia at least, this has arguably led to an excessive focus on consubstantiality and the body at the expense of the emotional and affective dimensions of sharing a meal. The returned hunter is not a guaranteed positive experience, and can sometimes evoke anxiety as it is not always certain that one will be invited to eat or given a share. Being denied an invitation can easily cause offense, though, which is why the hunter and his family will usually be quite discreet, and as secretive as possible, if they are not planning on sharing with everyone in the vicinity. For this reason, perhaps, the truly happy sight is of an animal sufficiently large, say a peccary or tapir, that one can be sure of not being overlooked, avoiding the added discomfort and indignity of growing still hungrier while others eat.

Hospitality and generosity are central to what comes next. The animal as a whole is a gift from the Creator, but as meat, raw or cooked, it takes the form of gifts from the hunter and his wife to neighbors and loved ones. Sometimes cuts of raw meat are given, but more commonly a large, thick soup (*corerajaa*) is made, from which everyone shares. The men of the village come together to eat at the house of the hunter, whose wife sends their children with portions for neighboring wives and children who stay in their homes. People eat only what they have been offered to eat, such that food sharing forms part of a hospitable exchange that will be reciprocated in the future. Hence the distinction between human eating (*lenoniha*) and animal feeding (*quiha*), which so many languages seem to make. Eating a meal together in the human style is an inherently humanizing activity, much as eating foods such as game animals designated for humans is at the heart of what distinguishes humans from other kinds of being—hence, for example, mythical accounts of transformation into animal form often describe the foods eaten (berries, leaves, grass) as the hallmarks of nonhuman existence.[1]

---

1. In Urarina, it is possible to say that humans "feed" (*quiha*), just as it is in English, but it sounds odd or amusing.

The moment of eating itself involves the stimulation and satisfaction of all the senses. Usually no condiments or flavorings are used other than salt, with the result that the flavor of the meat itself is very important. There is all the difference in the world between different species of animal, but while many people have their favorites, they would not mention this while eating, as this could seem ungrateful. Similarly, children always eat what they are given, without complaint; any hint of refusing food is met with extreme scorn. Eating is relaxing, an excuse to take a break from what one might have been doing, and sometimes to withdraw in a way, though eating is also, and perhaps more commonly, an excuse to enter into sociality. Women typically eat with their children, while men especially eat with other men, using this as an opportunity to sit together and talk, and this liminal phase approaches what Turner (1969) would have called "communitas." At the conclusion of a meal, a few words are said by the host to each guest in turn, and a short speech is made of thanksgiving to the Creator.

A good meal is prepared such that everyone eats his or her fill and is left with the slight heaviness that comes of a full belly, associated with a real sense of satiation and a readiness to relax. Eating well thus makes it easier to achieve a state of tranquility. Yet if we examine this feeling of satisfaction more closely, or more specifically our experience of moving past satisfaction from one activity to another, it becomes apparent that this is more than simply a moment of closure or fulfillment. One never becomes specifically aware of moving past fullness to emptiness, or from absence to presence. As phenomenologists have pointed out, the feeling of satisfaction does not mean an absolute limit has been reached, so much as that a new horizon has opened to us: we reach the threshold of one particular engagement with the world and enter into another (Jager 1999). We notice a shift in our attention, a turn in our interest, and the opening up of a new path that invites our exploration. In other words, "to be satisfied" means to give in to a new adventure and to approach the world from a different angle. There is a strong sense of flow here, in other words, such that the moment of joy is anything but cut off from the rhythms of social life which encompass it, as anticipation gives way to satiety while opening up new horizons of activity.

The returning hunter thus precipitates a cycle of desire and satisfaction, in which the shared quality of the experience is crucial. Rather like enjoying a great view, there is a sense of shame or loss if one cannot share the experience with another, and shared experience is often, I suspect, more highly valued than individual experience. It is not a static moment, and does not simply end in satiety.

While it certainly alleviates the anxieties that surround an uncertain food supply, thus paving the way for a state of tranquility, it also leads to an opening up of horizons, of new possibilities, in a continuous dynamic movement that orients daily life. The returned hunter might indeed be considered an example of what Mauss ([1925] 2002) termed a "total social fact," a unifying event or a symbol of core social values that integrates all aspects of Urarina life, economic, moral, religious, and aesthetic; at once eminently sensory, social, and cosmological. It brings together the values and practices that, taken together, comprise the Urarina vision of the good life, and condenses these into a short-lived but multifaceted and dynamic subjective experience that lies at the heart of their conception of happiness.

CONCLUSION

A distinction between short-term, affective or hedonic conceptions of happiness that emphasize satisfaction or "feeling good," and long-term, objective or eudaimonic conceptions of happiness that stress self-actualization, a life of virtue, and a wider sense of "flourishing," has pervaded Western thinking on the subject for millennia. While there is a growing sense that focusing on one of these contrastive aspects of happiness to the exclusion of the other is problematic, and that integrating them is necessary (e.g., Tomer 2011), exactly how they do or should inform people's life goals and motivations in differing cultural contexts remains unclear, as does the nature of the relationship between them. How does momentary pleasure, in short, involving enjoyable and positive experiences, relate to active involvement or engagement in life and all that it requires, and to having a higher purpose, a meaningful life? In seeking to answer this question for the Peruvian Urarina, I have shown how they manage two interrelated concepts of happiness, one of which is long term and is epitomised by a state of "tranquility"; the other of which is short term and is epitomized by the joyous sight of the successful hunter returned from the forest. These are not opposed concepts; in fact they imply each other in several ways. Interestingly, some similar distinctions appear to be made by at least some other Amazonian peoples: one is reminded of the distinction Piro people make between "having a good time, having a festival" and "living well, living quietly" (Gow 2000); as well as the contrast drawn by the Trio between *onken*, the condition of everyday contentment that implies calmness and quiet, and *sasame*, a more climactic state of ritual happiness, exemplified by joyous, collective dancing (Rivière 2000: 257). According to Peter Rivière, the latter might be understood as a kind of "aesthetic intensification" of the former.[2]

The Urarina concept of "tranquility" (*raotojoeein*) is central to their sense of a life well lived, and perhaps even more than short-term pleasure is a goal or ideal for which they actively strive. It must be understood, in the first instance, in relation to the uncertainty, danger, and violence that provide the backdrop of everyday sociality. In some ways, it recalls certain other, better-known concepts of happiness as tranquility, such as the ancient Greek concept of *ataraxia*, which is often described as a lucid state of robust tranquility, characterized by ongoing freedom from distress and worry. According to Epicurus, one reaches the pleasant state of tranquility by realizing that there are only a handful of desires that must be fulfilled in order to lead a pleasant life, and that those can easily be satisfied. Epicurean tranquility is "a state of contentment and inner calm that arises from the thought that one has or can easily get all that one needs, and has no reason to be afraid of anything in the future" (Striker 1990: 100).[3]

The Urarina sense of tranquility differs significantly from this emphasis on imperturbability, and from the Stoics' indifference to everything bodily or external, and consequent freedom from emotion (*apatheia*). For Urarina, tranquility is more an external condition, one that necessarily involves others, and it implies emotional engagement and spontaneity. It is the grounds from which an enjoyable but also virtuous life becomes possible, a collective resource, part of the immaterial commons. A state in which, to a casual outside observer, little seems to happen, it can easily seem rather boring, even if this boredom is recognized to be a purposive achievement, a space of calm carved out within a hostile

---

2. According to Rivière, *sasame* means "happy" in its simplest sense, but also has a deeper meaning that "implies a sense of inner contentment and the feeling of belonging not only to society but to the whole of nature and the universe" (ibid.: 254).

3. For Pyrrho and his followers in particular, tranquility was also closely linked to suspension of judgment concerning the true nature or essence of things. The things of the world are ultimately unfathomable and unknowable, and refusing to trust in our senses or judgments, especially as concerns goods and evils, is the best way to avoid anxiety and achieve peace of mind (Striker 1990: 102–4) . It is tempting to speculate whether the "highly transformational world" of native Amazonians, in which, as Rivière put it, "it is never entirely safe to believe the evidence of your own eyes" (1994: 261), might similarly be an attitude of skepticism, though it scarcely in this case seems conducive to tranquility.

cosmos pervaded by danger. Yet a quiet, calm but profound sense of enjoyment may be derived from going about one's tasks in the right kind of way, in accordance with one's attitudes to life, and I would suggest that the boredom of the anthropologist is directly proportional to his or her lack of practical mastery, a failure to develop the skills required to achieve small but meaningful goals from the materials at hand, and an inability to recognize opportunities for action and interaction. The only time I ever heard Urarina describe themselves as "bored" was when they were in the city, a place with few meaningful opportunities for the exercise of skill, and little if any available work that allows people to express their freedom and creativity. Work in the city for them was a drudgery, involving specialized routine tasks performed day in, day out, ad infinitum. Boredom, in short, is possible only in the absence of tranquility.

In their preferred forest environment, by contrast, work is freely chosen, flexible, and diverse. A happy, tranquil life is the result of creative activity developing in multiple directions, and where economic production just one form among others. Activity is not merely a means adapted to certain ends; it is an end in itself. People literally "do one thing today and another tomorrow," to invoke Marx and Engels' well-known (if half-joking) description of a nonalienated society, in which one might "hunt in the morning, fish in the afternoon, rear cattle in the evening, criticize after dinner . . . without ever becoming hunter, fisherman, herdsman or critic." ([1845–6] 1970: 53)[4] Through their work, which ideally becomes a free expression of their life, people affirm themselves as well as those nearby who use or enjoy what they produce, whose needs they satisfy, and who in turn complete and confirm the worker in their thoughts and love. This kind of work is thus inherently communal, even when performed alone. The flexibility and nonalienated character of work encourage people to focus on the activity at hand, allowing themselves to be absorbed into or lost in the interaction. This experience of flow is valuable precisely because of the way it steers a middle course between boredom and anxiety. Challenges are perceived not as threats, but as opportunities for action; put differently, goals and challenges imply each other, allowing people to achieve a feeling of control. Getting to this point requires discipline and determination, and does not come naturally. Over and above the material goods that are perhaps the most obvious outcome, such work is also directly responsible for the

---

4.   Alternatively, as Marx expressed the idea in an unpublished notebook: "The very activity of his work would enable him to enjoy his personality and realise his natural capacity and spiritual aims" (cited in McLellan 1969: 464).

production of those immaterial commons—affects, social relationships, forms of life—that are conveniently captured in the notion of tranquility.

The condition of tranquility allows people to act consistently and in accordance with their attitudes to life, their beliefs and emotions forming a harmonious whole. This means acting for others as much as for oneself, contributing to their wellbeing, exercising the virtues of hard work and generosity. Practical mastery in work is inextricably linked to fostering relatedness with others. In fact, these are mutually reinforcing: people work to meet the needs of their loved ones, but are loved in turn, respected by their spouse and family, because they work hard. Hence Rosa's account of her marriage to Lucho: "I'm happy with my husband because he works well. . . . Because of this, nothing ever happens." In its ideal, the entirety of life is transformed into a kind of single activity with unified goals that provide a constant sense of purpose. When thoughts, feelings, and actions are congruent with one another, when boredom and anxiety are absent, people find in themselves an admirable strength and serenity.

Within this broader state of tranquility (*raotojoeein*) arise fleeting moments of joy (*rachojoiha*), epitomized by the scene of the returned hunter. At first glance, the difference between joy and tranquility appears to correspond to a difference between subjective and objective conceptions of happiness, or between the positive affective state of feeling good and the objective conditions of the good life, which include scope for self-actualization and the practice of virtue. Yet I have argued instead that the difference lies more in the fact that the momentary experience of joy, in its purest form, is a crystallization and intensification of all the ingredients that make up the good life, allowing for a harmony between sensory pleasure or gratification, and moral, virtuous living with and through others. Pleasure is effectively a measure for judging moral goodness, as delight is taken in actions perceived to be worthy. This does not mean that tranquility can be reduced to joy, or vice versa, nor does it mean that there can be a single standard of hedonic value through which all forms of the good may be evaluated. It points instead to a different kind of achievement: the ability to find enjoyment in those fleeting moments in life that integrate one's convictions of the good.

ACKNOWLEDGMENTS

This research was supported by a British Academy Small Grant and the Suntory and Toyota International Centres for Economics and Related Disciplines

(STICERD). For helpful comments and suggestions I am grateful to Iza Kavedžija, five anonymous reviewers, and participants at seminars at the Institute of Latin American Studies and the London School of Economics and Political Science.

REFERENCES

Bateson, Gregory. 1972. "Style, grace, and information in primitive art." In *Steps to an ecology of mind*, 128–52. New York: Ballantine.

Belaunde, Luisa Elvira. 2001. *Viviendo bien: Género y fertilidad entre los Airo-Pai de la Amazonía Peruana*. Lima: Centro Amazónico de Antropología y Aplicación Práctica.

Cepek, Michael. 2008. "Bold jaguars and unsuspecting monkeys: The value of fearlessness in Cofán politics." *Journal of the Royal Anthropological Institute* (N.S.) 14: 334–52.

Csikszentmihályi, Mihály. 1992. *Flow: The psychology of happiness*. London: Rider.

Descola, Philippe. 1996. *In the society of nature: A native ecology in Amazonia*. Translated by Nora Scott. Cambridge: Cambridge University Press.

Fausto, Carlos. 2007. "If God were a jaguar: Cannibalism and Christianity among the Guarani (16th–20th centuries)." In *Time and memory in indigenous Amazonia: Anthropological perspectives*, edited by Carlos Fausto and Michael Heckenberger. Gainesville: University Press of Florida.

Gasché Suess, Jorge, and Napoleón Vela Mendoza. 2012. *Sociedad Bosquesina Tomo II: ¿Qué significa para los bosquesinos "autonomía," "libertad," "autoridad" y "democracia"?* Iquitos: Instituto de Investigaciones de la Amazonía Peruana.

Goldman, Irving. 1963. *The Cubeo*. Urbana: University of Illinois Press.

Gow, Peter. 2000. "Helpless: The affective preconditions of Piro social life." In *The anthropology of love and anger*, edited by Joanna Overing and Alan Passes, 46–63. London: Routledge

Hardt, Michael, and Antonio Negri. 2009. *Commonwealth*. Cambridge, MA: Harvard University Press.

Henderson, Luke Wayne, and Tess Knight. 2012. "Integrating the hedonic and eudaimonic perspectives to more comprehensively understand wellbeing and pathways to wellbeing." *International Journal of Wellbeing* 2 (3): 196–221.

High, Casey. 2010. "Warriors, hunters, and Bruce Lee: Gendered agency and the transformation of Amazonian masculinity." *American Ethnologist* 37 (4): 753–70.

Huta, Veronika, and Richard M. Ryan. 2010. Pursuing pleasure or virtue: The differential and overlapping well-being benefits of hedonic and eudaimonic motives. *Journal of Happiness Studies* 11: 735–62.

Izquierdo, Carolina. 2009. "Well-being among the Matsigenka of the Peruvian Amazon." In *Pursuits of happiness: Well-being in anthropological perspective*, edited by Gordon Matthews and Carolina Izquierdo, 67–87. Oxford: Berghahn Books.

Jager, Bernd. 1999. "Eating as natural event and as intersubjective phenomenon: Towards a phenomenology of eating." *Journal of Phenomenological Psychology* 30 (1): 66–116.

Kekes, John. 2008. *Enjoyment: The moral significance of styles of life*. Oxford: Oxford University Press.

Marx, Karl, and Friedrich Engels. (1845–6) 1970. *The German ideology*. New York: International Publishers Co.

Mauss, Marcel. (1925) 2002. *The gift: The form and reason for exchange in archaic societies*. Translated by W. D. Halls. London: Routledge.

McLellan, David. 1969. "Marx's view of the unalienated society." *The Review of Politics* 31 (4): 459–65.

Miles-Watson, Jonathan 2010. "Ethnographic insights into happiness." In *The practices of happiness: Political economy, religion and wellbeing*, edited by John Atherton, Elaine Graham, and Ian Steedman, 125–33.. London: Routledge.

Overing, Joanna. 1981. "Amazonian anthropology." *Journal of Latin American Studies* 13 (1): 151–65.

———. 1989. "The aesthetics of production: The sense of community among the Cubeo and Piaroa." *Dialectical Anthropology* 14 (3): 159–75.

Overing, Joanna, and Alan Passes, eds. 2000a. *The anthropology of love and anger: The aesthetics of conviviality in native Amazonia*. London: Routledge.

———. 2000b. Introduction: Conviviality and the opening up of Amazonian anthropology. In *The anthropology of love and anger: The aesthetics of conviviality in native Amazonia*, edited by Joanna Overing and Alan Passes, 1–30. London: Routledge.

Reyes-García, Victoria, and Tsimane' Amazonian Panel Study (TAPS). 2012. "Happiness in the Amazon: Folk explanations of happiness in hunter-horticulturalist society in the Bolivian Amazon." In *Happiness across cultures:*

Views of happiness and quality of life in non-Western cultures, edited by Helaine Selin and Gareth Davey, 209–26. Dordrecht: Springer.

Rivière, Peter. 2000. "The more we are together . . . ." In *The anthropology of love and anger: The aesthetics of conviviality in native Amazonia*, edited by Joanna Overing and Alan Passes, 252-67. London: Routledge.

Robbins, Joel. 2013. Beyond the suffering subject: Toward an anthropology of the good. *Journal of the Royal Anthropological Institute* 19 (3): 447–62.

Ryan, Richard M., and Edward L. Deci. 2001. "On happiness and human potentials: A review of research on hedonic and eudaimonic well-being." *Annual Review of Psychology* 52: 141–66.

Sahlins, Marshall. 1968. "Notes on the original affluent society." In *Man the hunter*, Edited by Richard. B. Lee and Irven DeVore, 85–89. New York: Aldine Publishing Company.

Santos Granero, Fernando. 2001. "The Sisyphus syndrome." In *The anthropology of love and anger: The aesthetics of conviviality in native Amazonia*, edited by Joanna Overing and Alan Passes, 268–87. London: Routledge.

Stasch, Rupert. 2008. "Knowing minds is a matter of authority: Political dimensions of opacity statements in Korowai moral psychology." *Anthropological Quarterly* 81 (2): 443–53.

Striker, Gisela. 1990. "*Ataraxia*: Happiness as tranquillity." *The Monist* 73 (1): 97–110.

Tomer, John F. 2011. "Enduring happiness: Integrating the hedonic and eudaimonic approaches." *Journal of Socio-Economics* 40: 530–7.

Turner, Victor. 1969. *The ritual process: Structure and anti-structure*. Chicago: Aldine Publishing Co.

Viveiros de Castro, Eduardo. 2001. "GUT feelings about Amazonia: Potential affinity and the construction of sociality." In *Beyond the visible and the material: The Amerindianization of society in the work of Peter Rivière*, edited by Laura M. Rival and Neil L. Whitehead, 19–43. Oxford: Oxford University Press.

Warren, James. 2002. *Epicurus and Democritean ethics: An archaeology of Ataraxia*. Cambridge: Cambridge University Press.

AFTERWORD

On happiness, values, and time
The long and the short of it

Joel Robbins

This collection on the values of happiness in part responds to the fact that happiness has made a major push recently to move itself up in the Euro-American hierarchy of values. Bhutan got there first, of course, but at the currently very busy crossroads of psychology, economics, and policy discourse, some Euro-American elites are lobbying hard to get happiness to the top of their own countries' evaluative charts. In a social critical mood, it is hard not to find all of this interest in happiness a little disappointing. One remembers almost wistfully the early years of the recent recession, when many people voiced the hope that the devastation the financial crisis was wreaking would finally provide an opening to reconsider the stark neoliberal version of the value of individualism that had until that moment seemingly become so entrenched as to be beyond challenge. Then the energy and rapid initial spread of the Occupy Movement appeared poised to go some way toward making this hope for a real effort at value change seem realistic. If the only innovation we end up with out of this ferment, at least on the elite academic and policy levels, is a concern with "nudging" us toward happiness regardless of the state of the world around us, one has to wonder how much will really have changed (Davies 2015).

It is also hard to imagine that the current vogue for happiness will not pass rather quickly. One expects that either the global economy will make stronger moves toward recovery and neoliberal individualism will confidently stride back to the very center of our value concerns (it is surely already taking giant steps in this direction, and it never had a long way to go to get there in any case), or things will get worse and happiness will come to look like too flimsy a goal to pursue by way of fixing them. Thus it is a relief that this collection, in both conception and realization, does not stake everything on happiness, and does not address only what Ross Abbinnett (2013: 32) calls the "neo-utilitarianism" at the heart of recently emergent versions of the science of happiness, but also responds to the resurgence of anthropological interest in the study of values (e.g., Graeber 2001; Pedersen 2008; Otto and Willerslev 2013). The ultimate goal of this afterword is to work along with the articles collected here to trace out some of the threads that tie discussions of happiness and of values to one another. In pursuit of that goal, I will push further some theoretical suggestions made in the articles, and put forward a few arguments of my own that build on them. But before I get to work on this, I also want to respond to the unusually ethnographically creative and compelling quality of most of the articles by making some observations about some aspects of what it means to take on happiness as an ethnographic object (or set of different objects). As Sara Ahmed (2010: 15) puts it in her book *The promise of happiness*, a work many of the contributors here cite, it is worth asking not only what happiness is, but also "what it does." In that spirit, I want to start by asking what happiness does to ethnography and ethnographic writing. As we will see, answering this question will lead us onward toward more theoretical concerns.

HAPPINESS: THE LONG AND THE SHORT OF IT

One thing that is striking about many of the articles collected here is that they show that a focus on happiness somewhat reworks the standard ethnographic construction of time. Borrowing an element of Jason Throop's elegant phenomenological description of the nature of happiness, an element Ahmed (2010) also elaborates, happiness as a modality of engagement with the world brings its own horizon(s) to bear on the way we understand what we encounter, and it is clear that this horizon or these horizons have informed to productive effect the way many of the ethnographic accounts collected here approach time.

Put straightforwardly, many of contributors to this collection are concerned either with intense moments of experienced happiness or with people's reckoning of their own or others' happiness over long spans of time. Some of them also take up the relationship between these two temporalities of happiness. So Dena Freeman shows us how Gamo Highlanders of Southern Ethiopia once aimed for the long-term pleasures of living with smooth social relations but have recently switched to seeking the strong momentary highs of Pentecostal ritual. In studying Bangladeshi migration to London, Katy Gardner similarly counterposes the "emotional high" that migration promises the would-be migrant will feel on arrival at a new home to the way in which family projects that involve migration for some members aim at "wellbeing" or "the good life"" as a much "longer-term" reward. Iza Kavedžija shows us that the elderly Japanese people she studies explicitly seek to balance pleasures of the present moment with the construction of narrative coherence across the life-course, while Harry Walker finds the Amazonian Urarina representing all that goes into defining a life well lived over time in their joyful response to the sight of a successful hunter returning to the village with a lot of game in hand. Finally, following what should by now begin to look like a pattern, Charles Stafford, working in China and Taiwan, compares families motivated by goals of long-term economic betterment with those who have opted for the rather narrower time horizon of the pleasures of decadence.

Even the ethnographic phenomena and accounts presented here that are not built on some or other opposition between long-term and short-term pleasures situate themselves at one extreme or the other. Thus we can contrast Throop's discussion of the Yapese concern that happiness narrows a person's temporal (and social horizons) too drastically with Michael Lambek's analytic decision in his study of one version of Swiss happiness to take as "the unit of happiness not a statement, bodily expression, or feeling, but a life." And in a related twist, Henrik Vigh builds his discussion of the motives that lead young Bissauan men to join a rather millitarily weak militia around the notion that these men volunteer out of a sense that it is worth trading short-term experiences of violence for the possibility of living out long lives of secure, happy social involvement

Even in an afterword, it is probably not good practice for a writer to overload two consecutive paragraphs with as much diverse ethnographic material as I just have. But I am hoping that the kaleidoscopic near-repetition of concerns with either or both the present instant and the very long term in sentence after sentence above can help me make in quite concrete terms my point that once anthropologists start to write about happiness, something interesting happens to the way they engage time. One might say that most ethnographic writing, whether phrased in the ethnographic present or not, at least implicitly constructs a kind of thick temporal middle ground between the moment and the long-term horizon. This is the temporal middle of routine actions and their expected consequences, of getting things done, of everyday social reproduction, and of, we might say, succeeding more or less at being a "normal" person of a certain social type living a "normal" life in local terms. In ethnographic accounts set in this temporal middle, time recedes into the analytic background, and it rarely appears as an important aspect of the motives that ethnographers demonstrate or imply drive the actions of those they are studying. But when it comes to studying happiness, this temporal middle does not appear to provide an adequate framework for ethnographic discussion. Gardner's and Stafford's articles, for example, stand out against the general run of ethnographic writing for the way their considerations of happiness allow them to integrate long, two or more generation time-spans and diverse temporal perspectives into their descriptions of what Stafford elegantly calls the "intergenerational coordination of goals and intentions." Most of the other pieces offer us detailed accounts of the way actors draw on culturally available materials to help them work out the relationship between living for or nonreflexively engaging in the moment and, by contrast, working toward longer-term projects thought to lead to the achievement of something like a good life. I would suggest that such complicated considerations of time are part of what makes these articles so fresh, and that this concern with the temporal lends these pieces a deep coherence beyond that which follows from the fact that they all focus on happiness.

To this point, I have wanted to make a descriptive claim: the articles collected here, all of which take happiness under one definition or another as their object, crowd around the ends of the temporal continuum upon which human lives are lived, and very few of them dwell much in the temporal middle that so commonly provides the setting of ethnographic work. Furthermore, many of the contributors also tell us that one of the projects that is important to the people they study is finding some way to relate the momentary and the long-term versions of happiness, or to decide how much energy they should devote to seeking each type. Staying on the descriptive level here, I would also note that the activity of work appears in a number of the articles as a practice that ideally relates these two modalities of happiness. Throop, for example, notes that the Yapese, often suspicious of happiness as too individualizing in its effects, still find it morally appropriate to take pleasure in work. The Urarina, Walker tells us, likewise find nonalienated labor productive of the momentary pleasure they call "joy" as well as the long-term tranquility that marks the good life. In Freeman's account, it is changing labor relations that in part account for the reorientation of Gamo approaches to happiness that she charts. We might say that work is usually by its nature an activity viscerally experienced in the present but also oriented to future goals. When people enjoy it in the moment, then, they never wholly lose sight of the longer term. Perhaps this is what gives work the ability to bind together the kinds of times to which happiness is relevant. Unlike work, sex only makes a few appearances in these articles (perhaps surprisingly in a collection on happiness). But in Vigh's discussion of it, the ability to engage in sexual relations assures young Bissauan men of the true social belonging they value, and so sex turns out, like work, to provide momentary pleasures without completely occluding long-term goods.

I consider the points I have just discussed to be some of the findings of these articles taken as a set: happiness in a wide range of diverse cultural settings appears to come in momentary and long-term forms, and people frequently feel themselves challenged to construct some relationship between them. Work and, maybe, sex stand out as activities that have been attractive to people living in some cultural settings for their ability to link these two temporalities of happiness. Simply figuring this much out in empirical terms is worth the price of admission here, especially since I, at least, have not seen these kinds of points made anywhere else. But findings are not theories, and so a crucial next step is to think about ways to get some theoretical purchase on the varied temporalities of happiness that these articles lay out. I want to suggest in what follows that turning to the question of values can help us in this endeavor.

I recognize that it might at first glance appear that, taken together, the articles already lay out a theoretical approach to the issue at hand, rendering a turn to the discussion of values superfluous. This appearance rests on the way that some of the contributors turn to the classic philosophical distinction between hedonism and eudaimonia to shape up the opposition between momentary and long-term happiness. This works well in many of the articles, but it is important to recognize that in itself this distinction does not constitute a theory of happiness per se but rather a classificatory device for distinguishing between different kinds of the purported phenonemena. Even when we draw on this philosophical distinction, we still have theoretical work to do. And the wager of the approach I will be taking here is that doing this work in anthropological and sociological terms, rather than in philosophical ones, may help us reach some new destinations in our thinking about happiness.

I should also note that difficulties for any theory of happiness arise for the fact that when confronted with its momentary and long-term temporalities, particularly when they are construed by means of the hedonism/eudaimonia distinction, it is fair to wonder whether happiness is not more than one kind of thing. Perhaps hedonism has to do with something like a feeling of joy, while eudaimonia is about a feeling of contentment. Or maybe eudaimonia is not about a feeling at all, but more about a culturally informed judgment on the nature of a particular life. In light of similar concerns, the philosopher Dan Haybron (2011: 3) suggests that philosophers have long pointed to, and often conflated, two distinct things in their discussions of happiness: "a state of mind" and "a life that goes well for the person living it." I bring this up because in reading the articles in this collection is it hard not to wonder whether if in fact the contributors do routinely conflate two different things under the term "happiness," then there is something confused at the very heart of the attempt to have an anthropology of happiness, and particularly one that relates happiness to values, that encompasses them both. Haybron, for his part, finds that it is only the "life going well" kind of happiness that is clearly about values, since "to ascribe happiness" in this sense "is to make a value judgment: namely, that the person has whatever it is that benefits a person" (ibid.: 4, emphasis removed). In response to this problem, I want to take a different tack and suggest that through the articles collected here, perhaps we can find a core element shared by these two kinds of happiness, and that this core has crucially to do with the way both kinds of happiness involve values. This is where my argument is headed.

EFFERVESCENCE, VALUE, AND EMOTION

What is the relationship between happiness and values? There are a number of ways one could approach answering this question. In this section, I want to take one that leads through the work of Émile Durkheim and which thus deploys materials with which anthropologists have long been familiar.

To accept values as a central theoretical concern means to follow James Laidlaw (2013: 60) in defining human beings as profoundly "evaluative" creatures and to agree with the philosopher Józef Tischner (2008: 50) that "our world is a hierarchically ordered world and our thinking, a preferential thinking." But even when we have gone only this far in thinking about values, we confront a problem that has beset the scholarly debate about values ever since it began to take something like its current shape in the nineteenth century (for a brief history, see Schnädelbach 1984): Are values essentially subjective, such that we as Laidlaw-like evaluative creatures add them to the world, or are they objective, in the sense that they are qualities of Tischner's hierarchically ordered world taken on its own terms? Is this not in some ways analogous to our problem of two kinds of happiness (each with its own distinct temporality)? Does not the hedonic, in-the-moment kind of happiness appear to be wholly subjective, and does not the eudaimoniac, life-span version of happiness, even if we can imagine it might find subjective expression in a feeling like contentment, seem ineradicably to involve some kind of "objective" or at least socially shared and stable judgment on what it means to live a good life?[1] The fact that this problematic of plausibly being considered both subjective and objective is shared by values and happiness alike is, I think, a clue that values and happiness are related and that examining them together can enrich our understanding of both.

Let us start with values. In the history of philosophy and the human sciences more generally, there are many answers to the question of whether value is a subjective or an objective phenomenon, and there are strong arguments on either side. There is no space to review much of this debate here. But as it happens, Durkheim took it up in a lecture entitled "Value judgments and judgments

---

1. A reviewer of this article took issue with this point, suggesting that if we take happiness only to be a feeling, then one can have "long-term happiness" as long as one feels such happiness, regardless of whether one realizes socially shared values or not—even mass murderers, on this argument, can have happy lives. I would not want to suggest that it is impossible to argue for this position, but I would point out that the position I am taking here is not idiosyncratic. It is often taken by philosophers interested both in happiness and in values. To refer to just two very recent examples, Roberts (2015) considers this very issue and argues for a position like the one I have argued for here, while May (2015) makes a strong argument for the need for values to be objective or socially shared if the realization of them is to contribute to a meaningful life (see also the quotation from and discussion of Durkheim immediately below in the main text, for his own grappling with some related issues). This reviewer is more generally worried that in connecting happiness to values, I fail to define happiness as only a feeling. I am not sure I would want to restrict the meaning of "happiness" in this way in any case—I have already noted that I take "happiness" to be a complex term—but I would point out that I do intend the following discussion of Durkheim's work to offer a novel way of connecting short-term and long-term happiness by tying them both to the experience (emotion?) of what Durkheim calls effervescence.

of reality" given in 1911, just before publishing his great book on religion (in English the lecture appears in Durkheim [1924] 1974 and the religion book as Durkheim [1912] 1995). As he puts the problem:

> One the one hand, all value presupposes appreciation by an individual in relation with a particular sensibility. What has value is in some way good; what is good is desired, and all desire is a psychological state. Nevertheless the values under discussion have the objectivity of things. How can these two characteristics, which at first blush appear contradictory, be reconciled? How, in fact, can a state of feeling be independent of the subject that feels it? (Durkheim [1924] 1974: 81–82)

As we might expect, especially if we are familiar with the Introduction to the *Elementary forms*, by drawing on his notions of social facts, shared representations, and effervescence, Durkheim finds an answer to this question that lets him have it both ways.

Durkheim begins by arguing that the value of something emerges when it is placed into relation with an "ideal" (ibid.: 90). Or, as he puts it somewhat more clearly, "value derives from the relation of things to different aspects of the ideal" (ibid.: 94). "Since ideals and their corresponding value systems vary with various human groups," Durkheim continues in a vein that should be a comfortable one for anthropologists, "does this not suggest a collective origin for both?" Turning then to an argument that will become very well known through the versions of it that appear in the *Elementary forms*, he suggests that sentiments that are shared among members of a social group have more "energy" than purely individual ones and thus appear to subjects as ideal ones by contrast to their more personal, less obviously shared "real" ones. Durkheim goes on to add that such powerful, shared sentiments and the ideals they produce arise in moments of "collective ferment" (ibid.: 91). Once created in such moments, these ideals are invested in concrete objects and shared concepts that allow them to be continually apprehended, even outside of moments of collective enthusiasm (ibid.: 94). In this way, things in the world come to be related to ideals, and thus to have value, and values come at once to be in us, as experiences and recollections of collective ferment, and to transcend us, as things in the world that we feel have a value of their own.

In the *Elementary forms*, the argument we have been tracing appears in a modified version as an account of how moments of collective "effervescence" produced by ritual elevate individuals, making them feel they are more than themselves and in touch with an external power greater than their own, and thereby give rise to the notions of religion and the sacred, which are in fact simply representations of the force of collectivity (society) itself (Durkheim [1912] 1995: 220). I have gone back to Durkheim's slightly earlier and less often discussed text because there this argument appears not as one primarily about the origin and nature of the sacred, but rather as one about the roots of ideals and values. Values and the sacred are surely not unrelated in Durkheim's thought, but I want to focus on the values argument here.

In particular, I want to suggest that we take Durkheim's feeling of effervescence as at least the paradigm case of what the contributors to this collection treat as happiness in the present moment, and as at most wholly equivalent to it. Durkheim would then be telling us that it is this kind of experience of happiness that produces values (or, to be precise, it produces ideals which then produce values). Sometimes he seems to want to suggest that this emotional state produces new ideals and values *de novo* (as in the Reformation or the French Revolution: Durkheim [1912] 1995: 215–16; [1924] 1974: 92). At other times, I think it is more compelling to read him as suggesting that experiences of intense happiness convince subjects beyond a doubt that they live in the objectively "hierarchically ordered" worlds Tischner describes in which some things are clearly better than others, rather than producing such worlds anew every time they occur. More importantly, we should also note the recursive element of Durkheim's argument. We experience effervescent happiness when we feel we are joined together with others in sharing the same representations and evaluations of a situation and are therefore acting in concert in relation to it. It is this sense of shared approach to the world that produces the feeling in question in the first place. Yet if we take objective values to be productive of shared judgments of the world and shared desires to act upon it in particular ways (remember that for Durkheim values elicit desires), we can also say that values produce collective effervescence as much as collective effervescence produces values. A corollary of this recursive quality of the relationship between values and effervescence/happiness is that subjects sometimes find themselves experiencing moments of happiness when they act in terms of a shared value, and they sometimes discover they are in the presence of a shared value when they feel such happiness.

A number of prominent philosophers in the phenomenological tradition have connected emotions to the discovery of values in a way that bears some relation to Durkheim's argument (though with no particular focus on the social production of such emotions). They have argued, as Fiorenza Toccafondi (2009: 150) puts it, that a "certain type of expressiveness [here taken as a quality of an object] and the emotional tonality connected to it discloses to us the value of what we are faced with, thus giving rise to certain axiological beliefs." Max Scheler ([1913–16] 1973) is the most prominent phenomenologist to hold a position of this kind, arguing that feelings of love and hate in particular are the "organs" of the perception of values, but arguments along these lines are common in this philosophical tradition more generally (see Gubser 2014). What makes Durkheim's position stand out, along with the role it gives to social experience and to effervescence or happiness rather than love or hate as a key emotion of value perception, is the fact that he goes beyond asserting that feelings disclose values to subjects to also offer an account of what it feels like to realize a shared value in the performance of a concrete activity. In Durkheim's recursive model, that is to say, effervescence attends not only the revelation of a value, but also the performative realization of it. This point becomes clear if we turn to ethnography.

I carried out fieldwork among the Urapmin of Papua New Guinea, a community of roughly four hundred persons. I have elsewhere argued that what I have called "relationalism" is one of the two most important contemporary Urapmin values (Robbins 2004). This is a value that defines the creation and maintenance of relationships as two of the best things a person can accomplish. One of the key ways Urapmin realize the value of relationalism is through carrying out exchanges of foodstuffs and other material items with one another, for they see such exchanges as the most powerful way of fostering relationships. In examining the relationship of values to happiness, it is worth noting that one kind of exchange the Urapmin find very pleasurable is that of feasts that consist of large platters of mashed taro covered in oil that has been squeezed from the seeds of pandanus palms.

All Urapmin families own stands of pandanus trees, and because these are situated at a wide range of altitudes and the fruiting of the trees is very sensitive to microclimate, different stands produce seeds at different times throughout the year. At any given time, only a few families will have trees with fruits that are in seed and ready to use for preparing a feast. When a family has pandanus trees in seed, it will invite friends and relatives to come to a feast. There follows several long hours of labor-intensive preparation on the part of the host family, both cooking and mashing the taro, and squeezing the thick red oil from the

Pandanus seeds. Once the dish is ready, the guests will crowd around the plat-
ter (made from a large slab of dried tree bark) and devour the food with great
speed, fending off as they do so the inevitable crowd of dogs eager for their
share. The consumption of the pandanus feast thus unfolds as a brief period of
intense fervor. The eating part of the event is always frantic and over quickly.
It is also emotionally very highly pitched. Urapmin find pandanus oil delicious
and highly satisfying; it is an extremely fat-rich component of a diet notably
lacking in fat. People are always excited to be invited to a pandanus feast, and in
my experience the events themselves are routinely happy and effervescent ones
that stand as a clear realization of the value of relationalism in Urapmin life.

If a group of people have been invited to a pandanus feast, it is also expected
that they will invite their host to a return feast when their own pandanus fruits
are ready for harvest. Often, at the initial feast, the guests will use some bark
string to measure the size of the dish prepared. They will give the hosts this
string to keep until they come for the return feast, when the second dish will
be measured to check if it is a true reciprocal match for the first one. (As I have
noted elsewhere, the Urapmin find the exchange of precisely matched items to
be an especially satisfying way of realizing the value of relationalism:Robbins
2009a.) At one return feast where I was present, the string was brought out and
it was discovered that the return dish was slightly larger than the original one
it was given to reciprocate. Everyone in attendance immediately became very
animated, producing a chorus of whooping exclamations that often indicates
moments of effervescence among the Urapmin. The source of this great happiness was the fact that because the return dish was larger than the first, the
original hosts would have to start the cycle again, since the exchange could not
be left in a non-matched state. What made this feast even more effervescent
than usual was that the discovery of the excess meant that this realization of the
value of relationalism, exciting enough in its own terms, pointed to another one
in the future.

Urapmin pandanus feasts, with their relation-enhancing quality and emotional intensity, are a good example of the way people experience moments of
intense happiness when they realize values they find important. Young Urapmin
who attend these feasts learn about the value of relationships from them in precisely the kind of effervescent setting in which Durkheim expects that people
will first come to recognize the values that hold in their communities. Older
people know this value already, but through the intense happiness they feel at its

realization, they reconfirm their sense that relationships, and particularly those of equivalent exchange, are some of the most valued things in their world.

The contributions to this collection are full of moments in which the realization of an important value is connected with strong feelings of happiness in precisely the way it is in Urapmin Pandanus feasts. Freeman, for example, tells us about the delight the Ethiopian Gamo take in "playing," the jocular kind of interaction they take to most directly realize the value of "smooth social relations." One similarly senses that the British humanists Matthew Engelke studies find themselves feeling quite happy when they realize their core value of reason as they publicly criticize those they take to be overly invested in religion or hold what they call "ethical juries." For the elderly Japanese people with whom Kavedžija works, achieving balance between the multiple values that call out to them appears to be their primary value, and they find happiness in accomplishing this by, for example, "properly" carrying out everyday tasks such as "preparing meals and growing vegetables," thereby demonstrating they can still balance the value of autonomy against the also valued dependence that increasingly marks their lives.

The connection between happiness and the realization of important values can also have an anticipatory or retrospective character. We have already seen the anticipatory side of this in the Urapmin excitement over the way too large a return of pandanus sets up a new round of feasting. In a major contribution to the anthropological study of values, Frederick Damon (2002) provides another example. He describes how the Muyuw people of Milne Bay Province in Papua New Guinea take the achievement of fame in kula exchange as their primary value (see also Munn 1986). As locally understood, the achievement of fame in kula is a temporally extended process. When one first gives (or "throws") a kula valuable to a partner, one's "name" (or fame) "falls" as that of one's partner "climbs" (Damon 2002: 129). It is only when one's partner gives one's valuable onward that one's own name will climb. Damon describes the emotions that attend kula exchanges in these terms:

> While the initial throwing of a valuable is experienced as a loss, and often an angry one, fairly soon my informants assumed an attitude that was more like dancing. "Mwon won" is the term employed for this condition, and it is reasonably well translated as "ecstacy" [sic]. It is a sense of coming back to life as one envisages a valuable moving on down a line of actors. This experience of being, perhaps like being blessed, is the realization of fame one imagines. (Ibid.: 130)

Though the time-scale is shorter, Walker illustrates a similar kind of happiness in the anticipation of the realization of a value when he discusses, in his contribution to this collection, the way the Urarina take the experience of seeing a hunter return to the village with a large game animal he has bagged as one that "epitomizes" intense short-term happiness. What the Urarina anticipate in this moment—a moment in which they know there will be enough meat for everyone to eat—is the performative realization of their core value of "tranquility." To explore an emotionally charged form of retrospection, rather than anticipation, we can turn to Lambek's discussion of the restaurant and ballroom (Rossfall) that is so important to Willi Preisig, the Swiss man whose life-history he narrates. This ballroom, the recurring site of youthful courtship in the region, and also, as a restaurant, the scene of visits by older adults, appears to represent, or to have represented during the course of Willi's life, the highly valued possibility of reproducing the local farming way of life. Finally, in Gardner's and Stafford's contributions, we catch glimpses of the ways in which anticipations and recollections of the production of happiness through the realization of values are managed in intergenerational and transnational social groupings. The two authors describe social situations rendered very complex either by migration or by rapid socioeconomic change or by both. But it is fair to assume that all societies must in part be bound together by intergenerational constructions of shared values and moments of anticipated, recollected, and presently experienced happiness of the kinds they discuss (on the creation of intergenerational sharing more generally, see Wentzer 2014).

Having brought time into my argument about effervescent happiness and value by looking at anticipation and recollection, I have begun to move toward returning to the problem of determining the relationship between momentary, hedonic bursts of feeling and more long-term, eudaimonic-type feelings of contentment and judgments of happiness. In the remainder of this section, I want to consider one way of thinking about this link from the Durkheimian perspective I have been developing here.

As it happens, Durkheim's notion of effervescence has recently received a good deal of attention from sociologists (Fish 2005 provides a good overview). One of the most important contributions to this renewed discussion has been Randall Collins' (2004) elaboration of a theory of what he calls "interaction ritual chains" (see also Robbins 2009b). Collins accepts Durkheim's assertion that collective actions produce effervescence and his further claim that rituals are a kind of action that is especially suited to generating this emotional state.

Noting that rituals can be characterized by their combination of a shared focus of attention and a high degree of mutual coordination between participants, Collins goes on to follow Erving Goffman (1967) in suggesting that all successful social interactions have a ritualized quality. Because this is so, Collins concludes, all well-formed social interactions must also produce at least some effervescence, or what he calls "emotional energy," among those who take part in them. If one is tempted to check Collins' argument against the evidence of one's own experience, one might think here of the elevated feeling one has after a good conversation with a friend, or a successful meeting with colleagues, or even after an unproblematic interaction with a stranger who stops to ask directions on the street.

On Collins' account, smooth social relations, even when they are not valued in themselves as among the Gamo, are productive of some quantum of the kind of happiness that we have tied to the disclosure and realization of values. In making this statement, I am suggesting that it is possible to bring Collins' argument about interaction ritual chains together with the one about the relation between values and happiness I am making here. To fully carry off a synthesis along these lines, I would have to show that many social interactions aim at the short- or long-run realization of some locally important value, for this would make a large number of social interactions capable of generating appropriate effervescence when successful. I do not have space to pursue such an argument here (though I have tried to do so in Robbins 2012), but I do not think it is at all far-fetched, and I hope it can be taken as a plausible hypothesis for the purposes of the present discussion.

If we accept that all successful social interactions not only produce at least some effervescence, but that in doing so they also reveal their links to values, then a final argumentative step that Collins takes can give us some help in finding a link between punctual experiences of happiness and the happiness of a life well lived. The step in question comes when Collins (2004: 44) argues that it is the effervescence or "emotional energy" produced by ritual interaction that propels us through life. Human beings actively seek such energy, Collins argues, and they use the energy produced by previous interactions to move themselves forward into new ones. The emotional links between interactions that result create the "chains" that Collins refers to in his titular phrase "interaction ritual chains." I want to suggest at this point that with Collins' claims in mind, we might take a life well lived to be one that produces a steady flow of effervescence by virtue of moving regularly through a wide range of successful interactions across the life-course. These interactions may realize any number of locally important values, and we know the values at stake will differ across cultures, but perhaps the form of a life well lived (rather than its content) could be said to be fairly stable in the way it links values and the production of happiness in the routine movement of a person through a large number of successful social interactions.

In defining a life well lived in this way, I do not mean to suggest that every social interaction a person engages in has to go smoothly in order for his or her life to go well (for a related point made in philosophical terms, see Roberts 2015: 42). This would be too high a bar to set for a life to be defined as good. The point is rather that a good life will be one in which social relations often tend to go well, to be oriented to and disclosive of important values, and therefore to produce a reasonable amount of effervescent happiness that can carry a person forward into the future. But even when the bar is lowered in this way, this account still leaves out one important feature of the way people live lives oriented toward values: the fact that people often find themselves confronted with values that conflict, or with the need to make choices between values which will lead them to set aside the pursuit of some important ones. How do people's negotiation of these kinds of complicated value situations factor into the question of how well their lives have gone? To address this question, we will have to set Durkheim's preoccupations aside and turn instead to those of Max Weber.

VALUE PLURALITY AND THE NATURE OF A LIFE WELL LIVED

Weber, more than Durkheim, is known as a sociological theorist of value. One of his most influential arguments, after all, is that there exist a number of different values in society (or at least in "modern" society), and that these are destined forever to conflict with one another like "warring gods" (Weber 1946: 147, 153). Economic and ethical values, for example, often pull in different directions, as do scientific and political ones, and so forth. If Weber's argument is correct, it raises problems for any theory that would want to relate in a simple way the kind of happiness that results from the realization of a single value to the kind of happiness that is supposed to characterize a life well lived. (Such problems are also taken up in slightly different terms in the introduction to this collection.) For if multiple values exist and sometimes conflict with one another, the happiness of a good life is going to have to follow in some respects not only from realizing particular values, but also from choosing to realize the right ones at the right time, even if that means failing to realize others. In this section, I want to take Weber's position to be partially though not wholly right, and I want to consider what the issues it raises mean for the anthropological analysis of short- and long-term happiness.

Even in the very simple form in which I have just presented Weber's argument about value conflict, it consists of two parts. The first asserts that there exist many values in society. Let us call this a claim of value plurality. In the rest of this section, I am going to assume that all social formations contain a plurality of values.[2] The second part of Weber's argument concerns not just the *existence* of multiple values, but also the nature of the *relationships* that hold between them. The relationships between values, he asserts, are destined to be ones of conflict, and this will mean that people living in these societies will often be faced with "tragic" choices that require them to forgo realizing one value in order to realize a conflicting one. Thus, for example, a person might choose to act on an ethical value at the expense of realizing an economic value he or she also holds to be important. The position that all societies will contain values that conflict in this way is know as "value pluralism" (see Lassman 2011 for an excellent discussion of value pluralism that also surveys the positions of Isaiah Berlin and others).

It is worth going to the trouble to distinguish value plurality from value pluralism because there is another theory of the relations between values that, like that of value pluralism, assumes the existence of value plurality, but that, unlike value pluralism, does not assume values are inevitably in conflict. This position is known as value monism, and its primary claim is that the various values present in any given society ultimately work harmoniously together. One way this can come about is if all of the diverse values ultimately serve one "supervalue." In hedonistic versions of utilitarianism, for example, happiness or pleasure stands as a supervalue in this way (Chang 2001). It can also come about because, properly understood, all of the values in a society work together, such that realizing one helps a person realize others (Dworkin 2011). And, finally, drawing on Dumont's crucial anthropological contributions to value theory, and simplifying

---

2.   I make an argument for this position, drawing on the work of Louis Dumont, in Robbins (2013). More generally, Robbins (2013) and (2014) offer much more developed accounts of the arguments of the next several paragraphs.

them a great deal, value monism can come about because society allocates the realization of different values to different social domains (or contexts), such that people do not in fact face tragic choices between values that in the abstract would conflict (Dumont 1986). For example, one can imagine societies in which ethical values are thought to apply most importantly to the domain of family life, while those of economic gain apply most fully to the market. If people properly identify the domains in which they are acting, they should be able without tragic difficulty to determine which values they should be realizing by their actions. Dumont further adds that different social domains are themselves ranked by values, such that while each domain sometimes provides the appropriate context for action, some are more important and widely relevant than others. Such relations between domains allow people to sort out how to act in situations in which more than one domain appears to apply: in a rough-and-ready way, one can assume that the more highly valued domain should govern action in such circumstances. A society that is exhaustively ordered by the kinds of value relations Dumont lays out would be a monist one in the sense that, as in the other monist formulations, tragic value conflicts would not arise.

I have argued elsewhere that social formations tend to display both monist and pluralist tendencies, but that at any given time some lean more in one direction or the other (Robbins 2013). The hypothesis I want to explore in the rest of this section is that the way punctual moments of happiness contribute to a life well lived will look somewhat different in societies with a more monist inclination than they will in those that are more tilted toward the pluralist side. In their introduction to this collection, Walker and Kavedžija argue that in practice conflicts between values do not tend to trouble people very much. As they put it, in "the everyday world of practical ethics, people routinely make judgments involving incommensurable values in a straightforward, formal, or schematic manner." I think this accurately describes the situation in largely monist social settings.[3] These are ones in which finding the right value to realize in any given

---

3.   I am less confident than Walker and Kavedžija that it also describes the situation in most pluralist settings, in which they suggest values frequently differ from one another but do not conflict. Perhaps they are thinking of situations of value plurality but not pluralism, as I have defined these terms. There are some important theoretical issues at stake here, such as whether the fact that values always involve ranking constrain the kinds of relations that can exist between them, so that situations of value plurality that are not ones of value pluralism must be monistic in some way, but these are not issues that need to be settled in the context of the argument I am making here.

situation is relatively straightforward. Where this is true, movement from one moment of happiness to another throughout life in the way Collins predicts ought to eventuate at the end of the day in having a lived a life socially understood to be "good."

We catch glimpses of the kind of good life more monistic social settings allow in some of the contributions to this collection. One senses, for example, that Willi Preisig, the Swiss farmer at the center of Lambek's article, has lived this kind of life. It is not that his life has been wholly free of difficult choices, but few of them appear to have been tragic, and the many momentary happinesses he has experienced appear to sum neatly and with little or no remainder into a quiet but secure sense of satisfaction with how his life has gone. Lambek does not make this argument, but it is possible to imagine that for many people of Willi's generation, *Le bonheur suisse* has taken this form. It is possible to catch a glimpse of a similar sense of long-term achievement among the elderly Japanese discussed in Kavedžija's article, where a high or even preeminent valuation of balance provides people with a very effective way of approaching conflicts that arise between their lower-level values; whenever faced with such conflict, finding a way to balance the realization of both values will count as having realized one that is higher than either of them. In this way, a wide range of value-linked experiences of momentary happiness that follow from the achievement of balance can feed into a life well lived. Even the militia volunteers of Vigh's study appear to have a pretty strong sense that social involvement is unchallenged as their primary value, and they thus aim for it with a monistic steadiness that, as Vigh shows to powerful effect, cuts against the apparent chaos of the world around them. Yapese altruistic suffering, in Throop's account here, similarly helps organize other values into what appears to be an at least partially monistic formation in which the route that connects momentary happiness to long-term eudaimonic success is not a hard one for people to identify (though it may be hard for some or even many of them to traverse).

Some of the other contributions to this collection, by contrast, paint portraits of social formations that seem better characterized as value pluralist. In these cases, the line that links momentary pleasures to notions of the good life does not run at all straight, and one senses that finding the good life in these places is less a matter of achieving the quiet satisfaction that comes from pursuing values that fit well together than it is one of making "heroic" efforts of practical judgment in the face of the significant challenges that follow from confronting values in conflict. In pluralistic formations, it is always possible to go astray not by failing to seek the good as one pursues the pleasures of the moment, but by indulging too much in some value-linked pleasures and too little in others. These kinds of concerns appear in the ethnographic portraits offered by Gardner and Stafford, where across spans of time and space people wrestle with choosing the values on which to focus. Should one aim for familial closeness or economic uplift, educational and artistic cultivation or the ascetic work routines that can bring greater wealth? And the people they discuss in their contributions further ask themselves if one person can make value choices for another, a particularly fraught question in situations in which tragic loss in some value dimension always accompanies gain in another. Similarly, though the tragic drama of choice has a different ethnographic feel in this case, Engelke shows us how humanists wrestle with the need to allow themselves to recognize the value of some emotional insights and experiences to ethical deliberation, even as they promote reason as their primary value (and as the one most conducive to the production of happiness). And finally, Freeman's article, focused on a situation of significant change, paints a picture of a settled Gamo monism built around the core value of smooth social relating displaced by Gamo entry into the market and exposure to pluralistic struggles that changing legal regimes and Pentecostal ritual help to address, but perhaps not to resolve into a new monist formation.

By means of this rapid marshaling of ethnography, I have meant to suggest that the nature of good lives is different in different places, and not just because of differences in the content of the values that exist in various societies, but also because of the differences in the ways those values relate to each other. I have suggested two ideal types of good life in this regard: one in which more monist formations allow moments of happiness to add up to good lives in a fairly straightforward manner; and one in which value pluralism and conflict mean that good lives are going to be at least different from, and maybe even felt by those who achieve them to be "more" than, the sum of the happy moments they have had in the course of arriving at them. No one lives in ideal-type worlds, so there is no question of reifying these accounts into a hard dichotomy. The point is to be aware as anthropologists of the different ways people can hope or seek to connect feelings of happiness to the accomplishment of happy lives in the social formations in which they live. In this way, we can acknowledge the ethnographic differences in kinds of notions of the good life that show up in this collection, and confirm the strong hunch, one that has guided me here, that these reflect real if subtle differences in the materials the contributors present, and not just differences in the way they have written them up. It is through being attentive to these differences that we can build on the progress made in this collection toward the goal of creating accounts that are adequate to both the long and the short of happiness.

CONCLUSION

Twenty years ago, at the height of the most recent wave of disciplinary particularism, anthropologists might have suspected that happiness is too much a culture-bound Western notion to be of much use in cross-cultural research (Keane 2003). I have sought to argue here that the consistency with which these articles raise issues of short- and longer-term temporal horizons, rather than simply relying on the unspoken temporal middle ground that provides the setting for most ethnographic discussions, gives the lie to this position. There is something about happiness and its relation to values that everywhere presents challenges to people seeking to integrate the various temporalities through which their lives unfold. If we focus on how people face those challenges, it is not difficult to shape up happiness and values as topics of comparative investigation, even as happiness may be understood differently in different places, and even as values and the relationships that hold between them clearly differ across diverse social settings.

In the past, anthropologists who have not focused on issues of happiness have arguably raised issues of the relation of long- and short-term temporalities similar to those found in these articles. Most notably, Maurice Bloch and Jonathan Parry's (1989) influential discussion of the various ways social formations use currencies to articulate the two transactional orders constructed by individual, short-term interests, on the one hand, and long-term, collective interests in the reproduction of social orders, on the other, strikes me as pointing to a similar area of investigation. And it is perhaps not accidental that although Bloch and Parry are not interested in happiness in their piece, they are interested in matters of certain kinds of value. Values on their own, this might suggest, render human temporality complex. Happiness without value, then, would not raise the same kinds of questions about time. But it is a great accomplishment of this collection that it shows us that happiness without value appears to be a rare occurrence. Even if there are very few societies in which happiness itself is the primary, overriding value people seek to realize—it is rarely the supervalue that rallies all others to its cause—we now know that happiness is routinely tied up with the disclosure and realization of values, and hence with the complexities of the personal and social management of time. This unusually rich collection of articles puts this important point before us, and in doing so redeems its promise of showing why happiness is an important subject of anthropological investigation.

REFERENCES

Abbinnett, Ross. 2013. *Politics of happiness: Connecting the philosophical ideas of Hegel, Nietzsche and Derrida to the political ideologies of happiness.* New York: Bloomsbury.

Ahmed, Sara. 2010. *The promise of happiness.* Durham, NC: Duke University Press.

Bloch, Maurice, and Jonathan Parry. 1989. "Introduction: Money and the morality of exchange." In *Money and the morality of exchange*, edited by Jonathan Parry and Maurice Bloch, 1–32. Cambridge, Cambridge University Press.

Chang, Ruth. 2001. "Value pluralism." In *International encyclopedia of the social and behavioral sciences*, edited by N. J. Smelser and P. B. Baltes, 16139–45. New York: Elsevier.

Collins, Randall. 2004. *Interaction ritual chains.* Princeton, NJ: Princeton University Press.

Damon, Frederick H. 2002. "Kula valuables: The problem of value and the production of names." *L'Homme* 162: 107–36.

Davies, William. 2015. *The happiness industry: How the government and big business sold us well being.* London: Verso.

Dumont, Louis. 1986. *Essays on individualism: Modern ideology in anthropological perspective.* Chicago: University of Chicago Press.

Durkheim, Émile. (1912) 1995. *The elementary forms of the religious life.* Translated by Joseph Ward Swain. New York: Free Press.

———. (1924) 1974. *Sociology and philosophy.* Translated by D. F. Pocock. New York: Free Press.

Dworkin, Ronald. 2011. *Justice for hedgehogs.* Cambridge, MA: Harvard University Press.

Fish, Jonathan S. 2005. *Defending the Durkheimian tradition: Religion, emotion and morality.* Aldershot: Ashgate.

Goffman, Erving. 1967. *Interaction ritual: Essays on face-to-face behavior.* Garden City, NY: Anchor Books.

Graeber, David. 2001. *Toward an anthropological theory of value: The false coin of our own dreams.* New York: Palgrave.

Gubser, Michael. 2014. *The far reaches: Phenomenology, ethics, and social renewal in Central Europe.* Stanford: Stanford University Press.

Haybron, Dan. 2011. "Happiness." *Stanford Encyclopedia of Philosophy.* http://plato.stanford.edu/entries/happiness/.

Keane, Webb. 2003. "Self-interpretation, agency, and the objects of anthropology: Reflections on a genealogy." *Comparative Studies in Society and History* 45: 222–48.

Laidlaw, James. 2013. *The subject of virtue: An anthropology of ethics and freedom.* Cambridge: Cambridge University Press.

Lassman, Peter. 2011. *Pluralism.* Cambridge, Polity.

May, Todd. 2015. *A significant life: Human meaning in a silent universe.* Chicago: University of Chicago Press.

Munn, Nancy D. 1986. *The fame of Gawa: A symbolic study of value transformation in a Massim (Papua New Guinea) society.* New York: Cambridge University Press.

Otto, Ton, and Rane Willerslev, eds. 2013. "Value as theory—Parts I and II." *HAU: Journal of Ethnographic Theory* 3 (1– 2). (Special issues.)

Pedersen, David E., ed. 2008. "Values of value." *Anthropological Theory* 8 (1). (Special Issue.)

Robbins, Joel. 2004. *Becoming sinners: Christianity and moral torment in a Papua New Guinea society.* Berkeley: University of California Press.

———. 2009a. "Conversion, hierarchy, and cultural change: Value and syncretism in the globalization of Pentecostal and charismatic Christianity." In *Hierarchy: Persistence and transformation in social formations,* edited by Knut M. Rio and Olaf H. Smedal, 65–88. New York: Berghahn.

———. 2009b. "Pentecostal networks and the spirit of globalization: On the social productivity of ritual forms." *Social Analysis* 53 (1): 55–66.

———. 2012. "Cultural values." In *A companion to moral anthropology,* edited by Didier Fasin, 117–32. Malden, MA: Wiley-Blackwell.

———. 2013. "Monism, pluralism and the structure of value relations: A Dumontian contribution to the contemporary study of value." *HAU: Journal of Ethnographic Theory* 3 (1): 99–115.

————. 2014. "Ritual pluralism and value pluralism: Ritual and the management of intercultural diversity." *Debates do NER* 15 (26): 15–41.

Roberts, Robert C. 2015. "How virtue contributes to flourishing." In *Current controversies in virtue theory*, edited by Mark Alfano, 36–49. New York: Routledge.

Scheler, Max. (1913–16) 1973. *Formalism in ethics and a non-formal ethics of values: A new attempt toward the foundation of an ethical personalism.* Evanston, IL: Northwestern University Press.

Schnädelbach, Herbert. 1984. *Philosophy in Germany 1831–1933.* Cambridge: Cambridge University Press.

Tischner, Józefa. 2008. "Thinking in values." *Thinking in Values: The Tischner Institute Journal of Philosophy* 2: 47–59.

Toccafondi, Fiorenza. 2009. "Facts, values, emotions, and perception." In *Values and ontology: Problems and perspectives*, edited by Beatrice Centi and Wolfgang Huemer, 137–54. Frankfurt, Ontos Verlag.

Weber, Max. 1946. *From Max Weber: Essays in Sociology.* Edited by Hans H. Gerth and C. Wright Mills. New York: Oxford University Press.

Wentzer, Thomas Schwarz. 2014. ""I have seen Königsberg burning': Philosophical anthropology and the responsiveness of historical experience." *Anthropological Theory* 14 (1): 27–48.

Index

phenomenology, 31, 36-38, 46, 100,
102, 124, 238, 282, 284, 294, 301, 302
play, 39, 49, 113-117, 119, 127, 199, 304
pleasure, 7, 10-12, 14, 15, 18, 24, 41, 46,
61, 62, 76, 85, 96, 98, 106, 133, 134,
139, 142, 149, 154, 156-160, 200, 220,
221, 240, 248, 268-270, 275, 278, 281,
285, 286, 288, 290, 297, 308
politics (see also: citizenship, government), 2, 3, 4, 5, 8, 12, 13, 22, 30, 34,
39, 65, 112, 113, 122, 139, 141, 153, 163,
164, 167-170, 173-178, 184, 195, 207,
215-217, 220-228, 232, 242, 250, 252,
253, 256, 258-261, 271, 279, 280, 307
prayer (see also: ritual), 126, 206, 224
private, 9, 11, 13, 62, 81, 93, 167, 180, 249
prosperity (see also: money, wealth),
2, 22, 45, 66, 131, 191, 192, 194, 195,
198-201, 203, 207, 208, 240
purpose, 3, 13, 21, 22, 51, 75, 85, 86, 99,
122, 140, 149, 157, 170, 174, 205, 208,
270, 272, 274, 285, 288
psychology, 3, 5, 18, 23, 25-27, 60, 106,
107, 120, 129-131, 161, 164, 168, 185,
187-189, 234, 235, 289-291, 293

R

rationality, 137, 151, 156
reason (see also: Enlightenment), 11,
22, 133, 134, 138, 146, 149-151, 156-
158, 304, 311
recognition, 6, 13, 63, 81, 104, 145, 224,
228, 269, 279
reconciliation, 15, 112, 113
reflection (see also: contemplation,
mindfulness), 47, 99, 101, 124, 142,
166, 172;
reflexivity, 101, 178
religion (see also: Christianity, Confucianism, God, ritual), 121, 122,
126, 137, 138, 143, 144-148, 151, 169,
216, 250, 261, 300, 301, 304

responsibility, 7, 9-13, 21, 22, 36, 39, 45,
49, 50, 54, 62, 63, 97, 103, 104, 121,
156, 164-167, 172-178, 185, 186, 189,
240, 250, 251, 253, 259
ritual (see also: communitas, prayer,
religion), 62, 71, 116, 121-126, 128,
196, 227, 243, 275, 286, 295, 300,
305, 306, 311

S

secularism, 12, 22, 134, 137, 139, 143,
147-151, 149, 160, 168, 172
security, 8, 16, 66, 71, 77, 118, 193, 194,
205, 211, 223-227, 229, 232
self (see also: personhood), 3, 6, 7, 10,
18, 19, 22, 31, 34, 39, 40, 43, 52-54,
74, 76, 84-87, 90, 95-96, 98, 102,
103, 105, 109, 122-128, 136, 137, 140,
146, 151, 152, 157, 163-168, 172, 173,
175-178, 182, 184, 208, 216, 220,
238-240, 242, 258, 261, 270, 273, 274,
276, 278-280, 285, 288
self-cultivation, 84, 95-96
sentiment, 5, 92, 96, 97, 139, 140, 149,
150, 222, 223, 238, 278, 300,
sex, 30, 142, 145, 146, 153, 182, 227, 228,
261, 269, 297
spirits, 32, 33, 44, 46, 53, 116, 122, 123,
275
stories, 12, 28, 33, 20, 48, 49, 65, 72, 81,
84, 85, 86, 92, 98, 99, 101-103, 106,
112, 124, 137, 195, 199, 200, 201, 204,
206, 208, 219, 221, 227, 228, 232, 234,
241, 255
suffering (see also: hardship, pain), 5,
12, 21, 29, 31, 33, 35, 36, 39-45, 48-54,
62, 88, 112, 124, 145-147, 150, 168,
169, 172, 174, 175, 177, 184, 191, 194,
195, 198, 205, 219, 220, 228, 229, 232,
239, 272, 274, 276, 310
support, 69, 71, 88, 91-95, 137, 144, 198,
202, 208

HAU Books is committed to publishing the most distinguished texts in classic and advanced anthropological theory. The titles aim to situate ethnography as the prime heuristic of anthropology, and return it to the forefront of conceptual developments in the discipline. HAU Books is sponsored by some of the world's most distinguished anthropology departments and research institutions, and releases its titles in both print editions and open-access formats.

www.haubooks.com

Supported by

Hau-N. E. T.
Network of Ethnographic Theory

University of Aarhus – EPICENTER (DK)
University of Amsterdam (NL)
University of Bergen (NO)
Brown University (US)
California Institute of Integral Studies (US)
University of Campinas (BR)
University of Canterbury (NZ)
University of Chicago (US)
University College London (UK)
University of Colorado Boulder Libraries (US)
CNRS – Centre d'Études Himalayennes (FR)
Cornell University (US)
University of Edinburgh (UK)
The Graduate Institute, Geneva Library (CH)
University of Helsinki (FL)
Indiana University Library (US)
Johns Hopkins University (US)
University of Kent (UK)
Lafayette College Library (US)
London School of Economics and Political Science (UK)
Institute of Social Sciences of the University of Lisbon (PL)
University of Manchester (UK)
The University of Manchester Library (UK)
Max-Planck Institute for the Study of Religious and Ethnic
Diversity at Göttingen (DE)
Musée de Quai Branly (FR)
Museu Nacional – UFRJ (BR)
Norwegian Museum of Cultural History (NO)
University of Oslo (NO)
University of Oslo Library (NO)
Pontificia Universidad Católica de Chile (CL)
Princeton University (US)
University of Queensland (AU)
University of Rochester (US)
Universidad Autónoma de San Luis Potosi (MX)
SOAS, University of London (UK)
University of Sydney (AU)
University of Toronto Libraries (CA)

www.haujournal.org/haunet